D0192799

THE
# SNOWDEN
# READER

WITHDRAWN

WITHDRAWN

# THE
# SNOWDEN
## READER

EDITED BY
## DAVID P. FIDLER

FOREWORD BY SUMIT GANGULY

INDIANA UNIVERSITY PRESS
BLOOMINGTON · INDIANAPOLIS

This book is a publication of

Indiana University Press
Office of Scholarly Publishing
Herman B Wells Library 350
1320 East 10th Street
Bloomington, Indiana 47405 USA

www.iupress.indiana.edu

© 2015 by Indiana University Press
All rights reserved

No part of this book may be reproduced or utilized in any form or by any means, electronic
or mechanical, including photocopying and recording, or by any information storage and
retrieval system, without permission in writing from the publisher. The Association of American
University Presses' Resolution on Permissions constitutes the only exception to this prohibition.

The paper used in this publication meets the minimum requirements of
the American National Standard for Information Sciences—Permanence
of Paper for Printed Library Materials, ANSI Z39.48–1992.

Manufactured in the United States of America

Cataloging is available from the Library of Congress.

ISBN 978-0-253-01731-4 (cloth)
ISBN 978-0-253-01737-6 (paperback)
ISBN 978-0-253-01738-3 (ebook)

1 2 3 4 5   20 19 18 17 16 15

*To my students, whose generation has so much at stake when national security dangers, innovative technologies, and commitment to civil liberties converge.*

When the people of America reflect that they are now called upon to decide a question, which, in its consequences, must prove one of the most important that ever engaged their attention, the propriety of their taking a very comprehensive, as well as serious, view of it, will be evident.

*The Federalist Papers, No. 2*

# CONTENTS

*Norms of Responsible Behavior in Cyberspace?*
*U.S. Cyber Operations*

*"Worse than the U.S."?*
*Surveillance by the UK's Government Communications Headquarters*

**B. Reviews and Recommendations**

*U.S. Federal Court Decisions on NSA Programs*

*Reports from U.S. Advisory and Oversight Bodies*

# Foreword

Public disclosures of classified information have long played a role in U.S. national security politics, raising questions about secrecy in a democracy, the propriety of government actions, and the protection of civil rights. Until recent events, perhaps the most famous episode involved Daniel Ellsberg, a civilian Pentagon analyst, who released in April 1971 nearly seven thousand pages of a classified study called "History of U.S. Decision-Making Process on Viet Nam Policy" to the *New York Times* and the *Washington Post*. After the *Times* began publishing excerpts from what became known as the "Pentagon Papers," the Nixon administration attempted to prevent the newspapers from publishing more classified information. The Supreme Court, in a striking decision, held that the U.S. government failed to satisfy the First Amendment's requirements for imposing a prior restraint on freedom of speech. The government's prosecution of Ellsberg for violating the Espionage Act also failed because evidence emerged of the government's clandestine efforts to discredit him with documents obtained from burgling his psychiatrist's safe.

In June 2013, another historic episode involving disclosure of classified information began when the *Guardian*, a British newspaper, began publishing stories about secret documents provided to it by Edward J. Snowden, who had worked as a private contractor for the National Security Agency (NSA). To much consternation in national security circles, these stories revealed that Snowden had made available to journalists a vast trove of material pertaining to the NSA's surveillance and espionage activities. Snowden's actions embarrassed the U.S. government, raised fears about damage to U.S. national security, sparked controversies about the possible abuse of civil liberties in the United States, and angered citizens and leaders of foreign countries, including U.S. allies, who discovered the NSA had access to their communications.

Snowden's release of classified documents was of momentous significance because of the political, legal, and ethical issues it raised in the United States and around the world. Given the magnitude of the disclosures and their impact, on September 6, 2013, the Center on American and Global Security at Indiana University organized a panel of leading IU faculty to examine the historical, legal, policy, and ethical dimensions of Snowden's actions. At the suggestion of Rebecca Tolen of Indiana University Press and under the editorship of David P. Fidler, the panel presentations were revised, expanded, and updated as essays reflecting on Snowden's disclosures and their aftermath. These essays form part I of this book. To supplement these contributions, *The Snowden Reader* includes, in part II, a selection of primary documents disclosed by Snowden, released by the U.S. government or other affected actors, or produced in the wake of the controversies during the first year of this affair. *The Snowden Reader* combines critical analysis of major issues Snowden's disclosures generated with primary sources at the heart of the controversies. It provides expert perspectives and access to documents that have become, in various ways, historic.

The contributions in part I range across the spectrum of political, legal, and ethical matters affected by Snowden's actions. In the introduction, David P. Fidler sets the stage by reviewing the Snowden disclosures and analyzing how the disclosures generated pressure on "fault lines" in U.S. national security politics, precipitating a potential historic shift in U.S. policy and law on foreign intelligence.

In "Security and Liberty: The Imaginary Balance," Nick Cullather focuses on the frequent use of the metaphor of "balance" between liberty and security in Snowden-related debates and provides a historical perspective on the idea of striking a balance between these objectives. What many people believe is a concept rooted in the republic's founding is actually of more recent vintage, dating from the crafting of new U.S. national security architecture, including the NSA, in the early Cold War period. Cullather observes that the "balance" metaphor arose in the development of a system of classified information and security clearances. According to Cullather, this system has produced "a country divided between those who know and cannot speak, and those who can speak but do not know"—a division at the heart of the politics stirred up by Snowden. This division produced oversight failures within the community of people with security clearances, making leakers "an indispensable but criminalized link, mediating a vexed relationship between the public and the cleared."

Fred H. Cate analyzes five issues in "Edward Snowden and the NSA: Law, Policy, and Politics"—the scope of the NSA's legal authority for collecting telephone metadata in the United States, problems with the trustworthiness of U.S. officials, the hypocrisy of the U.S. government concerning cyber espionage, the weakening of cyber security by U.S. activities, and the impact on privacy of U.S. surveillance programs. His critique of the U.S. government's interpretation of applicable law, surveillance policies, and responses to Snowden is withering. He roots his criticisms in principles he believes are central to the nation's politics, including the Fourth Amendment and the importance of ensuring that interpretations of law not remain secret from the American people.

Former congressman and vice chair of the 9/11 Commission, Lee H. Hamilton, concentrates on the failure of oversight concerning the government power revealed in Snowden's disclosures. In "From Passivity to Eternal Vigilance: NSA Surveillance and Effective Oversight of Government Power," Hamilton discusses the expansion of government power apparent in NSA surveillance programs, criticizes the government's record in exercising this power, and warns about potential abuse of this power. He predicts NSA surveillance programs will not undergo radical reforms, which necessitates, in his opinion, much stronger and more sustained oversight within the legislative and judicial branches as the most effective way to address "an unprecedented challenge to hold the government accountable and to constrain its reach into our lives."

David P. Fidler addresses "U.S. Foreign Policy and the Snowden Leaks." He lays out U.S. foreign policy approaches to cyberspace and cyber security before Snowden, especially U.S. support for "Internet freedom," and analyzes how these leaks have adversely affected them. The damage arises from revelations about the NSA's surveillance activities within the United States, the NSA's electronic surveillance targeting foreign nationals outside the United States, U.S. cyber espionage against other governments, U.S. offensive cyber operations, and NSA activities perceived to threaten global cyber security. Fidler argues the Snowden disclosures have diminished U.S. credibility in cyberspace affairs, an outcome that coincides, worryingly, with an erosion of U.S. influence in geopolitical matters in Europe, Asia, and the Middle East.

William E. Scheuerman explores Snowden's contributions to political thinking about civil disobedience in "Taking Snowden Seriously: Civil Disobedience for an Age of Total Surveillance." Grounding his analysis in the theory and practice of civil disobedience, Scheuerman unpacks how "Snowden has articulated a powerful defense of why he was morally obligated to engage in politically motivated lawbreaking." He assesses Snowden's actions against the tradition of civil disobedience and argues that his actions hold up well under scrutiny. Scheuerman also believes Snowden has contributed to this tradition in how he linked his disobedience with matters of global concern, expressed in principles of international law.

Part II provides a selection of primary documents associated with the Snowden disclosures. The documents are organized in three categories: Revelations and Reactions, covering documents Snowden released and responses to such disclosures from various sources, including the U.S. and foreign governments;

Reviews and Recommendations, including documents that contain legal analysis, policy evaluation, and recommendations for reforms concerning issues raised by the Snowden disclosures and the reactions to them; and Reforms and a Reflection, providing documents from the executive and legislative branches proposing policy and legal reforms and Snowden's reflection on the first anniversary of the publication of his initial disclosures.

The purpose of part II is not to provide a comprehensive archive but to make accessible documents that reflect issues, problems, controversies, and positions that arose during the first year of Snowden's disclosures. To achieve this objective, part II includes a diversity of documents, including classified documents and briefing slides leaked by Snowden, responses from the U.S. government, opinions of federal courts, reactions of foreign leaders and governments, and activities in the United Nations. Each document is preceded by a brief note introducing it, putting it into context, and explaining its significance.

*The Snowden Reader* captures the historic importance of Snowden's actions. But everyone involved in this project has been acutely aware that the story is not finished. More disclosures from Snowden continue to be made, debates about reform continue, and what the post-Snowden landscape for surveillance, espionage, secrecy, and individual rights will look like remains uncertain. Nevertheless, *The Snowden Reader* makes an important contribution to our understanding of what transpired in the United States and globally after June 2013 and the enduring significance of how governments and citizens respond to the challenges now apparent.

Sumit Ganguly
Professor of Political Science
Rabindranath Tagore Chair in Indian Cultures and Civilizations
Director, Center on American and Global Security
Indiana University

# Acknowledgments

As editor of *The Snowden Reader,* I would like to acknowledge and thank people who made this book possible. The book originated in a panel conceived and organized by Sumit Ganguly in September 2013, and he took the initiative, with Rebecca Tolen at Indiana University Press, to begin the process of turning the panel presentations into contributions for a book. Nick Cullather, Fred Cate, Lee Hamilton, and William Scheuerman were an editor's dream in terms of contributors, and I thank them for making my task easier. I am grateful to David Delaney for answering questions and providing advice to me throughout the book's development. Ashley Ahlbrand and Cindy Dabney in the Maurer School of Law's library provided valuable assistance in helping identify and organize the documents Edward Snowden disclosed and the responses to his revelations. Stacey Kaiser patiently endured and professionally fulfilled all my requests for help in transforming primary documents into manuscript texts. Rebecca Tolen and her staff, including Mollie Ables and Darja Malcolm-Clarke, deserve my thanks for moving the manuscript to publication in such an efficient and effective way. Finally, thanks to my family for understanding all the times I was Snowdened under in completing this book.

David P. Fidler
Bloomington, Indiana

# Editor's Note

Part II of *The Snowden Reader* was organized to provide an overview of the revelations by Edward Snowden that began in June 2013 and what the disclosures generated during the months that followed. The selections in part II roughly come from the first year of the "Snowden affair," with updates made as permitted by the publication schedule. The documents selected represent only samplings of the vast quantity of documents that have been generated and disseminated by various parties. Selections were made with the goal of providing a diversity of accessible materials and with the nonspecialist reader in mind. For the most part, the volume does not address specialists in the policy, law, and technology of foreign intelligence, which meant that a number of fascinating but technically challenging documents had to be left out. I can only beg the reader's forgiveness if the selections have left out documents you think are more important, interesting, or entertaining. In part II, "as of this writing" means approximately December 10, 2014.

Before each selection, I have included a short introductory note to provide context and to connect it with other documents and developments in the Snowden saga. Except where documents appear in their original forms (e.g., NSA briefing slides), the selections have been edited, with ellipses used to indicate where material has been omitted. Except where indicated, the documents in part II are in the public domain.

# Abbreviations

| | |
|---|---|
| ACLU | American Civil Liberties Union |
| AG | Attorney General |
| AUS | Australia |
| C | Classified |
| CAN | Canada |
| CIA | Central Intelligence Agency |
| COMINT | Communications Intelligence |
| CT | Counterterrorism |
| DHS | Department of Homeland Security |
| DNI | Director of National Intelligence |
| DOC | Department of Commerce |
| DOD | Department of Defense |
| DOE | Department of Energy |
| DOJ | Department of Justice |
| DSD | Defence Signals Directorate (now Australian Signals Directorate) |
| ECHR | European Convention on Human Rights |
| EO or E.O. | Executive Order |
| EU | European Union |

| | |
|---|---|
| FBI | Federal Bureau of Investigation |
| FISA | Foreign Intelligence Surveillance Act |
| FISC | Foreign Intelligence Surveillance Court |
| FISCR | Foreign Intelligence Surveillance Court of Review |
| FOUO | For Official Use Only |
| FVEY | Five Eyes |
| GBR | Great Britain |
| GCHQ | Government Communications Headquarters (UK's signals intelligence agency) |
| GPS | Global Positioning System |
| HUMINT | Human Intelligence |
| IC | Intelligence Community |
| ICCPR | International Covenant for Civil and Political Rights |
| IPT | Investigatory Powers Tribunal |
| ISA | Intelligence Services Act |
| ISC | Intelligence and Security Committee |
| ISP | Internet Service Provider |
| IT | Information Technology |
| NF | No Foreign Nationals |
| NOFORN | No Foreign Nationals |
| NSA | National Security Agency |
| NSL | National Security Letter |
| NZL | New Zealand |
| ODNI | Office of the Director of National Intelligence |
| PCLOB | Privacy and Civil Liberties Oversight Board |
| PPD | Presidential Policy Directive |
| RAS | Reasonable Articulable Suspicion |
| RIPA | Regulation of Investigatory Powers Act |
| REL | Release to |
| S | Secret |
| SI | Sensitive Information |
| SID | Signals Intelligence Directorate (NSA) |
| SIGAD | Signals Intelligence Activity Designator |

| | |
|---|---|
| SIGDEV | Signals Intelligence Development |
| SIGINT | Signals Intelligence |
| SWIFT | Society for Worldwide Interbank Financial Telecommunication |
| TAO | Tailored Access Operations (NSA) |
| TTIP | Transatlantic Trade and Investment Partnership Agreement (being negotiated between the United States and the EU) |
| TS | Top Secret |
| TSP | Terrorist Surveillance Program |
| U | Unclassified |
| UK | United Kingdom |
| UN | United Nations |
| US or U.S. | United States |
| USA FREEDOM Act | Uniting and Strengthening America by Fulfilling Rights and Ending Eavesdropping, Drag-Net Collection, and Online Monitoring Act |
| USA PATRIOT Act | Uniting and Strengthening America by Providing Appropriate Tools Required to Intercept and Obstruct Terrorism Act |
| U.S.C. | United States Code |
| WCIT | World Conference on International Telecommunications |

# THE
# SNOWDEN
# READER

# Introduction

DAVID P. FIDLER

## Into a Secret World

On June 5, 2013, Edward J. Snowden entered history with the first of a series of disclosures about the activities of the National Security Agency (NSA). Over the months that followed, Snowden continued to leak documents he obtained while working as a contractor for the NSA. Through these revelations, Snowden opened a secret world, and we were at once disconcerted and amazed at what we saw. We responded, emotionally and analytically, in attempts to make sense of Snowden, what he did, what he revealed, and what we should do now that he has made us direct participants in deliberations about protecting national security and respecting individual rights. Snowden's actions, and their impact in the United States and internationally, are unprecedented and constitute a seminal event for many areas of policy and politics, including cyber security, cyberspace, national security, the roles and responsibilities of Congress, foreign policy, constitutional and statutory law, international law, and the ethics of civil disobedience.

Pausing to assess history-making events that continue to make history may be misguided, but it is an overpowering impulse. More than a year into the journey into this secret world, and as events continue to unfold, we do not have clarity about what it all means, but we do have enough documentation, analysis, and perspective to warrant looking back and capturing some of the unprecedented things that have happened. This book explores the nature and significance of Snowden's leaks and the challenges they have created for the United States and other countries.

During his employment as a contractor for the NSA and in earlier jobs in the U.S. intelligence community, Snowden came to the conclusion that electronic surveillance undertaken by the NSA violated U.S. and international law on a massive scale, with the violations hidden from public scrutiny by secrecy rules imposed and enforced by the U.S. government. According to Snowden, his alarm about the power and practices of the NSA ripened into civil disobedience when NSA officials did not take his concerns seriously. He believed his only choice was to expose the NSA activities in order to spark public debate about what the NSA was doing, and to stimulate reforms.

With access to classified information on NSA computer systems, Snowden surreptitiously obtained a collection of secret documents later estimated to total 1.7 million pages of material. While gathering his trove of documents, Snowden made contact with journalist Glenn Greenwald at the *Guardian* newspaper in the United Kingdom, documentary filmmaker Laura Poitras, and—through Poitras— reporter Barton Gellman at the *Washington Post* to develop channels to disclose the information.[1] Snowden left the United States for Hong Kong in mid-May 2013, where Greenwald and Poitras met him for the first time in early June. A few days later, on June 5, the *Guardian* published the first of Greenwald's stories based on documents provided by Snowden.

When the disclosures began, the newspaper stories did not identify the leaker. Snowden revealed himself as the source of the leaked documents on June 9 while he was still in Hong Kong. Reeling from the shock waves caused by the disclosures, the U.S. government sought to get custody of Snowden by asking Hong Kong to extradite him under the U.S.-Hong Kong extradition treaty. Officials in Hong Kong refused the American request, claiming it did not meet the requirements of the treaty, and permitted Snowden to leave on a flight to Moscow, where he arrived on June 23. Although Snowden did not intend to stay in Russia, the U.S. government's revocation of his passport and pressure on other countries not to grant Snowden asylum left Snowden in limbo in the transit area of Sheremetyevo Airport. Russia eventually granted Snowden temporary asylum for one year in early August, allowing him to leave the airport to live in Moscow. At the end of this temporary asylum, Russia gave Snowden permission to reside in Russia for three more years.

During and after the Moscow airport ordeal, disclosures based on documents Snowden provided to journalists continued to make news around the world. Media stories based on Snowden-leaked information appeared in, among other places, Brazil, China, Germany, Spain, United Kingdom, and the United States.

The disclosures have been nearly relentless and have produced a body of documents, reactions, and commentary about diverse issues that is overwhelming in scale, substance, and significance. Snowden introduced people unfamiliar with intelligence activities to baffling code names for complex secret programs, such as BULLRUN, DROPMIRE, FOXACID, MUSCULAR, QUANTUMTHEORY, TURBINE, and XKEYSCORE. As Snowden intended, the revelations provoked intense controversies and heated debates in the United States and other countries about the surveillance conducted by the NSA, the relationships between other national intelligence agencies and the NSA, and the surveillance activities of other governments, especially the United Kingdom.

Among other things, the leaks prompted the U.S. intelligence community to increase transparency about its activities, including by establishing a website—IC on the Record[2]—and releasing dozens of previously classified documents. The leaks also infuriated U.S. technology companies; damaged U.S. relations with fellow democracies; provided the basis for litigation in U.S. courts, British tribunals, and the European Court of Human Rights; and forced the Obama administration to retreat from its initial staunch defense of the NSA and embrace the need for reforms. The whirlwind generated by Snowden has been astonishing in its intensity, political contentiousness, and global scope. This impact makes trying to understand the Snowden affair and its implications all the more important for the United States, international relations, and the future of civil rights and liberties in an increasingly digital world.

## The Significance of the Snowden Affair

The political choices, national security challenges, legal rules, and technologies implicated by Snowden's revelations had been years in the making, and this created complicated backstories for everything Snowden exposed. Figuring out why the NSA was engaging in the activities Snowden disclosed involved asking how these capabilities and programs came to be, but confusion about what exactly the NSA was doing frustrated attempts to answer these "why" and "how" questions. Provocative headlines exasperated NSA officials frustrated with the incomplete, misleading, and misinterpreted information they believed was being released. The nature and magnitude of what Snowden divulged overwhelmed normal patterns of domestic and international politics, which discombobulated dynamics inside the Beltway and diplomacy abroad. The world Snowden made more accessible had its own difficult history, shadows between fact and fiction, and confusion caused by political compasses going haywire. Many people worried by Snowden's leaks doubted his guidance in navigating this difficult terrain because he took refuge in Russia, a place generally not associated with the values he proclaimed to be defending.

In the long term, the most significant features of Snowden's actions arise from neither the intense emotions they aroused nor the specific secrets he divulged, but rather from the enormous pressure his disclosures put on already existing fault lines in the national security politics of democratic governments. Snowden's actions transcend the "hero v. traitor" debate because they disrupted the trajectory of political affairs and forced democratic societies to reconsider fundamental questions the answers to which help define the quality of the democratic experience. Analyzing Snowden's agitation of these fault lines is agnostic on whether Snowden is a brave defender of American ideals,[3] a "useful idiot" who has helped democracy's enemies,[4] or a perplexing bit of both.

The fault lines in national security politics affected by Snowden's actions include the tension between secrecy and transparency and between material power and political principle. Although phrased or described in different ways, the same tensions appear throughout the essays in part I of this book, which provide perspectives on what Snowden did and the importance of his actions from leading experts on U.S. history and politics, cyber security, political science, privacy, and international law. Part II contains key primary documents released by Snowden or produced in response to what he revealed. These documents capture for a general readership how Snowden's disclosures disturbed the political status quo, caused political earthquakes in the United States and beyond, and exposed problems, issues, and questions that governments and societies are still working through.

## NSA Activities under the Foreign Intelligence Surveillance Act

The center of gravity of Snowden's leaks is the NSA, and much of the information made public exposes NSA programs, policies, procedures, partnerships, and capabilities. Created in 1952, the NSA became the U.S. intelligence community's premier entity for collecting signals intelligence (SIGINT), or "the production of foreign intelligence through the collection, processing, and analysis of communications or other data, passed or accessible by radio, wire, or other electromagnetic means."[5] The organization was so secret (and secretive) that the NSA's existence was not acknowledged until 1957, leading to the joke that the initials stood for "No Such Agency." To the general public, the NSA's role and importance have usually been overshadowed by the better-known Central Intelligence Agency (CIA). When most Americans think of scandals in the U.S. intelligence community, the CIA typically comes to mind, whether the controversies occurred during the Cold War (covert operations to overthrow foreign governments) or in the years following the terrorist attacks of 9/11 (use of "enhanced interrogation techniques" against suspected terrorists).

But the NSA did not avoid scrutiny during investigations in the mid-1970s of abuses in the U.S. intelligence community. The famous Church Committee found,

## Box 1. Key U.S. Laws in the Snowden Disclosures

*Fourth Amendment to the U.S. Constitution*

"The right of the people to be secure in their persons, houses, papers, and effects, against unreasonable searches and seizures, shall not be violated, and no warrants shall issue, but upon probable cause, supported by oath or affirmation, and particularly describing the place to be searched, and the persons or things to be seized."

*Section 215 of the USA PATRIOT Act (50 U.S.C. §1861)*

Section 215 authorizes the Director of the Federal Bureau of Investigation to "make an application for an order requiring the production of any tangible things (including books, records, papers, documents, and other items) for an investigation to obtain foreign intelligence information not concerning a United States person or to protect against international terrorism or clandestine intelligence activities, provided that such investigation of a United States person is not conducted solely upon the basis of activities protected by the first amendment to the Constitution." Any such application must include "a statement of facts showing that there are reasonable grounds to believe that the tangible things sought are relevant to an authorized investigation (other than a threat assessment) . . . to obtain foreign intelligence information not concerning a United States person or to protect against international terrorism or clandestine intelligence activities[.]"

*Section 702 of the Foreign Intelligence Surveillance Act (50 U.S.C. §1881a)*

"Notwithstanding any other provision of law, . . . the Attorney General and the Director of National Intelligence may authorize jointly, for a period of up to 1 year from the effective date of the authorization, the targeting of persons reasonably believed to be located outside the United States to acquire foreign intelligence information." Before implementing any such authorization, the Attorney General and Director of National Intelligence must submit to the Foreign Intelligence Surveillance Court for its review and approval a "written certification" that includes (1) targeting procedures to "ensure that any acquisition . . . is limited to targeting persons reasonably believed to be located outside the United States; and . . . prevent the intentional acquisition of any communication to which the sender and all intended recipients are known at the time of acquisition to be located in the United States"; and (2) minimization procedures that, among other things, "minimize the acquisition and retention, and prohibit the dissemination, of nonpublicly available information concerning unconsenting United States persons consistent with the need of the United States to obtain, produce, and disseminate foreign intelligence information[.]"

---

**Box 2. The Right to Privacy in International Legal Texts**

*Universal Declaration of Human Rights (1948)*

Article 12

No one shall be subjected to arbitrary interference with his privacy, family, home or correspondence, nor to attacks upon his honour and reputation. Everyone has the right to the protection of the law against such interference or attacks.

---

*European Convention on Human Rights (1950)*

Article 8—Right to respect for private and family life

1. Everyone has the right to respect for his private and family life, his home and his correspondence.

2. There shall be no interference by a public authority with the exercise of this right except such as is in accordance with the law and is necessary in a democratic society in the interests of national security, public safety or the economic well-being of the country, for the prevention of disorder or crime, for the protection of health or morals, or for the protection of the rights and freedoms of others.

---

*International Covenant on Civil and Political Rights (1966)*

Article 17

1. No one shall be subjected to arbitrary or unlawful interference with his privacy, family, home or correspondence, nor to unlawful attacks on his honour and reputation.

2. Everyone has the right to the protection of the law against such interference or attacks.

---

for example, that the NSA had violated policy and law in intercepting domestic communications (such as telegrams),[6] findings which led Congress to adopt the Foreign Intelligence Surveillance Act (FISA) in 1978. FISA regulated government surveillance for foreign intelligence purposes conducted in the United States by, among other things, requiring prior review and approval of such surveillance by a special court, the Foreign Intelligence Surveillance Court (FISC).

Snowden made it clear that one of his primary objectives in disclosing classified documents was to expose NSA activities authorized under FISA that he believes violate statutory law and the constitutional rights of Americans, namely what came to be called the "telephone metadata program" (or "telephony metadata program") and "Section 702 surveillance." Under the FISC-approved telephone metadata program, the NSA collected telephone metadata (telephone numbers and the duration of calls, but not the content of calls) on virtually all calls made in the United States. Snowden holds that neither FISA nor the Fourth Amendment of the Constitution supports the collection of telephone metadata on every U.S. citizen. "Section 702 surveillance" refers to NSA activities under Section 702 of

FISA, which permits, with FISC review, NSA surveillance from within the United States targeting non-U.S. persons believed to be located outside the country. Snowden thinks that Section 702 surveillance makes Americans' communications with foreigners overseas subject to NSA data collection, use, and dissemination in violation of the Fourth Amendment. See Box 1 for the texts of these key U.S. laws implicated in the Snowden disclosures.

Snowden's hostility to Section 702 surveillance does not end with U.S. law. He also made it clear that Section 702 has become the source of authority for the NSA to engage in bulk or mass surveillance of the communications of foreigners located outside the United States when collection occurs in the United States (such as a foreigner using Google mail). He believes that such mass surveillance violates the human right to privacy in international law, enshrined in the Universal Declaration of Human Rights and the International Covenant on Civil and Political Rights. Others made similar claims under the European Convention on Human Rights. The global scope of his concern about the right to privacy connects to the global nature of the manner in which he made disclosures about NSA activities. See Box 2 for the principles on the right to privacy in leading international legal instruments implicated by Snowden's leaks.

## NSA Cooperation with Foreign Intelligence Agencies

Snowden also released information about NSA activities with the intelligence agencies of other countries, including Australia, Canada, Germany, Israel, the Netherlands, New Zealand, Norway, Sweden, and—most prominently—the United Kingdom. These disclosures came in two basic forms. Many leaked NSA documents indicated that the U.S. government had shared them among the so-called "Five Eyes," the intelligence agencies of the United States, Australia, Canada, New Zealand, and the United Kingdom. Collaboration among the Five Eyes originated in the aftermath of World War II, but, as numerous documents disclosed by Snowden show, the relationship remains active and important to the intelligence agencies of each government.

Snowden's leaks also included documents exposing collaboration between the NSA and the intelligence agencies of foreign governments. Sometimes these documents revealed information about NSA work with Five Eyes countries, most notably Australia, Canada, and the United Kingdom. We also learned about NSA relationships with the intelligence agencies of Germany and other governments beyond the Five Eyes. Through these documents, Snowden communicated that the NSA's reach and influence went beyond its own activities and affected the intelligence practices of other governments. Based on documents from Snowden and its own reporting, *Der Spiegel* observed that, as between the NSA and the German intelligence agency (the Bundesnachrichtendienst (BND)), "the exchange of data, spying tools and knowhow is much more intense than previously thought." This raised concerns among German legal experts that "the BND is potentially violating the German constitution by working with data received from the NSA."[7]

## Revelations about UK's Government Communications Headquarters

Although the NSA constituted Snowden's primary target, he revealed a significant amount of information about the activities of the United Kingdom's signals intelligence body, the Government Communications Headquarters (GCHQ). This information included documents exposing not only the close relationship between the NSA and GCHQ but also some of GCHQ's own surveillance activities. Specifically, Snowden provided the *Guardian* with documents about GCHQ's TEMPORA project, under which GCHQ gained access to massive streams of telephone and Internet communications by tapping fiber-optic cables. The nature and scale of this surveillance prompted Snowden to argue that GCHQ is "worse than the U.S."[8] Snowden's revelations about GCHQ's cooperation with the NSA and its own surveillance programs provoked claims in the United Kingdom that GCHQ was violating British law, including obligations under the right to privacy in the European Convention on Human Rights.

## NSA Spying on Foreign Countries

Another major feature of Snowden's disclosures involved exposing NSA espionage targeting foreign countries, including close allies and fellow democracies, and spying on international institutions, such as the European Union (EU) and the United Nations (UN). These revelations proved embarrassing and, in many cases, damaging to U.S. foreign policy and bilateral relations with the affected countries. China, a political and economic rival of the United States and a country the U.S. government had accused of cyber espionage, did not miss the opportunity to hit back at the United States, citing in particular Snowden's release of information about the scale and intensity of U.S. cyber espionage against China. Brazil and Germany, friends of the United States, reacted angrily to news that the NSA had spied on their leaders, Brazilian president Dilma Rousseff and German chancellor Angela Merkel. The Obama administration's responses in both cases made the spats even worse. Rousseff rejected the explanation that the NSA spied on her as part of U.S. global counterterrorism efforts. President Obama stated he did not know that the NSA tapped Merkel's mobile phone, suggesting that either the NSA was out of control or that spying on Germany's top leader was not important enough for the president to know.

## NSA Capabilities

Other Snowden disclosures revealed technological capabilities the NSA had or was developing. These capabilities included online metadata harvesting, storage of massive amounts of metadata, data mining, mobile phone tracking, cracking encrypted communications, smart phone surveillance, mapping social networks of targets, overcoming online anonymity tools, collecting contact lists from Internet services, acquiring foreign mobile phone location data, hacking computers not connected to the Internet, bulk collection of foreign text messages, and implanting malware on the computers of surveillance targets. These capabilities reveal the NSA developing tools to manage, mine, and manipulate digital data and communications, efforts that reflect how much digital technologies and the Internet have transformed the ways individuals and institutions communicate locally, nationally, and globally. The NSA's formidable technological capabilities, and their robust use, led critics to argue that U.S. policy appeared to embrace what was technologically possible at the expense of what was politically principled and/or prudent, contributing to expedient or aggressive interpretations of relevant laws.

## Responses to Snowden's Disclosures

In interviews and written statements, Snowden made it clear that part of his motivation for revealing NSA secrets was to provoke public debate in the United States and other countries about governments' power to conduct surveillance of digital communications on a massive scale. And provoke debates he did. The responses to his actions fall into three broad areas of debate—about Snowden himself, about the secret programs and activities he exposed, and about what should be done in light of what we learned from his revelations.

To say Snowden became a divisive figure would be something of an understatement. His actions fueled antagonistic "patriot" and "traitor" narratives about the man, his motivations, his impact, and his place in history. While other episodes in American history involve individuals breaking the law to reveal classified information, there has never been anyone like Snowden, what he did, and how he did it. Even though Snowden held government and private-sector positions that gave him access to classified information,[9] he is not a Cold War–type "mole," planted by a foreign intelligence agency to pass secret information from the U.S. government directly to an adversary. Although often compared to Bradley/Chelsea Manning, who provided Julian Assange and Wikileaks with thousands of classified U.S. government documents, Snowden is not, as Manning became, an overwhelmed, troubled, and marginalized person in the events he precipitated. Snowden has been a far more consequential figure in explaining his actions, engaging his detractors, and attracting supporters around the world. In that sense, in the eyes of some, Snowden has been linked with the tradition of civil disobedience and has been connected, for example, with Daniel Ellsberg's violation of U.S. laws to make public the classified Pentagon Papers on U.S. policy in Vietnam in the early 1970s.

For others, Snowden violated important laws, betrayed his country, damaged its interests and capabilities, helped its adversaries, fled like a coward, and—under the protection of Vladimir Putin—anointed himself guardian of American ideals and global human rights. Indeed, the dissonance between what Snowden claims to be defending—fundamental individual rights enshrined in the Constitution and protected in international law—and his acceptance of temporary asylum for one year and then a three-year residency in Russia has, to many, tarnished his credibility. An investigation by nongovernmental organizations concerned about the right to privacy described Russia in fall 2013—when Snowden began his temporary asylum—as a "surveillance state" that intercepts "all electronic utterances" through "an Orwellian network that jeopardizes privacy and the ability to use telecommunications to oppose the government."[10]

Although Snowden could not get to Venezuela, his willingness to accept asylum from Nicolás Maduro, president of Venezuela, did not improve matters in this regard. In its World Report 2014, Human Rights Watch noted that under Maduro and his predecessor, Hugo Chávez, Venezuela experienced "the accumulation of power in the executive branch and the erosion of human rights guarantees that enabled the government to intimidate, censor, and prosecute its critics."[11] Under Maduro, Venezuela withdrew from the American Convention on Human Rights (a decision condemned by Amnesty International[12]) and—with Ecuador and Bolivia (two other countries Snowden thanked for their human rights stance)— "supported a campaign to undermine the independence of the Inter-American Commission on Human Rights, and limit the funding and effectiveness of its special rapporteur on freedom of expression."[13]

The intensity of the debate about Snowden has counterparts in the back-and-forth arguments about the NSA activities he exposed. Although generalizing about these arguments is risky, debates about the NSA programs, interpretations of law and policy, and capabilities oscillated between narratives of clarity and complexity. NSA critics and Snowden supporters often emphasized what they believed were obvious abuses of power and glaring violations of law cloaked in unjustifiable secrecy. Defenders of the NSA often tried to explain all the rules, procedures, institutions, and oversight that applied to the activities Snowden disclosed, with this deliberate layering of authority, restraint, and secrecy carefully safeguarding the nation's security interests and privacy rights. Snowden believed the telephone metadata program was so illegal and wrong that it triggered his obligation to break the law. NSA supporters wondered how a program outside the ambit of the Fourth Amendment under Supreme Court jurisprudence, overseen by a federal court, repeatedly briefed to and approved by Congress, and subject to executive branch policies and rules could be as illegal and immoral as Snowden and others claimed.

Another prominent debate has been about reform—what should the United States and other countries do now the disclosures have been made? Part of Snowden's legacy includes all the proposals for change made in the United States and around the world directly related to what he exposed. He triggered a vibrant, captivating, and—many would acknowledge, even if reluctantly—a needed normative exploration of many political, legal, and ethical issues. In January 2014, President Obama announced reforms to end the existing telephone metadata program and increase protections for the privacy interests of foreign nationals overseas affected by U.S. signals intelligence activities. More changes may be in the works, either through proposals before legislative bodies or rulings by national or international courts. The reform debate is not free from complexities and controversies, especially surrounding questions such as whether reform means tinkering with the status quo or radically revising the laws and practices governing surveillance activities. Many observers question whether Snowden-prompted reform in the United States and other democracies will have any spillover effect for international law or the surveillance practices of authoritarian governments, which prior to Snowden had been the leading human rights worry in this area.

## Stressing Fault Lines in National Security Politics

In the national security politics of democratic countries, the enduring challenge is to meet security threats without diminishing individual liberty. Snowden's actions accuse the U.S. government of damaging liberty through NSA programs ostensibly designed to keep America and its allies safe. The relationship between security and liberty can be unstable in democratic governance because it involves various political "fault lines," places where the alignment of policies and laws shifts, settles, endures stress, and shifts again as a consequence of domestic and international developments. For example, perceived abuses by the U.S. intelligence community in the 1960s and 1970s produced political pressure that led to, among other things, enactment of FISA. The 9/11 terrorist attacks, combined with emerging challenges to national security posed by digital communications transiting cyberspace, produced another seismic shift, resulting in passage of the USA PATRIOT Act, creation of the telephone metadata program, and adoption of Section 702 of FISA in 2008.

Snowden's disclosures have created sufficient political pressure to precipitate another shift in national security politics in the United States and, perhaps, in other democratic states. Snowden exerted pressure along six key fault lines:

Secrecy / Transparency
Elitism / Populism
Legalism / Rule of law
Duty / Responsibility
National security / International cooperation
Material power / Political principle

His leaks increased transparency at the expense of secrecy and in doing so challenged pervasive secrecy in national security politics. His actions privilege transparency over secrecy in how democracies handle national security threats. His revelations have forced the U.S. intelligence community—and the NSA in particular—to become more transparent, and proposals for reform seek greater transparency in the future.

Snowden's leaks have a populist quality because he claims the American people should debate and determine NSA surveillance powers rather than having such powers defined and exercised by elites operating in secret. The tension between popular participation in national security and foreign policy and elite management of such affairs is not new, but Snowden's actions brought this issue to the fore again. And he can claim some vindication on this point with respect to the telephone metadata program, which elites across all three branches of government crafted and implemented in secret but which, when exposed, did not survive unchanged the political uproar that ensued.

Snowden's actions drew attention to friction between legalism and the rule of law in national security politics. Defenders of NSA activities often stress that the programs comply with existing legal rules, and they argue that the NSA has followed the complex rules and procedures laid down by Congress, the president, and the courts. Snowden started a different conversation, one focused on the rule of law. Uninterested in legalities—such as whether the NSA complied with the law—he challenged the law more fundamentally. How, Snowden asked, can laws interpreted secretly by a secret court, implemented secretly by the executive branch, and considered in secret by legislative bodies comport with the rule of law? Given the scale of the NSA surveillance programs exposed, this question carries extra wallop in a polity that embraces the rule of law as part of its governing ethos.

Snowden's decision to violate laws prohibiting the release of classified information highlighted tensions between duty and responsibility frequently encountered in national security contexts. Given the dangers the country faces, the need for individuals working on national security issues to follow the rules is significant, including rules about protecting certain types of sensitive information. But we know the pitfalls of blind obedience when power is abused and no outlet to disclose such abuses exists. Snowden has argued that NSA officials paid no attention to the concerns he raised and that because he was a private contractor for the NSA, U.S. law provided him none of the protections provided for "whistleblowers."

Although the NSA disputes his account, the larger point here is that Snowden's actions have refocused attention on the duty/responsibility problem and highlighted the potential need for rethinking whistleblower rules and procedures in the intelligence community. The director of national intelligence issued a new directive (in the works before Snowden appeared) on whistleblower protection in the intelligence community in March 2014.[14] Reactions to Snowden's leaks in the European Union also led to discussion about crafting European-wide protections for whistleblowers.

Snowden's disclosures also highlight tensions between national security interests and prospects for international cooperation. Fairly or unfairly, Snowden's disclosures painted a picture of a United States willing and able to engage in signals intelligence on a massive scale against adversaries and allies alike, exploiting for national security advantages its position as a leader in the development of cyber technologies and services. In the wake of the leaks, the fears of adversaries were confirmed, cooperation with allies strained, and U.S. leadership in cyber technologies damaged. Whether Snowden is a hero or a traitor does not enter into the calculations of countries trying to process what they have learned and how they might relate to the U.S. government and the NSA in the future. Although some blame Snowden for this predicament, others ask whether some of the programs Snowden disclosed made sense in terms of U.S. relationships with other countries and the U.S. need for international cooperation on a host of cyberspace and other political and economic challenges.

Snowden's actions also touch age-old tensions between the exercise of material power and fidelity to political principles. Lee Hamilton observes in his essay in this volume that the United States "cannot proceed on the basis that our spying is necessary or appropriate simply because we can technologically do it." This sentiment captures what many people thought when exposed to the NSA's formidable capabilities—amazement at what the NSA could do, but with questions about whether the United States should engage in some of these SIGINT activities. We know from history that the advent of new technologies can increase the material power countries wield, and such technological enhancements entice governments to reinterpret rules, procedures, and principles to accommodate what the new instruments of power can do. A common refrain in NSA responses to Snowden's revelations about its technological capabilities was that media stories rarely observed that the NSA only uses its capabilities in compliance with established policies and laws. But Snowden's disclosures prompted people to wonder whether the availability of new technological power in the cyber and digital realms has unduly influenced how the U.S. government shapes, interprets, and applies policies and laws.

Interestingly, Snowden's leaks did not touch on other fault lines in U.S. national security politics, most notably the tension between the executive and legislative branches. Tensions here routinely appear, for example, in relation to war powers. Clashes have occurred in the surveillance context as well, often centered on presidential claims of authority to conduct warrantless surveillance inside the United States for foreign intelligence and national security purposes. The surveillance program eventually authorized under Section 702 of FISA was started by President George W. Bush as the Terrorist Surveillance Program (TSP) under his interpretation of presidential authority to conduct foreign intelligence surveillance in the United States outside FISA and without judicial involvement. The controversy that exploded when the press disclosed the TSP in 2005 placed stress on the executive-legislative fault line. The controversies around the telephone metadata and Section 702 programs leaked by Snowden did not create such stress because these programs involved participation from all three branches of the government.

Although Snowden put significant pressure on fault lines in U.S. national security politics that affect the security-liberty relationship, this does not mean he was right to do so or that what emerges, if a shift occurs, will reflect what he wants or produce a more stable or legitimate outcome. Nevertheless, Snowden's legacy includes the increasing political strain he put on these long-standing fault lines and the possibility of another historic realignment in U.S. national security policy and law.

Disclosures from Snowden are likely to continue, but future leaks might not top the shock, awe, anger, and action generated after the first story appeared on June 5, 2013. Some observers noted "Snowden fatigue" in the relative lack of media coverage of, and political and public interest in, new disclosures made in the fall of 2014, such as the one on AURORAGOLD, an NSA operation to gain access to cellphone networks and technologies worldwide.[15] Other surveillance controversies might emerge, but not necessarily ones caused by Snowden. For example, U.S. government officials believed a "second Snowden" leaked classified documents to journalists involved in Snowden's disclosures.[16] In addition, a former State Department official and the American Civil Liberties Union both argued that Americans should be more concerned about the U.S. government's collection of their communications under Executive Order 12333 than under FISA.[17]

These developments have prompted speculation about what Snowden will leave behind. Will Snowden's impact fade under the rush of other national security crises that require governments to exploit powerful surveillance and intelligence capabilities at home and abroad?[18] If so, the Snowden affair might appear years from now more as a historical curiosity than a turning point. Or has Snowden triggered changes in national security politics that produce more governmental transparency, deliberative democracy, and whistleblower protections? If so, then the secret world Snowden exposed might, in years hence, seem like a relic of a time and place no longer valuable to those responsible for meeting security threats without diminishing individual liberty.

# Notes

1. Glenn Greenwald, *No Place to Hide: Edward Snowden, the NSA, and the U.S. Surveillance State* (New York: Macmillan, 2014); Laura Poitras, Citizenfour, 2014, https://citizenfourfilm.com.

2. Office of the Director of National Intelligence, IC on the Record, http://icontherecord .tumblr.com/, accessed August 13, 2014.

3. This perspective informs, for example, Greenwald, *No Place to Hide.*

4. This interpretation informs, for example, Edward Lucas, *The Snowden Operation: Inside the West's Greatest Intelligence Disaster* (London: Amazon, 2014).

5. National Security Agency, "The National Security Agency: Missions, Authorities, Oversight and Partnerships," National Security Agency document, August 9, 2013, 2.

6. *Intelligence Activities and the Rights of Americans: Final Report of the Select Committee to Study Governmental Operations with Respect to Intelligence Activities,* Book II (Washington, D.C.: U.S. Government Printing Office, 1976), 12.

7. "Spying Together: Germany's Deep Cooperation with the NSA," *Der Spiegel,* June 18, 2014, http://www.spiegel.de/international/germany/the-german-bnd-and-american-nsa-cooperate -more-closely-than-thought-a-975445.html.

8. Quoted in Ewen MacAskill, Julian Borger, Nick Hopkins, and James Ball, "GCHQ Taps Fibre-Optic Cables for Secret Access to World's Communications," *Guardian,* June 21, 2013, http:// www.theguardian.com/uk/2013/jun/21/gchq-cables-secret-world-communications-nsa.

9. For more on Snowden's biography, see Luke Harding, *The Snowden Files: The Inside Story of the World's Most Wanted Man* (New York: Vintage Books, 2014).

10. Andrei Soldatov and Irina Borogan, "Russia's Surveillance State," *World Policy Journal* (Fall 2013), http://www.worldpolicy.org/journal/fal12013/Russia-surveillance.

11. Human Rights Watch, "Venezuela," in *World Report 2014,* http://www.hrw.org/world -report/2014/country-chapters/venezuela?page=1.

12. Amnesty International, "Venezuela's Withdrawal from Regional Human Rights Instrument a Serious Setback," September 6, 2013, http://www.amnesty.org/en/news/venezuela-s-withdrawal -regional-human-rights-instrument-serious-setback-2013-09-06.

13. Human Rights Watch, "Venezuela."

14. Director of National Intelligence, "Intelligence Community Directive 120 on Intelligence Community Whistleblower Protection," March 20, 2014, http://www.dni.gov/files/documents /ICD/ICD%20120.pdf.

15. See, for example, the lack of mainstream coverage of the disclosure of the secret 2009 *Quadrennial Intelligence Community Review* in Glenn Greenwald, "The U.S. Government's Secret Plans to Spy for American Corporations," *The Intercept,* September 5, 2014, https://firstlook.org /theintercept/greenwald/. On AURORAGOLD, see Ryan Gallagher, "Operation AURORAGOLD: How the NSA Hacks Cellphone Networks Worldwide," *The Intercept,* December 4, 2014, https:// firstlook.org/theintercept/2014/12/04/nsaauroragold-hack-cellphones/.

16. Arit John, "U.S. Officials Say There's a Second Snowden Leaking Documents," *The Wire,* August 5, 2014, http://www.thewire.com/politics/2014/08/us-official-says-theres-a-second -snowden-leaking-security-documents/375613/. In October 2014, news reports indicated the FBI had identified a suspect and conducted an investigation of his home. Andrea Peterson, "The 'Second Source' for Snowden Reporters," *Washington Post,* October 29, 2014, http://www.washington post.com/blogs/the-switch/wp/2014/10/29/the-second-source-for-snowden-reporters-explained/.

17. First issued in 1981, Executive Order 12333 is the key document guiding U.S. surveillance and intelligence activities outside the United States. For the arguments warning about this executive order, see John Napier Tye, "Meet Executive Order 12333: The Reagan Rule That Lets the NSA Spy on Americans," *Washington Post,* July 18, 2014, http://www.washingtonpost.com/opinions /meet-executive-order-12333-the-reagan-rule-that-lets-the-nsa-spy-on-americans/2014/07/18 /93d2ac22-0b93-11e4-b8e5-d0de80767fc2_story.html; American Civil Liberties Union, "New NSA Documents Shine More Light into Black Box of Executive Order 12333," October 30, 2014, https://

www.aclu.org/blog/national-security/new-nsa-documents-shine-more-light-black-box-executive -order-12333.

18. My chapter in this volume identifies dramatic developments in international politics in 2014 that increased interest in the use of extensive surveillance and intelligence capabilities to address mounting national security threats.

PART I

PERSPECTIVES ON THE

# SNOWDEN
# DISCLOSURES

# 1

# Security and Liberty:
# The Imaginary Balance

### NICK CULLATHER

If one truism captures the tenor of discussion surrounding the Snowden revelations, it is the recurring metaphor of balance between liberty and security. In May 2013, three days after Snowden fled to Hong Kong but before his disclosures began, President Obama maintained his administration was "working hard to strike the appropriate balance between our need for security and preserving those freedoms that make us who we are."[1] Later, as the magnitude of National Security Agency's mass surveillance became clear from Snowden's leaks, editorialists condemned the president in almost the same words: George W. Bush had "tipped the balance too far from liberty towards security," wrote *The Economist*, "and it has stayed there under Barack Obama."[2]

On December 16, 2013, a federal district judge ruled the NSA's domestic telephony metadata program "probably unconstitutional," and observed that the case was "the latest chapter in the Judiciary's continuing challenge to balance the national security interests of the United States with the individual liberties of our citizens.... In the months ahead, other Article III courts, no doubt will wrestle to find the proper balance consistent with our constitutional system."[3] On December 27, 2013, another judge in a different circuit upheld the NSA's telephony metadata program in dismissing a lawsuit from the American Civil Liberties Union. Referring to the 9/11 Commission, this judge stated that "[t]he choice between liberty and security is a false one, as nothing is more apt to imperil civil liberties than the success of a terrorist attack on American soil."[4]

Extending the meme beyond America's borders, Silicon Valley giants—including Google, Facebook, and Twitter—objected in an open letter in December 2013 that the "balance in many countries has tipped too far in favor of the state and away from the rights of the individual."[5] The contexts in which the "balance" metaphor has arisen in responses to Snowden's disclosures all refer to government's need to protect official secrets as central to the maintenance of "security." Through repetition, the balance cliche has gained an aura of probity, even wisdom. It appears to be a neutral framing of the problem of official secrecy, but the perception that liberty and security sit in the teetering pans of a beam scale comes laden with assumptions that deserve examination.

This perception implies that security and liberty are competing considerations and that a responsible government has an obligation to restrict civil liberties to meet a minimum standard of diligence in pursuit of security. It also carries connotations of quantity and precision, as if security and liberty are two columns in a ledger in which incremental deductions can be measured or recorded.[6]

The metaphor also gives primacy to administration over law or principle, conveying a notion that the process of balancing is a matter of bureaucratic fine-tuning, not a job for politicians or citizens but for experts. And, finally, it implies a permanence to the process, as if balancing ("a continuing challenge") has always gone on and always will. In December 2013, Senator Ron Wyden attributed "what's always been the constitutional teeter-totter" to "the founding fathers, it really comes back to that. They always said, our system works when you have liberty and security in balance."[7]

## The Invented History of Balance

Wyden felt no need to specify which founding father invented the teeter-totter image or in which of the *Federalist Papers* it appeared. Nor did Senator Charles Schumer, who told *Face the Nation* that the "balance" issue was "age-old . . . since the Constitution was written."[8] Although the image gains much of its rhetorical power from its presumed antiquity, it does not appear in any of the founding documents, the debates in the *Congressional Globe,* or the speeches of Abraham Lincoln. Oliver Wendell Holmes, who limited free speech to those not yelling fire in crowded theaters, did not mention it. Perhaps more strikingly, Americans weathered three existential crises in the first half of the twentieth century—World War I, the Great Depression, and World War II—without discussing or attempting to balance security and liberty.

In facing dangers more dire than terrorism, previous administrations pushed for suspension or modification of conceptions of liberty by arguing either that the circumstances required it or the Constitution allowed it. Woodrow Wilson's administration, in securing passage of the 1917 espionage laws under which Snowden is charged, stated plainly that the Bill of Rights was suspended for the duration of the war. Wilson noted that "a time of war must be regarded as wholly exceptional, and that it is legitimate to regard things which would in ordinary circumstances be innocent as very dangerous."[9]

Franklin Roosevelt, in asking for a vast expansion of executive power to meet the twin emergencies of the Depression and war persuasively argued that the Constitution was expansive enough to accommodate the requirements of liberty as well as the need to act in the national defense. "Our Constitution is so simple and practical," he explained in his first inaugural, "that it is possible always to meet extraordinary needs by changes in emphasis and arrangement without loss of essential form."[10] Wilson and Roosevelt each violated civil liberties on a frightful scale, but these older justifications had the advantage of requiring politicians to acknowledge the violation, to say when the public could expect its full rights to be restored, and to explain their interpretation of their obligations under the Constitution.

## Balance and the Politics of Secrecy

It was only in the 1940s that the term "security" came to mean protecting state secrets, or, as the *Oxford English Dictionary*'s earliest record of this usage put it, "the Army term for what normal people call secrecy."[11] The apparatus of official secrecy in the United States, as well as the balance metaphor used to justify it, emerged in the particular cultural setting of the nuclear age, the Red Scare, wiretapping by the Federal Bureau of Investigation (FBI), and the Cold War. Its inventor was Harry S. Truman, under attack for tolerating a State Department riddled with communist spies and for overzealously enforcing the loyalty codes intended to keep spies out. On January 23, 1951, he named Admiral Chester Nimitz to head a presidential commission on secrecy and enjoined him to "seek the wisest balance that can be struck between security and freedom."[12] It was the first recorded use of the balance image.

The balance trope, thus, emerged in a specific policy context. The Nimitz Commission was the first of a series of panels that dismantled the patchwork of McCarthy-era loyalty programs and replaced them with a unified, professionalized system of security clearances. This system classified two things, documents and personnel. Documents were divided into three primary and other exceptional levels of secrecy, and personnel were given "clearance" at corresponding levels. The classification system emerged as a solution to the divisive politics of loyalty, which subjected the Truman and Eisenhower administrations to repeated charges of harboring subversives and sympathizers and which subjected officials, writers, educators, and anyone of influence to unsubstantiated charges against their integrity.

The loyalty programs began in 1941, when Roosevelt authorized the FBI to fingerprint and investigate the backgrounds of all federal employees. In 1947, Truman created an extensive apparatus of commissions to enforce the "complete and unswerving loyalty" of all federal employees.[13] Dismissal was mandated on the basis of any "derogatory information" or simply by the subject's inability to refute unsubstantiated charges. Loyalty was a universal category, and anyone positioned anywhere in the government, from the Manhattan Project to the Bureau of Weights and Measures, could be fired on the basis of mere accusation. The FBI pushed the program outside government, sending "blind memoranda" to private companies fingering suspect employees on their payrolls.[14]

By 1951, Truman faced a rising public backlash against indiscriminate investigations and reckless allegations of disloyalty. At the same time, Senator Joseph McCarthy was accusing the administration of harboring hundreds of known communists. The security clearance system was designed to narrow investigations to a smaller set of officials who had access to high-level secrets. The press generally applauded the move, but editorials hit at Truman's framing of the issue as one of balance. The *New York Times* argued, "We do not have to choose between sedition or treason on the one hand and a sterile conformity on the other. We do not have to endure either."[15] "Security and freedom are not in conflict," insisted the *Washington Post,* "they are, on the contrary, complimentary."[16] Editorials maintained that the government was responsible for ensuring both security and liberty, but they welcomed a more civil and methodical process for granting security clearances.

Begun by the Nimitz Commission, the work of establishing a nonpolitical system for rationing security clearances was implemented through presidential Executive Orders 10290 and 10450 and finalized by the Wright Commission in 1957. This solution turned the fractious issue of loyalty into an issue of "suitability" assessed through a system of uniform procedures. "All loyalty cases are security cases, but the converse is not true," the Wright Commission observed. "A man who talks too freely when in his cups or a pervert who is vulnerable to blackmail may both be security risks although both may be loyal Americans."[17] The polygraph, psychological profiling, and background investigations were tools for drawing a harder, more scientific line between the suitable and the unsuitable.

The new system changed loyalty from a political question to a procedural one and changed "clearance" from a verdict—exoneration before a Loyalty Board— into a credential. By the late 1950s, it was being used as an ordinary noun, a "security clearance," something everyone in defense or intelligence work had to have. This strategy did not fully end the injustices of the loyalty screenings. In fact, it replaced the Red Scare with a Lavender Scare as the government searched for evidence of unsuitability in bedrooms.[18] But, consequentially for the Snowden case, it introduced new hierarchies, between sensitive jobs and nonsensitive ones, those with a clearance and those without, and, eventually, between those with various levels of clearance.

## The Cleared and the Uncleared

The language of balance was, thus, introduced to describe the proper relation between the small group of people with a security clearance and the remainder of the American public, which now had no legitimate recourse to the growing system of hidden knowledge their government was creating and using. That is what the balance idea still describes. Snowden justifies his actions as an attempt to redress what he sees as a widening imbalance of power between the cleared and the uncleared. "These things need to be determined by the public, not by somebody who was simply hired by the government," he explained in his first statement from Hong Kong. "The public needs to decide whether these programs and policies are right or wrong."[19]

Today, five million Americans hold security clearances, 1.5 percent of the population. They are seen as government insiders, but they attain that status by sacrificing a substantial share of their rights. Most are subject to lifetime confidentiality contracts that prohibit them from ever speaking about what they know. Those without clearances also sacrifice rights; they live in a country divided between those who know and cannot speak, and those who can speak but do not know.

The politics of the Snowden case rests on this division. Leaks have become the prime driver of reform in the intelligence establishment, not because illegal or improper acts were necessarily committed, but because the public has been left in the dark about what is legal and proper under the applicable rules. The oversight procedures in the executive, legislative, and judicial branches, operating within the confines of the secrecy regime, were satisfied that the system was working and that adequate and effective checks were in place. It was only those outside the clearance wall—the press, foreign leaders, and the public—who were outraged by the nature and scale of the NSA's activities.

The leaker is now an indispensable but criminalized link, mediating a vexed relationship between the public and the cleared. Snowden is charged, and Bradley/Chelsea Manning was convicted in the Wikileaks affair, with disclosing classified information to "unauthorized persons." The charge refers not only to the Russians or Chinese, but also to the 308 million Americans without a security clearance. Obama's vigorous pursuit of leakers, the Department of Justice's use of subpoenas to obtain information about press contacts, and the administration's ongoing prosecution of *New York Times* correspondent James Risen for shielding a confidential source are all attempts to police a crumbling boundary between the suitable and unsuitable sectors of the American polity.

There have been other rationales for drawing arbitrary lines between Americans, and they have proven more or less durable. "Separate but Equal" lasted sixty years; "Don't Ask Don't Tell" lasted considerably less. When such barriers fall, they do so abruptly, resting as they do on a kind of common sense that suddenly makes no sense.

Snowden's most politically damaging revelation was the complicity of the watchdogs charged with protecting the public interest, the oversight committees and the FISA court, which acquiesced when the NSA overstepped even the residual safeguards left standing after 9/11. When it became clear that there was no balancer, no effective advocate for the uncleared majority, NSA surveillance lost legitimacy. To continue, former NSA chief Michael Hayden explained, the president needed to regain "the consent of the governed." The NSA and the administration scrambled to put forward transparency proposals and shift some collection activities from intelligence agencies to telecom providers.[20] This was, Hayden told Chris Wallace of Fox News Sunday, "a PR move." The president needed to restore an appearance of balance, "but the objective . . . is to keep on doing what he's doing."[21]

# Notes

1. Kevin Clarke, "Obama Seeks Balance Between Liberty and Security," *America,* May 23, 2013, http://new.americamagazine.org/node/155623.

2. "Liberty's Lost Decade," *The Economist,* August 3, 2013, 11.

3. *Klayman v. Obama,* 957 F.Supp.2d 1, 43 (D.D.C. 2013). A notable dissent from this perspective appeared in a report released to the public on December 18, 2013, from a special White House panel established to examine issues raised by Snowden's disclosures. This panel cautioned that while "[t]he idea of 'balancing' has an important element of truth . . . it is also inadequate and misleading. . . . In the American tradition, liberty and security need not be in conflict." President's Review Group on Intelligence and Communications Technologies, "Liberty and Security in a Changing World," December 12, 2013, 16, 259. See part II.B for excerpts from the *Klayman* case and the executive summary of the report of the President's Review Group.

4. *ACLU v. Clapper,* 959 F.Supp.2d 724, 757 (S.D.N.Y. 2013). See part II.B for excerpts from the *Clapper* case.

5. AOL, Apple, Dropbox, Facebook, Google, LinkedIn, Microsoft, Twitter, and Yahoo, "An Open Letter to Washington," December 9, 2013, https://www.reformgovernmentsurveillance.com /#111614, accessed July 7, 2014. See part II.A for the text of this letter.

6. Jeremy Waldron, "Security and Liberty: The Image of Balance," *Journal of Political Philosophy* 11 (2003): 191–210.

7. "Sen. Ron Wyden on Balancing the 'Teeter-Totter' of Security and Liberty," *PBS Newshour,* December 13, 2013, http://www.pbs.org/newshour/bb/government_programs-july-dec13-nsa2 _12-13/.

8. "Face the Nation," *CBS News*, August 4, 2013, http://www.cbsnews.com/news/face-the-nation-transcripts-august-4-2013-schumer-ryan-and-mccaul/.

9. "The Press Under Post Office Censorship," *Current History*, November 1, 1917, 235–36.

10. Ira Katznelson, *Fear Itself: The New Deal and the Origins of Our Time* (New York: Liveright, 2013), 121.

11. Security, definition d, *Oxford English Dictionary* (Oxford: Oxford University Press, 3rd ed., 2011), http://www.oed.com/view/Entry/174661?redirectedFrom=security#eid, accessed July 10, 2014.

12. "Text of Truman Order and Statement on Security and Rights Board," *New York Times*, January 24, 1951, 12.

13. Executive Order 9835, Prescribing Procedures for the Administration of an Employees Loyalty Program in the Executive Branch of the Government, March 21, 1947, 1.

14. Ellen Schrecker, *Many Are the Crimes: McCarthyism in America* (Boston: Little, Brown, 1998).

15. "Freedom and Security," *New York Times*, January 25, 1951, 24.

16. "Loyalty and Liberty," *Washington Post*, January 20, 1953, 14.

17. Commission on Protecting and Reducing Government Secrecy, *Secrecy: Report of the Commission on Protecting and Reducing Government Secrecy* (Washington, D.C.: U.S. Government Printing Office, 1997), A-51.

18. David K. Johnson, *The Lavender Scare: The Cold War Persecution of Gays and Lesbians in the Federal Government* (Chicago: University of Chicago Press, 2004).

19. Quoted in David Cole, "The Three Leakers and What to Do About Them," *New York Review of Books*, February 6, 2014, 7.

20. See, e.g., President Obama, Remarks on Review of Signals Intelligence, January 17, 2014. See part II.C for the text of this speech.

21. Chris Wallace, "Interview with Michael Hayden," *Fox News Sunday*, January 19, 2014, http://www.foxnews.com/on-air/fox-news-sunday-chris-wallace/2014/01/19/hayden-leahy-debate-presidents-proposed-nsa-reforms-obamacare-website-security-getting#p//v/3076728835001.

# 2

# Edward Snowden and the NSA: Law, Policy, and Politics

## FRED H. CATE

The disclosures by Edward Snowden have revealed a great deal about the National Security Agency, its surveillance activities, and the oversight provided by the president, the Foreign Intelligence Surveillance Court (FISC), and Congress. Snowden's disclosures, and subsequent responses (or lack thereof) by government officials, focus attention on five significant sets of issues that confront the American people and their government: the scope of the NSA's legal authority, problems with the honesty of U.S. officials, the hypocrisy of the U.S. government concerning cyber espionage, the undermining of cyber security by U.S. actions, and the impact of U.S. surveillance activities on personal privacy.

## The NSA's Legal Authority

The first set of issues concerns the authority under which the NSA has conducted the sweeping surveillance programs Snowden disclosed. Thanks to the documents Snowden leaked, we have learned about more and more NSA practices, including how it undertakes surveillance activities, introduces security vulnerabilities into products and services, or compels the private sector to cooperate in these activities. In each case, we want to know under *what legal authority* is the NSA acting. To date, the only surveillance activities we know about in legal detail are the ones the Obama administration has addressed publicly—compelling phone companies to disclose metadata about all telephone calls under Section 215 of the USA PATRIOT Act and the PRISM program operated under Section 702 of the Foreign Intelligence Surveillance Act (FISA), which is addressed elsewhere in this book.

## The Meaning of Section 215 of the USA PATRIOT Act

The first Snowden disclosure was an order from the FISC compelling Verizon (and, we later learned, AT&T and Sprint) to turn over to the NSA on a daily basis metadata on "all calls," including calls "wholly within the United States including local telephone calls."[1] The FISC issued the order under Section 215 of the USA PATRIOT Act, a broad provision of law empowering the FISC to issue secret orders "requiring the production of any tangible things (including books, records, papers, documents, and other items)."[2]

The use of Section 215 to require telephone companies to collect and disclose information about all calls made on their networks (other than calls taking place wholly outside of the United States, which the NSA collects through other means) raises many questions about the applicability of this legal authority. For example, Section 215 on its face only applies to the FBI, yet the orders Snowden revealed require disclosure to the NSA. Does "any tangible things" include surveillance of metadata? The statute describes tangible things as "books, records, papers, documents, and other items." As originally drafted, this legal provision was called the "Business Records Provision" and only applied to the records already kept by commercial entities. Businesses could not be required to create records for the government, only to provide the FBI with access to records that already existed. When the USA PATRIOT Act expanded this provision to include "any tangible things," the language and legislative history suggested that it meant tangible things that already existed. Yet the FISC orders revealed by Snowden applied to information that did not yet exist.

Most importantly, in the process of expanding what Section 215 covered, Congress specifically limited when Section 215 applied by only permitting the FISC to issue orders where there were "reasonable grounds to believe that the tangible things sought are relevant to an authorized investigation (other than a threat assessment) . . . to obtain foreign intelligence information not concerning a United States person or to protect against international terrorism or clandestine intelligence activities."[3]

There are important limits in that cumbersome phrase, and it simply strains credulity to believe that there was any basis, much less "reasonable grounds," to believe that metadata on all calls made by all Americans were "relevant to an authorized investigation." If data on everyone could be relevant to an "authorized investigation," then the limits enacted by Congress mean nothing.

We subsequently learned through congressional testimony and statements by Obama administration officials that neither the government nor the court claimed that the metadata about all calls were "relevant to an authorized investigation," but rather were being collected by the NSA only so that those metadata later, in the words of the director of national intelligence (DNI), may be "queried when there is a reasonable suspicion, based on specific facts, that the particular basis for the query is associated with a foreign terrorist organization."[4]

Rather than limit the FISC orders, as FISA requires, to collecting only the "tangible things" for which there are "reasonable grounds to believe are relevant to an authorized investigation," the NSA instead sought vastly more data, the majority of which, according to the DNI's general counsel, are "never going to be responsive to one of these terrorism-related queries."[5] The standard the NSA applied *after* collection is, in fact, the standard required by Section 215 *before* the data are collected. This failure to follow the law as written further casts into doubt as to whether the FISC had the authority to the issue the surveillance orders or whether the government followed the law in seeking them.

## Independent Reviews of the Meaning of Section 215

Two independent reviews sanctioned by the U.S. government of the NSA's activities prompted by the Snowden disclosures concluded that the NSA lacked the authority to act as it did under Section 215. The Privacy and Civil Liberties Oversight Board (PCLOB), originally established by Congress in 2007 to exercise independent oversight of intelligence and homeland security activities, found "the government's interpretation of the word 'relevant' in Section 215 to be unsupported by legal precedent and a subversion of the statute's manifest intent."[6]

But the PCLOB went further and identified four reasons for its conclusion that "Section 215 does not provide an adequate legal basis to support the program":

> First, the telephone records acquired under the program have no connection to any specific FBI investigation at the time of their collection. Second, because the records are collected in bulk—potentially encompassing all telephone calling records across the nation—they cannot be regarded as "relevant" to any FBI investigation as required by the statute without redefining the word relevant in a manner that is circular, unlimited in scope, and out of step with the case law from analogous legal contexts involving the production of records. Third, the program operates by putting telephone companies under an obligation to furnish new calling records on a daily basis as they are generated (instead of turning over records already in their possession)—an approach lacking foundation in

the statute and one that is inconsistent with FISA as a whole. Fourth, the statute permits only the FBI to obtain items for use in its investigations; it does not authorize the NSA to collect anything.[7]

In addition, the PCLOB concluded that the metadata surveillance program violates the Electronic Communications Privacy Act: "That statute prohibits telephone companies from sharing customer records with the government except in response to specific enumerated circumstances, which do not include Section 215 orders."

The other review was conducted by the President's Review Group on Intelligence and Communications Technologies (Review Group), made up of legal and security professionals appointed by the president to examine surveillance activities and oversight in the wake of Snowden's leaks. The Review Group took an equally negative view of the NSA's use of Section 215:

> In our view, the current storage by the government of bulk meta-data creates potential risks to public trust, personal privacy, and civil liberty. We recognize that the government might need access to such meta-data, which should be held instead either by private providers or by a private third party. This approach would allow the government access to the relevant information when such access is justified, and thus protect national security without unnecessarily threatening privacy and liberty.[8]

The Review Group endorsed "a broad principle for the future: as a general rule and without senior policy review, the government should not be permitted to collect and store mass, undigested, non-public personal information about US persons for the purpose of enabling future queries and data-mining for foreign intelligence purposes." And the Review Group recommended "important restrictions on the ability of the Foreign Intelligence Surveillance Court (FISC) to compel third parties (such as telephone service providers) to disclose private information to the government."

## The Candor of Government Officials

The documents disclosed by Snowden provide convincing and disturbing evidence that senior intelligence officials have not been honest with the public or with Congress. It is important to be clear here: Most of what happens with national security and intelligence is classified, and we are not told about it. While reasonable people might disagree about how much information should be classified, a great deal necessarily will be, and I believe this is reasonable and appropriate.

Respect for necessary secrecy, however, never justifies lying to the public or to Congress. Intelligence officials may say "no comment" or decline to answer difficult questions, but when they do speak, and especially when they speak under oath, they should tell the truth.

Snowden's leaks cast serious doubt on the accuracy of numerous statements by senior intelligence officials. For example, James Clapper, director of national intelligence, testified before Congress in March 2013 that the NSA was not collecting data on U.S. persons, when in fact it was collecting data on billions of U.S. person calls every day.[9] After the Snowden disclosures began, he tried to explain away the statement by saying it was the "least most untruthful" response possible,[10] as if there is a meaningful difference between untrue statements and least untrue statements. Both the false statement and the explanation by the nation's senior intelligence official were embarrassing.

General Keith Alexander, NSA director, testified before Congress in March 2012 for the explicit purpose of denying a *Wired* story claiming that the NSA was conducting surveillance on U.S. persons. He made the definitive statement, "We're not authorized to do it [collect data on U.S. citizens], nor do we do it."[11] It turns out only the first part of his statement was true. In July 2012, General Alexander told an American Enterprise Institute audience that the NSA does not "hold data on U.S. citizens,"[12] when, in fact, it did at the time and was collecting more every day. General Alexander spoke to the Reuters Cybersecurity Summit in May 2013 and said that "[t]he great irony is we're the only ones not spying on the American people,"[13] when we now know that the NSA has been conducting extensive surveillance involving data generated by U.S. citizens.

The occasional misstatement by government personnel is unavoidable, but a pattern of deceiving Congress and the public requires some official response. To date, however, the president has refused to prosecute, dismiss, or even reprimand any administration official for dishonest public statements.

The president could have sent a strong, and I think desirable, signal to the public, Congress, and our allies, which have been outraged by NSA surveillance of their leaders, had he said: "Dishonesty with the public and with Congress, which is constitutionally charged with oversight, is something this administration will not tolerate. You may not lie to Congress. You can say, 'I cannot answer that question' or 'I can only answer it in a closed hearing,' but you may not deceive or mislead Congress or the public."

James Goodale, the attorney who represented the *New York Times* in the famed Pentagon Papers case, wrote that "[w]e expect the NSA to have a culture that lies to and deceives the enemy. But the American public is not the enemy."[14] He recommended that the president should "fire officials who lie."

But that has not happened in the case of any senior official, nor in the case of NSA employees or Justice Department attorneys who the FISC found repeatedly misled the court.[15] In one opinion, Judge Reggie B. Walton wrote that "[t]he government has compounded its noncompliance with the court's orders by repeatedly submitting inaccurate descriptions of the alert list process" to the court.[16] Yet the Justice Department declined even to investigate the misconduct, much less take action to punish it or create disincentives for similar conduct in the future.[17]

We have other examples resulting from Snowden's disclosures that are equally troubling. For example, the FBI spent a fair amount of time in congressional testimony talking about the problem of the Internet going "dark"—what the FBI describes as "a potentially widening gap between our legal authority to intercept electronic communications pursuant to court order and our practical ability to actually intercept those communications."[18] It turns out that as a result of the NSA's extraordinary access to digital communications, the Internet is not going dark for the government. We are left with two possibilities. First, the FBI officials who testified before Congress that this was a critical national security issue were not telling the truth. Second, the NSA had not told the FBI about the agency's capabilities. Neither one is a very comfortable outcome—our national security officials are either not honest or are not cooperating with each other.

A final example concerns the U.S. negotiations with European allies. It now turns out that the NSA was spying on some of our closest allies, such as German chancellor Angela Merkel, but while doing so were apparently misrepresenting our surveillance capabilities and activities. In 2010, for example, European officials objected to the U.S. Treasury Department's sweeping, secret subpoenas requiring U.S. financial institutions to hand over transactional data from the Brussels-based Society for Worldwide Interbank Financial Telecommunication (SWIFT). In response to these objections, the U.S. negotiated an agreement with the European Union providing for strict limits on American access to the SWIFT system. But disclosures by Snowden make clear that despite this agreement, the NSA was secretly collecting SWIFT data. Such disingenuousness has not done much to enhance our nation's credibility with our allies and trading partners.

## Hypocrisy on Cyber Espionage

A third problem falls under the term "hypocrisy." Not only was the U.S. government misleading its allies, but it was also embarking on a foreign policy the Snowden revelations suggest is directly at odds with its own behavior. The first disclosure by Snowden, before we even knew his identity, occurred just before President Obama met with President Xi Jinping of China at a summit in California.

For months prior to the summit, the administration followed a carefully orchestrated plan making the case that China was the source of successful attacks on the Department of Defense (DOD) and other government agencies, major defense contractors, Google and other major technology companies, the International and

U.S. Olympic Committees, the *New York Times* and other U.S. media, and human rights groups—a tactic *The Economist* described as "naming and shaming."[19] In May 2013, the DOD for the first time specifically named the Chinese *government* and *military* as the source of significant cyber attacks against the United States.[20] On May 7, 2013, the *New York Times*, typical of many U.S. newspapers, editorialized about "China and Cyberwar," arguing that "there seems little doubt that China's computer hackers are engaged in an aggressive and increasingly threatening campaign of cyber espionage directed at a range of government and private systems in the United States."[21] All this effort was leading up to the first summit between President Xi and President Obama during the first week of June 2013, at which it was widely anticipated that the United States would air its long-standing grievances against Chinese surveillance and hacking activities.

Ultimately, Snowden's early June 2013 leaks about the U.S. government's own cyber attacks and online surveillance activities dampened the vigor with which the U.S. president pressed the topic.[22] Ironically, the Chinese delegation refused to stay at the Sunnylands estate where the summit was held, reportedly out of fear that the U.S. government would spy on them.

The leaks that began immediately prior to the U.S.-China summit revealed U.S. surveillance activities around the world (including within the United States). They also exposed cyber exploits by the NSA designed to facilitate surveillance, launch cyber attacks, and interfere with online transactions. According to documents provided by Snowden and widely reported in the press, the United States has been attacking "hundreds" of targets in Hong Kong and mainland China as part of the U.S. government's cyber attacks on sixty-one thousand targets worldwide.[23] Those attacks include incursions into Chinese telecommunications companies, the owner of China's most extensive fiber-optic submarine cable network, and Beijing University.[24] One prominent target, according to documents reviewed by the *New York Times*, was Chinese telecommunications giant Huawei. The NSA installed back doors into networks operated by Huawei, which reportedly serve a third of the world's population, not merely to collect information from the Chinese, but to surveil users in other countries that used Huawei's networks and to conduct offensive cyber operations.[25]

"Load stations" operated by U.S. intelligence agencies around the world—including at least two in China[26]—allowed those agencies to interdict computers and related accessories, load malware or hardware components on to them, and then arrange for the delivery of the now-compromised equipment to their intended recipients.[27] In addition, the NSA's Tailored Access Operations (TAO) group used "covert implants"—"sophisticated malware transmitted from far away, in computers, routers and firewalls on tens of thousands of machines every year," with plans to expand exponentially.[28] According to officials interviewed by *BusinessWeek*,

TAO implants access two petabytes of data an hour, the equivalent of "hundreds of millions of pages of text."[29]

The scope of the attacks is so vast that they are managed by an automated system—codenamed "TURBINE"—intended, according to leaked NSA documents, to provide "intelligent command and control capability" for "industrial-scale exploitation" by the NSA.[30] The NSA documents tout TURBINE as a tool for increasing the agency's ability to gather intelligence and disrupt, damage, or destroy systems through "potentially millions of implants." The documents detail the agency's ability to use the implants covertly to

- "take over a targeted computer's microphone and record conversations taking place near the device";
- "take over a computer's webcam and snap photographs";
- "record[] logs of Internet browsing histories and collect[] login details and passwords used to access websites and email accounts";
- "log keystrokes"; and
- "exfiltrate[] data from removable flash drives that connect to an infected computer."

Leaked NSA documents also describe the NSA infecting computers with malware to infiltrate data through "man-in-the-middle" attacks in which NSA servers impersonated real websites.

Even machines never connected to the Internet can be compromised, according to Snowden's revelations, thanks to miniature technologies U.S. intelligence agencies install on target computers that transmit information by radio to nearby briefcase-sized relay stations. Targets include not only traditional computers, but also mobile phones and large network servers, including those made by the Chinese. Among frequent targets of the NSA's sophisticated attacks reportedly is the Chinese army, which the United States accuses of launching cyber attacks against the U.S. government and the American private sector.[31]

U.S. officials have tried to argue that it only conducts cyber operations against governments to collect military and other government information, while the Chinese are hacking businesses for trade secrets and commercial information. But this argument has proved a tough sell. Revelations about U.S. cyber operations against Huawei and other networks in China and elsewhere, as well as leaked information about U.S. efforts to obtain information on Indonesian trade negotiations and Brazil's largest energy company, Petrobas, cast doubt on U.S. claims. As Jack Goldsmith, former assistant attorney general and special counsel to the DOD during the George W. Bush administration, noted, "the Huawei revelations are devastating rebuttals to hypocritical U.S. complaints about Chinese penetration of U.S. networks, and also make USG [U.S. government] protestations about not stealing intellectual property to help U.S. firms' competitiveness seem like the self-serving hairsplitting that it is."[32]

Chinese officials and those from other nations do not see the clear divide that the United States is trying to articulate between espionage for national security and industrial espionage. Peter Singer of the Brookings Institution observed that "to the Chinese, gaining economic advantage is part of national security."[33] Moreover, the U.S. campaign against Huawei—prohibiting the company from operating in the United States, pressing U.S. companies not to purchase Huawei equipment, and lobbying other countries to exclude the company from their markets—has clear competitive and economic effects, whether or not it is motivated by national security concerns.[34]

There is also the question of whether the distinction between traditional espionage and economic espionage matters, especially in international law. "Economic espionage is expressly prohibited by U.S. domestic law, but is not prohibited by international law, written or unwritten, and it is widely practiced," Goldsmith argues.[35] U.S. complaints about China engaging in the wrong type of espionage "amount to the claim that the Chinese are not playing by the rules that suit the USG [U.S. government]."[36]

Whatever the merits of the U.S. arguments, the unavoidable reality is that in the wake of months of Snowden revelations about U.S. surveillance and cyber operations, those arguments did not fare well. When President Obama raised the topic of hacking at the June 2013 summit, President Xi reportedly cited the *Guardian*'s first report on Snowden's revelations as "proof that America should not be lecturing Beijing about abusive surveillance."[37] After the revelations about U.S. intrusions into Huawei's networks, William Plummer, a senior Huawei executive, observed that "the irony is that exactly what they are doing to us is what they have always charged that the Chinese are doing through us."[38]

Irrespective of distinctions about targeting government versus corporation information, and even of the accuracy of Chinese denials of involvement in cyber espionage, revelations about NSA activities have compromised the credibility and the effectiveness of U.S. claims about Chinese hacking, even as those attacks are reportedly increasing.[39] "Snowden changed the argument from one of 'The Chinese are doing this, it's intolerable' to 'Look, the U.S. government spies, so everybody spies,'" according to Richard Bejtlich, former chief security officer at Mandiant, a private cybersecurity firm.[40] Jason Healey, director of the Cyber Statecraft Initiative at the Atlantic Council, observed that "no one cares anymore about our whining about Chinese espionage. The time we had for making the case on that is long gone. Internationally, I don't see how we recover."[41]

One of the lasting images revealed by Snowden was that of the NSA breaking into computers at the United Nations to spy on diplomatic activities there.

Reportedly, when they broke into the UN system, U.S. hackers found the Chinese already there conducting their own surveillance.[42] But because the United States was engaged in exactly the same arguably illegal activity, the U.S. government had no standing to call out the Chinese.

On May 19, 2014, U.S. attorney general Eric Holder revealed that the Justice Department had obtained a sealed indictment of five Chinese military officials for conducting economic cyber espionage against U.S. companies.[43] This desperate effort to regain the upper hand in U.S. dealings with China over electronic spying at least suggested that however little the Obama administration might appreciate the meaning of hypocrisy, it at least understood irony.

## Increasing Insecurity in Cyberspace

The Snowden revelations also raise fundamental questions about the extent to which the NSA may be weakening, rather than enhancing, cyber security. Beginning in 2013, the annual *Worldwide Threat Assessment of the U.S. Intelligence Community* has identified cyber threats, even more than terrorist attacks, as the greatest threats facing the United States.[44] The key challenge, according to analysts, "is the often losing battle to stop cyber incursions into US networks."[45]

To help guard against that threat, the Obama administration in February 2013 published Executive Order 13636 on Improving Critical Infrastructure Cybersecurity, which asserted:

> Repeated cyber intrusions into critical infrastructure demonstrate the need for improved cybersecurity. The cyber threat to critical infrastructure continues to grow and represents one of the most serious national security challenges we must confront. The national and economic security of the United States depends on the reliable functioning of the Nation's critical infrastructure in the face of such threats."[46]

Although worded in terms of "consultation" and "voluntary" adoption of a cybersecurity framework, which the National Institute of Standards and Technology released in February 2014,[47] the Executive Order called for federal agencies to consider incentives, including changes to the federal acquisition regulations, for encouraging adoption of the framework.[48] It required agencies to report on the extent of private-sector participation in the framework program.[49] And, most significantly, the Executive Order directed agencies to "determine if current cybersecurity regulatory requirements are sufficient given current and projected risks"; report on "whether or not the agency has clear authority to establish requirements based upon the Cybersecurity Framework to sufficiently address current and projected cyber risks to critical infrastructure, the existing authorities identified, and any additional authority required"; and "propose prioritized, risk-based, efficient, and coordinated actions . . . to mitigate cyber risk" if current regulatory requirements are "insufficient."[50]

While the president ordered federal agencies to strengthen cyber defenses, and the intelligence community identified weaknesses in those defenses as part of the greatest threat the country faces, documents leaked by Snowden suggest the NSA has actually been weakening cyber security. According to a number of the documents, in its quest for tools to break into the communications of other countries and industries, the NSA has worked deliberately to weaken cyber security.

The *New York Times* cataloged some of the ways disclosed in NSA documents in which the NSA seeks to create and exploit cyber vulnerabilities. These include:

> The NSA's SIGINT Enabling Project, "a $250 million-a-year program that works with Internet companies to weaken privacy by inserting back doors into encryption products . . . to undermine encryption used by the public."
> - NSA insertion of "vulnerabilities into commercial encryption systems, IT systems, networks, and endpoint communications devices used by targets."
> - NSA efforts to "[i]nfluence policies, standards and specifications for commercial public [encryption] key technologies."
> - NSA work "with the manufacturers of the [encryption] chips to insert back doors or by exploiting a security flaw in the chips' design."[51]

These and other methods of weakening cyber security to advance the NSA's surveillance mission are profoundly problematic because, in the words of cyber security expert Bruce Schneier, "It's sheer folly to believe that only the NSA can exploit the vulnerabilities they create."[52]

Ironically, the NSA is charged with two missions: securing the cyber infrastructure of the DOD and related agencies, and gathering foreign intelligence. Privacy and security advocates have long worried that in pursuit of the latter, increasingly dominant mission, the agency would learn about software and other vulnerabilities. Rather than disclose or attempt to fix them, the agency would exploit them, thus compromising its cyber defense mission. What we now know is that the agency went a step further and actively introduced vulnerabilities into commercial security products and services to enhance its ability to collect intelligence, even though this actively weakens both government and private-sector cyber infrastructure. This problem is particularly challenging not only because the NSA holds two conflicting missions, but also because it is problematic to introduce vulnerabilities into the cyber ecosystem if cyber security is as important as the president and intelligence officials claim.

And what the NSA is doing has huge costs for industry, individuals, and our nation. Industry is hurt because foreign business partners and government agencies are refusing to do business with U.S. information technology and telecommunications companies out of fear those companies are cooperating with, or are susceptible to, legal or financial pressure from, the NSA. Individuals are hurt because the software, hardware, and services that secure our data—our financial transactions, health records, and personal communications—are less secure from intrusions by the NSA and anyone else taking advantage of the NSA's meddling. Our nation is hurt whenever our economy or civil liberties are attacked. Our entire governmental system—our tax records, benefit payments, air traffic control systems, fire and police protection, nuclear safety, and thousands of other vital functions—depends on networks and technologies that, thanks to the NSA, are less secure today.

## The Impact of Government Surveillance on Personal Privacy

Snowden's disclosures focused new attention on the inadequacy of U.S. privacy law. That law has long been described as fragmented, inadequate, and often unworkable. It continues to deny privacy rights to non-U.S. persons, which is inconsistent with the administration's position on human rights in cyberspace. In addition, it is often impossible to determine the nationality of the source or subject of digital information, an ambiguity the NSA has exploited aggressively. In fact, under current U.S. law, the citizens and leaders of our closest allies get the same level of privacy protection as terrorist suspects and the nation's most bitter foes.

Under the Supreme Court's "third party doctrine," constitutional protection for data is denied to information that is held by a third party. The doctrine originated in 1976 in *United States v. Miller,* where the court held that there can be no reasonable expectation of privacy in information shared with a third party. The case involved canceled checks, to which, the court noted, "respondent can assert neither ownership nor possession." Such documents "contain only information voluntarily conveyed to the banks and exposed to their employees in the ordinary course of business," and, therefore, the court found that the Fourth Amendment is not implicated when the government sought access to them:

> The depositor takes the risk, in revealing his affairs to another, that the information will be conveyed by that person to the Government. This Court has held repeatedly that the Fourth Amendment does not prohibit the obtaining of information revealed to a third party and conveyed by him to Government authorities, even if the information is revealed on the assumption that it will be used only for a limited purpose and the confidence placed in the third party will not be betrayed.[53]

The Court reinforced its holding in *Miller* in the 1979 case of *Smith v. Maryland,* involving metadata about telephone calls. The Supreme Court found that the Fourth Amendment is inapplicable to telecommunications "attributes" (e.g., the number dialed, the time the call was placed, the duration of the call, etc.) because that information is necessarily conveyed to, or observable by, third parties involved in connecting the call: "[T]elephone users, in sum, typically know that they must convey numerical information to the phone company; that the phone company has facilities for recording this information; and that the phone company does in fact record this information for a variety of legitimate business purposes."[54]

Excluding data held by third parties from the protection of the Fourth Amendment is problematic today because of the extraordinary increase in both the volume and sensitivity of information about individuals necessarily held by third parties. In today's networked world, almost all information we generate—our e-mail, voice mail, documents, pictures, recordings, etc.—is held by third parties. The Supreme Court's exemption from the Fourth Amendment of records held by third parties today means that virtually all personal information is removed from the protection of the Fourth Amendment. As a result, individuals are more exposed than ever to government scrutiny. In addition, the Supreme Court also has repeatedly found that there is no constitutional protection against the government's *use* of data it already possesses, even if it collected the data illegally.[55]

Snowden's disclosures shone new and brilliant light on the inadequacies of U.S. privacy protection against government surveillance by making it clear that despite that protection, the FISC granted secret orders authorizing the collection of "metadata" about all U.S. domestic and international calls despite the absence of any "authorized investigation" to which such a sweeping set of data could be relevant. Subsequent disclosures showed that the NSA was using authorized access to data about non-U.S. persons collected abroad to obtain data on U.S. persons. The NSA was exploiting ambiguity about whether data concerned a U.S. person in order to collect and retain the data, and it was keeping data about U.S. persons erroneously collected for up to five years. This behavior furthered calls for clarifying and strengthening U.S. privacy law.[56]

This issue is of more than merely domestic importance. Before Snowden, provinces in Canada and a growing range of national governments in the European Union cited the U.S. government's broad access to private-sector records as a basis for blocking the export of personal data to the United States.[57] After Snowden, U.S. information technology, telecommunications, and financial companies reported significant pushback from foreign clients concerned about their data being stored in a "U.S. cloud." The German government canceled a long-standing agreement with Verizon because of NSA surveillance. Addressing this issue is critical to building stronger, more cooperative relationships with our allies in the quest for better security.

The Technology and Privacy Advisory Committee, the blue-ribbon, bipartisan committee secretary of defense Donald Rumsfeld appointed to examine privacy and security issues, reported in 2004 that "[l]aws regulating the collection and use of information about US persons are often not merely disjointed, but outdated." They "fail to address extraordinary developments in digital technologies, including the Internet." As a result, "[i]t is time to update the law to respond to new challenges."[58] Also as a result, privacy is often not protected. Public and legislative concerns about the proper line between privacy and security have also led to political firestorms over proposed security programs and created great uncertainty and even a sense of personal risk among security professionals in the government. The National Academy of Sciences echoed the call for updating U.S. privacy laws in 2008, again to no avail.[59]

Government officials often respond to calls for stronger privacy laws by claiming that any restraints will diminish the effectiveness of national security, foreign intelligence, or other important activities. This does not have to be the case: building discipline, thoughtfulness, and focus into our nation's surveillance efforts might actually enhance our nation's security. After all, in the aftermath of the 9/11 attacks, no one claimed that we lacked information about the hijackers, but rather that we could not work effectively with the data we already had, could not "connect the dots," or find the needles buried in the government's own haystacks of existing intelligence information. So while the Obama administration talked about the need to find more information—more hay—that very assertion suggests how misguided our surveillance efforts may be because it ignores a critical lesson from the 9/11 attacks. It also suggests the government has forgotten that the end goal of surveillance should be to find needles, not merely more hay.

Even if protecting our rights and other national interests makes security more difficult, that is the case with all constitutionally protected rights. Trials by juries, for example, take more time and cost more money than trials before judges. The presumption of innocence inevitably results in guilty people going free. Free speech can cause great harm. Important civic values are rarely without cost. But the framers of the Constitution thought that protecting those values was worth the costs those protections imposed. This belief is especially clear in the case of privacy, as the Supreme Court noted in its unanimous June 2014 opinion in *Riley v. California,* striking down warrantless searches of cellphones: "Privacy comes at a cost."[60]

One of the most potent grievances that led the colonists to declare independence more than two centuries ago was the practice of British officials conducting "general" searches. British troops and customs officials would go door to door and person to person, searching everything and everyone in their path. The hostility to general searches found powerful expression in the Fourth Amendment to the Constitution. The amendment established the "right of the people to be secure in their persons, houses, papers, and effects" and to be free from "unreasonable searches and seizures." But it goes further. It gives meaning to that constitutional right by requiring that to obtain a warrant to conduct a search, the government must "particularly describ[e] the place to be searched, and the persons or things to be seized" and demonstrate under oath that it has "probable cause" a crime has been or is likely to be committed and that the search is germane to that crime.

The NSA surveillance programs ignore the Fourth Amendment. But they ignore something else as well: the courage of the Americans who crafted that amendment and the rest of the Bill of Rights. Too often, government officials today argue that the threat of terrorism has made everything different or that the values of the Fourth Amendment must give way in dangerous times. But the times in which the Fourth Amendment was adopted were hardly tranquil. In 1783, the Treaty of Paris ended the Revolutionary War. The former colonies were in economic and physical shambles. The Articles of Confederation, enacted in 1781, were failing; it looked as though the new nation would disintegrate before it ever got started. In this setting, when the new nation was hanging by a thread, the Fourth Amendment was adopted. In fact, just four days after the amendment was adopted in 1789, Congress created a standing army for the new nation, and within twenty-three years the British would burn the White House in the War of 1812.

The danger to the survival of the nation seemed far greater then than now, yet in the midst of that turmoil, the founders of the United States enacted their most vigorous protections for fundamental rights. Congress and the administration would do well to remember the importance of those values and of the tools to protect them, from not only attack from without but also erosion from within.

The question whether Snowden is a villain or a hero continues to be hotly debated. The truth is more complicated than this simple question might suggest.

As an intelligence gathering agency, many—perhaps most—of the NSA's activities must be conducted in secret. But this reality does not mean that intelligence activities should be conducted free from effective oversight or that they should be immune from careful scrutiny about whether appropriate benefits outweigh their considerable costs. Perhaps most importantly, intelligence activities should not operate outside the law or be conducted in ways that are unnecessarily intrusive, costly, or damaging to personal privacy, the U.S. economy, the nation's integrity and standing, or the values Americans purport to uphold. While intelligence activities may need to be secret, the law and legal interpretations that guide them must not be. As former congressman and 9/11 Commission vice chair Lee Hamilton has argued, "secret power is dangerous power." Clearly we can and should do better, and government task forces, commissions, and expert panels have frequently recommended ways to do so.

The disclosures by Snowden demonstrate that the NSA has violated these basic principles. It has engaged in dozens of secret programs, many of which were totally unknown not merely to the public, but to expert oversight boards, such as the President's Foreign Intelligence Oversight Board. It has done so under secret legal interpretations with no precedent in published law. In fact, the idea that the NSA could, under existing law, collect data on all Americans had been actively and repeatedly denied by senior government officials until Snowden made it clear that the NSA was doing it. Such sweeping changes in the application of the law, the large-scale surveillance and cyber incursions undertaken under these changes, and the lies that obscured what was being done, should all be the subject of public debate. Thanks to Snowden, whatever his virtues and failings, that debate is now happening.

# Notes

1. Foreign Intelligence Surveillance Court, *In re Application of the FBI for an Order Requiring the Production of Tangible Things from Verizon Business Network Services, Inc. on Behalf of MCI Communication Services, Inc. D/B/A Verizon Business Services,* Docket No. BR 13–80 (RV) (April 25, 2013). See part II.A for the text of this FISC order.

2. Uniting and Strengthening America by Providing Appropriate Tools Required to Intercept and Obstruct Terrorism Act, § 215, October 26, 2001 (codified at 50 U.S.C. §1861).

3. 50 U.S.C. §1861(b)(2)(A).

4. Office of the Director of National Intelligence, "DNI Statement on Recent Unauthorized Disclosures of Classified Information," June 6, 2013, http://www.dni.gov/index.php/newsroom /press-releases/191-press-releases-2013/868-dni-statement-on-recent-unauthorized-disclosures-of -classified-information.

5. Office of the Director of National Intelligence, "Newseum Special Program—NSA Surveillance Leaks: Facts and Fiction," June 26, 2013 (statement of Robert Litt), http://www.dni.gov/index .php/newsroom/speeches-and-interviews/195-speeches-interviews-2013/887-transcript-newseum -pecial-program-nsa-surveillance-leaks-facts-and-fiction.

6. Privacy and Civil Liberties Oversight Board, "Report on the Telephone Records Program Conducted under Section 215 of the USA PATRIOT Act and on the Operations of the Foreign Intelligence Surveillance Court," January 23, 2014, 81. See part II.B for the executive summary of this PCLOB report.

7. Ibid., 10.

8. President's Review Group on Intelligence and Communications Technologies, "Liberty and Security in a Changing World," December 12, 2013, 17–18. See part II.B for the executive summary of the Review Group's report.

9. Glenn Kessler, "James Clapper's 'Least Untruthful' Statement to the Senate," *New York Times,* June 12, 2013, http://www.washingtonpost.com/blogs/fact-checker/post/james-clappers -least-untruthful-statement-to-the-senate/2013/06/11/e50677a8-d2d8-11e2-a73e-826d299ff459 _blog.html.

10. James R. Clapper, interview with Andrea Mitchell, June 8, 2013, http://www.dni.gov/index .php/newsroom/speeches-and-interviews/195-speeches-interviews-2013/874-director-james-r -clapper-interview-with-andrea-mitchell.

11. Andy Greenberg, "NSA Chief Denies Wired's Domestic Spying Story (Fourteen Times) in Congressional Hearing," *Forbes,* March 10, 2012, http://www.forbes.com/sites/andygreenberg /2012/03/20/nsa-chief-denies-wireds-domestic-spying-story-fourteen-times-in-congressional -hearing/2/.

12. "Cybersecurity Threats to the U.S.," *C-SPAN,* July 9, 2012, http://www.c-span.org/video /?306956-1/cybersecurity-threats-us.

13. Andrea Shalal-Esa, "Four-Star General in Eye of U.S. Cyber Storm," *Reuters,* May 26, 2013, http://www.reuters.com/article/2013/05/26/us-cybersecurity-nsa-alexander-idUSBRE94 P06S20130526.

14. James Goodale, "To Reform the NSA, Fire Officials Who Lie," *Guardian,* September 25, 2013, http://www.theguardian.com/commentisfree/2013/sep/25/nsa-reform-fire-officials-lied.

15. Foreign Intelligence Surveillance Court, Memorandum Opinion (Judge John D. Bates), October 3, 2011, http://www.lawfareblog.com/wp-content/uploads/2013/08/162016974-FISA-court -opinion-with-exemptions.pdf; Foreign Intelligence Surveillance Court, Order (Judge Reggie B. Walton), March 2, 2009, http://www.dni.gov/files/documents/section/pub_March%202%202009 %20Order%20from%20FISC.pdf. See part II.A for the FISC order from Judge Walton.

16. FISC, Order (Judge Reggie B. Walton), 6.

17. Brad Heath, "Justice Dept. Watchdog Never Probed Judges' NSA Concerns," *USA Today,* September 19, 2013, http://www.usatoday.com/story/news/nation/2013/09/19/nsa-surveillance -justice-opr-investigation/2805867/.

18. *Going Dark: Lawful Electronic Surveillance in the Face of New Technologies. Testimony Before the Judiciary Committee, Subcommittee on Crime, Terrorism, and Homeland Security,* House of Representatives, 112th Cong., 1st Sess. (February 17, 2011) (statement of Valerie Caproni, FBI general counsel), http://www.fbi.gov/news/testimony/going-dark-lawful-electronic-surveillance -in-the-face-of-new-technologies.

19. "Admit Nothing and Deny Everything," *The Economist,* June 8, 2013, http://www.economist .com/news/china/21579044-barack-obama-says-he-ready-talk-xi-jinping-about-chinese-cyber -attacks-makes-one.

20. Ellen Nakashima, "Confidential Report Lists U.S. Weapons System Designs Compromised by Chinese Cyberspies," *Washington Post,* May 27, 2013, http://www.washingtonpost.com/world /national-security/confidential-report-lists-us-weapons-system-designs-compromised-by -chinese-cyberspies/2013/05/27/a42c3e1c-c2dd-11e2-8c3b-0b5e9247e8ca_story.html.

21. Editorial, "China and Cyberwar," *New York Times,* May 7, 2013, http://www.nytimes .com/2013/05/08/opinion/china-and-cyberwar.html?ref=stuxnet&_r=0.

22. Tim Walker, "'Positive' US-China Summit Stumbles Over Cyber Security," *Independent* (London), June 9, 2013, http://www.independent.co.uk/news/world/americas/positive-uschina -summit-stumbles-over-cyber-security-8651256.html.

23. Kelvin Chan, "Leaker Snowden Alleges NSA Hacking on China, World," *South China Morning Post,* June 18, 2013, http://www.scmp.com/news/hong-kong/article/1260074/leaker -snowden-alleges-nsa-hacking-china-world.

24. Kurt Eichenwald, "How Edward Snowden Escalated Cyber War with China," *Newsweek,* November 1, 2013, http://www.newsweek.com/how-edward-snowden-escalated-cyber-war-1461.

25. David E. Sanger and Nicole Perlroth, "N.S.A. Breached Chinese Servers Seen as Security Threat," *New York Times,* March 22, 2014, http://www.nytimes.com/2014/03/23/world/asia/nsa -breached-chinese-servers-seen-as-spy-peril.html?_r=0.

26. David E. Sanger and Thom Shanker, "N.S.A. Devises Radio Pathway into Computers," *New York Times,* January 14, 2014, http://www.nytimes.com/2014/01/15/us/nsa-effort-pries-open -computers-not-connected-to-internet.html.

27. "Inside TAO: Documents Reveal Top NSA Hacking Unit," *Der Spiegel,* December 29, 2013, http://www.spiegel.de/international/world/the-nsa-uses-powerful-toolbox-in-effort-to-spy-on -global-networks-a-940969.html.

28. Ibid.

29. Michael Riley, "How the U.S. Government Hacks the World," *Businessweek,* May 23, 2013, http://www.businessweek.com/articles/2013-05-23/how-the-u-dot-s-dot-government-hacks-the -world.

30. Ryan Gallagher and Glenn Greenwald, "How the NSA Plans to Infect 'Millions' of Computers with Malware," *The Intercept,* March 12, 2014, https://firstlook.org/theintercept/article/2014/03

/12/nsa-plans-infect-millions-computers-malware/. Part II.A contains NSA slides that illustrate use of the TURBINE system.

31. Sanger and Shanker, "N.S.A. Devises Radio Pathway into Computers."

32. Jack Goldsmith, "The NYT on NSA's Huawei Penetration (UPDATED)," *Lawfare Blog,* March 22, 2014, http://www.lawfareblog.com/2014/03/the-nyt-on-nsas-huawei-penetration/.

33. Quoted in Sanger and Shanker, "N.S.A. Devises Radio Pathway into Computers."

34. Sanger and Perlroth, "N.S.A. Breached Chinese Servers Seen as Security Threat."

35. Jack Goldsmith, "Why the USG Complaints Against Chinese Economic Cyber-Snooping Are So Weak," *Lawfare Blog,* March 25, 2013, http://www.lawfareblog.com/2013/03/why-the-usg -complaints-against-chinese-economic-cyber-snooping-are-so-weak/#.UtZzldJDuSo.

36. Jack Goldsmith, "More Questions About the USG Basis for Complaints about China's Cyber Exploitations," *Lawfare Blog,* May 30, 2013, http://www.lawfareblog.com/2013/05/more-questions -about-the-usg-basis-for-complaints-about-chinas-cyber-exploitations/.

37. Eichenwald, "How Edward Snowden Escalated Cyber War with China."

38. Quoted in Sanger and Perlroth, "N.S.A. Breached Chinese Servers Seen as Security Threat."

39. Ibid.

40. Quoted in Eichenwald, "How Edward Snowden Escalated Cyber War with China."

41. Quoted in ibid.

42. Eric Linton, "NSA Bugged United Nations Headquarters in New York, Der Spiegel Reports," *International Business Times,* August 25, 2013, http://www.ibtimes.com/nsa-bugged-united -nations-headquarters-new-york-der-spiegel-reports-1398203.

43. Timothy M. Phelps and Julie Makinen, "U.S. Indicts Five Chinese Military Officials on Cyberspying Charges," *Los Angeles Times,* May 19, 2014, http://www.latimes.com/business/la-fi -china-cyberspying-justice-20140520-story.html#page=1. See part II.A for the FBI "Wanted" poster for these individuals.

44. *Worldwide Threat Assessment of the US Intelligence Community. Testimony Before the Senate Select Committee on Intelligence,* Washington, D.C. (March 12, 2013) (statement of James R. Clapper, director of national intelligence), http://www.intelligence.senate.gov/130312/clapper.pdf.

45. Anna Mulrine, "Top 3 Threats to the United States: The Good and Bad News," *Christian Science Monitor,* March 13, 2013, http://www.csmonitor.com/USA/Military/2013/0313/Top-3-threats -to-the-United-States-the-good-and-bad-news/Cyberwarfare.

46. White House, Improving Critical Infrastructure Cybersecurity (Executive Order), February 12, 2013, §1, http://www.whitehouse.gov/the-press-office/2013/02/12/executive-order-improving -critical-infrastructure-cybersecurity.

47. National Institute of Standards and Technology, "Framework for Improving Critical Infrastructure Cybersecurity (Version 1.0)," February 12, 2014.

48. Executive Order on Improving Critical Infrastructure Cybersecurity, §8.

49. Ibid., §8(c).

50. Ibid., §10.

51. "Secret Documents Reveal N.S.A. Campaign Against Encryption," *New York Times,* September 5, 2013 (analyzing NSA 2013 budget request), http://www.nytimes.com/interactive/2013/09 /05/us/documents-reveal-nsa-campaign-against-encryption.html?_r=0.

52. David Talbot, "Bruce Schneier: NSA Spying Is Making Us Less Safe," *MIT Technology Review,* September 23, 2013, http://www.technologyreview.com/news/519336/bruce-schneier-nsa -spying-is-making-us-less-safe/.

53. *United States v. Miller,* 425 U.S. 435, 440, 442–443 (1976).

54. *Smith v. Maryland,* 442 U.S. 735, 743 (1979).

55. *United States v. Leon,* 468 U.S. 897 (1984); *United States v. Calandra,* 414 U.S. 338, 354 (1974); *Walder v. United States,* 347 U.S. 62 (1954).

56. "U.S. Confirms Warrantless Searches of Americans," *USA Today,* April 2, 2014, http://www .usatoday.com/story/news/politics/2014/04/01/us-confirms-warrantless-searches-nsa/7176749/;

Edward Moyer, "NSA Taps into Google, Yahoo Clouds, Can Collect Data 'at Will,' says Post," *CNET,* October 30, 2013, http://www.cnet.com/news/nsa-taps-into-google-yahoo-clouds-can -collect-data-at-will-says-post/; James Risen and Laura Poitras, "N.S.A. Gathers Data on Social Connections of U.S. Citizens," *New York Times,* September 28, 2013, http://mobile.nytimes.com /2013/09/29/us/nsa-examines-social-networks-of-us-citizens.html; Glenn Greenwald and James Ball, "The Top Secret Rules that Allow NSA to Use US Data without a Warrant," *Guardian,* June 20, 2013, http://www.theguardian.com/world/2013/jun/20/fisa-court-nsa-without-warrant.

57. Fred H. Cate, James X. Dempsey, and Ira S. Rubinstein, "Systematic Government Access to Private-Sector Data," *International Data Privacy Law* 2, no. 4 (2012): 195–99.

58. U.S. Department of Defense, Technology and Privacy Advisory Committee, "Safeguarding Privacy in the Fight Against Terrorism" (March 2004), 5–6.

59. National Academy of Sciences, Committee on Technical and Privacy Dimensions of Information for Terrorism Prevention and Other National Goals, *Protecting Individual Privacy in the Struggle Against Terrorists: A Framework for Program Assessment* (Washington, D.C.: National Academies Press, 2008).

60. *Riley v. California,* 134 S.Ct. 2473 (June 25, 2014).

# 3

# From Passivity to Eternal Vigilance: NSA Surveillance and Effective Oversight of Government Power

LEE H. HAMILTON

Like most Americans, I cherish privacy on personal matters, and I do not like it when my privacy is invaded. But the threats against our country and the vulnerabilities of our government are real and need to be taken seriously. Our government has legitimate reasons to monitor cyberspace for national security and foreign policy reasons. Our democracy needs intelligence agencies that operate with a fair amount of secrecy. The disclosures made by Edward Snowden, however, demonstrate we have not had nearly the checks and balances on programs of the National Security Agency that we should have had and will need in the future. NSA surveillance programs should not be abolished; they are a vital national security tool. But they must be reformed and made subject to active, sustained oversight by Congress and the courts in order to ensure that such programs serve our national interests and keep faith with the privacy and civil liberties of the American people.

## Extensive Capabilities, Expansive Power

Snowden's leaks have helped us understand the extent of the surveillance. It is astounding. The capabilities of the intelligence community to learn what we are doing have knocked our socks off! The government gathers an enormous amount of data about you and all Americans. With each leak we learned more about how much the government does and knows. It has for years collected, and can to this day log, metadata on every phone call made by every American. It gains access to e-mail and instant messaging contact lists. In some cases, the government gathers the content of e-mail communications sent by and between citizens of the United States. The government can scan messages Americans send or receive from overseas. Every time we use an electronic device to communicate brings us potentially into the scope of NSA surveillance. Millions of Americans, who have done nothing wrong and have no connection to terrorism or foreign governments, are being watched.

What the NSA has done is flip the traditional way of gathering intelligence. This approach involved collecting information about identified people believed to pose threats to U.S. national security or foreign policy interests. Now the NSA gathers data on large numbers of people in massive amounts and applies the mind-boggling capabilities of the intelligence community to sift through all the data looking for links to terrorism or other threats. But all this metadata and data can reveal a great deal about the personal behavior of people who pose no security problems. These intelligence activities in the world of digital data—a world we are going to be living in for the rest of our lives—require justification because they represent a massive extension of government power without precedent in the modern era.

What does the government say about all of this? The government believes its expansive power to monitor and conduct surveillance is necessary to protect your safety and the security of the country. It claims that collecting all this data is necessary to prevent terrorism. It asserts that the programs have been effective in preventing terrorist acts. It argues that the manner in which it exercises this power must be kept secret because any leaks—even revealing the mere existence of surveillance programs—will benefit our adversaries and cause significant harm to the United States. Government officials say, "Trust us. We can deal with these matters and protect you."

To some, this approach is comforting. For others, it is worrying. I am worried. The activities, capabilities, and power of the NSA have expanded much faster than its judgment. Its technology has outrun its policy. The operating principle seems to be that if the intelligence community has the technical ability to gather information, it ought to do so. Government officials have argued that the safeguards NSA programs have are quite extensive and adequately protect the public.

These checks, however, are currently dominated by the executive branch and have proved inadequate for this kind of government power.

## The Government's Track Record Exercising This Power

We have evidence that reinforces skepticism about executive branch oversight of its secret activities. The amount of misinformation from the government on surveillance programs has simply been astounding and appalling. The director of national intelligence told Congress the government was not collecting data on millions of Americans. I am still waiting for the attorney general to indict him for a clear-cut case of perjury. The Foreign Intelligence Surveillance Court (FISC) found NSA programs to be operating in violation of the law and NSA information to be misleading. The NSA itself uncovered thousands of violations of its rules. Claims about the effectiveness of NSA surveillance programs have proven inaccurate or, given the lack of transparency, impossible to verify or assess.

Until Snowden, all this was unknown to the American people because of the secrecy surrounding these activities. In the wake of the leaks, the Obama administration stated it welcomes public debate, but it did nothing on its own initiative to enable a debate before Snowden. And, concerning the leaks, time and again the administration refused to be transparent and provided misstatements about the surveillance efforts.

Despite pushing back in some contexts, judicial oversight by the FISC has largely consisted of a deferential, secret, and unchallenged body of law that supported the expansion of government power. Incredibly, the FISC has repeatedly signed off on an expedient stretching of the USA PATRIOT Act, thus permitting collection of metadata on essentially all Americans.

Legislative oversight by Congress has been no better. I am astounded that members of Congress were informed over a period of many years about the NSA programs—and the enormous expansion of staggering government power it entails—and failed to see the urgent need for public debate, especially during a time when skepticism about government has been high in almost all other matters. Members of the House Select Intelligence Committee, on which I once served, even failed to distribute information from the executive branch on NSA activities to other House members. Congress did not enact the Foreign Intelligence Surveillance Act (FISA) and the USA PATRIOT Act to give the government boundless surveillance powers that would sweep up data on millions of innocent Americans.

Congressional passivity shows that members of Congress are too often captivated, captured, and seduced by representatives of the intelligence community they are supposed to be supervising. I know how good, how persuasive, and how patriotic officials in the intelligence community are.

The executive branch's management of our foreign intelligence activities also deserves criticism. Our aggressive espionage has unnecessarily damaged our relations with friendly and allied nations and put their leaders in politically difficult situations. What appears to be out-of-control snooping on foreign leaders should not happen. The United States must engage in foreign intelligence, sometimes even against our allies. But we cannot proceed on the basis that our spying is necessary or appropriate simply because we can technologically do it. This type of arrogance undercuts the real sources of our power. Our spy network and its activities must be subject to greater scrutiny, heightened sensibility about political context, and limits.

Again, it took the actions of a leaker to spur activity in Washington, D.C., and in the nation as a whole. Now Snowden has caused me heartburn. He did wrong in mishandling classified information. But his disclosures have made us more educated about how our government operates and how much privacy we have lost. Whatever we might think about him, we are in a better position to ensure that in the future lawbreaking is not required to address the exercise of secret, expansive government power.

## Beware the Potential for the Abuse of Power

My greatest concern is the potential for the abuse of power. When you give power to government, it is a rare thing indeed for government to give it up. When that power is exercised in secret, dangers multiply. Power is not only given to the existing incumbents in office but also to those who will hold office in the future. When you look at these NSA programs, you have to look at their impact now, but you have to think about their impact in perpetuity. The potential for someone at some point to abuse that power and turn it against the American people is worrisome.

Even if we concede that those in positions of authority today have acted carefully, correctly, and honorably (and I do not make that concession), there is a potential slippery slope here. The temptation for government to use vast intelligence capabilities and unmatched spying technologies is strong. This power could be extended and abused in all sorts of areas—policing payment of taxes, preventing terrorism, addressing child abuse, or predicting illegal behavior. Who watches the watchers? Not just today, but for generations to come? We must be constantly on guard for abuse.

## A Prediction

Given my concerns, my next point might be disconcerting. I believe that politicians in Washington, D.C., will make only modest changes to NSA surveillance programs and will essentially preserve them. Some constraints on government power might be enacted, but the policy of massive collection of data and surveillance of cyber communications will not fundamentally change. The main reason is that all the nation's key political actors and institutions have repeatedly approved these programs.

Two presidents have backed them. Reforms that President Obama has taken or proposed largely address *how* the programs operate, not *whether* the exercise of such expansive power is appropriate. That distinction is important because it shows that the president supports far-reaching surveillance and intelligence programs.

The intelligence community—a powerful voice on national security issues—has resolutely defended these powers and programs and has resisted many changes, despite claims to the contrary. The various agencies that make up the intelligence community are convinced of the value of these surveillance programs and are determined to defend them. The FISC and other federal courts that are supposed to keep NSA activities in line with the Constitution have largely been deferential to national security authorities. For years, Congress supported the NSA programs. Although hearings have been held and bills proposed, as of this writing Congress still has not adopted any surveillance reform legislation because legislators remain seriously at odds about what to do.

Then we have the American people. The lack of outrage is palpable and perhaps signals they accept the expansion of government power and how the NSA exercises such powers. Even though on many matters they do not trust the government, here the majority of the American people appear to favor security over liberty.

## What Must Be Done

Given that the government is likely to retain expansive surveillance powers, what do we do? We need to understand that the increased need in a democracy for secret intelligence activities creates heightened requirements for more robust debate, transparency, scrutiny, and oversight of such activities from all three branches of government. When this kind of extraordinary power is concentrated in the intelligence community, we have to make sure this power is subject to constitutional constraints managed through the checks and balances of our constitutional system. The checks on this power within the executive branch are commendable, but they are not sufficient in a government with separation of powers. What we have now does not reflect this principle. To make progress, we need much more vigorous oversight from the FISC, Congress, and the Privacy and Civil Liberties Oversight Board (PCLOB).

FISA, and especially the FISC role under that legislation, does not provide adequate accountability or privacy protections. The FISC should hear more than the government's side. It must require more from the executive branch in terms of explaining the need for massive surveillance. It should analyze less intrusive alternatives for achieving the desired goals. It should make its legal opinions public. Its operations need more visibility. We have to lift the veil of secrecy from this court because secret judicial processes do not produce due process. We must get away from secret courts making secret rulings and creating secret law.

So far, I do not believe Congress has provided sufficient oversight of, or demanded enough accountability from, the intelligence community on NSA surveillance programs. I want congressional oversight that is robust, demanding, and sustained. Such oversight needs to produce clarity in facts, transparency in purposes and consequences, and accountability in the executive branch to the people's elected representatives. Ask hard questions, demand and critically evaluate answers, explore alternative possibilities to achieve the ends sought, and regulate the exercise of surveillance power. All members of Congress—not just the few who sit on the select intelligence committees—have responsibilities here. This type of congressional engagement will stimulate more public involvement and produce legislation that more effectively balances the need for intelligence activities with other political interests and civil liberties.

The PCLOB was established on the basis of a recommendation from the 9/11 Commission. But the story of its establishment underscores the serious challenge of producing the kind of oversight needed in this context. For years, the recommendation to create this board was ignored. Every time I testified during this period, and that was many times, and in every conversation I have had with presidents, I urged action on this recommendation. Even with all my persuasive powers, it took twelve years before this board was finally established. But, when established, it was not given a budget or a staff. Eventually, the board got a budget and a staff.

The PCLOB has started to function in the wake of the Snowden leaks, producing reports on the telephone metadata program under Section 215 of the USA PATRIOT Act and surveillance of foreign targets conducted under Section 702 of FISA. These are important—and long overdue—steps that demonstrate the importance of the PCLOB. Subjecting surveillance and intelligence programs to external, independent review inserts more discipline, transparency, critical analysis, alternative approaches, and shared responsibility into this area of policy and law. The PCLOB must build on this promising start, and the president must take seriously its recommendations.

None of what I have suggested would, if implemented, guarantee that every violation of the law, procedural irregularity, or bad program will be prevented, detected, investigated, reported, or stopped. But stronger oversight rooted in the constitutional tradition of checks and balances will significantly improve the chances that we engage in surveillance and intelligence programs that protect national security, help our country internationally, and strike a better domestic balance between privacy and security.

With the vast expansion of our intelligence agencies, their aggressive exploitation of their extensive and intrusive powers, their astounding surveillance and monitoring capabilities, and the excessive secrecy wrapped around their activities, you and I are confronted with an unprecedented challenge to hold the government accountable and to constrain its reach into our lives.

It is true today as it was at our founding: The price of liberty is eternal vigilance.

# 4

# U.S. Foreign Policy and the Snowden Leaks

DAVID P. FIDLER

The proposition that Edward Snowden's disclosures of information about the National Security Agency have damaged U.S. national security and foreign policy is not controversial.[1] Since June 2013, the U.S. government has been reeling at home and abroad from Snowden's disclosures. These revelations harmed U.S. relations with allies and friendly nations, hurt U.S. technology companies globally, and helped U.S. adversaries.

The impact has been so significant that the leaks undermined the strategic U.S. foreign policy approach on cyberspace developed before Snowden entered history. This approach—captured by the "Internet freedom" idea—emphasizes protecting individual rights in cyberspace, promoting democracy through cyber means, accessing the economic benefits and technological innovations a global Internet generates, and strengthening multistakeholder Internet governance. The Snowden disclosures, by contrast, created the perception that the United States prioritizes national security over individual rights, spies on democracies and dictatorships alike, subjects technological innovation to its interests, and exploits the Internet without restraint to protect its security and project its power.

The strategic damage to U.S. foreign policy is bad enough, but even worse is that it occurred when the international system was transitioning to a more dangerous context characterized by increasing Chinese and Russian assertiveness, growing worries about global terrorism and extremism, and retreating U.S. influence. This transition is not anchored in the Snowden controversies; it reflects geopolitical and other political trends related to, among other things, the American withdrawal from Afghanistan, Russian intervention in Crimea and Ukraine, Chinese power and behavior in maritime disputes with Asian countries, and renewed concerns about conflicts and terrorism in the Middle East. Many countries believe the balance of power is shifting in ways detrimental to the United States and its allies, and U.S. foreign policy faces eroding credibility in both cyberspace and geopolitical space.

And, unfortunately, it gets worse. The damage complicates U.S. responses to the mounting foreign policy challenges. Historically, great powers have responded to intensified competition and perceived threats with heightened emphasis on material power, especially intelligence and military capabilities. Controversies created by Snowden, however, might handicap the cyber power of the United States but not that of its rivals. Unlike China and Russia, the United States is debating how to integrate cyber technologies as instruments of national security with its constitutional values, international legal commitments, and universalistic political ideology. What will emerge from this debate is not clear because of the acrimonious nature of American politics and the lack of easy answers. The rising tide of geopolitical and other threats heightens the urgency of U.S. foreign policy problems Snowden's disclosures produced.

## Once Upon a Time: U.S Foreign Policy on Cyberspace before Snowden

In *Man, the State and War,* Kenneth Waltz analyzed the causes of war through three levels of analysis, or "images."[2] The "first image" explanation grounded the cause of war at the individual level, with Waltz exploring human nature. The "second image" focused on the nature of domestic political regimes as the cause of war. The "third image" identified the anarchical international system as the font of war. These levels of analysis prove useful in examining how U.S. foreign policy conceives of cyberspace in international relations.

Before Snowden, U.S. foreign policy characterized cyberspace in "first" and "second" image terms; policy should empower individual liberty and promote democracy in this new political ecosystem. These preferences informed U.S. support for the involvement of nonstate actors in managing the Internet, as manifested in multistakeholder processes that have characterized Internet governance from its earliest days.[3] The main threat to individual liberty, democracy, and multistakeholder governance in cyberspace came from authoritarian regimes, a "second image" threat. These regimes wanted government control over Internet governance, posed cyber security problems for democracies, and repressed individual liberty through censorship and other infringements of civil and political rights in cyberspace.

Secretary of state Hillary Clinton's speech on Internet freedom in January 2010 captured this perspective. Clinton described the Internet as "a new nervous system for our planet" and argued that U.S. policy supports "a single Internet where all of humanity has equal access to knowledge and ideas." Recalling the Four Freedoms enunciated by President Franklin Roosevelt—freedom of speech, freedom of religion, freedom from fear, and freedom from want—she proposed a fifth freedom, the "freedom to connect—the idea that governments should not prevent people from connecting to the internet, to websites, or to each other."[4]

Clinton described how the U.S. government promoted the freedom to connect through assistance to "individuals silenced by oppressive governments" in order to "enable citizens to exercise their rights of freedom of expression by circumventing politically motivated censorship." Internet freedom, Clinton argued, "supports the peace and security that provides a foundation for global progress" because "asymmetrical access to information is one of the leading causes of interstate conflict." This speech, and its promotion of individual rights and democratic politics in cyberspace, came after a controversy about the Chinese government's infiltration of Google to collect information about dissidents,[5] which reinforced the "second image" perspective infusing Clinton's remarks.

The Obama administration's International Strategy for Cyberspace (May 2011) reinforced Clinton's Internet freedom speech. The strategy highlighted U.S. support for fundamental freedoms in cyberspace and for information flowing on an open, interoperable, and accessible Internet—objectives that empower individuals and the private sector. In addition, the strategy emphasized that multistakeholder Internet governance is integral to the U.S. vision for cyberspace because it preserves the Internet's open, decentralized architecture, which "fuels the freedom of innovation that enables economic growth [and] . . . fuels the freedom of expression and association that enables social and political growth and the functioning of democratic societies worldwide."[6] Reflecting concerns about the cyber behavior of China and other authoritarian states, the Obama administration highlighted its commitment to "norms for state conduct in cyberspace" and working "internationally to forge consensus regarding how norms of behavior apply to cyberspace, with the understanding that an important first step in such efforts is applying the broad expectations of peaceful and just interstate conduct to cyberspace."[7]

Pre-Snowden cyberspace controversies reinforced U.S. foreign policy framings of the Internet. The major disputes in the months before Snowden's disclosures began included battles over Internet governance and mounting U.S. pressure against Chinese economic cyber espionage. Concerning Internet governance, China, Russia, and other countries pushed, at the end of 2012, to shift Internet governance toward more government control. This effort occurred at the World Conference on International Telecommunications (WCIT) held by the International Telecommunication Union to revise the International Telecommunication Regulations.[8] The WCIT ended acrimoniously, with the United States opposing what the negotiations produced. The U.S. government objected to revisions that potentially opened new avenues for Internet censorship and for "government control over internet governance," which the United States believes "can only be legitimately handled through multi-stakeholder organizations."[9]

Following the WCIT came confrontation between the United States and China over allegations that the Chinese government engages in advanced, persistent, and large-scale economic cyber espionage against companies in the United States and other countries. In February 2013, Mandiant, a private cyber security firm, identified a Shanghai-based unit of the Chinese People's Liberation Army as the source of intensive economic cyber espionage.[10] Although the U.S. government expressed displeasure about Chinese economic cyber espionage before Mandiant's report,[11] the report increased pressure on the U.S. government to respond more vigorously to Chinese behavior. After the Mandiant report, the Obama administration released a new strategy to protect trade secrets of U.S. companies from cyber and other kinds of theft.[12] The Obama administration ratcheted up the diplomatic stakes by announcing that President Obama would confront Chinese leaders about economic cyber espionage at the Sino-American summit in early June 2013.[13] Snowden's first disclosures began as this summit convened.

This overview of U.S. foreign policy on cyberspace before Snowden began his leaks is not comprehensive; it does not, for example, cover U.S. positions on military, trade, and development issues concerning cyberspace. The overview was intended to communicate the leading U.S. foreign policy perspective, which framed international cyberspace challenges in terms of individual liberty, democracy promotion, and multistakeholder Internet governance. Concerns about U.S. intelligence and military cyber activities existed in the pre-Snowden period,[14] but they tended to be less prominent than the "first image" and "second image" narratives U.S. cyberspace policymaking used.

## And Now for Something Completely Different: Snowden's Disclosures and U.S. Foreign Policy

Snowden's leaks transformed the context for U.S. foreign policy on cyberspace. The disclosures rampaged over the Internet freedom perspective and forced the U.S. government to defend itself against what the leaks unleashed at home and abroad. The transformation was painful no matter how one perceived Snowden's actions. Responses from the Obama administration often compounded the discomfort and the adverse consequences.

The damage to U.S. foreign policy has been both tactical and strategic. Tactical damage flows from the impact Snowden's disclosures have had on U.S. relations with, and America's reputation in, many countries, including allied and friendly nations. Strategic damage emerges from how the leaks strengthened U.S. adversaries and signaled that realpolitik, not Internet freedom, characterizes American behavior in cyberspace.

Rather than anything China or Russia did, U.S. actions exposed by Snowden drew attention to "third image" analysis, where the anarchical nature of the international system explains state behavior in cyberspace. Snowden's leaks played into the hands of authoritarian rivals of the United States and hung an albatross around the neck of Internet freedom in U.S. foreign policy on cyberspace.

### NSA Domestic Surveillance Activities

Comprehensively describing Snowden's many disclosures is beyond this chapter's scope. Identifying categories of leaks, however, can communicate the damage done by these disclosures to U.S. foreign policy. The first category involves disclosures that sparked domestic debates in the United States about NSA activities. The first of these leaks was the initial revelation Snowden made—exposure of the domestic telephone metadata program.[15] Although this category of leaks is domestic, the foreign policy implications are serious.

The world watched the champion of global Internet freedom become embroiled in a domestic debate about individual rights and national security in the cyber age. Rather than showing the United States as a paragon of respect for civil and political rights and open democratic governance in cyberspace, Snowden's leaks exposed the workings of a "secret court" rendering "secret case law" permitting the NSA to collect metadata on every American's telephone calls, with secrecy laws blocking elected representatives from raising concerns. The intensity of arguments over whether the NSA's domestic surveillance was legal only exacerbated the spectacle of the United States struggling with challenges cyber technologies create for the government's national security responsibilities.

Let me be clear: The adverse international implications from U.S. political turmoil do not mean NSA domestic surveillance activities were illegal. Although many experts argued that the Foreign Intelligence Surveillance Act (FISA) did not authorize the telephone metadata program,[16] most of those opposed to the NSA's statutory interpretation do not believe the NSA perpetrated a Watergate-style abuse of power. Regarding constitutional law, U.S. federal district courts have, to date, rendered different opinions on whether the telephone metadata program violates the Fourth Amendment, another marker of the complexities of the U.S. legal issues.[17]

The back and forth between U.S. legal experts, however, has not mitigated the adverse consequences for U.S. foreign policy. The Obama administration's argument that NSA domestic surveillance activities were legal has not been convincing, as demonstrated by the controversies Snowden's leaks generated in the United States, controversies deepened by the conclusion of the Privacy and Civil Liberties Oversight Board (PCLOB) that the telephone metadata program was not legal.[18] The administration's retreat from, and eventual modification of, the telephone metadata program undermined prior assertions that the program was both vital for national security and compliant with U.S. law.[19] To many outside the United States, the episode justified Snowden's lawbreaking because it brought about something the U.S. government had not facilitated—an open, democratic deliberation on NSA domestic programs affecting the relationship between civil and political rights and national security in the cyber age.

### NSA Electronic Surveillance Targeting Foreigners

The second category of leaks involves revelations about the NSA's electronic surveillance against foreign persons outside the United States. This category includes the PRISM program operated under provisions added to FISA in 2008, particularly the addition of Section 702 to FISA.[20] The 2008 FISA amendments generated controversy[21] and litigation before Snowden, culminating in the U.S. Supreme Court's decision in *Clapper v. Amnesty International* (2013) that the plaintiffs did not have standing to challenge the constitutionality of the FISA amendments.[22]

Despite this pre-existing context, revelations of NSA electronic surveillance of foreign nationals did not create the frenzy in the United States that news of the telephone metadata program sparked. For example, the PCLOB, which concluded that the domestic telephone metadata program was not legal, determined that surveillance of foreign nationals under Section 702 of FISA did not violate U.S. law.[23] Much of the controversy in the United States about NSA surveillance under Section 702, both before and after Snowden, focused on the communications of U.S. persons incidentally collected in this surveillance. But the disclosures about PRISM and other large-scale surveillance programs targeting foreign nationals angered other countries, including traditional U.S. friends and allies, and created problems for U.S. foreign policy.

The scale and intensity of NSA electronic surveillance of cyber communications of foreigners surprised many people and revealed how the United States respected the privacy of foreigners less than the privacy of U.S. nationals. Reactions coalesced around efforts by offended countries, led by Germany and Brazil, to push in diplomatic venues, including the United Nations (UN), for governments to respect the international human right to privacy not only within but also beyond territorial borders.[24] The United States was caught between its support of Internet freedom and universal respect for civil and political rights (including privacy) and the U.S. position that its obligations under human rights treaties, including the International Covenant on Civil and Political Rights (ICCPR),[25] do not extend beyond U.S. borders.[26]

Other countries interpreted the U.S. stance to mean that American intelligence agencies could ignore the right to privacy in international law outside the United States on a massive scale, an awkward position given that Internet freedom was an American rallying cry for universal individual liberty in cyberspace. As happened with the domestic controversies over the telephone metadata program, the Obama administration fell back on legal arguments, claiming it did not violate international law because (1) U.S. obligations under the ICCPR to respect privacy did not apply extraterritorially, and (2) the surveillance was lawful under the ICCPR because U.S. law authorized it. The U.S. delegation to the UN used these reasons to counter German and Brazilian efforts to condemn bulk or mass surveillance targeting foreigners as a violation of the "human right to privacy in the digital age."[27] The U.S. legal arguments struck many in other countries as an expedient reading of international law permitting the NSA to conduct electronic surveillance against foreigners on a massive and intrusive scale. Further, the U.S. position meant any country could do likewise without violating international human rights law.

Sensing its legal arguments were not helping, the Obama administration tried to repair the damage. In Presidential Policy Directive/PPD-28 (January 2014), President Obama instructed the U.S. intelligence community to protect the privacy of foreign nationals in ways approximating protections U.S. nationals receive.[28] Although heralded as unprecedented,[29] this decision raised more concerns. First, PPD-28 used the phrase "privacy interests" rather than "privacy rights," meaning the United States was not recognizing the privacy of foreigners as an individual right vis-à-vis U.S. intelligence activities. Second, PPD-28's protections applied *after* information was collected, which did not address anger about U.S. intelligence agencies conducting mass surveillance against foreigners in the first place. Third, the attempt to accommodate "privacy interests" of foreigners after denying that U.S. behavior violated international law on privacy looked like an expedient maneuver rather than a commitment to norms embedded in the Internet freedom ideology.

The controversies over U.S. surveillance of foreign nationals also damaged U.S. foreign policy because they diverted attention from a primary target of American cyber policy—authoritarian governments—and generated scrutiny of U.S. behavior under U.S.-enunciated principles. The Obama administration's position that international law does not impose extraterritorial obligations with respect to the right to privacy is plausible, especially given how intelligence agencies around the world behave.[30] Plausible legal arguments, though, could not obscure erosion of U.S. credibility. To many around the world, how the United States handled disclosures about its surveillance of foreign nationals revealed a gap between U.S. rhetoric about Internet freedom and the reality of American intelligence activities.

## NSA Cyber Espionage against Foreign Governments

The third category of Snowden's disclosures centers on leaks about the scale, intensity, and sophistication of U.S. cyber espionage against other governments. The leaks included information about U.S. cyber espionage against adversaries, such as China, and against friendly nations, such as Germany, Mexico, and Brazil. These disclosures damaged U.S. foreign policy in various ways. To begin, revelations about U.S. cyber espionage against China and other adversaries were not shocking, but they blunted U.S. complaints that it was under constant "cyber attack" by foreign intelligence agencies.

For example, in responding to pre-Snowden U.S. criticism about its cyber espionage, China complained it was a victim of large-scale, persistent, and skilled U.S. cyber espionage. As the Chinese noted after Snowden's leaks began, the leaks confirmed China's claims. Such confirmation did not generate sympathy for China, but China did not need sympathy to score strategic points. That China and the United States were perceived as engaging in the same type of intelligence activities was enough to undermine the American attempt to distinguish democracies from nondemocratic governments in terms of international cyberspace politics.

This "equivalence" effect also arose with disclosures about U.S. cyber espionage against allied and friendly governments, with Germany and Brazil in particular responding angrily. Democracies spying on democracies did not communicate the democratic solidarity supposedly animating Internet freedom. The Obama administration's response constituted various formulations of "every country engages in espionage." This response resonated with the desire of China, Russia, and other authoritarian countries to drain from cyberspace the "democracies v. dictatorships" trope. The leaks about U.S. cyber espionage underscored that international law does not seriously constrain state espionage, including economic espionage. This reality also reinforced equivalence among democracies and authoritarian regimes, making U.S. complaints about Chinese violations of international norms empty as a matter of international law.

The U.S. effort to distinguish traditional espionage (states spying on states) from economic espionage (states stealing intellectual property and trade secrets from foreign companies) also suffered from Snowden's disclosures. Some leaks revealed U.S. cyber espionage meant to gain information from foreign companies in order to help U.S. trade negotiators achieve better deals for American businesses.[31]

Although such espionage is not what the U.S. government considers economic espionage, other countries, before and after Snowden, have proven unwilling to follow the U.S. government's approach. The fallout from Snowden's disclosures worsened prospects that other nations will support what the U.S. government means by "economic espionage."

Reactions of other countries to revelations of U.S. cyber espionage included feigned umbrage that made eyes roll in intelligence agencies around the world. Behind the posturing was opportunism, as governments sensed the chance to snatch business from U.S. technology companies, such as Google, that have dominated innovation and globalization in cyber goods and services. However one views such behavior, it represents a problem for U.S. foreign policy because U.S. companies face adverse consequences from disclosures about U.S. cyber espionage.

## U.S. Offensive Cyber Operations

A fourth category of leaks involves U.S. offensive cyber operations. Snowden disclosed the classified Presidential Policy Directive/PPD-20 on U.S. Cyber Operations Policy, which defined different cyber operations and established rules for their conduct.[32] Among other things, PPD-20 addressed "offensive cyber effects operations," defined as operations, other than defensive and espionage activities, the U.S. government conducts outside U.S. government networks to manipulate, disrupt, deny, degrade, or destroy computers, information, communication systems, networks, or physical or virtual infrastructure controlled by computers or information systems.[33] PPD-20 revealed the U.S. government's belief in the utility of offensive cyber operations, ordered development of offensive capabilities, and instructed executive branch agencies to identify targets for offensive cyber operations.[34]

In leaks about the "Black Budget" for U.S. intelligence activities, Snowden revealed that in 2011, the United States conducted 231 offensive cyber operations.[35] Although this controversial disclosure relates to a period before PPD-20's finalization, PPD-20 provides the best idea of what the intelligence community meant in reporting how many offensive cyber operations took place in 2011.

For many other governments, these disclosures confirmed what they previously believed was happening—the United States was developing intelligence and military capabilities to engage in covert and overt offensive cyber operations. Indeed, the United States had previously been identified as responsible for the covert Stuxnet cyber attack, which damaged centrifuges at an Iranian nuclear facility from 2008 through 2010.[36] Creation of a new military command, U.S. Cyber Command, in 2010 signaled development of offensive military cyber capabilities and their integration with other instruments of U.S. military power.

Even so, leaks about U.S. offensive cyber operations and capabilities created problems for U.S. foreign policy. These leaks raised questions about the United

States launching hundreds of offensive operations to manipulate, damage, degrade, or destroy cyber systems in other countries. How did the United States justify such operations under international law? Could this level of offensive cyber operations be reconciled with the U.S. desire for international norms of responsible state behavior in cyberspace? Through development and use of offensive cyber capabilities, was the United States contributing to the militarization of cyberspace rather than Internet freedom? Was U.S. activity a "green light" for other states to undertake offensive cyber operations with equivalent intensity and consequences?

More broadly, the leaks suggest U.S. pursuit of offensive cyber capabilities signals how seriously great powers are interested in cyber weapons and covert or military cyber attacks. The United States is leavening its material power with cyber capabilities, suggesting cyber technologies are coming of age as instruments of covert action and military force. Other countries, including China, Iran, and Russia, are moving down the same path, creating conditions for a "cybersecurity dilemma" to emerge. The United States could be fueling systemic cyber actions and reactions that reflect realpolitik more than the U.S. vision of Internet freedom.

## U.S. Activities Perceived to Threaten Global Cybersecurity

The fifth category includes leaks identifying U.S. activities experts believe threaten the security of the Internet and cyberspace. Revelations about NSA efforts to manipulate encryption technologies and U.S. policies on "zero-day vulnerabilities" gained notoriety. Some of Snowden's disclosures indicated the NSA tried to overcome or undermine encryption used to protect the security and privacy of cyber communications.[37] These disclosures raised concerns that the NSA was weakening the roles encryption plays in enhancing security and privacy in cyberspace.

Similarly, Snowden's leaks helped focus attention on how the U.S. government deals with zero-day vulnerabilities—software flaws that criminals, intelligence and law enforcement agencies, or militaries can exploit before the software vendor learns about and fixes them. The U.S. and other governments discover zero days through research and buy them from companies that hunt for such flaws.[38] U.S. policy on zero days received scrutiny after Stuxnet because this attack used four zero days,[39] illustrating the utility of exploiting such vulnerabilities. Retaining zero days, however, means not disclosing them to software makers, leaving users vulnerable to exploitation. Tension exists, therefore, between disclosure as a way to strengthen cyber defenses and retention as a strategy for enhancing offensive cyber opportunities.

Snowden-related controversies brought more attention to U.S. policy on zero days. The President's Review Group on Intelligence and Communications Technologies, established to make recommendations in light of Snowden's leaks, urged U.S. policy in December 2013 to shift toward greater disclosure of zero days to improve cyber defenses, with retention "[i]n rare instances" for "high priority intelligence collection."[40] President Obama's response to the review group's recommendations in early 2014 did not address zero days. But questions concerning whether the U.S. government knew about the Heartbleed zero-day vulnerability in Internet security software identified in April 2014 prompted Michael Daniel, President Obama's special assistant and cyber security coordinator, to clarify U.S. policy. Daniel stressed "in the majority of cases, responsibly disclosing a newly discovered vulnerability is clearly in the national interest" and important to "an open and interoperable, secure and reliable Internet[.]"[41] Daniel argued, however, that not disclosing some zero days for national security purposes was legitimate, and the U.S. government used a "disciplined, rigorous and high-level decision-making process" to evaluate when to disclose or withhold zero-day information. For many, this explanation raised as many questions as it answered about how the United States balances the defensive benefits disclosure provides and the offensive opportunities retention creates.

The perception generated by the encryption and zero-day controversies and other NSA practices Snowden disclosed (e.g., malware implants, manipulating hardware) was that the U.S. government weakens cyber defenses nationally and globally when it suits U.S. national security. This perception linked with post-Snowden concerns that the United States projects its material power unilaterally in cyberspace through unrestrained surveillance, espionage, and offensive operations. Reconciling this perspective with America's pre-Snowden emphasis on adherence to international norms in cyberspace proved difficult because the United States rejected the application of international law (surveillance of foreigners), took advantage of its absence (cyber espionage), or violated it (offensive operations).

## U.S. Foreign Policy and Cyberspace after Snowden

Snowden's leaks challenged the idea that U.S. foreign policy supported Internet freedom. The leaks created the impression that the U.S. government exploited the Internet to achieve its own foreign policy and national security objectives. U.S. policy did not recognize privacy of non-U.S. nationals as a constraint on its cyber intelligence, which undercut the rights-based universalism in the Internet freedom agenda. U.S. cyber espionage targeted democracies as well as authoritarian regimes, which diluted the Internet freedom emphasis on democratic solidarity in cyberspace. Pre-Snowden complaints about cyber security threats from authoritarian governments lost force when the U.S. government engaged in activities that undermined cyber defenses at home and abroad. The U.S. call for an open, global Internet governed by multistakeholder processes suffered as countries, including fellow democracies, reacted to Snowden's leaks with strategies to reduce American power in cyberspace, creating a potential "splinternet" effect.[42] The U.S. emphasis on state adherence to norms of responsible behavior in cyberspace rang hollow in light of the nature, scale, and intensity of activities Snowden exposed.

U.S. government responses often confirmed rather than countered the perceptions Snowden's leaks created around the world. Complaints that neither Snowden nor the media provided accurate accounts of U.S. intelligence activities had difficulty gaining traction for a number of reasons, including (1) the U.S. government often did not provide better information because it remained classified, and (2) Snowden's leaks contained enough accurate information to leave the U.S. government struggling to explain or defend exposed activities. Announced reforms more in tune with Internet freedom tenets, such as according more protection to the privacy interests of non-U.S. nationals, looked like post hoc damage control when the U.S. had government acted differently before being exposed.

Certainly, the twelve months following Snowden's initial disclosures became an *annus horribilis* for U.S. foreign policy concerning cyberspace. Whether the leaks continue to inflict damage on U.S. foreign policy will depend on many factors, including what else Snowden discloses. Analyzing the future for post-Snowden U.S. foreign policy on cyberspace, however, needs to include more than a focus on cyberspace.

## There's an App for That: Multipolarity, Geopolitics, and the Future of Cyberspace Policy

Snowden's disclosures highlight cyberspace's importance in world affairs, and they offer glimpses of U.S. behavior, interests, and power in this realm. However, the focus on the United States means the leaks do not provide insights about how cyberspace fits into broader trends in international relations. During the first year of Snowden's leaks, more indicators have appeared that a multipolar international system now prevails. The most powerful indicators involve, first, increased assertions of power by China, Russia, and Islamic insurgent groups hostile to the United States, and, second, a widely perceived decline in U.S. influence and leadership.[43] Although Snowden's leaks damaged the United States, the most significant events in multipolarity's multiplying manifestations involve developments related to physical space rather than cyberspace.

Both China and Russia have become more assertive with respect to disputes concerning control of physical spaces. China's behavior vis-à-vis other Asian countries in controversies about sovereignty over islands has raised fears in the region about Chinese power.[44] Russia's annexation of Crimea and involvement with pro-Russian insurgents in Ukraine likewise prompted anxieties across Europe about Russia's strategic intentions.[45] The continuing U.S. drawdown in Afghanistan, and advances by the Taliban insurgents, created worries about what happens to this strategic region when U.S. military forces are completely gone. The seizure of Syrian and Iraqi territory by the self-proclaimed "Islamic State" threatens to shatter the territorial integrity of these two states, is sending shock waves across the Middle East, and has triggered a large-scale campaign of aerial bombing of Islamic State forces in Iraq and Syria by the United States and allied nations.

Compounding these worries are growing perceptions that the ability of the United States to counter Chinese and Russian power, dangerous insurgencies in strategically important areas, and resurgent extremist terrorism is weakening, in both material terms and political willingness.[46] These developments suggest that Asian, European, and Middle Eastern leaders sense the balance of power shifting in ways adverse to the interests of the United States and its allies in countering China, Russia, or extremist threats.[47]

The "return of geopolitics,"[48] with great powers maneuvering for strategic advantage over physical control of territory and political domination of strategic regions, has little to do with the fallout caused by Snowden. For sure, the damage the U.S. government has endured over the leaks has benefited China and Russia, especially in how the leaks created gaps between American behavior and the Internet freedom agenda. These gaps drained U.S. policy of the pre-Snowden emphasis on individual rights and democracy in cyberspace, leaving the impression that the United States acted in the same ways it accused authoritarian governments of behaving, namely infringing on rights domestically, engaging in unrestrained cyber espionage, and developing offensive cyber capabilities and strategies.

What emerges from this equivalence perception is a "third image" outlook— the great powers behave similarly in cyberspace because of the anarchical nature of the international system. For authoritarian governments, a "third image" framing is better than approaches that focus on the domestic political regime and how it treats citizens. For China and Russia, the "third image" application for cyberspace politics converges with the return of balance-of-power thinking created by their geopolitical projections of power. Authoritarian governments prefer international relations when countries perceive that power politics determines the fates of nations.

By contrast, this convergence spells trouble for the United States. Not only has it lost credibility in cyberspace through the Snowden leaks, but its ability to counter Chinese and Russian geopolitical moves, exercise influence in strategic regions where it fought two wars, and confront the dangers posed by the Islamic State and terrorism is also in question. Countries nervous about the balance of power want the United States to project more material power and reverse a perceived withdrawal of American influence. Doing so in a multipolar context will lessen the U.S. government's ability to push countries on individual rights and democracy issues, which elevates "third image" thinking and handicaps U.S. ideological preferences.

Moving to counter Chinese and Russian geopolitical challenges and Islamic State–related terrorism will require the United States to project its power in different ways, including through enhanced espionage activities and military capabilities. This requirement has to involve action in cyberspace, producing, ironically, the need for the United States not to forgo strategies and capabilities criticized in the wake of Snowden's leaks. In September 2014, the UN Security Council required UN member states to prevent foreign fighters from joining the forces of the Islamic State,[49] and compliance with this mandate will require extensive surveillance and intelligence activities for counterterrorism purposes. In October and November 2014, news reports about possible Russian government involvement in breaches of computer systems of JP Morgan Chase (a major U.S. financial institution), the White House, and U.S. energy companies reinforced the sense of intensifying geopolitical competition in cyberspace.

Even more ironically, the geopolitical and terrorist challenges facing the United States and other countries might mitigate the strategic damage to U.S. foreign policy caused by Snowden. Put another way, Chinese and Russian behavior and government vulnerabilities to extremist terrorism have reminded many countries that the United States remains, for them, the indispensable counterweight in the emerging multipolar balance of power and against the threat of global terrorism. For example, Russia's actions in Crimea and Ukraine in 2014 constitute more dangerous events for Germany than the spat with the United States over NSA surveillance in Germany.

Against this reality, U.S. cyber power—glimpses of which Snowden provided—does not appear as threatening as initial reactions to the leaks suggested. Geopolitics and the resurgent terrorist threat help, therefore, put the cyber controversies wrought by Snowden into a different perspective, one that does not see them as damaging U.S. foreign policy strategically for the long term in the context of multipolar, balance-of-power politics and extremist threats posed by the Islamic State.[50] Similarly, U.S. officials, confronted with the responsibility of global leadership, might calibrate Snowden-related criticism and calls for reform against the need for the United States to use its cyber power in countering threats from China, Russia, the Islamic State, and other adversaries.

Domestic political debates about cyber issues, however, might interfere with the U.S. government's thinking clearly about the exercise of its cyber power in the context of emerging security challenges amidst multipolarity. The political climate Snowden's leaks have created is not conducive to such calculations. Although the most serious changes are likely to happen in domestic surveillance programs, what effects, if any, the NSA controversies will have on U.S. strategic considerations concerning cyber's role in geopolitics and counterterrorism is not yet clear.

## iMorgenthau?

The damage to U.S. foreign policy caused by Snowden's disclosures is apparent when pre-Snowden U.S. policy on cyberspace is compared to the revealed U.S. behavior and the negative perceptions created around the world. Comparing Internet freedom as a U.S. policy objective and the surveillance, espionage, and offensive activities Snowden exposed highlights why the U.S. government was criticized and lost credibility in cyberspace policy. Emerging geopolitical and terrorist challenges, however, might ameliorate the foreign policy damage Snowden produced because the cyber capabilities displayed in the leaks form part of the instruments of U.S. power needed to counteract the assertiveness of China and Russia and the extremist threats emerging in regions of U.S. strategic interest.

This argument does little to lessen anxieties of those worried about great-power politics running roughshod over cyberspace and transforming the Internet into another technological pawn of realpolitik. The ideas of individual rights, democracy, and multistakeholder governance associated with Internet freedom face an increasingly difficult international political environment for two reasons: the damage to U.S. foreign policy done by Snowden's leaks and problems geopolitics and terrorism create for the United States and countries that rely on American power for security.

Both U.S. behavior and the unfolding security challenges reduce the prospect that states will treat cyberspace differently from terrestrial, oceanic, air, and extraterrestrial spaces that earlier technological innovations opened for human use. In what Snowden disclosed, and in how balance-of-power politics appears to be evolving, it is increasingly hard not to paraphrase Hans Morgenthau by observing that "statesmen think and act in terms of cyber defined as power."[51]

## Notes

1. In October 2013, General Keith Alexander, NSA director, stated that Snowden's leaks will cause "irreversible damage to our nation." Quoted in Hayley Tsukayama, "In Speech to Telecom Industry, NSA's Alexander Criticizes Coverage of Surveillance," *Washington Post,* October 9, 2013, http://www.washingtonpost.com/business/technology/in-speech-to-telecom-industry -nsas-alexander-criticizes-coverage-of-surveillance/2013/10/09/3c2449c6-30f7-11e3-8627 -c5d7de0a046b_story.html. A Department of Defense review of the impact of Snowden's leaks concluded in December 2013 "with high confidence that the information compromise by a former NSA contractor . . . will have a GRAVE impact on U.S. national defense." Department of Defense Review Task Force-2, "Initial Assessment—Impacts Resulting from the Compromise of Classified Material by a Former NSA Contractor," December 18, 2013, 3.

2. Kenneth Waltz, *Man, the State and War* (New York: Columbia University Press, 1959).

3. These multistakeholder processes include the Internet Engineering Task Force (IETF) and the Internet Corporation for Assigned Names and Numbers (ICANN).

4. Hillary Clinton, "Remarks on Internet Freedom," January 21, 2010, http://www.state.gov /secretary/20092013clinton/rm/2010/01/135519.htm.

5. Tania Branigan, "Google to End Censorship in China Over Cyber Attacks," *Guardian*, January 10, 2010, http://www.theguardian.com/technology/2010/jan/12/google-china-ends -censorship.

6. White House, "International Strategy for Cyberspace" May 2011, http://www.whitehouse .gov/sites/default/files/rss_viewer/international_strategy_for_cyberspace.pdf, 22.

7. Ibid., 9.

8. David P. Fidler, "Internet Governance and International Law: The Controversy Concerning Revision of the International Telecommunication Regulations," *American Society of International Law Insights*, February 7, 2013, http://www.asil.org/insights/volume/17/issue/6/internet -governance-and-international-law-controversy-concerning-revision.

9. Terry Kramer, "Remarks on the World Conference on International Telecommunications," December 13, 2013, http://www.state.gov/e/eb/rls/rm/2012/202040.htm.

10. Mandiant, "APT 1: Exposing One of China's Cyber Espionage Units," February 2013, http:// intelreport.mandiant.com/Mandiant_APT1_Report.pdf, accessed July 10, 2014.

11. Office of the National Counterintelligence Executive, "Foreign Spies Stealing US Economic Secrets: Report to Congress on Foreign Economic Collection and Industrial Espionage, 2009–2011" October 2011, http://www.ncix.gov/publications/reports/fecie_all/Foreign_Economic _Collection_2011.pdf.

12. White House, "Administration Strategy on Mitigating the Theft of U.S. Trade Secrets," February 2013, http://www.whitehouse.gov/sites/default/files/omb/IPEC/admin_strategy_on _mitigating_the_theft_of_u.s._trade_secrets.pdf.

13. Steve Holland and Matt Spetalnick, "Cyber Hacking to Overshadow Summit Between Obama and China's Xi," *Reuters*, June 1, 2013, http://www.reuters.com/article/2013/06/02/us-usa -china-idUSBRE95101H20130602.

14. Mary Ellen O'Connell, "Cyber Security without Cyber War," *Journal of Conflict and Security Law* 17, no. 2 (2012): 187–209.

15. Glenn Greenwald, "NSA Collecting Phone Records of Millions of Verizon Customers Daily," *Guardian*, June 5, 2013, http://www.theguardian.com/world/2013/jun/06/nsa-phone -records-verizon-court-order.

16. Brief of *Amicus Curiae* Professors of Information Privacy and Surveillance Law in Support of Petitioner, *In re Electronic Privacy Information Center*, No. 13–58, August 9, 2013, http://www .law.indiana.edu/front/etc/section-215-amicus-8.pdf. This author and Fred H. Cate participated in this *amicus* brief.

17. Compare *Klayman v. Obama*, 957 F.Supp.2d 1 (D.D.C. 2013) (stating the program probably violated the Fourth Amendment), and *ACLU v. Clapper*, 959 F.Supp.2d 724 (S.D.N.Y. 2013) and *Smith v. Obama*, Case No. 2:13-CV-257-BLW, U.S. District Court, District of Idaho, June 3, 2014 (both holding the program did not violate the Fourth Amendment). Part II.B contains excerpts from the *Klayman* and *Clapper* cases.

18. Privacy and Civil Liberties Oversight Board, "Report on the Telephone Metadata Program Conducted Under Section 215 of the USA PATRIOT Act and on the Operations of the Foreign Intelligence Surveillance Court," January 23, 2014, 81. Part II.B includes the executive summary of this report.

19. President Barack Obama, Remarks on Review of Signals Intelligence, January 17, 2014, http://www.whitehouse.gov/the-press-office/2014/01/17/remarks-president-review-signals -intelligence. Part II.C reprints this speech.

20. Glenn Greenwald and Ewen MacAskill, "NSA Prism Program Taps in to User Data of Apple, Google and Others," *Guardian*, June 6, 2013, http://www.theguardian.com/world/2013/jun /06/us-tech-giants-nsa-data. Part II.A includes NSA slides Snowden disclosed on PRISM.

21. In 2008, the American Civil Liberties Union argued the FISA Amendments Act "gave the NSA virtually unchecked power to conduct warrantless, dragnet collection of Americans'

international communications." American Civil Liberties Union, "America's Surveillance Society," November 18, 2008, https://www.aclu.org/national-security/americas-surveillance-society.

22. *Clapper v. Amnesty International,* 133 S.Ct. 1138 (2013).

23. Privacy and Civil Liberties Oversight Board, "Report on the Surveillance Program Operated Pursuant to Section 702 of the Foreign Intelligence Surveillance Act," July 2, 2014, 8–9. Part II.B includes the executive summary of this report.

24. UN General Assembly, "The Right to Privacy in the Digital Age," UNGA Res. 68/167, December 18, 2013. Part II.B includes the text of this resolution.

25. International Covenant on Civil and Political Rights, December 16, 1966, 999 United Nations Treaty Series 171.

26. Beth Van Schaack, "The United States' Position on Extraterritorial Application of Human Rights Obligations: Now Is the Time for Change," *International Law Studies* 90 (2014): 20–65.

27. Colum Lynch, "Inside America's Plan to Kill Online Privacy Everywhere," *Foreign Policy,* November 20, 2013, http://thecable.foreignpolicy.com/posts/2013/11/20/exclusive_inside _americas_plan_to_kill_online_privacy_rights_everywhere.

28. Presidential Policy Directive/PPD-28 on Signals Intelligence Activities, January 17, 2014, 5.

29. President Obama, Remarks on Review of Signals Intelligence.

30. For the argument that international law imposes extraterritorial obligations concerning privacy, see Human Rights Council, "The Right to Privacy in the Digital Age: Report of the Office of the United Nations High Commissioner for Human Rights," UN Doc. A/HRC/27/37, June 30, 2014; UN General Assembly, "Report of the Special Rapporteur on the Promotion and Protection of Human Rights and Fundamental Freedoms while Countering Terrorism," UN Doc. A/69/397, September 23, 2014.

31. David E. Sanger, "Fine Line Seen in U.S. Spying on Companies," *New York Times,* May 20, 2014, http://www.nytimes.com/2014/05/21/business/us-snooping-on-companies-cited-by-china .html?hp&_r=0.

32. Glenn Greenwald and Ewen MacAskill, "Obama Orders US to Draw Up Overseas Target List for Cyber-Attacks," *Guardian,* June 7, 2013, http://www.theguardian.com/world/2013/jun /07/obama-china-targets-cyber-overseas.

33. Presidential Policy Directive/PPD-20 on U.S. Cyber Operations Policy, October 16, 2012, 3. Part II.A includes the text of PPD-20.

34. Ibid., 9.

35. Barton Gellman and Ellen Nakashima, "U.S. Spy Agencies Mounted 231 Offensive Cyber-Operations in 2011, Documents Show," *Washington Post,* August 30, 2013, http://www.washington post.com/world/national-security/us-spy-agencies-mounted-231-offensive-cyber-operations-in -2011-documents-show/2013/08/30/d090a6ae-119e-11e3-b4cb-fd7ce041d814_story.html.

36. David E. Sanger, *Confront and Conceal: Obama's Secret Wars and Surprising Use of American Power* (New York: Crown Publishers, 2012).

37. Nicole Perlroth, Jeff Larson, and Scott Shane, "N.S.A. Able to Foil Basic Safeguards of Privacy on Web," *New York Times,* September 5, 2013, http://www.nytimes.com/2013/09/06/us/nsa -foils-much-internet-encryption.html?pagewanted=all.

38. Nicole Perlroth and David E. Sanger, "Nations Buying as Hackers Sell Flaws in Computer Code," *New York Times,* July 13, 2013, http://www.nytimes.com/2013/07/14/world/europe/nations -buying-as-hackers-sell-computer-flaws.html?pagewanted=all.

39. Ryan Naraine, "Stuxnet Attackers Used 4 Windows Zero-Day Exploits," ZDNet.com, September 10, 2010, http://www.zdnet.com/blog/security/stuxnet-attackers-used-4-windows-zero-day -exploits/7347.

40. President's Review Group on Intelligence and Communications Technologies, "Liberty and Security in a Changing World," December 12, 2013, 37. Part II.B includes the executive summary of this report.

41. Michael Daniel, "Heartbleed: Understanding When We Disclose Cyber Vulnerabilities," *The White House Blog,* April 28, 2014, http://www.whitehouse.gov/blog/2014/04/28/heartbleed -understanding-when-we-disclose-cyber-vulnerabilities.

42. Tabassum Zakaria and David Ingram, "Google Warns of 'Splinter Net' Fallout from U.S. Spying," *Reuters,* November 13, 2013, http://www.reuters.com/article/2013/11/13/us-usa-security -hearing-idUSBRE9AC0S720131113.

43. Jay Soloman and Carol E. Lee, "Obama Contends with Arc of Instability Unseen since '70s," *Wall Street Journal,* July 13, 2014, http://online.wsj.com/articles/obama-contends-with-arc-of -instability-unseen-since-70s-1405297479?mod=e2tw.

44. James Steinberg and Michael E. O'Hanlon, "Don't Be a Menace to South (China Sea)," *Foreign Policy,* April 21, 2014, http://www.foreignpolicy.com/articles/2014/04/21/obama_china_japan _asia_abe_pivot_rebalance_resolve.

45. Jeffrey Mankoff, "Russia's Latest Land Grab," *Foreign Affairs* (May/June 2014), http://www .foreignaffairs.com/articles/141210/jeffrey-mankoff/russias-latest-land-grab.

46. Max Boot, "Why Russia's Other Neighbors Are Worried," *Commentary,* June 3, 2014, http:// www.commentarymagazine.com/2014/06/03/why-russias-other-neighbors-are-worried/; Helene Cooper and Jane Perlez, "U.S. Sway in Asia Imperiled as China Challenges Alliances," *New York Times,* May 30, 2014, http://www.nytimes.com/2014/05/31/world/asia/us-sway-in-asia-is-imperiled -as-china-challenges-alliances.html.

47. Steven Metz, "Strategic Horizons: Russia's Ukraine Invasion Signifies a Changing Global Order," *World Politics Review* (March 5, 2014), http://www.worldpoliticsreview.com/articles/13607 /strategic-horizons-russia-s-ukraine-invasion-signifies-a-changing-global-order.

48. Walter Russell Mead, "The Return of Geopolitics: The Revenge of the Revisionist Powers," *Foreign Affairs* (May/June 2014), http://www.foreignaffairs.com/articles/141211/walter-russell -mead/the-return-of-geopolitics.

49. UN Security Council Resolution 2178 (2014), September 24, 2014, http://www.security councilreport.org/atf/cf/%7B65BFCF9B-6D27-4E9C-8CD3-CF6E4FF96FF9%7D/s_res_2178.pdf.

50. In June 2014, comments by the new NSA director, Admiral Michael S. Rogers, revealed "an absence of alarm about the long-term effects of the Snowden revelations." David E. Sanger, "New N.S.A. Chief Calls Damage from Snowden Leaks Manageable," *New York Times,* June 29, 2014, http://www.nytimes.com/2014/06/30/us/sky-isnt-falling-after-snowden-nsa-chief-says.html?_r=0.

51. Hans Morgenthau, *Politics Among Nations,* 5th ed. (New York: Knopf, 1978), 5.

# 5

# Taking Snowden Seriously: Civil Disobedience for an Age of Total Surveillance

WILLIAM E. SCHEUERMAN

Edward Snowden's revelations about surveillance by the National Security Agency have dominated global news like few events in recent years. A hero to some and traitor to others, his disclosures unleashed, as he hoped, a worldwide debate about state surveillance in the context of technological advances, the implications of which most policy makers, let alone ordinary people, barely fathom. Hardly a week has passed since the initial disclosures in June 2013 without headline-grabbing reports about new leaks, followed by polarized elite and public reactions. Media have painted a vivid portrait of Snowden's background and career, supplemented with expert commentary. Politicians and pundits have eagerly proffered sound bites deriding and attacking Snowden. Vociferous responses have come from those—often abroad and viewing themselves as victims of NSA surveillance—more sympathetic to his cause.

Unfortunately, the hoopla has obscured a more vital part of the story, namely the *moral and political seriousness* with which Snowden acted to make covert NSA surveillance public knowledge. As we now know, and as Snowden anticipated, his decision came at a huge personal cost. The Obama administration's abrupt cancellation of his passport rendered him effectively stateless, dependent on a Russian government more focused on flexing its weakening muscles as a global power than ending high-tech spying. Sadly, one of our most eloquent critics of state surveillance found himself, partly because of the Obama administration's draconian response, at the whim of a former KGB spymaster.[1]

While media sources reported on his quest for asylum and travails in Putin's Russia, they failed to impart a sense of the moral and political reflections that induced Snowden to give up his six-figure salary and comfortable life in Hawaii. Snowden's public declarations—especially an illuminating yet neglected statement at the Moscow airport on July 12, 2013,[2] when reluctantly accepting Russia's offer of asylum—show that Snowden thought long and hard about the question of when and how citizens of a liberal democratic state are morally and politically obliged to violate the law.

A nineteenth-century critic of militarism and slavery, Henry David Thoreau, is widely, albeit misleadingly, credited with coining the term "civil disobedience."[3] At least since the middle of the twentieth century, when Mahatma Gandhi and Martin Luther King mesmerized global attention by articulating robust defenses of nonviolent lawbreaking,[4] political activists in many national contexts have adapted Gandhi's and King's ideas and techniques to local conditions. For their part, major political theorists and philosophers—including liberals like John Rawls and radical democrats like Jürgen Habermas—have struggled to make sense of this form of protest, especially the conditions under which civil disobedience should be seen as indispensable in a mature liberal and democratic political culture. The media's failure to report on Snowden's contributions to that debate notwithstanding, they deserve our careful attention.

I argue that Snowden's actions meet most of the demanding tests outlined in political thinking about civil disobedience. To be sure, some have already described his actions as legitimate civil disobedience,[5] but these efforts have yet to justify this view sufficiently, which will strike many of Snowden's critics as counterintuitive and tendentious. Like Thoreau, Gandhi, King, and countless other activists, Snowden has articulated a powerful defense of why he was morally obligated to engage in politically motivated lawbreaking.

Snowden has also undertaken impressive efforts to explain how his actions are distinguishable from ordinary criminality and why they need not culminate in reckless lawlessness. In fact, his example can perhaps help *advance* liberal and democratic ideas about civil disobedience. First, it highlights reasons why the acceptance of punishment by those engaging in civil disobedience should *not* be a precondition of its legitimacy. Second, Snowden reminds us that in our era, intensified globalization processes shape every feature of political existence. Defenders of civil disobedience need to update their reflections accordingly.

## Snowden as Civil Disobedient

If we start with the usual definition of civil disobedience as a "public, nonviolent, conscientious yet political act contrary to the law usually done with the aim of bringing about a change in the law or policies of the government,"[6] Snowden's revelations fall under its rubric.

From the outset, Snowden anticipated that his disclosures would be taken by the U.S. government as evidence "that I have broken the Espionage Act and helped our enemies." In an early interview with the journalists who helped break the story, Snowden predicted not only that he would be accused of illegality, espionage, and even treason, but also that the U.S. government would marshal its power to discredit and punish him.[7] Later, Snowden conceded that he signed the obligatory government classified information nondisclosure agreement and that his actions might be construed as violating his "civil contract" with the U.S. government.[8] In short, he has always acknowledged that the U.S. government would describe his actions as illegal while conceding that it has some legal leg to stand on.

In fact, the U.S. government revoked Snowden's passport and deterred a number of foreign countries from granting asylum, effectively leaving him with no choice except Russian exile. Attorney General Eric Holder then announced that Snowden would be charged with violations of the Espionage Act. As Snowden predicted, and as it had with other whistleblowers (such as Thomas Andrew Drake[9] and Bradley/Chelsea Manning[10]), the Obama administration threw the book at him.

More importantly, Snowden's actions represent what the philosopher Hugo Adam Bedau characterized as *indirect* yet potentially legitimate resistance or civil disobedience—illegal acts undertaken at "one (or even several) remove(s), e.g., blacks violate a trespass ordinance to protest racial injustice," in contrast to *direct* disobedience aimed at preventing enforcement of an unfair or unjust law (e.g., blacks violating segregation statutes).[11] Though Snowden admits to violating his nondisclosure agreement, and even though he is skeptical of Attorney General Holder's recourse to the Espionage Act, his main target was U.S. policies undergirding NSA surveillance. He violated prohibitions on whistleblowing because doing so offered an effective—and in his view necessary—way to bring the injustices of U.S. surveillance policies to public attention, not because he aspires to discredit government nondisclosure rules or the Espionage Act. He went so far as to claim that "I am not trying to bring down the NSA, [but instead] I am working to improve the NSA" by making sure it abides by proper legal and constitutional limits.[12]

Snowden sketched out this basic position at the Moscow airport, where he explained why he felt morally and legally obliged to pursue acts likely to be perceived as "contrary to the law." Most obviously, his was an *open* and *public* intervention because it entailed "a moral decision to tell the public about spying that affects all of us." Such disclosure was imperative if policies about which most people—even most political elites—remained in the dark were to gain public attention. Addressing not only U.S. citizens but also others around the globe, Snowden "took what he knew to the public, so what affects all of us can be discussed by all of us in the light of day." Hoping to generate awareness about surveillance policies and the necessity of reform, his act's public character was essential to that aim. As he also told *Guardian* reporters, "[m]y sole motive is to inform the public as to that which is done in their name and that which is done against them."[13]

Snowden's Moscow statement appealed to U.S. constitutional and international human rights law. He asserted that NSA programs constitute "a serious violation of the law," including the Fourth and Fifth Amendments to the U.S. Constitution (prohibiting unreasonable searches and seizures and guaranteeing basic due process), various U.S. statutes, Article 12 of the Universal Declaration of Human Rights (protecting against arbitrary interference with a person's privacy), and treaties banning legally unchecked state surveillance, which he believes the NSA recklessly pursued.[14] Snowden is hardly condoning illegality or lawlessness. On the contrary, he has regularly insisted that he is *upholding* fundamental laws and basic rights, which in his view trump fidelity to U.S. anti-whistleblowing statutes and regulations.

Like earlier civil disobedients, Snowden condones the violation of local or particular laws because of their incongruity with higher—and more fundamental—law. In a *Washington Post* interview in December 2013, he reiterated the claim that his obligations to the U.S. Constitution override any "civil contract," meaning the nondisclosure agreement he signed. When such agreements conflict with constitutional law, Snowden believes, we are obliged to violate them.[15]

Against those who view NSA activities as lawful and legitimate, Snowden's Moscow statement asserts that the legal foundation of these activities remains the secret rulings of the controversial Foreign Intelligence Surveillance Court (FISC), "which the world is not permitted to see." Elsewhere, Snowden stated his opposition to what he dubbed "the federation of secret law, unequal pardon, and irresistible executive power."[16] Secret jurisprudence, arbitrary power, and burgeoning executive discretion go hand in hand and need to be countered. Given what we now know about problems with judicial oversight of the NSA, including the FISC's chief judge conceding that the court is badly equipped to perform its job and evidence suggesting that the NSA often ignored the court's rulings,[17] Snowden's worries seem credible.[18]

The illegality of NSA spying was confounded, the Moscow statement continues, by the Obama administration's decision to place him on no-fly lists and prevent foreign countries from granting asylum. This behavior included "the unprecedented step of ordering military allies to ground a Latin American president's plane."[19] According to Snowden, this move constituted an attack on "the basic rights shared by every person, every nation, to live free from persecution, and to seek and enjoy asylum," as guaranteed by human rights treaties to which the U.S. government subscribes.

In striking contrast to the open character of *his* actions, Snowden asserted, the secrecy of the NSA's activities corrupts "the most basic notion of justice—that it must be seen to be done. The immoral cannot be made moral through use of secret laws." Publicity is fundamental to the rule of law and constitutional government, whereas secret law tends to be corrosive, as it risks veiling government action from individual and collective scrutiny. As the legal theorist Lon Fuller once noted, secret laws and courts provide an easy cover for arbitrary and immoral state action.[20] Not surprisingly, such laws and courts remain a favorite device for those who prefer to keep unjust and heinous actions from the public eye. Secret law tends to proliferate in authoritarian regimes.

To be sure, and as Snowden might concede, some government activities need to be veiled from *direct* public scrutiny; every liberal democracy carves out some place for government secrecy in the context of national security. Yet secrecy still poses a principled threat to any political order committed to basic liberal and democratic values.[21]

Snowden's main claim is that *his* actions not only protect fundamental—but systematically endangered—rights and laws, but they also embody core legal virtues (e.g., publicity and openness) on which any legitimate liberal and democratic legal order depends. In contrast, NSA surveillance, as well as the Obama administration's heavy-handed response to his protests, makes a mockery of such virtues.

## Recipe for Lawlessness?

Snowden's position is unlikely to satisfy anyone worried about the dangers of reckless and potentially destructive illegality. Are not citizens of a more-or-less well-functioning liberal democracy obliged to respect laws adopted through normal political channels? What is to prevent them from irresponsibly abrogating laws and policies they deem unsatisfactory in the name of some "higher" law? The familiar answer from modern liberal and democratic theory is that politically motivated lawbreaking needs to pass tough, additional tests. Snowden's comments at the Moscow airport and elsewhere show that he has made a good faith effort to do so.

Significantly, it seems ungenerous to deny that his actions, whatever one's assessment of their political merits, are morally serious and thus *conscientious*. His behavior reflects a "moral decision" deriving "from what I believed right," made after internal, moral reflection, or what Gandhi and King described as "self-purification." His "willingness to act in public and to offer explanations to other people suggest also a willingness to reflect upon and worry about the possible consequences,"[22] which attests to his moral seriousness.

The fact that his moral reflections cost him what he characterized as a comfortable "life in paradise" belies accusations of "narcissism" leveled at him by journalists and pundits,[23] as does his refusal to enrich himself by selling U.S. secrets or partnering with foreign governments. On the contrary, his selfless actions demonstrate a morally praiseworthy willingness to sacrifice the private for the public good. If what Snowden did constitutes immoral narcissism, contemporary democracies probably could use more of it.

In his June 2013 conversation with *Guardian* journalists, Snowden also claimed to "have carefully evaluated every single document I disclosed to ensure that each was in the public interest," in part to avoid "harming people."[24] In fact, Snowden's actions have been nonviolent, because they constitute "disobedience to law within the limits of fidelity to law."[25] His aim is neither violent criminality nor revolution, but instead a peaceful transformation of U.S. policy—and even the NSA itself—so that it might better accord with his interpretations of the U.S. Constitution and international law.

As Snowden grasps, nonviolence is essential to this project because injury and harm clash with the objective of *persuading* other political actors of injustices in need of correction. Coercion and force would deny others their basic rights, undermining the possibility of political agency on which democratic persuasion rests. Nonviolence is essential to what Bedau described as an "ideal political discourse" predicated on rational exchange, tolerance, and patience along the lines any public-minded responsible civil disobedient hopes to instigate.[26]

To be sure, Snowden's critics—including President Obama and British prime minister Cameron—accused him of placing people in harm's way, if only by increasing the odds of terrorist attacks.[27] Yet the evidence in support of this position seems paltry, as many observers and even a U.S. federal judge have pointed out.[28] Reasonable observers might disagree about the likely *long-term* political consequences of Snowden's actions. Yet *all* political activity generates unexpected and unforeseeable consequences.[29] Similar criticisms were directed against more-or-less universally praised exemplars of civil disobedience. Even King was accused of "inciting" violence because his nonviolent acts would produce a violent backlash from segregationists. The problem with the criticism, however, is that it rendered King culpable for the irresponsibility and violent disposition of his racist opponents. As he countered, "[i]sn't this like condemning the robbed man because his possession of money precipitated the evil act of robbery?"[30]

No political actor can be held responsible for all of her act's long-term consequences, even though she should ponder their likely character and minimize unnecessary harm to others. If Snowden devoted attention to avoiding such harm, as he claims, he probably has met this test. Until governments provide some unambiguous evidence to the contrary, there is no a priori reason to assume Snowden has endangered anyone.

## Snowden and Liberal and Republican Theories of Civil Disobedience

In scholarly debate, both those who provide a *liberal* gloss on civil disobedience and those seeking to give it a *democratic* and *republican* face insist that the legitimacy of civil disobedience is necessarily limited to a *special* case of injustices. The liberal philosopher John Rawls dubbed such injustices "serious infringements" and "blatant violations" of basic liberal rights.[31] More democratic and republican theorists describe these injustices as *fundamental* threats to the political process, in contrast to mere policy disagreements vis-à-vis governing political majorities.

Under the demanding tests outlined by liberal *and* republican theorists, Snowden's actions provide fodder for both sides. Simultaneously, they provide a reminder that scholarly attempts to contrast democratic (or republican) with competing liberal models of civil disobedience only get us so far when applied to real-life examples. In a liberal democratic political context, elements of both perspectives fuse together.

On the one hand, Snowden justifies his acts by what he holds to be sustained attacks on core rights, especially the Fourth and Fifth Amendments to the U.S. Constitution. In sync with the liberal model of civil disobedience, his actions can be interpreted as representing an attempt to counter serious and systemic infringements of basic liberties. Politically *defensive* in nature, they also follow the liberal model by emanating from an *individual,* whose *voice of conscience* demands action regardless of costs or consequences.[32]

On the other hand, Snowden's acts fit the republican view, which envisions civil disobedience as a collective undertaking by political actors working in concert with express political purposes.[33] As noted, his main goal has always been to ignite public debate, and however solitary he may appear, Snowden's is hardly the voice of an isolated moral agent unconcerned with public affairs or the common good. Interestingly, his appeals to individual conscience lack the overt religious tones found, for example, in parallel statements from Gandhi and King; his seems to be a secular and *political* conscience.

In the republican view, civil disobedience's main function is to challenge political complacency by bringing public attention to issues that may never have been meaningfully deliberated in the first place, or where privileged, vested interests and institutional stasis stymie re-examination of policy. This situation "may occur because the policy was never approved by the democratic sovereign at all but instead arose in some other way, as through a slow and unattended transformation of an initially very different policy."[34]

For republicans, the chief dilemma is not that a political majority approved legislation that violates individual rights, as the liberal model suggests. Instead, the needed public debate and exchange perhaps never occurred. Institutional inertia, rather than a legislative decision by a self-conscious political majority, haphazardly drives government action, perhaps tangentially linked to some previous but outdated expression of the popular will. For the republican, civil disobedience is only legitimate when there are pressing reasons for believing that a polity has failed to engage vital issues or when its political institutions and their dominant players have conspired to keep the public from taking a fresh look at existing policy. Solely in settings plagued by far-reaching political apathy and/or institutional inertia is nonviolent lawbreaking a justifiable strategy.

Snowden's actions arguably pass this test as well. Their open and public character stems from the quest to provoke debate in a context where he judged that mass and elite ignorance about government spying was ubiquitous. His Moscow statement characterizes U.S. surveillance policies as affecting "all of us," and thus of common and perhaps universal interest. As he anticipated, his revelations proved explosive, chiefly because only a tiny group of national security and political elites were familiar with the scope and scale of NSA activities. Further, the legal foundations for these activities partly consist of judicial rulings on the Fourth Amendment's application to telephony metadata dating back to 1979,[35] well before computers transformed communication and information technology. The "slow and unattended" evolution of such increasingly obsolete rulings into a legal veneer for massive NSA spying raises difficult questions for democratic legitimacy.[36]

In the June 2013 *Guardian* conversation, Snowden recalled his frustration following Obama's 2008 election at the failure to reverse his predecessor's surveillance policies. Snowden "watched as Obama advanced the very policies that I thought would be reined in," despite Obama's promises to pursue major changes in U.S. counterterrorism policy.

Faced with the task of taming government surveillance, the much-touted U.S. system of institutional checks and balances has performed erratically after the 9/11 terrorist attacks.[37] Even though President Bush assured the American people his administration only engaged in domestic surveillance when in possession of a judicial warrant, it aggressively initiated warrantless domestic spying. When news of the administration's illegal actions reached Congress, it responded, but arguably only by providing some of the administration's more controversial policies with a stronger legislative base and by immunizing telecommunications companies that cooperated with executive branch illegality. For its part, the secret FISC has pretty much given the NSA a free hand, rarely challenging even some of the NSA's most far-reaching assertions of authority. In Snowden's view, the FISC has served as a "graveyard of judgment."[38] Rather than reining in executive power, the legislative and judicial branches effectively colluded with the executive branch to condone massive domestic and foreign surveillance while excusing wrongdo-ers.[39] Nor have attempts by human rights organizations to focus attention on the resulting dangers gained much traction in Washington, D.C.

Observing this troublesome downward spiral at close quarters, Snowden de-cided that "you can't wait around for someone else to act. I had been looking for leaders, but I realized that leadership is about being the first to act."[40] He reached this conclusion, however, after political leaders failed at making NSA spying a theme for public discussion.

Snowden has, thus, also satisfied the "last resort" test. Civil disobedience only represents a legitimate option after normal political and legal channels have been exhausted or in situations Rawls characterized as where:

> the legal means of redress have proved of no avail. Thus, for example, the existing political parties have shown themselves indifferent to the claims of the minor-ity or have proved unwilling to accommodate them. Attempts to have the laws repealed have been ignored and legal protests and demonstrations have had no success.[41]

With some justification, Snowden believes that the failure of the U.S. polity to address NSA spying falls into this category. Consequently, he had no choice as a conscientious and public-minded citizen but to leak the ugly facts of NSA spy-ing. What alternatives were available to him? A donation to the American Civil Liberties Union (ACLU) or Human Rights Watch? A letter to his congressional representative, or perhaps to President Obama himself? Or maybe a collegial conversation with his superiors?

Interestingly, Snowden claims to have shared his misgivings with his bosses. But they ignored him, "almost certainly because the agency and its leaders don't consider these collection programs to be an abuse."[42] In light of the effectively nonexistent legal protections provided to whistleblowing NSA private contractors, the *New York Times* concluded, "Mr. Snowden was clearly justified in believing that the only way to blow the whistle on this kind of intelligence gathering was to expose it to the public."[43]

Even those with a more benign assessment of our political system's operations should recall Rawls' additional proviso that:

> Some cases may be so extreme that there may be no duty to use first only legal means of political opposition. If, for example, the legislature were to enact some outrageous violation of equal liberty, say by forbidding the religion of a weak and defenseless minority, we surely could not expect that sect to oppose the law by normal political procedures.[44]

To be sure, NSA spying differs in important ways from discriminatory laws against defenseless minorities. Sound arguments, however, buttress the view that unchecked NSA surveillance is proving disturbingly ruinous of fundamental liberties.

## Civil Disobedience Without Penalties?

Despite the conventional wisdom that civil disobedients should accept the legal ramifications of their actions, Snowden fled the United States and refused to turn himself in to U.S. authorities. This scenario poses problems for any attempt to interpret his deeds as a legitimate case of civil disobedience. For Gandhi, nonviolence demanded "voluntary submission to the penalty for non-cooperation with evil."[45] King penned a "Letter from a Birmingham Jail," not "Letter on the Run from a Birmingham Jail."

Yet, as critical voices in a protracted legal and philosophical debate have posited, the grounds for assenting to punishment as an unavoidable consequence of civil disobedience are perhaps less airtight than typically recognized.[46] Snowden's example, in my view, strengthens this dissenting position. In any event, U.S. officials are obliged to offer clemency to Snowden. The penalties they hope to impose are inappropriate.

Those who insist that civil disobedience entails enduring its legal repercussions offer a potent—yet ultimately unwieldy—brew of principled reasons, along with strategic and tactical reasons. Most fundamentally, they argue that undergoing punishment allows lawbreakers to evince what King described as the "very highest respect for law."[47] By accepting punishment for breaking an unjust law, lawbreakers express their fidelity to the idea of legality, or the rule of law, as well as appreciation for the legitimacy of a legal or constitutional order. In contrast to the criminal or revolutionary, both of whom try to avoid getting caught when violating the law, a responsible civil disobedient anticipates criminal prosecution, its potentially unjust character notwithstanding.

Typically, this argument gets fused with the related notion that civil disobedience must be open or public, which—as we have seen—plays a decisive role in distinguishing it from other varieties of illegality. King, for example, suggested that accepting "the penalty by staying in jail to arouse the conscience of the community" was essential to "openly, lovingly" breaking the law. He juxtaposed this approach to segregationists who torched black churches under the cover of darkness and did everything in their power to avoid prosecution.[48]

Academic theorists of civil disobedience have defended the punishment requirement in more strategic or tactical terms. Accepting punishment is how lawbreakers provide evidence of their unselfishness and public-mindedness, their moral seriousness, the intensity of their concerns, and their moral and political sincerity.[49] On one view, they should neither expect nor seek special treatment because fidelity to the rule of law demands strict nondiscrimination. Because of their commitment to the idea of legality and the overall legitimacy of the existing legal order, it would be inconsistent to expect better treatment than others—including ordinary criminals—who broke the law.[50]

According to the conventional view, criminal punishment also serves a deterrent function: without its looming specter, the costs of lawbreaking would be cheapened.[51] Irresponsible illegality lacking in the requisite moral seriousness might ensue.

This account rests on a rich tradition arguably dating to Plato's *Crito*. At closer examination, however, it raises as many questions as it answers. Most immediately, to the degree that the arguments are strategic or tactical in character, they imply that dissenting lawbreakers might follow alternative paths in order to bring about the desired moral and political results.

Exiled to Putin's Russia, with no likelihood of returning home, has Snowden not provided sufficient evidence of his moral seriousness and public-mindedness? Though he has never appeared in a U.S. courtroom, the open and public character of his actions can hardly be denied. Even absent criminal punishment, his disclosures continue to rivet public attention, generating a worldwide debate about not only U.S. surveillance, but also the moral responsibilities of individuals in an age of unprecedented technological possibilities for state surveillance. Can we be so sure that better, or even equivalent, results would have been achieved if Snowden had remained in the United States and assented to prosecution under the Espionage Act?

As for the thesis that punishment serves a deterrent function, it hardly seems self-evident that Snowden's example will lead to a dramatic increase in irresponsible and morally intemperate lawbreaking. On the contrary, the world can see what he has sacrificed and that his moral decision came at a high personal cost—even absent criminal punishment—most of us would not willingly bear.

Nor is it clear that previous practitioners of civil disobedience followed this orthodox view of punishment. Thoreau neither advertised his illegal acts nor sought punishment for them; his readers will look in vain for a celebratory description of the penalty meted out to him by his Massachusetts jailers.[52] Gandhi accepted the legal repercussions of his acts, but not out of respect for the legitimacy of British colonial law in India, which he despised.[53] And when the framework of a legal order is polluted by corrosive forms of secret law and court rulings, as Snowden believes is the case for U.S. law, can we be sure that accepting legal punishment will buttress the rule of law rather than help bury it?

Though rarely mentioned, the core intuition that acceptance of legal penalties is related to respect for the law only makes sense if disobedients can count on criminal proceedings embodying the virtues of the rule of law.[54] Evasion of punishment should probably remain the exception to the norm, but if peaceful lawbreakers face a situation where there is "no right of public trial, and no possibility of using punishment for publicity purposes, or if punishments were made draconian in order to prevent dissenters from publicizing their views," then evasion could prove justified because it might best guarantee the requisite publicity.[55] When criminal proceedings rest on vague and poorly defined legal norms, suffer from excessive politicization that impairs possibility of a fair trial, and mete out draconian sentences, then a conscientious disobedient's decision to escape is potentially supportive and not destructive of the rule of law.

Unfortunately, as the German jurist Merkel observed, such concerns are pertinent to the Obama administration's decision to prosecute Snowden under the Espionage Act. This infamous statute's main accomplishment has been its inadvertent contributions to the creation of twentieth-century U.S. civil liberties movements.[56] Since World War I, when it functioned as an "efficient tool for the blanket suppression of antiwar views," the Espionage Act has allowed the executive branch to clamp down on unwanted dissident voices, in ways often recognized as legally dubious and politically counterproductive.[57] As Harold Edgar and Benno Schmidt chronicled, the act is riddled with vague and often incomprehensible language that provides the executive with arbitrary power over a stunning range of activities related to the undefined terrain of "national security."[58] Because the ideal of the rule of law is tied to the quest for legal clarity and consistency, the Espionage Act is inconsonant with it. Not surprisingly, Edgar, Schmidt, and others have argued that it is probably unconstitutional.

In part because of its legal failings, most presidents have been reluctant to enforce the Espionage Act. President Obama, however, has been more aggressive than his predecessors in doing so. Among liberal-minded law professors and civil libertarians, this development has proven contentious. Another prominent whistleblower prosecuted under the Espionage Act, Bradley/Chelsea Manning, is serving a thirty-five-year sentence.

The problem here goes beyond the Espionage Act's legal failings. As Snowden is aware, and as the Manning case reminded him, whistleblowers in national security institutions enjoy few legal protections. As civil libertarians and others have noted, the legal status of national security personnel is precarious at best, and the area most relevant to Snowden's case, basic rule of law virtues, remains underdeveloped.[59] And, just in case any ambiguity remained, Attorney General Holder made it clear the U.S. government considers Snowden guilty and would fight for him to receive at least a thirty-year sentence or, if possible, life imprisonment. Is it any wonder Snowden decided his chances of a fair trial in the United States were close to nil?[60]

Pushing back against the Obama administration's hard line, major voices in the United States—including the *New York Times* editorial staff—have called on Obama to encourage Snowden to return home in exchange for clemency or amnesty.[61] The debate on civil disobedience suggests some pressing reasons why this approach would represent a humane and intellectually sound course of action.

All legal systems—and especially the U.S. system—provide for leniency in the law's application. Prosecutors and judges allow plea bargaining, reduction of charges, or mitigation of penalties under special circumstances (as when an offender is young, lives in extreme poverty, or in other special circumstances).[62] The orthodox view that disobedients should not be treated differently from ordinary criminals obscures that they *are* different. Snowden did not break the law for private gain or to aid foreign terrorists, but instead to bring violations of the law to the attention of his compatriots in order to generate public debate. The Obama administration's decision to enforce the Espionage Act against him as it would against "ordinary" spies constitutes a spurious application of legal generality incongruent with basic legal and constitutional ideals.

The view that "the law is the law"—and that Snowden's acts require strict prosecution—also downplays that he explained why *his* actions were required by constitutional and international law. Obviously, the Obama administration does not share Snowden's legal views, but many others in the United States and elsewhere do, in part because he has persuaded them.

There are sound reasons why reasonable people disagree about how state surveillance is best regulated by the U.S. Constitution and international law. We face a situation where "the law is uncertain, in the sense that a plausible case can be made on both sides."[63] As legal philosopher Ronald Dworkin wrote in a similar context, "then a citizen who follows his own judgment is not behaving unfairly." Liberal democracy should not only permit but also encourage citizens to cultivate their judgments about complex constitutional issues. Fidelity to the law cannot be equated with blind loyalty to an official's or institution's legal views. Thus, with respect to a civil disobedient, "our government has a special responsibility to try to protect him, and soften his predicament, whenever it can do so without great damage to other policies." Of course, no government can guarantee immunity to those who violate the law in the name of conscience. "But it does follow," Dworkin argued, "that when the practical reasons for prosecuting are relatively weak in a particular case, or can be met in other ways, the path of fairness lies in tolerance."[64]

After revealing that NSA officials regularly broke the law and then succeeding in igniting a much-needed political debate about the modern surveillance state, Snowden deserves better than Russian exile or thirty years in a U.S. prison.

## Civil Disobedience in a Global Age

One of the most striking traits of Snowden's Moscow statement is how he acknowledges the global parameters of contemporary law and politics. The statement appeals to the U.S. Constitution, the Universal Declaration of Human Rights, the Law of Nations, and the international legal principle of *non-refoulement*, which prohibits countries from rendering victims of persecution to their persecutors. According to Snowden, Attorney General Holder's attempt to force Hong Kong to return him to the United States in June 2013 violated international law. He even references the Nuremberg war crimes tribunal and its ruling that:

> Individuals have international duties which transcend the national obligations of obedience. Therefore individual citizens have the duty to violate domestic laws to prevent crimes against peace and humanity from occurring.

Snowden not only believes that he acted in accordance with the Nuremberg principles, but that his actions have been conducive to international peace.

The Moscow statement addresses not just U.S. citizens but a global public: "I asked the world for justice." Snowden lauds the governments and peoples of Russia, Venezuela, Bolivia, Nicaragua, and Ecuador—each of which sought to grant him asylum before facing a backlash from the United States—for having "earned the respect of the world." Snowden has mobilized not only specific national publics but also an emerging worldwide public in support of his cause.

From one perspective, this strategy is familiar from the annals of modern civil disobedience. Gandhi and King sought to influence foreign governments and shape global opinion, while appealing to supranational norms and moral values. During the Vietnam War, politically motivated lawbreakers in the antiwar movement similarly described the Nuremberg trials as offering a basis for a "higher" law they envisioned as superordinate to U.S. law.[65]

Yet Snowden's statement evinces some significant novelty. Even if earlier civil disobedients hinted at our increasingly global condition, Snowden takes it as a given, as his appeal to international law attests. Revealingly, Snowden's actions not only have had worldwide political ramifications, but he is also more attuned than his historical predecessors to prominent global political and legal innovations, some of which offer a launching pad for checking unjust state action. International human rights lawyers risk conflating their normative wishes with political realities when describing international human rights law as "humanity's law," where human security trumps state sovereignty or national security.[66] By the same token, it would be equally misleading to obfuscate how supranational political and legal institutions—including the human rights regime—are core pillars of the evolving global order. Even if the global system remains messy, contradictory, too often driven by power politics, and faced with tasks suggesting its obsolescence, its main features rest on cosmopolitan moral and political aspirations.[67]

This observation points to an alternative reading of Snowden's actions and whether civil disobedients should submit to criminal prosecution. Crucially, he has never claimed that he should be immune from punishment. Instead, he has accused the U.S. government of trying to deny him a fair trial. He has insisted that his actions are consonant with international law, whereas the United States has abrogated it in spying on foreign countries and violating his rights in seeking asylum. As Snowden understands, he has no chance of validating the legality of his position given the power inequalities plaguing the global order. We still lack a global legal system in which Snowden and others could defend their legal claims and where they might have a reasonable chance of defeating major global players in a court of law.

Given that lacuna, Snowden perhaps concluded that his only option was to seek asylum. Yet his actions point to an important constructive political task. We need to build a stronger global legal and human rights system, where the rights of those who take on the great powers garner real protection. If such a system existed and was able to secure the requisite fairness and impartiality likely to be missing from U.S. legal proceedings under the Espionage Act, Snowden could appear before it to make his case and be subject to applicable penalties should he lose.

We lack a global legal system and none seems likely to emerge in the near future. The great powers prefer the status quo. In the meantime, we are forced to accept makeshift solutions, recognizing their political necessity and unsatisfactory normative character. Americans should demand the U.S. government treat Snowden with clemency. If the United States fails to do the right thing, Snowden should have somewhere to go besides Putin's Russia. Politicians in other countries who tapped into public anger about U.S. spying need to back up their rhetoric with deeds. His contributions to the democracy and the rule of law, in striking juxtaposition to those who have tried to silence him, remain auspicious.

## Notes

1. The evidence suggests President Putin is envious of U.S. surveillance capacities, and the predictable result will be an arms race in these capacities, as in so many other areas of the U.S.-Russia rivalry.

2. Part II.A includes this statement by Snowden.

3. In fact, an unnamed editor chose the term for a posthumously published version (1866) of Thoreau's famous (1849) essay, "Resistance to Civil Government," which was retitled "Civil Disobedience." In the aftermath of the U.S. Civil War, the original title probably seemed too incendiary! Lewis Perry, *Civil Disobedience: An American Tradition* (New Haven, Conn.: Yale University Press, 2013), 65.

4. Bidyut Chakrabarty, *Confluence of Thought: Mahatma Gandhi and Martin Luther King* (New York: Oxford University Press, 2013).

5. The Hamburg law professor Reinhard Merkel defended Snowden on the basis of liberal theories of civil disobedience, including that of John Rawls. David Hugendick, "Snowdens Strafe wäre existenzvernichtend" [Interview with Reinhard Merkel], *Die Zeit*, June 27, 2013, http://www.zeit.de/kultur/2013-06/Interview-Reinhard-Merkel-Moral.

6. John Rawls, "Definition and Justification of Civil Disobedience," in *Civil Disobedience in Focus*, ed. Hugo Adam Bedau, 104 (New York: Routledge, 1991).

7. Quoted in Glenn Greenwald, Ewen MacAskill, and Laura Poitras, "Edward Snowden: The Whistleblower Behind the NSA Surveillance Revelations," *Guardian*, June 9, 2013, http://www.theguardian.com/world/2013/jun/09/edward-snowden-nsa-whistleblower-surveillance.

8. Barton Gellman, "Edward Snowden, After Months of NSA Revelations, Says His Mission's Accomplished," *Washington Post,* December 23, 2013, http://www.washingtonpost.com/world /national-security/edward-snowden-after-months-of-nsa-revelations-says-his-missions -accomplished/2013/12/23/49fc36de-6c1c-11e3-a523-fe73f0ff6b8d_story.html.

9. Drake was a high-level NSA official who believed the NSA was committing crimes and who leaked information to the media. He was charged under the Espionage Act. In the aftermath of a May 22, 2011, *60 Minutes* report on his case, the Obama administration dropped most of the charges. Snowden appears to have paid close attention to Drake's case and the Obama administration's attempt to prosecute him under the Espionage Act. Luke Harding, *The Snowden Files* (New York: Vintage, 2014), 51–52.

10. Bradley/Chelsea Manning was convicted in 2013 by a military court of various criminal charges, including violations of the Espionage Act, for his role in disseminating classified documents in what became known as the Wikileaks affair.

11. Hugo Adam Bedau, "Civil Disobedience and Personal Responsibility for Injustice," in *Civil Disobedience in Focus,* ed. Hugo Adam Bedau, 50 (New York: Routledge, 1991).

12. Quoted in Gellman, "Edward Snowden, After Months of NSA Revelations."

13. Quoted in Greenwald, MacAskill, and Poitras, "Edward Snowden."

14. This critical assessment of NSA policy is shared by former vice president Al Gore and a federal judge, Richard Leon, appointed by President George W. Bush. See *Klayman v. Obama,* 957 F.Supp.2d 1 (D.D.C. 2013). Part II.B contains excerpts from Judge Leon's decision in *Klayman.*

15. Gellman, "Edward Snowden, After Months of NSA Revelations."

16. Quoted in Greenwald, MacAskill, and Poitras, "Edward Snowden."

17. Carol D. Leonnig, "Court: Ability to Police U.S. Spying Limited," *Washington Post,* August 15, 2013, http://www.washingtonpost.com/politics/court-ability-to-police-us-spying-program-limited/2013/08/15/4a8c8c44-05cd-11e3-a07f-49ddc7417125_story.html; Charles Savage and Scott Shane, "Secret Court Rebuked N.S.A. on Surveillance," *New York Times,* August 21, 2013, http://www.nytimes.com/2013/08/22/us/2011-ruling-found-an-nsa-program-unconstitutional.html ?pagewanted=all&_r=0.

18. Statements by civil libertarian and human rights organizations echo similar concerns.

19. Suspected of transporting Snowden to Bolivia, on July 3, 2013, a plane carrying the Bolivian president was forced to land in Austria, allegedly because of U.S. political pressure.

20. Lon Fuller, *The Morality of Law* (New Haven, Conn.: Yale University Press, 1964), 40–41, 157–59.

21. Norberto Bobbio, *The Future of Democracy,* trans. Robert Griffin (Minneapolis: University of Minnesota Press, 1987), 79–97.

22. Michael Walzer, *Obligations: Essays on Disobedience, War, and Citizenship* (New York: Simon & Schuster, 1970), 20.

23. On *Face the Nation* (June 16, 2013), Bob Schieffer of CBS called Snowden a narcissist. Jeffrey Toobin did so in "Edward Snowden Is No Hero," *New Yorker,* June 10, 2013, http://www.newyorker .com/online/blogs/comment/2013/06/edward-snowden-nsa-leaker-is-no-hero.html. Other commentators noted Snowden has endorsed right-leaning, antistatist "libertarian" views. Sean Wilentz, "Operation Mayhem," *New Republic,* February 3, 2014, 14–25; Harding, *The Snowden Files.*

24. Quoted in Greenwald, MacAskill, and Poitras, "Edward Snowden."

25. Rawls, "Definition and Justification of Civil Disobedience," 106.

26. Hugo Adam Bedau, "Introduction," in *Civil Disobedience in Focus,* ed. Hugo Adam Bedau, 8 (New York: Routledge, 1991).

27. Snowden's leaks show that the Government Communications Headquarters (GCHQ), a British intelligence agency, engaged in spying and has served as the NSA's junior partner. Speaking before Parliament on October 15, 2013, Prime Minister Cameron criticized the *Guardian* for publishing Snowden's story, accusing its writers and Snowden of endangering national security and handing "the advantage to the terrorists." The *Guardian* has been subjected to intrusive

government searches. Alan Rusbridger, "The Snowden Leaks and the Public," *New York Review,* November 21, 2013, 31–34. In an interview, Obama accused Snowden of "putting our people at risk." David Remnick, "Going the Distance: On and Off the Road with Barack Obama," *New Yorker,* January 27, 2014, 59.

28. *Klayman v. Obama.*

29. On the irreversibility and unpredictability of political action, see Hannah Arendt, *The Human Condition* (Chicago: University of Chicago Press, 1958), 175–247, esp. 236–47.

30. Martin Luther King, "Letter from a Birmingham Jail," in *Civil Disobedience in Focus,* ed. Hugo Adam Bedau, 76 (New York: Routledge, 1991). As King added, "society must protect the robbed and punish the robber."

31. Rawls, "Definition and Justification of Civil Disobedience," 108–9.

32. This description of competing liberal and republican models draws on Jean L. Cohen and Andrew Arato, *Civil Society and Political Theory* (Cambridge, Mass.: MIT Press, 1992), 564–604. Representatives of the liberal position include Rawls and Ronald Dworkin, *Taking Rights Seriously* (Cambridge, Mass.: Harvard University Press, 1977), 206–22.

33. A powerful statement of this view was formulated by Hannah Arendt, *Crises of the Republic* (New York: Harcourt Brace and Jovanovich, 1973), 49–102. A republican theory of civil disobedience is also developed in Daniel Markovits, "Democratic Disobedience," *Yale Law Journal* 114 (2005): 1897–1952. Elements of Markovits' theory overlap with a democratic-deliberative account inspired by Jürgen Habermas by Will Smith, "Civil Disobedience and the Public Sphere," *Journal of Political Philosophy* 19, no. 2 (2011): 145–66.

34. Markovits, "Democratic Disobedience," 1933.

35. See *Smith v. Maryland,* 442 U.S. 735 (1979).

36. Ryan Lizza, "State of Deception: Why Won't the President Rein in the Intelligence Community?" *New Yorker,* December 16, 2013, 48–61.

37. For a contrary view, see Jack Goldsmith, *Power and Constraint: The Accountable Presidency After 9/11* (New York: Norton, 2012). For a critical response to Goldsmith, see my "Obama's War on Terror," *Constitutional Commentary* 28 (Spring 2013): 519–38.

38. Quoted in Gellman, "Edward Snowden, After Months of NSA Revelations."

39. Jonathan Schell, "The Surveillance Net," *The Nation,* July 8/15, 2013, 3–6.

40. Quoted in Greenwald, MacAskill, and Poitras, "Edward Snowden."

41. Rawls, "Definition and Justification of Civil Disobedience," 110.

42. "Edward Snowden, Whistle-Blower: Considering the Value of His Leaks, He Should be Offered Clemency or a Plea Bargain," *New York Times,* January 2, 2014, A18. The NSA has disputed this claim.

43. Ibid.

44. Rawls, "Definition and Justification of Civil Disobedience," 110.

45. Mahatma Gandhi, "Nonviolence," in *Civil Disobedience and Violence,* ed. Jeffrie G. Murphy, 93 (Belmont, Calif.: Wadsworth, 1971).

46. See the debate between David Lefkowitz, "On a Moral Right to Civil Disobedience," *Ethics* 117, no. 2 (2007): 202–33, and Kimberley Brownlee, "Penalizing Public Disobedience," *Ethics* 118, no. 4 (2008): 711–16. Its key insight is that criminal punishment contains elements of moral disapprobation inappropriate to the legal treatment of civil disobedients.

47. King, "Letter from a Birmingham Jail," 74. The idea that the acceptance of a legal penalty demonstrates respect for the law was endorsed by many academics. See Bedau, "Introduction," 8; Carl Cohen, "Civil Disobedience and the Law," *Rutgers Law Review* 21, no. 1 (1966): 5–7; and Rawls, "Definition and Justification of Civil Disobedience," 106–7. For a critical discussion, see Gene G. James, "The Orthodox Theory of Civil Disobedience," *Social Theory and Practice* 2, no. 4 (1973): 475–98.

48. King, "Letter from a Birmingham Jail," 74.

49. Bedau, "Introduction," 8; Cohen, "Civil Disobedience and the Law," 5–7; Rawls, "Definition and Justification of Civil Disobedience," 106–7; Smith, "Civil Disobedience and the Public Sphere," 161–63.

50. Cohen, "Civil Disobedience and the Law," 5–7; James, "The Orthodox Theory of Civil Disobedience," 491–95.

51. Smith, "Civil Disobedience and the Public Sphere," 163.

52. Henry D. Thoreau, "Resistance to Civil Government," in *The Higher Law: Thoreau on Civil Disobedience and Reform,* ed. Howard Zinn, 63–90 (Princeton, N.J.: Princeton University Press, 2004).

53. Arendt, *Crises of the Republic,* 77. Arendt criticized the orthodox view that civil disobedients should necessarily accept criminal punishment, hoping that it would "be possible to find a recognized niche for civil disobedience in our institutions of government." Ibid., 99.

54. The rule of law is a contested concept. For an overview, see Brian Z. Tamanaha, *On the Rule of Law: History, Politics, Theory* (Cambridge: Cambridge University Press, 2004).

55. Peter Singer, *Democracy and Disobedience* (Oxford: Clarendon Press, 1973), 83–84.

56. The Espionage Act provoked creation of the National Civil Liberties Bureau, forerunner of the ACLU.

57. Geoffrey R. Stone, *Perilous Times: Free Speech in Wartime—From the Sedition Act of 1787 to the War on Terrorism* (New York: Norton, 2004), 173.

58. Harold Edgar and Benno C. Schmidt Jr., "The Espionage Statutes and Publication of Defense Information," *Columbia Law Review* 73, no. 5 (1973): 929–1087.

59. The ACLU and Human Rights Watch have used Snowden's case as a rallying cry for strengthening whistleblowing protections in the national security context. For an account of the existing legal regime, see David E. Pozen, "The Leaky Leviathan: Why the Government Condemns and Condones Unlawful Disclosures of Information," *Harvard Law Review* 127 (2013–14): 512–635.

60. Interestingly, Snowden's father initially hoped his son would return home to face criminal proceedings, but the Obama administration's presumption of guilt led him to change his views. Associated Press, "Edward Snowden Better Off in Russia than US, His Father Says," *Guardian,* July 26, 2013, http://www.theguardian.com/world/2013/jul/27/nsa-snowden-father-justice-russia. The fact that politicians described his son as a traitor, and even joked about assassinating him, probably did not inspire much confidence either.

61. "Edward Snowden, Whistle-Blower."

62. Dworkin, *Taking Rights Seriously,* 207.

63. Ibid., 215.

64. Ibid., 215–16.

65. Harrop Freeman, "Response to Carl Cohen," *Rutgers Law Review* 21, no. 1 (1966): 17–27; Telford Taylor, *Nuremberg and Vietnam: An American Tragedy* (New York: Bantam, 1971).

66. Ruti G. Teitel, *Humanity's Law* (New York: Oxford University Press, 2011).

67. David Held, *Democracy and the Global Order: From the Modern State to Cosmopolitan Governance* (Stanford, Calif.: Stanford University Press, 1995).

PART II

THE SNOWDEN AFFAIR THROUGH
# PRIMARY
# DOCUMENTS

## A. Revelations and Reactions

The first year of Snowden's disclosures brought remarkable revelations, facilitated by Snowden's collaboration with journalists, and elicited a cacophony of reactions to the leaks by affected parties. The primary documents in this section are organized into categories of important issues Snowden's disclosures generated, with a sampling of documents from each category. This selection of documents provides a panorama of what Snowden did and how the U.S. government, foreign governments, private companies, and civil society groups responded.

*Unconstitutional Abuse of Power or*
*Legitimate and Necessary Security Measures?*
*NSA Programs under the Foreign*
*Intelligence Surveillance Act*

# 1

# The Verizon Order

It all started with disclosure of this document, which came to be known as the "Verizon Order." In it, the Foreign Intelligence Surveillance Court (FISC) ordered Verizon to produce to the NSA on a daily basis records of telephone calls—telephony or telephone metadata—between the United States and foreign countries and wholly within the United States, pursuant to Section 215 of the USA PATRIOT Act (codified as 50 U.S.C. §1861). Information sought under Section 215 for foreign intelligence purposes or to protect against international terrorism must be "relevant to an authorized investigation." The Verizon Order revealed that the FBI, NSA, and FISC interpreted this requirement to mean the NSA could collect from Verizon, and from other telephone companies under similar FISC orders, metadata on millions of telephone calls made by Americans every day. Exposure of the telephone metadata program, and the associated interpretation of Section 215, triggered a political and legal controversy in the United States.

TOP SECRET//SI//NOFORN

UNITED STATES

FOREIGN INTELLIGENCE SURVEILLANCE COURT

WASHINGTON, D.C.

---

IN RE APPLICATION OF THE
FEDERAL BUREAU OF INVESTIGATION
FOR AN ORDER REQUIRING THE          Docket Number: BR 13–80
PRODUCTION OF TANGIBLE THINGS
FROM VERIZON BUSINESS NETWORK SERVICES,
INC. ON BEHALF OF MCI COMMUNICATION
SERVICES, INC. D/B/A VERIZON
BUSINESS SERVICES

---

## SECONDARY ORDER

This Court having found that the Application of the Federal Bureau of Investigation (FBI) for an Order requiring the production of tangible things from **Verizon Business Network Services, Inc. on behalf of MCI Communication Services Inc., d/b/a Verizon Business Services (individually and collectively "Verizon")** satisfies the requirements of 50 U.S.C. § 1861,

IT IS HEREBY ORDERED that, the Custodian of Records shall produce to the National Security Agency (NSA) upon service of this Order, and continue production on an ongoing daily basis thereafter for the duration of this Order, unless otherwise ordered by the Court, an electronic copy of the following tangible things: all call detail records or "telephony metadata" created by Verizon for communications (i) between the United States and abroad; or (ii) wholly within the United States, including local telephone calls. This Order does not require Verizon to produce telephony metadata for communications wholly originating and terminating in foreign countries. Telephony metadata includes comprehensive communications routing information, including but not limited to session identifying information (*e.g.*, originating and terminating telephone number, International Mobile Subscriber Identity (IMSI) number, International Mobile station Equipment Identity (IMEI) number, etc.), trunk identifier, telephone calling card numbers, and time and duration of call. Telephony metadata does not include the substantive content of any communication, as defined by 18 U.S.C. § 2510(8), or the name, address, or financial information of a subscriber or customer.

IT IS FURTHER ORDERED that no person shall disclose to any other person that the FBI or NSA has sought or obtained tangible things under this Order, other than to: (a) those persons to whom disclosure is necessary to comply with such Order; (b) an attorney to obtain legal advice or assistance with respect to the production of things in response to the Order; or (c) other persons permitted by the Director of the FBI or the Director's designee. A person to whom disclosure is made pursuant to (a), (b), or (c) shall be subject to the nondisclosure requirements applicable to a person to whom an Order is directed in the same manner as such person. Anyone who discloses to a person described in (a), (b), or (c) that the FBI or NSA has sought or obtained tangible things pursuant to this Order shall notify such person of the nondisclosure requirements of this Order. At the request of the Director of the FBI or the designee of the Director, any person making or intending to make a disclosure under (a) or (c) above shall identify to the Director or such designee the person to whom such disclosure will be made or to whom such disclosure was made prior to the request.

IT IS FURTHER ORDERED that service of this Order shall be by a method agreed upon by the Custodian of Records of Verizon and the FBI, and if no agreement is reached, service shall be personal.

This authorization **requiring the production of certain call detail records or "telephony metadata" created by Verizon** expires on the <u>19th</u> day of July, 2013, at 5:00 p.m., Eastern Time.

Signed <u>04–25–2013</u> P<u>O2:26</u> Eastern Time
      Date       Time

                             **ROGER VINSON**

                             Judge, United States Foreign
                             Intelligence Surveillance Court

Foreign Intelligence Surveillance Court, Secondary Order, In Re Application of the Federal Bureau of Investigation for an Order Requiring the Production of Tangible Things from Verizon Business Network Services, Inc. on Behalf of MCI Communication Services, Inc. d/b/a Verizon Business Services, April 25, 2013 [disclosed June 5, 2013].

*Source:* "Verizon Forced to Hand Over Telephone Data—Full Court Ruling," *Guardian,* June 5, 2013, http://www.theguardian.com/world/interactive/2013/jun/06/verizon-telephone-data-court -order.

# 2

# NSA PRISM and UPSTREAM Briefing Slides

People were still processing the June 5 exposure of the telephone metadata pro-gram when the next day brought a significant disclosure about NSA surveillance conducted under Section 702 of FISA. This FISA provision authorizes the U.S. government to conduct electronic surveillance within the United States for in-telligence purposes against foreign nationals reasonably believed to be located outside the United States. Unlike the secret interpretation of Section 215 of the USA PATRIOT Act revealed by the Verizon Order, Section 702 was debated by Congress during consideration of the FISA Amendments Act of 2008 and in the courts during litigation that produced a February 2013 Supreme Court decision, *Clapper v. Amnesty International,* which held that the plaintiffs could not chal-lenge the constitutionality of Section 702. Well before Snowden, Section 702 was understood to provide authority for the U.S. government to engage in broad, ex-tensive surveillance against targets believed to be located outside the United States that would incidentally capture communications of persons in the United States.

Many of the documents released by Snowden were slides prepared by NSA personnel for internal intelligence community briefings that contained clas-sified information to which Snowden had access as a contractor for the NSA. NSA briefing slides revealed two NSA activities under Section 702: the PRISM and UPSTREAM programs. Under PRISM, the NSA required U.S. companies, including those identified in the slides, to provide communications they managed to or from its foreign targets. Under UPSTREAM, the NSA tapped into privately owned fiber-optic cables carrying information to and from the United States to conduct surveillance on foreign targets. Both PRISM and UPSTREAM provided the NSA with communications metadata and content. As the slides indicate, the dominance of U.S. cyber companies meant that a significant portion of the world's communications transited the United States, providing the NSA with a rich surveillance source. The first slide declares PRISM to be the signals intelligence activity used the most in NSA analytical reports. Disclosure of these Section 702 programs fanned the flames of concern ignited by the Verizon Order about the civil liberties of U.S. persons, and it provoked anger in foreign countries about NSA surveillance of their citizens' communications.

★ ★ ★

# PRISM/US-984XN
## Overview

OR

*The SIGAD Used **Most** in NSA Reporting*
Overview

April 2013

Derived From: NSA/CSSM 1-52
Dated: 20070108
Declassify On: 20360901
TOP SECRET//SI//ORCON//NOFORN

TOP SECRET//SI//ORCON//NOFORN

**(TS//SI//NF) Introduction**

*U.S. as World's Telecommunications Backbone*

- Much of the world's communications flow through the U.S.
- A target's phone call, e-mail or chat will take the **cheapest** path, **not the physically most direct** path – you can't always predict the path.
- Your target's communications could easily be flowing into and through the U.S.

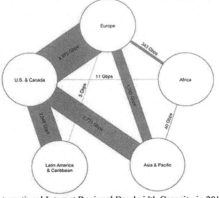

International Internet Regional Bandwidth Capacity in 2011
Source: Telegeography Research

TOP SECRET//SI//ORCON//NOFORN

---

TOP SECRET//SI//ORCON//NOFORN

**(TS//SI//NF) PRISM Collection Details**

**Current Providers**

What Will You Receive in Collection
(Surveillance and Stored Comms)?
It varies by provider. In general:

- Microsoft (Hotmail, etc.)
- Google
- Yahoo!
- Facebook
- PalTalk
- YouTube
- Skype
- AOL
- Apple

- E-mail
- Chat – video, voice
- Videos
- Photos
- Stored data
- VoIP
- File transfers
- Video Conferencing
- Notifications of target activity – logins, etc.
- Online Social Networking details
- **Special Requests**

Complete list and details on PRISM web page:
Go PRISMFAA

TOP SECRET//SI//ORCON//NOFORN

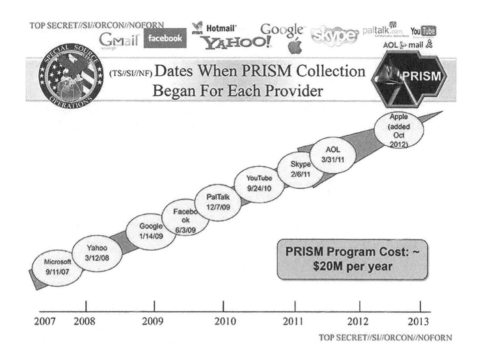

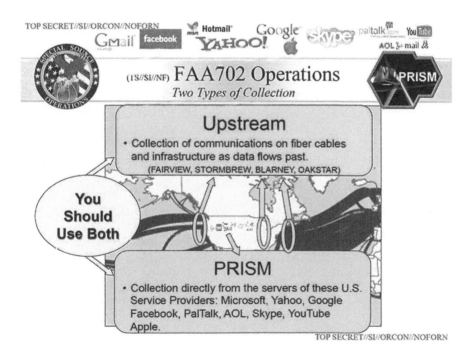

★ ★ ★

NSA Briefing Slides on Surveillance Programs Undertaken Pursuant to Section 702 of FISA, April 2013 [disclosed June 6, 2013].

*Source:* "NSA Slides Explain the PRISM Data-Collection Program," *Washington Post,* June 6, 2013 (updated July 10, 2013), http://www.washingtonpost.com/wp-srv/special/politics/prism-collection -documents/.

# 3

# Robert S. Litt, General Counsel, Office of the Director of National Intelligence, Speech at Brookings Institution

Snowden's disclosures about the telephone metadata and Section 702 programs, and the controversies the disclosures created, prompted U.S. government officials to react. This speech from the top lawyer in the Office of the Director of National Intelligence explains NSA activities under U.S. law, especially the telephone metadata program and PRISM surveillance conducted under FISA, and it defends their legality, effectiveness, and fidelity to the democratic values of the United States. The speech is a synthesis of the government's early response to the firestorms caused by Snowden's exposure of the telephone metadata and Section 702 programs.

# I. Introduction

I wish that I was here in happier times for the Intelligence Community. The last several weeks have seen a series of reckless disclosures of classified information about intelligence activities. These disclosures threaten to cause long-lasting and irreversible harm to our ability to identify and respond to the many threats facing our Nation. And because the disclosures were made by people who did not fully understand what they were talking about, they were sensationalized and led to mistaken and misleading impressions. I hope to . . . correct some of these misimpressions today.

My speech today is prompted by disclosures about two programs that collect valuable foreign intelligence that has protected our Nation and its allies: the bulk collection of telephony metadata, and the so-called "PRISM" program. Some people claim that these disclosures were a form of "whistleblowing." But . . . [t]hese programs are not illegal. They are authorized by Congress and are carefully overseen by the Congressional intelligence and judiciary committees. They are conducted with the approval of the Foreign Intelligence Surveillance Court and under its supervision. And they are subject to extensive, court-ordered oversight by the Executive Branch. In short, all three branches of Government knew about these programs, approved them, and helped to ensure that they complied with the law. . . .

Nevertheless, I fully appreciate that it's not enough for us simply to assert that our activities are consistent with the letter of the law. Our Government's activities must always reflect and reinforce our core democratic values. . . . But security and privacy are not zero-sum. We have an obligation to give full meaning to both: to protect security while at the same time protecting privacy and other constitutional rights. But although our values are enduring, the manner in which our activities reflect those values must necessarily adapt to changing societal expectations and norms. Thus, the Intelligence Community continually evaluates and improves the safeguards we have in place to protect privacy, while at the same time ensuring that we can carry out our mission of protecting national security.

. . .

# II. Legal Framework

Let me begin by discussing . . . the legal framework that governs intelligence collection activities. And it is a bedrock concept that those activities are bound by the rule of law. . . . We begin, of course, with the Constitution. Article II makes the President the Commander in Chief and gives him extensive responsibility for the conduct of foreign affairs. The ability to collect foreign intelligence derives from that constitutional source. The First Amendment protects freedom of speech. And the Fourth Amendment prohibits unreasonable searches and seizures.

I want to make a few points about the Fourth Amendment. First, under established Supreme Court rulings a person has no legally recognized expectation of privacy in information that he or she gives to a third party.... Second, the Fourth Amendment doesn't apply to foreigners outside of the United States. Third, the Supreme Court has said that the "reasonableness" of a warrantless search depends on balancing the "intrusion on the individual's Fourth Amendment interests against" the search's "promotion of legitimate Governmental interests."

In addition to the Constitution, ... statutes govern our collection activities ... in particular, the Foreign Intelligence Surveillance Act, or FISA. FISA was passed by Congress in 1978 and significantly amended in 2001 and 2008. It regulates electronic surveillance and certain other activities carried out for foreign intelligence purposes....

A final important source of legal restrictions is Executive Order 12333.... Section 2.3 of EO 12333 provides that elements of the Intelligence Community "are authorized to collect, retain, or disseminate information concerning United States persons only in accordance with procedures ... approved by the Attorney General ... after consultation with" the Director of National Intelligence. These procedures must ... establish strict limits on collecting, retaining or disseminating information about U.S. persons, unless that information is actually of foreign intelligence value, or in certain other limited circumstances ... , such as to protect against a threat to life. These so-called "U.S. person rules" are basic to the operation of the Intelligence Community....

. . .

## III. Impact of Changing Societal Norms

Let me turn now to the impact of changing technology on privacy. Prior to the end of the nineteenth century there was little discussion about a "right to privacy." ... Indeed, in the 1890 article that first articulated the idea of a legal right to privacy, Louis Brandeis and Samuel Warren explicitly grounded that idea on changing technologies:

> Recent inventions and business methods call attention to the next step which must be taken for the protection of the person, and for securing to the individual what Judge Cooley calls the right "to be let alone." Instantaneous photographs and newspaper enterprise have invaded the sacred precincts of private and domestic life; and numerous mechanical devices threaten to make good the prediction that "what is whispered in the closet shall be proclaimed from the house-top."

Today, as a result of the way digital technology has developed, each of us shares massive amounts of information about ourselves with third parties. . . . All in all, there's little doubt that the amount of data that each of us provides to strangers every day would astonish Brandeis and Warren—let alone Jefferson and Madison.

And this leads me to what I consider to be the key question. Why is it that people are willing to expose large quantities of information to private parties but don't want the Government to have the same information? Why . . . don't we care if the telephone company keeps records of all of our phone calls . . . , but we feel very differently about . . . the same information being on NSA servers? This does not seem to me to be a difficult question: we care because of what the Government could do with the information.

Unlike a phone company, the Government has the power to audit our tax returns, to prosecute and imprison us, to grant or deny licenses to do business, and many other things. And there is an entirely understandable concern that the Government may abuse this power. . . . [T]here is no question that the Government, because of its powers, is properly viewed in a different light.

On the other hand, just as consumers . . . make extensive use of modern technology, so . . . do potentially hostile foreign governments and foreign terrorist organizations. Indeed, we know that terrorists and weapons proliferators are using global information networks to conduct research, to communicate and to plan attacks. Information that can help us identify and prevent terrorist attacks or other threats to our security is often hiding in plain sight among the vast amounts of information flowing around the globe. New technology means that the Intelligence Community must continue to find new ways to locate and analyze foreign intelligence. . . .

One approach to protecting privacy would be to limit the Intelligence Community to a targeted, focused query looking for specific information about an identified individual based on probable cause. But from the national security perspective, that would not be sufficient. . . . Rather than attempting to solve crimes that have happened already, we are trying to find out what is going to happen before it happens. We may have only fragmentary information about someone who is plotting a terrorist attack, and need to find him and stop him. We may get information that is useless to us without a store of data to match it against, such as when we get the telephone number of a terrorist and want to find out who he has been in touch with. Or we may learn about a plot that we were previously unaware of, causing us to revisit old information and find connections that we didn't notice before—and that we would never know about if we hadn't collected the information and kept it for some period of time. . . .

So . . . there are vast amounts of data that contain[] intelligence needed to protect us not only from terrorism, but from cyber attacks, weapons of mass destruction, and good old-fashioned espionage. . . . [G]iving the Intelligence Community access to this data has obvious privacy implications. We achieve both security and privacy . . . by a framework that establishes appropriate controls on what the Government can do with the information it lawfully collects, and appropriate oversight to ensure that it respects those controls. . . . In this way we can allow the Intelligence Community to acquire necessary foreign intelligence, while providing privacy protections that take account of modern technology.

## IV. FISA Collection

In showing that this approach is in fact the way our system deals with intelligence collection, I'll use FISA as an example. . . . First, . . . FISA is an important mechanism through which Congress has legislated in the area of foreign intelligence collection. Second, . . . it covers a wide range of activities, and involves all three sources of law I mentioned earlier: constitutional, statutory and executive. . . .

. . .

I want to emphasize that the United States, as a democratic nation, takes seriously th[e] requirement that collection activities have a valid foreign intelligence purpose. We do not . . . steal the trade secrets of foreign companies in order to give American companies a competitive advantage. We do not indiscriminately sweep up and store the contents of the communications of Americans, or of the citizenry of any country.

We do not use our intelligence collection for . . . repressing the citizens of any country because of their political, religious or other beliefs. We collect metadata— information about communications—more broadly than we collect the actual content of communications, because it is less intrusive . . . and in fact can provide us information that helps us more narrowly focus our collection of content on appropriate targets. But it simply is not true that the United States Government is listening to everything said by every citizen of any country.

Let me turn now to FISA. I'm going to talk about three provisions of that law: traditional FISA orders, the FISA business records provision, and Section 702. These provisions impose limits on what kind of information can be collected and how it can be collected, require procedures restricting what we can do with the information we collect and how long we can keep it, and impose oversight to ensure that the rules are followed. This sets up a coherent regime in which protections are afforded at the front end, when information is collected; in the middle, when information is reviewed and used; and at the back end, through oversight, all working together to protect both national security and privacy. . . .

So let's begin by talking about traditional FISA collection. Prior to the passage of FISA in 1978, the collection of foreign intelligence was essentially unregulated by statutory law. It was viewed as a core function of the Executive Branch. In fact, when the criminal wiretap provisions were originally enacted, Congress expressly provided that they did not "limit the constitutional power of the President . . . to obtain foreign intelligence information . . . deemed essential to the national security of the United States." However, ten years later, as a result of abuses revealed by the Church and Pike Committees, Congress imposed a judicial check on some aspects of electronic surveillance for foreign intelligence purposes. This is what is now codified in Title I of FISA, sometimes referred to as "traditional FISA."

FISA established a special court, the Foreign Intelligence Surveillance Court, to hear applications by the Government to conduct electronic surveillance for foreign intelligence purposes. Because traditional FISA surveillance involves acquiring the content of communications, it is intrusive . . . and because it can be directed at individuals inside the United States, including American citizens, it implicates the Fourth Amendment. In FISA, Congress required that to get a "traditional" FISA electronic surveillance order, the Government must establish probable cause to believe that the target of surveillance is a foreign power or an agent of a foreign power, a probable cause standard derived from the standard used for wiretaps in criminal cases. And if the target is a U.S. person, he or she cannot be deemed an agent of a foreign power based solely on activity protected by the First Amendment. . . .

Moreover, by law the use of information collected under traditional FISA must be subject to minimization procedures, a concept that is key throughout FISA. Minimization procedures are procedures, approved by the FISA Court, that must be "reasonably designed in light of the purpose and technique of the particular surveillance, to minimize the acquisition and retention, and prohibit the dissemination, of nonpublicly available information concerning unconsenting United States persons consistent with the need of the United States to obtain, produce, and disseminate foreign intelligence information." For example, they generally prohibit disseminating the identity of a U.S. person unless the identity itself is necessary to understand the foreign intelligence or is evidence of a crime. . . . These tailored minimization procedures are an important way in which we provide appropriate protections for privacy.

So let me explain . . . how traditional FISA surveillance works in practice. Let's say that the FBI suspects someone inside the United States of being a spy, or a terrorist, and they want to conduct electronic surveillance. . . . [A]s a general rule they have to present an application to the FISA Court establishing probable cause to believe that the person is an agent of a foreign power. . . . That application . . . is reviewed at several levels within both the FBI and Department of Justice before it is submitted to the Court. Now, the target may have a conversation with a U.S. person that has nothing to do with the foreign intelligence purpose of the surveillance, such as talking to a neighbor about a dinner party.

Under the minimization procedures, an analyst who listens to a conversation involving a U.S. person that has no foreign intelligence value cannot generally share it or disseminate it unless it is evidence of a crime. Even if a conversation has foreign intelligence value—let's say a terrorist is talking to a confederate—that information may only be disseminated to someone with an appropriate need to know the information pursuant to his or her mission.

. . .

Now let me turn to the second activity, the collection of business records. After FISA was passed, it became apparent that it left some significant gaps in our intelligence collection authority. In particular, while the Government had the power in a criminal investigation to compel the production of records with a grand jury subpoena, it lacked similar authority in a foreign intelligence investigation. So a provision was added in 1998 to provide such authority, and was amended by Section 215 of the USA-PATRIOT Act passed shortly after 9/11. This provision, which is generally referred to as "Section 215," allows us to apply to the FISA Court for an order requiring production of documents or other tangible things when they are relevant to an authorized national security investigation. . . . Moreover, as with traditional FISA, records obtained pursuant to the FISA business records provision are subject to court-approved minimization procedures that limit the retention and dissemination of information about U.S. persons. . . .

Now, of course, the FISA business records provision has been in the news because of one particular use of that provision [the disclosed telephone metadata program]. The FISA Court has repeatedly approved orders directing several telecommunications companies to produce certain categories of telephone metadata. . . . It's important to emphasize that under this program we do not get the content of any conversation; we do not get the identity of any party to the conversation; and we do not get any cell site or GPS [Global Positioning System] locational information.

The limited scope of what we collect has important legal consequences. As I mentioned earlier, the Supreme Court has held that if you have voluntarily provided this kind of information to third parties, you have no reasonable expectation of privacy in that information. All of the metadata we get under this program is information that the telecommunications companies obtain and keep for their own business purposes. As a result, the Government can get this information without a warrant, consistent with the Fourth Amendment.

Nonetheless, I recognize that there is a difference between getting metadata about one telephone number and getting it in bulk. . . . Section 215 only allows us to get records if they are "relevant" to a national security investigation, and from a privacy perspective people worry that . . . the government could apply data mining techniques to a bulk data set and learn new personal facts about them—even though the underlying set of records is not subject to a reasonable expectation of privacy for Fourth Amendment purposes.

On the other hand, this information is clearly useful from an intelligence perspective. . . . It's important to understand the problem this program was intended to solve. Many will recall that one of the criticisms made by the 9/11 Commission was that we were unable to find the connection between a hijacker who was in California and an al-Qaida safe house in Yemen. Although NSA had collected the conversations from the Yemen safe house, they had no way to determine that the person at the other end of the conversation was in the United States. . . . This collection program is designed to help us find those connections.

In order to do so, however, we need to be able to access the records of telephone calls, possibly going back many years. However, telephone companies have no legal obligation to keep this kind of information, and they generally destroy it after a period of time. . . . And the different telephone companies have separate datasets in different formats, which makes analysis of possible terrorist calls involving several providers considerably slower and more cumbersome. That could be a significant problem in a fast-moving investigation where speed and agility are critical, such as the plot to bomb the New York City subways in 2009.

The way we fill this intelligence gap while protecting privacy illustrates the analytical approach I outlined earlier. From a subscriber's point of view, . . . the difference between a telephone company keeping records of his phone calls and the Intelligence Community keeping the same information is what the Government could do with the records. That's an entirely legitimate concern. We deal with it by limiting what the Intelligence Community is allowed [to] do with the information we get under this program—limitations that are approved by the FISA Court:

- First, we put this information in secure databases.
- Second, the only intelligence purpose for which this information can be used is counterterrorism.
- Third, we allow only a limited number of specially trained analysts to search these databases.
- Fourth, even those trained analysts are allowed to search the database only when they have a reasonable and articulable suspicion that a particular telephone number is associated with particular foreign terrorist organizations that have been identified to the Court. The basis for that suspicion has to be documented in writing and approved by a supervisor.
- Fifth, they're allowed to use this information only in a limited way, to map a network of telephone numbers calling other telephone numbers.
- Sixth, because the database contains only metadata, even if the analyst finds a previously unknown telephone number that warrants further investigation, all she can do is disseminate the telephone number. She

doesn't even know whose number it is. Any further investigation of that number has to be done pursuant to other lawful means, and in particular, any collection of the contents of communications would have to be done using another valid legal authority, such as a traditional FISA.

- Finally, the information is destroyed after five years.

The net result is that although we collect large volumes of metadata under this program, we only look at a tiny fraction of it, and only for a carefully circumscribed purpose—to help us find links between foreign terrorists and people in the United States. The collection has to be broad to be operationally effective, but it is limited to non-content data that has a low privacy value and is not protected by the Fourth Amendment. . . . Only the narrowest, most important use of this data is permitted; other uses are prohibited. In this way, we protect both privacy and national security.

Some have questioned how collection of a large volume of telephone metadata could comply with the statutory requirement that business records obtained pursuant to Section 215 be "relevant to an authorized investigation." . . . First, remember that the "authorized investigation" is an intelligence investigation, not a criminal one. The statute requires that an authorized investigation be conducted in accordance with guidelines . . . [that] allow the FBI to conduct an investigation into a foreign terrorist entity if there is an "articulable factual basis . . . that reasonably indicates that the [entity] may have engaged in . . . international terrorism or other threat to the national security," or may be planning or supporting such conduct. . . . And in this case, the Government's applications to collect the telephony metadata have identified the particular terrorist entities that are the subject of the investigations.

Second, the standard of "relevance" required by this statute is not the standard that we think of in a civil or criminal trial under the rules of evidence. The courts have recognized in other contexts that "relevance" can be an extremely broad standard. . . .

In each of these contexts, the meaning of "relevance" is sufficiently broad to allow for . . . requests that encompass large volumes of records in order to locate within them a smaller subset of material that will be directly pertinent to or actually be used in furtherance of the investigation or proceedings. . . .

When it passed the business records provision, Congress made clear that it had in mind such broad concepts of relevance. The telephony metadata collection program meets this relevance standard because . . . the effectiveness of the queries . . . based on "reasonable and articulable suspicion" . . . depends on collecting and maintaining the data from which the narrowly focused queries can be made. . . . While the scope of the collection at issue here is broader than typically might be acquired through a grand jury subpoena or civil discovery request, the basic principle is similar: the information is relevant because you need to have the broader set of records in order to identify within them the information that is actually important to a terrorism investigation. . . .

I want to repeat that the conclusion that the bulk metadata collection is authorized under Section 215 is not that of the Intelligence Community alone. Applications to obtain this data have been repeatedly approved by numerous judges of the FISA Court, each of whom has determined that the application complies with all legal requirements. And Congress reauthorized Section 215 in 2011, after the Intelligence and Judiciary Committees of both Houses had been briefed on the program, and after information describing the program had been made available to all Members. In short, all three branches of Government have determined that this collection is lawful and reasonable—in large part because of the substantial protections we provide for the privacy of every person whose telephone number is collected.

The third program I want to talk about is Section 702. . . . Again, a little history is in order. . . . Title I of FISA, or traditional FISA, governs electronic surveillance conducted within the United States for foreign intelligence purposes. When FISA was first passed in 1978, Congress did not intend it to regulate the targeting of foreigners outside of the United States for foreign intelligence purposes.

This kind of surveillance was generally carved out of coverage under FISA by the way Congress defined "electronic surveillance." Most international communications in 1978 took place via satellite, so Congress excluded international radio communications from the definition of electronic surveillance covered by FISA, even when the radio waves were intercepted in the United States, unless the target of the collection was a U.S. person in the United States.

Over time, that technology-based differentiation fell apart. By the early twenty-first century, most international communications travelled over fiber optic cables and thus were no longer "radio communications" outside of FISA's reach. At the same time there was a dramatic increase in the use of the Internet for communications purposes, including by terrorists. As a result, Congress's original intention was frustrated; we were increasingly forced to go to the FISA Court to get individual warrants to conduct electronic surveillance of foreigners overseas for foreign intelligence purposes.

After 9/11, this burden began to degrade our ability to collect the communications of foreign terrorists. Section 702 created a new, more streamlined procedure to accomplish this surveillance. So Section 702 . . . extended the FISA Court's oversight to a kind of surveillance that Congress had originally placed outside of that oversight: the surveillance, for foreign intelligence purposes, of foreigners overseas. This American regime imposing judicial supervision of a kind of foreign intelligence collection directed at citizens of other countries is a unique limitation that . . . goes beyond what other countries require of their intelligence services when they collect against persons who are not their own citizens.

The privacy and constitutional interests implicated by this program fall between traditional FISA and metadata collection. On the one hand we are collecting the full content of communications; on the other hand we are not collecting information in bulk and we are only targeting non-U.S. persons for valid foreign intelligence purposes. And the information involved is unquestionably of great importance for national security: collection under Section 702 is one of the most valuable sources of foreign intelligence we have. Again, the statutory scheme, and the means by which we implement it, . . . allow us to collect this intelligence, while providing appropriate protections for privacy. Collection under Section 702 does not require individual judicial orders authorizing collection against each target. Instead, the FISA Court approves annual certifications submitted by the Attorney General and the Director of National Intelligence that identify categories of foreign intelligence that may be collected, subject to Court-approved "targeting" procedures and "minimization" procedures.

The targeting procedures are designed to ensure that we target someone only if we have a valid foreign intelligence purpose; that we target only non-U.S. persons reasonably believed to be outside of the United States; that we do not intercept wholly domestic communications; and that we do not target any person outside the United States as a "back door" means of targeting someone inside the United States. The procedures must be reviewed by the Court to ensure that they are consistent with the statute and the Fourth Amendment. . . .

The concept of minimization procedures should be familiar to you by now: they are the procedures that limit the retention and dissemination of information about U.S. persons. We may incidentally acquire the communications of Americans even though we are not targeting them, for example if they talk to non-U.S. persons outside of the United States who are properly targeted for foreign intelligence collection. . . . But the incidental acquisition of non-pertinent information is not unique to Section 702. It is common whenever you lawfully collect information, whether it's by a criminal wiretap (where the target's conversations with his friends or family may be intercepted) or when we seize a terrorist's computer or address book, either of which is likely to contain non-pertinent information. In passing Section 702, Congress recognized this reality and required us to establish procedures to minimize the impact of this incidental collection on privacy.

How does Section 702 work in practice? . . . Let's say that the Intelligence Community gets information that a terrorist is using a particular email address. NSA analysts look at available data to assess whether that email address would be a valid target under the statute—whether the email address belongs to someone who is not a U.S. person, whether the person with the email address is outside the United States, and whether targeting that email address is likely to lead to the collection of foreign intelligence relevant to one of the certifications. Only if all three requirements of the statute are met, and validated by supervisors, will the email address be approved for targeting. . . .

Any communications that we collect under Section 702 are placed in secure databases, again with limited access. Trained analysts are allowed to use this data for legitimate foreign intelligence purposes, but the minimization procedures require that if they review a communication that they determine involves a U.S. person or information about a U.S. person, and they further determine that it has no intelligence value and is not evidence of a crime, it must be destroyed. In any case, conversations that are not relevant are destroyed after a maximum of five years. So under Section 702, we have a regime that involves judicial approval of procedures that are designed to narrow the focus of the surveillance and limit its impact on privacy. I've outlined three different collection programs, under different provisions of FISA. . . . In each case, we protect privacy by a multi-layered system of controls on what we collect and how we use what we collect, controls that are based on the nature and intrusiveness of the collection, but that take into account the ways in which that collection can be useful to protect national security. But we don't simply set out a bunch of rules and trust people to follow them. There are substantial safeguards in place that help ensure that the rules are followed.

These safeguards operate at several levels. The first is technological. The same technological revolution that has enabled this kind of intelligence collection and made it so valuable also allows us to place relatively stringent controls on it. . . . Second, we have secure databases to hold this data, to which only trained personnel have access. Finally, modern information security techniques allow us to create an audit trail tracking who uses these databases and how. . . . And I want to emphasize that there's no indication so far that anyone has defeated those technological controls and improperly gained access to the databases containing people's communications. . . .

We don't rely solely on technology. NSA has an internal compliance officer, whose job includes developing processes that all NSA personnel must follow to ensure that NSA is complying with the law. In addition, decisions about what telephone numbers we use as a basis for searching the telephone metadata are reviewed first within NSA, and then by the Department of Justice. Decisions about targeting under Section 702 are reviewed first within NSA, and then by the Department of Justice and by my agency, the Office of the Director of National Intelligence, which has a dedicated Civil Liberties Protection Officer who actively oversees these programs. . . . Finally, independent Inspectors General also review the operation of these programs. . . .

But wait, there's more. . . . As I've said, the FISA Court has to review and approve the procedures by which we collect intelligence under FISA, to ensure that those procedures comply with the statute and the Fourth Amendment. In addition, any compliance matter, large or small, has to be reported to the Court. Improperly collected information generally must be deleted, subject only to some exceptions set out in the Court's orders, and corrective measures are taken and reported to the Court until it is satisfied.

And I want to correct the erroneous claim that the FISA Court is a rubber stamp. Some people assume that because the FISA Court approves almost every application, it does not give these applications careful scrutiny. In fact the exact opposite is true. The judges and their professional staff review every application carefully, and often ask extensive and probing questions, seek additional information, or request changes, before the application is ultimately approved. Yes, the Court approves the great majority of applications at the end of this process, but before it does so, its questions and comments ensure that the application complies with the law.

Finally, there is the Congress. By law, we are required to keep the Intelligence and Judiciary Committees informed about these programs, including detailed reports about their operation and compliance matters. . . . For example, when Congress reauthorized Section 215 in 2009 and 2011 and Section 702 in 2012, information was made available to every member of Congress, by briefings and written material, describing these programs in detail.

. . .

And make no mistake, our intelligence collection has helped to protect our Nation from a variety of threats—and not only our Nation, but the rest of the world. We have robust intelligence relationships with many other countries. These relationships go in both directions, but it is important to understand that we cannot use foreign intelligence to get around the limitations in our laws, and we assume that our other countries similarly expect their intelligence services to operate in compliance with their own laws. . . . [W]e have provided the Congress a list of 54 cases in which the bulk metadata and Section 702 authorities have given us information that helped us understand potential terrorist activity and even disrupt it, from potential bomb attacks to material support for foreign terrorist organizations. . . .

I believe that our approach to achieving both security and privacy is effective and appropriate. It has been reviewed and approved by all three branches of Government as consistent with the law and the Constitution. It is not the only way we could regulate intelligence collection, however. Even before the recent disclosures, the President [in a May 2013 speech] said that we welcomed a discussion about privacy and national security, and we are working to declassify more information about our activities to inform that discussion. In addition, the Privacy and Civil Liberties Oversight Board—an independent body charged by law with overseeing our counterterrorism activities—has announced that it intends to provide the President and Congress a public report on the Section 215 and 702 programs[.] . . .

This discussion can, and should, have taken place without the recent disclosures, which have brought into public view the details of sensitive operations that were previously discussed on a classified basis. . . . The level of detail in the current public debate certainly reflects a departure from the historic understanding that the sensitive nature of intelligence operations demanded a more limited discussion. . . . As the debate about our surveillance programs goes forward, I hope that my remarks today have helped provide an appreciation of the efforts that have been made—and will continue to be made—to ensure that our intelligence activities comply with our laws and reflect our values.

. . .

★ ★ ★

Robert S. Litt, General Counsel, Office of the Director of National Intelligence, "Privacy, Technology & National Security: An Overview of Intelligence Collection," Remarks at the Brookings Institution, July 18, 2013 (references omitted).

*Source:* Office of the Director of National Intelligence, IC on the Record, http://icontherecord .tumblr.com/post/57724442606/privacy-technology-national-security-an.

# 4

# U.S. House of Representatives, Amash-Conyers Amendment Debate

This document provides excerpts from a July 2013 debate in the House of Representatives on a proposal to end the telephone metadata program disclosed by Snowden. Formulated as an amendment to the Department of Defense Appropriations Act of 2014, the proposal from representatives Justin Amash (R-MI) and John Conyers (D-MI) represented, at the time, the highest-profile legislative effort to prevent the U.S. government from collecting bulk telephone metadata on Americans. Passage of the amendment would have been a rebuke of the White House, FBI, NSA, and FISC for interpreting and using Section 215 to run the telephone metadata program. The arguments reveal a divided House of Representatives struggling to come to terms with what Snowden had disclosed and how the country should move forward. The House did not adopt the amendment, voting it down 217–205, but the close vote demonstrated that the telephone metadata program was politically vulnerable less than two months after exposure.

AMENDMENT NO. 100 OFFERED BY MR. AMASH

. . .

The text of the amendment is as follows:

At the end of the bill . . . insert the following new section:

SEC. _____. None of the funds made available by this Act may be used to execute a Foreign Intelligence Surveillance Court order pursuant to section 501 of the Foreign Intelligence Surveillance Act of 1978 (50 U.S.C. 1861) that does not include the following sentence:

> This Order limits the collection of any tangible things (including telephone numbers dialed, telephone numbers of incoming calls, and the duration of calls) that may be authorized to be collected pursuant to this Order to those tangible things that pertain to a person who is the subject of an investigation described in section 501 of the Foreign Intelligence Surveillance Act of 1978 (50 U.S.C. 1861).

. . .

Mr. AMASH. Mr. Chairman, . . . We are here today for a very simple reason: to defend the Fourth Amendment, to defend the privacy of each and every American.

As the Director of National Intelligence has made clear, the government collects the phone records without suspicion of every single American in the United States.

My amendment makes a simple, but important change. It limits the government's collection of the records to those records that pertain to a person who is the subject of an investigation pursuant to section 215.

Opponents of this amendment will use the same tactic that every government throughout history has used to justify its violation of rights—fear. They will tell you that the government must violate the rights of the American people to protect us against those who hate our freedoms. They will tell you there is no expectation of privacy in documents that are stored with a third party. Tell that to the American people. Tell that to our constituents back home.

We are here to answer one question for the people we represent: Do we oppose the suspicionless collection of every American's phone records?

. . .

Mr. ROGERS of Michigan. . . .

Mr. Chairman, I think the American people and, certainly, some well-intentioned Members in this Chamber have legitimate concerns. They should be addressed. We should have time and education on what actually happens in the particular program of which we speak.

I will pledge to each one of you today and give you my word that this fall, when we do the Intel authorization bill, that we will work to find additional privacy protections with this program which have no email, no phone calls, no names, and no addresses.

Fourteen Federal judges [serving on the FISC] have said, yes, this comports with the Constitution; 800 cases around the 1979 case [*Smith v. Maryland,* 442 U.S. 735 (1979)] have affirmed the underpinnings of the legality of this case—800. So 14 judges are wrong, and 800 different cases are wrong. The legislators on both Intelligence committees—Republicans and Democrats—are all wrong.

Why is it that people of both parties came together and looked at this program at a time when our Nation was under siege by those individuals who wanted to bring violence to the shores of the United States?

It is that those who know it best support the program because we spend as much time on this to get it right, to make sure the oversight is right. No other program has the legislative branch, the judicial branch, and the executive branch doing the oversight of a program like this. If we had this in the other agencies, we would not have problems.

Think about who we are in this body. Have 12 years gone by and our memories faded so badly that we've forgotten what happened on September 11?

This bill turns off a very specific program. It doesn't stop so-called "spying" and other things that this has been alleged to do. That's not what's happening. It's not a surveillance bill. It's not monitoring. It doesn't do any of those things.

What happened after September 11 that we didn't know on September 10—again, passing this amendment takes us back to September 10, and afterwards we said, wow, there is a seam, a gap—was somebody leading up to the September 11 attacks who was a terrorist overseas, called a "terrorist," living amongst us in the United States, and we missed it because we didn't have this capability.

What if we'd have caught it?

The good news is we don't have to what-if. It's not theoretical. Fifty-four times this and the other program [Section 702 surveillance] stopped and thwarted terrorist attacks both here and in Europe—saving real lives. This isn't a game. This is real. . . .

Think about the people who came here before us in this great body—Madison, Lincoln, Kennedy served here—and about the issues they dealt with and about the politics of "big" and of moving America forward while upholding . . . the general defense of the United States. . . .

Are we so small that we can only look at our Facebook "likes" today in this Chamber, or are we going to stand up and find out how many lives we can save?

Let us get back to the big politics of protecting America and of moving America forward. Soundly reject this amendment. Let's do this right in the Intel authorization bill.

. . .

Mr. CONYERS. . . . Ladies and gentlemen of the House, this amendment will not stop the proper use of the PATRIOT Act or stop the FISA authorities from conducting terrorism and intelligence investigations. I'd never block that.

All this amendment is intending to do is to curtail the ongoing dragnet collection and storage of the personal records of innocent Americans. It does not defund the NSA, and it will continue to allow them to conduct full-fledged surveillance as long as it relates to an actual investigation.

Our joining together on this bipartisan amendment demonstrates our joint commitment to ensure that our fight against terrorism and espionage follows the rule of law and the clear intent of the statutes passed by this Congress. I urge my colleagues on both sides of the aisle to vote for this amendment.
. . .

Mrs. BACHMANN [of Minnesota]. . . . Madam Chair, this is a very important issue that we are taking up today because the number one duty of the Federal Government is the safety of the American people. . . . As we know all too well, national security is a real and present danger, and it is something that we have to take quite seriously. We can't deal in false narratives.

A false narrative has emerged that the Federal Government is taking the content of Americans' phone calls. It's not true. It's not happening.

We need to deal in facts. The facts are real, and the facts are these:

The only people who have benefited from the revelation of classified information by someone who worked for this government—who intentionally and without authorization declassified some of the most sensitive national security information that we have—are those who are engaged in Islamic jihad. . . .

Consider this:

There is more information about each one of us contained in the phone book that sits at home on your kitchen counter than information that is in the National Security Database that we're talking about today. Your name, your address are in the phone book. Your name, your address are not in this National Security Database.

No other nation in the world has the advantage that the United States of America has on national security—no other nation—and we by this amendment today would agree to handcuff ourselves and our allies by restricting ourselves? Let it not be. Let us not deal in false narratives. Let us deal in facts that will keep the American people safe.

When you look at an envelope, when a letter is put in the mail, is there a privacy right as to what has been written on that envelope? No, there isn't. There is a privacy right as to what is contained inside that envelope. That's a Fourth Amendment right.

Is there a Fourth Amendment right to the record that you called someone on a certain day? No, there isn't—that's a record—but there is a Fourth

Amendment right to what's in that phone call. Let's deal in reality, not in false narratives.

. . .

Mr. SENSENBRENNER [of Wisconsin]. Madam Chair, I rise in strong support of the Amash amendment. I do so as the person who was the principal author of the PATRIOT Act in 2001, who got that law through quickly after 9/11 and who supported and managed its 2006 reauthorization.

Let me make this perfectly clear that . . . this amendment does not stop the collection of data under section 215—the people who are subject to an investigation of an authorized terrorist plot. What it does do is to prevent the collection of data of people who are not subject to an investigation. . . . The time has come to stop it, and the way we stop it is to approve this amendment.

. . .

Mr. POLIS [of Colorado]. . . . Madam Chair, reports of the NSA surveillance program have broad and far-reaching consequences.

Many Americans feel that our fundamental liberties as a country and our constitutional rights are threatened. In addition, it has ruined and hurt our reputation abroad—threatening our trade relationships with allies, threatening American jobs as a result, and putting in danger our cooperative security relationships that we need to fight the war on terror.

The responsible thing to do is to show some contrition. Let's pass this amendment. Let's make sure that we can have a practical approach that shows that protecting our liberties and securities are consistent and critical for the United States of America. . . .

. . .

Mr. MULVANEY [of South Carolina]. Madam Chair, here is the question:

It's a question of balancing privacy versus security. It's a question beyond that. It's a question of who will do the balancing.

Right now, the balancing is being done by people we do not know, by people we do not elect and, in large part right now, by somebody [James Clapper, Director of National Intelligence] who has admitted lying to this body at a hearing. That's wrong.

We should be doing the balancing. We were elected to do that. We need to pass this amendment so that we can do the balancing, not the folks who are not elected and whom we do not know.

. . .

Ms. LOFGREN [of California]. I want to talk about the much ballyhooed oversight.

Every year, there is a report to the Judiciary Committee, an annual report, on section 215. This year, the report was eight sentences—less than a full page. To think that the Congress has substantial oversight of this program is simply incorrect. . . . I do agree that when we wrote the PATRIOT Act relevance had a meaning.

. . .

Mr. BARTON [of Texas]. . . . Madam Chair, this is not about how sincere the NSA people are in implementing this technique. It is not about how careful they are. It is whether they have a right to collect the data in the first place on every phone call on every American every day.

The PATRIOT Act did not specifically authorize it. Section 215 talks about tangible things that are relevant to an authorized security investigation. In the NSA's interpretation of that, "relevant" is all data all the time. That is simply wrong. We should support the Amash amendment and vote for it.

. . .

Mr. POE of Texas. Warrants need to be particular and specific about the place to be searched and the items to be seized.

No judge would ever sign a general search warrant like the British did, allowing the police to search every house on the block, much less seize everybody's phone records, but this is what has happened under section 215. . . .

The government has gone too far in the name of security and the Fourth Amendment has been bruised.

Rein in government invasion. No more dragnet operations. Get a specific warrant based on probable cause, or stay out of our lives.

. . .

Mr. NADLER [of New York]. Madam Chairperson, this amendment stops the government from misusing section 215, to engage in the dragnet collection of all of our personal telephone records. Congress did not grant the executive the authority to collect everything it wants so long as it limits any subsequent search of that data.

This amendment restores the requirement that records sought are relevant to an authorized foreign intelligence or terrorist investigation. It restores the minimal relevant standard required by Congress but ignored by successive administrations.

No administration should be permitted to operate above or beyond the law as they have done in this respect. I therefore urge all of my colleagues to vote in favor of the Amash-Conyers amendment.

. . .

Mr. GRIFFITH of Virginia. General warrants, writs of assistance, that's what we're looking at, and the Founding Fathers found that to be anathema. What they're doing does violate the Fourth Amendment. We took an oath to uphold the Constitution, and we're supposed to rely on a secret agency that deals with a secret court that deals with a selective secrecy committee; and

Members of Congress are limited to their access to the actions of that committee, but we're supposed to trust them.

. . .

Ms. GABBARD [of Hawaii]. Madam Chairwoman, countless men and women from my State of Hawaii and all across the country have worn the uniform and put their lives on the line to protect our freedoms and our liberties. I cannot in good conscience vote to take a single dollar from the pockets of hardworking taxpayers from across the country to pay for programs which infringe on the very liberties and freedoms our troops have fought and died for.

Ben Franklin said:

> They who give up essential liberty to obtain a little temporary safety deserve neither liberty nor safety.

. . .

Mr. COTTON [of Arkansas]. Madam Chairwoman, I rise to strongly urge opposition to the Amash amendment.

This program has stopped dozens of terrorist attacks. That means it's saved untold American lives.

This amendment is not simple. It does not limit the program. It does not modify it. It does not constrain the program. It ends the program. It blows it up. . . . You will not have this program if this amendment passes. . . .

This program is constitutional under Supreme Court precedent. . . . This program is approved by large bipartisan majorities of this body on the statute—text that they approved, not their secret intents or wishes.

It is overseen by article III judges who have been confirmed by the Senate and are independent of the executive branch. It is reviewed by the Intelligence Committees, and it is executed primarily by military officers, not generals, but the majors and the colonels who have been fighting and bleeding for this country for 12 years.

What is it, metadata? It sounds kind of scary. It's nothing more than an Excel spreadsheet with five columns: called to, called from, date, time, and the duration. Five columns, billions of rows. It's in a lockbox. It can't be searched unless you have specific suspicion of a number being used by a terrorist. Only then do they go into that database and do they run a search for what that number has been calling.

Why do you need it? Verizon, AT&T, [and] other companies will not keep this data for the years necessary. Secondly, you need it quickly. When I was in Iraq as a platoon leader with the 101st Airborne, if we rolled up a bad guy and we found a cell phone or we found a thumb drive, we would immediately upload that data so intelligence professionals could search it so they could go roll up another bad guy, because you only have a few hours to stop a terrorist once you catch another terrorist.

Folks, we are at war. You may not like that truth. I wish it weren't the truth. But it is the truth. We're at war. Do not take this tool away from our warriors on the frontline.

. . .

U.S. House of Representatives, Debate on the Amash-Conyers Amendment to Change the Telephone Metadata Program, July 24, 2013.

*Source: Congressional Record,* July 24, 2013, H5023–H5027.

*Hero or Villain?*
*Persecuting a Defender*
*of Human Rights v. Prosecuting a*
*Criminal Suspect*

# 5

# Edward Snowden,
# Statement at the Moscow Airport

When the first stories about NSA activities appeared from June 5 to 8, 2013, the world did not know who provided the documents and information to journalists. Snowden, who had been working as a private contractor for the NSA in Hawaii, revealed himself as the source on June 9, 2013, from Hong Kong, where he had flown to avoid U.S. law enforcement. Once he was identified, arguments about whether Snowden was a hero or traitor began, focusing attention on his background and motivations for leaking classified documents and for leaving the United States. Snowden began explaining his actions in interviews in Hong Kong with the *Guardian* and the *South China Morning Post*. William Scheuerman (chapter 5) and others have identified Snowden's statement at the Moscow airport in July 2013 as important for understanding what he did and why he did it. When he made this statement, Snowden was not sure where he would get asylum from the persecution he feared from the U.S. government for his defense of the Constitution and international law. Snowden eventually accepted temporary asylum in Russia in August 2013 and a three-year residency in Russia when this asylum ended.

Hello. My name is Ed Snowden. A little over one month ago, I had family, a home in paradise, and I lived in great comfort. I also had the capability without any warrant to search for, seize, and read your communications. Anyone's communications at any time. That is the power to change people's fates.

It is also a serious violation of the law. The 4th and 5th Amendments to the Constitution of my country, Article 12 of the Universal Declaration of Human Rights, and numerous statutes and treaties forbid such systems of massive, pervasive surveillance. While the US Constitution marks these programs as illegal, my government argues that secret court rulings, which the world is not permitted to see, somehow legitimize an illegal affair. These rulings simply corrupt the most basic notion of justice—that it must be seen to be done. The immoral cannot be made moral through the use of secret law.

I believe in the principle declared at [the] Nuremberg [war crimes tribunal] in 1945: "Individuals have international duties which transcend the national obligations of obedience. Therefore individual citizens have the duty to violate domestic laws to prevent crimes against peace and humanity from occurring."

Accordingly, I did what I believed right and began a campaign to correct this wrongdoing. I did not seek to enrich myself. I did not seek to sell US secrets. I did not partner with any foreign government to guarantee my safety. Instead, I took what I knew to the public, so what affects all of us can be discussed by all of us in the light of day, and I asked the world for justice.

That moral decision to tell the public about spying that affects all of us has been costly, but it was the right thing to do and I have no regrets.

Since that time, the government and intelligence services of the United States of America have attempted to make an example of me, a warning to all others who might speak out as I have. I have been made stateless and hounded for my act of political expression. The United States Government has placed me on no-fly lists. It demanded Hong Kong return me outside of the framework of its laws, in direct violation of the principle of non-refoulement—the Law of Nations. It has threatened with sanctions countries who would stand up for my human rights and the UN asylum system. It has even taken the unprecedented step of ordering military allies to ground a Latin American president's plane in search for a political refugee. These dangerous escalations represent a threat not just to the dignity of Latin America, but to the basic rights shared by every person, every nation, to live free from persecution, and to seek and enjoy asylum.

Yet even in the face of this historically disproportionate aggression, countries around the world have offered support and asylum. These nations, including Russia, Venezuela, Bolivia, Nicaragua, and Ecuador have my gratitude and respect for being the first to stand against human rights violations carried out by the powerful rather than the powerless. By refusing to compromise their principles in the face of intimidation, they have earned the respect of the world. It is my intention to travel to each of these countries to extend my personal thanks to their people and leaders.

I announce today my formal acceptance of all offers of support or asylum I have been extended and all others that may be offered in the future. With, for example, the grant of asylum provided by Venezuela's President Maduro, my asylee status is now formal, and no state has a basis by which to limit or interfere with my right to enjoy that asylum. As we have seen, however, some governments in Western European and North American states have demonstrated a willingness to act outside the law, and this behavior persists today. This unlawful threat makes it impossible for me to travel to Latin America and enjoy the asylum granted there in accordance with our shared rights.

This willingness by powerful states to act extra-legally represents a threat to all of us, and must not be allowed to succeed. Accordingly, I ask for your assistance in requesting guarantees of safe passage from the relevant nations in securing my travel to Latin America, as well as requesting asylum in Russia until such time as these states accede to law and my legal travel is permitted. I will be submitting my request to Russia today, and hope it will be accepted favorably.

. . .

Edward Snowden, Statement to Human Rights Groups at Moscow's Sheremetyevo Airport, July 12, 2013.

*Source:* Wikileaks, https://wikileaks.org/Statement-by-Edward-Snowden-to.html.

# 6

# Attorney General Eric Holder,
# Letter to the Russian Minister of Justice

On July 23, 2013, Attorney General Eric Holder sent a letter to his Russian counterpart explaining the U.S. government's position regarding Snowden; rejecting Snowden's claim of stateless, refugee, or asylee status; and offering assurances about how the U.S. government would treat Snowden in a criminal trial. The United States and Russia have no extradition treaty, so Russia had no international legal obligation to process U.S. requests for Snowden to be returned to the United States. Holder's letter emphasizes the criminal nature of Snowden's actions, including violations of the Espionage Act, as well as the constitutional rights and legal protections he would receive in the U.S. criminal justice system. Much to the chagrin of U.S. officials, Russia refused to return Snowden and instead offered him temporary asylum—actions which contributed to worsening relations between the two countries.

**Office of the Attorney General**
**Washington, D. C. 20530**

July 23, 2013

His Excellency Alexander Vladimirovich Konovalov
Minister of Justice
The Russian Federation
14 Zhitnaya Ulitsa
Moscow 119991
Russia

Dear Mr. Minister:

I am writing concerning the current status of Edward Snowden. As you know, Mr. Snowden has been charged with theft of government property (in violation of Title 18, United States Code, Section 641), unauthorized communication of national defense information (in violation of Title 18, United States Code, Section 793(d)), and willful communication of classified communications intelligence information to an unauthorized person (in violation of Title 18, United States Code, Section 798(a)(3)). According to news reports and information provided by your government, Mr. Snowden is currently in the transit zone of the Sheremetyevo Airport.

We understand from press reports and prior conversations between our governments that Mr. Snowden believes that he is unable to travel out of Russia and must therefore take steps to legalize his status. That is not accurate; he is able to travel. Despite the revocation of his passport on June 22, 2013, Mr. Snowden remains a U.S. citizen. He is eligible for a limited validity passport good for direct return to the United States. The United States is willing to immediately issue such a passport to Mr. Snowden.

We also understand from press reports that Mr. Snowden has filed papers seeking temporary asylum in Russia on the grounds that if he were returned to the United States, he would be tortured and would face the death penalty. These claims are entirely without merit. Nonetheless, I can report that the United States is prepared to provide to the Russian government the following assurances regarding the treatment Mr. Snowden would face upon return to the United States:

First, the United States would not seek the death penalty for Mr. Snowden should he return to the United States. The charges he faces do not carry that possibility, and the United States would not seek the death penalty even if Mr. Snowden were charged with additional, death penalty-eligible crimes.

Second, Mr. Snowden will not be tortured. Torture is unlawful in the United States. If he returns to the United States, Mr. Snowden would promptly be brought before a civilian court convened under Article III of the United States Constitution and supervised by a United States District Judge. Mr. Snowden would receive all the protections that United States law provides to persons charged with federal criminal offenses in Article III courts. In particular, Mr. Snowden would be appointed (or, if he so chose, could retain) counsel. Any questioning of Mr. Snowden could be conducted only with his consent: his participation would be entirely voluntary, and his legal counsel would be present should he wish it. Mr. Snowden would have the right to a public jury trial; he would have the right to testify if he wished to do so; and the United States would have to prove his guilt beyond a reasonable doubt to a unanimous jury. If convicted, Mr. Snowden would have the right to appeal to the United States Court of Appeals.

We believe that these assurances eliminate these asserted grounds for Mr. Snowden's claim that he should be treated as a refugee or granted asylum, temporary or otherwise. Please ensure that this letter reaches the head minister for the Federal Migration Service, as well as any other Russian Federation agency responsible for receiving and considering Mr. Snowden's application for asylum.

Sincerely,

Eric H. Holder, Jr.
Attorney General

★ ★ ★

Attorney General Eric H. Holder Jr., Letter to Alexander Konovalov, Minister of Justice, Russian Federation, July 23, 2013.

*Source:* Politico, http://images.politico.com/global/2013/07/26/attorney_genral_letter_to_russian_justice_minister.pdf.

*Rubber Stamp or Robust Tribunal?*
*The Foreign Intelligence Surveillance Court*

# 7

# FISC Order on the
# Telephone Metadata Program, 2009

Controversies stirred up by the leaks of the telephone metadata and Section 702 programs included debates about the Foreign Intelligence Surveillance Court, a court unknown to most people and opaque even to those who study U.S. national security law. Congress established the FISC and the Foreign Intelligence Surveillance Court of Review in 1978 when it enacted FISA, but this secret court did not draw much attention until after 9/11. The FISCR heard its first appeal of a FISC decision in 2002 and published redacted, unclassified versions of decisions in 2002 and 2008. In the wake of Snowden's disclosures about the telephone metadata and Section 702 programs, critics called the FISC a "rubber stamp"—a charge amplified by citing the FISC's approval of almost every FISA application it reviewed. As seen in Robert Litt's speech (Document 3), supporters argued that the FISC is a serious court that provides robust oversight. The U.S. government released the next document in September 2013 to counter the "rubber stamp" accusation. In this 2009 decision, the FISC suspends the NSA's access to telephone metadata because the U.S. government violated FISC orders and made misrepresentations to the FISC. The U.S. government also declassified a 2011 decision (not included here) in which the FISC criticized the NSA for misrepresenting aspects of "upstream" surveillance conducted under Section 702 and held that NSA's targeting and minimization procedures for such surveillance did not comply with the Fourth Amendment. The seriousness of the FISC's analyses and decisions in these cases did not fit the "rubber stamp" critique. Critics, however, emphasized the NSA's violations and misrepresentations as evidence that the FISC process needed major reform.

★ ★ ★

TOP SECRET//COMINT//NOFORN//MR

UNITED STATES

FOREIGN INTELLIGENCE SURVEILLANCE COURT

WASHINGTON, D.C.

IN RE PRODUCTION OF TANGIBLE THINGS
FROM [REDACTED]                                    Docket Number: BR 08–13

**ORDER**
On December 12, 2008, the Foreign Intelligence Surveillance Court ("FISC" or "Court") re-authorized the government to acquire the tangible things sought by the government. . . . Specifically, the Court ordered [RE-DACTED] to produce, on an ongoing daily basis for the duration of the order, an electronic copy of all call detail records or "telephony metadata" created by those companies. . . . The Court found reasonable grounds to believe that the tangible things sought are relevant to authorized investigations being conducted by the Federal Bureau of Investigation ("FBI") to protect against international terrorism. . . . In making this finding, the Court relied on the assertion of the National Security Agency ("NSA") that having access to the call detail records "is vital to NSA's counterterrorism intelligence mission" because "[t]he only effective means by which NSA analysts are able continuously to keep track of [REDACTED], and all affiliates of one of the aforementioned entities [who are taking steps to disguise and obscure their communications and identities], is to obtain and maintain an archive of metadata that will permit these tactics to be uncovered." . . . NSA also averred that

[t]o be able to exploit metadata fully, the data must be collected in bulk. . . .
The ability to accumulate a metadata archive and set it aside for carefully controlled searches and analysis will substantially increase NSA's ability to detect
and identify members of [REDACTED].

. . .

Because the collection would result in NSA collecting call detail records
pertaining to . . . communications of United States ("U.S.") persons located
within the U.S. who are not the subject of any FBI investigation and whose
metadata could not otherwise be legally captured in bulk, the government proposed stringent minimization procedures that strictly controlled the acquisition, accessing, dissemination, and retention of these records by the NSA and
the FBI. . . . The Court . . . directed the government to strictly adhere to these
procedures. . . . [and] ordered that:

> access to the archived data shall occur only when NSA has identified a known
> telephone identifier for which, based on the factual and practical consider-
> ations of everyday life on which reasonable and prudent persons act, there are
> facts giving rise to a reasonable, articulable suspicion that the telephone iden-
> tifier is associated with [REDACTED]; provided, however, that a telephone
> identifier believed to be used by a U.S. person shall not be regarded as associ-
> ated with [REDACTED] solely on the basis of activities that are protected by
> the First Amendment to the Constitution. . . . (emphasis added)

In response to a Preliminary Notice of Compliance Incident dated January
15, 2009, this Court ordered further briefing on the non-compliance incident
to help the Court assess whether its Orders should be modified or rescinded;
whether other remedial steps should be directed; and whether the Court should
take action regarding persons responsible for any misrepresentations to the
Court or violations of its Orders. . . .

A. NSA's Unauthorized Use of the Alert List

The government reported . . . that, prior to the Court's initial authorization
[of the telephone metadata program] on May 24, 2006 . . . , the NSA had developed an "alert list process" to assist the NSA in prioritizing its review of the telephony metadata it received. . . . Following the Court's initial authorization, the
NSA revised this alert list process so that it compared the telephone identifiers
on the alert list against incoming FISC-authorized Business Record metadata
("BR metadata") and SIGINT collection from other sources, and notified NSA's
counterterrorism organization if there was a match between an identifier on the
alert list and an identifier in the incoming data. . . . The revised NSA process
limited any further analysis of . . . the BR metadata to those telephone identifiers

determined to have met the "reasonable articulable suspicion" standard (hereafter "RAS-approved identifiers"). . . . However, because the alert list included all identifiers (foreign and domestic) that were of interest to counterterrorism analysts who were . . . tracking [REDACTED], most of the telephone identifiers compared against the incoming BR metadata were not RAS-approved. . . . Thus, since the earliest days of the FISC-authorized collection of call-detail records . . . , the NSA has on a daily basis, accessed the BR metadata for purposes of comparing thousands of non-RAS approved telephone identifiers on its alert list against the BR metadata in order to identify any matches. Such access was prohibited by the governing minimization procedures under each of the relevant Court orders, as the government concedes. . . .

The government's submission suggests that its non-compliance . . . resulted from a belief by some personnel within the NSA that some of the Court's restrictions on access to the BR metadata applied only to "archived data." . . . That interpretation . . . strains credulity. It is difficult to imagine why the Court would intend the applicability of the RAS requirement—a critical component of the procedures proposed by the government and adopted by the Court—to turn on whether or not the data being accessed has been "archived." . . . Indeed, to the extent that the NSA makes the decision about where to store incoming BR metadata and when the archiving occurs, such an illogical interpretation . . . renders compliance with the RAS requirement merely optional.

The NSA also suggests that the NSA OGC's [Office of General Counsel] approval of procedures allowing the use of non-RAS-approved identifiers on the alert list to query BR metadata not yet in the NSA's "archive" was not surprising, since the procedures were similar to those used in connection with other NSA SIGINT collection activities. . . . If this is the case, . . . the non-compliance is not a terminological misunderstanding, but the NSA's decision to treat the accessing of all call detail records . . . no differently than other collections under separate NSA authorities, to which the Court-approved minimization procedures do not apply.

B. Misrepresentations to the Court

The government has compounded its non-compliance . . . by repeatedly submitting inaccurate descriptions of the alert list process to the FISC. Due to the volume of U.S. person data being collected . . . , the FISC's orders have all required that any renewal application include a report on the implementation of the Court's prior orders, including a description of the manner in which the NSA applied the minimization procedures. . . .

In its report to the FISC accompanying its first renewal application . . . on August 18, 2006, the government described the alert list process as follows:

NSA has compiled . . . an "alert list" of telephone numbers used by members of [REDACTED]. This alert list serves as a body of telephone numbers employed to query the data. . . .

[ . . . ] Each of the foreign telephone numbers that comes to the attention of the NSA as possibly related to [REDACTED] is evaluated to determine whether the information about it provided to NSA satisfies the reasonable articulable suspicion standard. If so, the foreign telephone number is placed on the alert list; if not, it is not placed on the alert list.

The process . . . applies also to newly discovered domestic telephone numbers considered for addition to the alert list, with the additional requirement that NSA's Office of General Counsel reviews these numbers and affirms that the telephone number is not the focus of the analysis based solely on activities that are protected by the First Amendment. . . .

. . .

As of the last day of the reporting period . . . , NSA had included a total of 3980 telephone numbers on the alert list, . . . after concluding that each of the foreign telephone numbers satisfied the [RAS standard], and each of the domestic telephone numbers was either a FISC approved number or in direct contact with a foreign seed that met those criteria. . . .

To summarize the alert system: every day new contacts are automatically revealed with the 3980 telephone numbers contained on the alert list described above, which themselves are present on the alert list either because they satisfied the reasonable articulable suspicion standard, or because they are domestic numbers that were either a FISC approved number or in direct contact with a number that did so. These automated queries identify any new telephone contacts between the numbers on the alert list and any other number, except that domestic numbers do not alert on domestic-to-domestic contacts. . . . (emphasis added).

This description was included in . . . all subsequent reports to the Court. . . .

The NSA attributes these material misrepresentations to the failure of those familiar with the program to correct inaccuracies in a draft of the report prepared in August 2006 by . . . the NSA's Office of General Counsel. . . . Further, the NSA reports:

it appears there was never a complete understanding among the key personnel who reviewed the report for the SIGINT Directorate and the Office of General Counsel regarding what each individual meant by the terminology used in the report. Once this initial misunderstanding occurred, the alert list description was never corrected since neither the SIGINT Directorate nor the Office of General Counsel realized there was a misunderstanding. As a result, NSA never revisited the description of the alert list that was included in the original report to the Court.

. . . Finally, the NSA reports that "from a technical standpoint, there was no single person who had a complete technical understanding of the BR FISA system architecture. This probably also contributed to the inaccurate description of the alert list that NSA included in its BR FISA reports to the Court." . . .

Regardless of what factors contributed to making these misrepresentations, the Court finds that the government's failure to ensure that responsible officials adequately understood the NSA's alert list process, and to accurately report its implementation to the Court, has prevented, for more than two years, both the government and the FISC from taking steps to remedy daily violations of the minimization procedures . . . designed to protect [REDACTED] call detail records pertaining to telephone communications of U.S. persons located within the United States who are not the subject of any FBI investigation and whose call detail information could not otherwise have been legally captured in bulk.

C. Other Non-Compliance Matters

Unfortunately, the universe of compliance matters . . . extends beyond the events described above. On October 17, 2008, the government reported to the FISC that, after the FISC authorized the NSA to increase the number of analysts authorized to access the BR metadata to 85, the NSA trained those newly authorized analysts on Court-order procedures. . . . Despite this training, however, the NSA subsequently determined that 31 NSA analysts had queried the BR metadata during a five day period in April 2008 "without being aware they were doing so." . . . (emphasis added) As a result, the NSA analysts used 2,373 foreign telephone identifiers to query the BR metadata without first determining that the reasonable articulable suspicion standard had been satisfied. . . .

Upon discovering this problem, the NSA undertook a number of remedial measures, including suspending the 31 analysts' access pending additional training, and modifying the NSA's tool for accessing the data so that analysts were required specifically to enable access to the BR metadata and acknowledge such access. . . . Despite taking these corrective steps, on December 11, 2008, the government informed the FISC that one analyst had failed to install the modified access tool and, as a result, inadvertently queried the data using five identifiers for which NSA had not determined that the reasonable articulable suspicion standard was satisfied. . . . Then, on January 26, 2009, the government informed the Court that, from approximately December 10, 2008, to January 23, 2009, two NSA analysts had used 280 foreign telephone identifiers to query the BR metadata without determining that the Court's reasonable articulable suspicion standard had been satisfied. . . . It appears that these queries were conducted despite full implementation of the above-referenced software modifications to the BR metadata access tool, as well as the NSA's additional training of its analysts. . . . And, . . . the NSA continues to uncover examples of systematic noncompliance.

In summary, . . . the FISC's authorizations of this vast collection program have been premised on a flawed depiction of how the NSA uses BR metadata. This misperception by the FISC existed from the inception of its authorized collection in May 2006, buttressed by repeated inaccurate statements made in the government's submissions, and despite a government-devised and Court-mandated oversight regime. The minimization procedures proposed by the government . . . and approved and adopted as binding by the orders of the FISC have been so frequently and systematically violated that it can fairly be said that this critical element of the overall BR regime has never functioned effectively.

D. Reassessment of BR Metadata Authorization

In light of the foregoing, the Court returns to fundamental principles underlying its authorizations. In order to compel the production of tangible things to the government, the Court must find that there are reasonable grounds to believe that the tangible things sought are relevant to an authorized investigation . . . to obtain foreign intelligence information not concerning a U.S. person or to protect against international terrorism or clandestine intelligence activities, provided that such investigation of a U.S. person is not conducted solely on the basis of activities protected by the First Amendment. . . .

The government's applications have all acknowledged that, of the [RE-DACTED] call detail records NSA receives per day . . . nearly all . . . pertain to communications of non-U.S. persons who are not the subject of an FBI investigation to obtain foreign intelligence information, are communications of U.S. persons who are not the subject of an FBI investigation to protect against international terrorism or clandestine intelligence activities, and are data that otherwise could not be legally captured in bulk by the government. Ordinarily, this alone would provide sufficient grounds for a FISC judge to deny the application.

Nevertheless, the FISC has authorized bulk collection of call detail records in this case based upon: (1) the government's explanation, under oath, of how the collection of and access to such data are necessary to analytical methods that are vital to the national security of the United States; and (2) minimization procedures that carefully restrict access to the BR metadata and include specific oversight requirements. Given the Executive Branch's responsibility for and expertise in determining how best to protect our national security, and in light of the scale of this bulk program, the Court must rely heavily on the government to monitor this program to ensure that it continues to be justified, in view of those responsible for our national security, and that it is being implemented in a manner that protects the privacy interests of U.S. persons as required by applicable minimization procedures. To approve such a program, the Court must have every confidence that the government is doing its utmost to ensure that those responsible for implementation fully comply with the Court's orders. The Court no longer has such confidence.

With regard to the value of the BR metadata program, the government points to the 275 reports that the NSA has provided to the FBI identifying 2,549 telephone identifiers associated with the targets. . . . The government's submission also cites three examples in which the FBI opened three new preliminary investigations of persons in the U.S. based on tips from the BR metadata program. . . . However, the mere commencement of a preliminary investigation, by itself, does not seem particularly significant. . . . [T]his program has been ongoing for nearly three years. The time has come for the government to describe to the Court how . . . the value of the program to the nation's security justifies the continued collection and retention of massive quantities of U.S. person information.

Turning to the government's implementation of the Court-ordered minimization procedures and oversight regime, the Court takes note of the remedial measures being undertaken by the government. . . . In particular, the Court welcomes the Director of the NSA's decision to order "end-to-end system engineering and process reviews (technical and operational) of NSA's handling" of BR metadata. . . . However, the Court is very disturbed to learn that this ongoing exercise has identified additional violations of the Court's orders, including the routine accessing of BR metadata from May 2006 to February 18, 2009 . . . using telephone identifiers that had not been determined to meet the reasonable articulable suspicion standard. . . .

In its last submission, the government describes technical measures implemented . . . to prevent any recurrences of the . . . non-compliance uncovered to date. . . . On the strength of these measures, the government submits that "the Court need not take any further remedial action." . . . After considering these measures in the context of the historical record of non-compliance and in view of the Court's authority and responsibility to "determine [and] enforce compliance" with Court orders and Court-approved procedures, . . . the Court has concluded that further action is, in fact, necessary.

The record before the Court strongly suggests that, from the inception of this FISA BR program, the NSA's data accessing technologies and practices were never adequately designed to comply with the governing minimization procedures. From inception, the NSA employed two separate automated processes— the daily alert list and the [REDACTED] tool—that routinely involved queries based on telephone identifiers that were not RAS-approved. . . . As for manual queries, the minimization procedures required analysts to use RAS-approved identifiers whenever they accessed the BR metadata, yet thousands of violations resulted from the use of identifiers that had not been RAS-approved by analysts who were not even aware that they were accessing BR metadata. . . .

Moreover, . . . the NSA . . . [is] still in the process of determining how the NSA's own systems and personnel interact with the BR metadata. Under these circumstances, no one inside or outside of the NSA can represent with adequate certainty whether the NSA is complying with these procedures. In fact, the government acknowledges that, as of August 2006, "there was no single person who had a complete understanding of the BR FISA system architecture." . . . This situation evidently had not been remedied as of February 18, 2009, when "NSA personnel determined," only as a result of the "end-to-end review of NSA's technical infrastructure" . . . that the [REDACTED] tool accessed the BR metadata on the basis of telephone identifiers that had not been RAS-approved. . . .

This end-to-end review has not been completed. . . . Nonetheless, the government submits that the technical safeguards implemented . . . "should prevent recurrences" of the identified forms of non-compliance, . . . and "expect[s] that any further problems NSA personnel may identify with the infrastructure will be historical," rather than current . . . (emphasis added). However, until this end-to-end review has been completed, the Court sees little reason to believe that the most recent discovery of a systemic, ongoing violation . . . will be the last. Nor does the Court share the government's optimism that technical safeguards implemented to respond to one set of problems will fortuitously be effective against additional problems identified in the future.

Moreover, . . . there is reason to question whether the newly implemented safeguards will be effective. For example, . . . the NSA reported on October 17, 2008, that it had deployed software modifications that would require analysts to specifically enable access to BR metadata when performing manual queries, but these modifications did not prevent hundreds of additional violations by analysts who inadvertently accessed BR metadata through queries using telephone numbers that had not been RAS-approved. . . .

. . .

In light of what appear to be systemic problems, this Court cannot accept the mere introduction of technological remedies as a demonstration that a problem is solved. More is required . . . to protect the privacy of U.S. person information acquired and retained pursuant to the FISC orders. . . . However, given the government's repeated representations that the collection of BR metadata is vital to national security, . . . the Court concludes it would not be prudent to order that the government's acquisition of the BR metadata cease at this time. However, except as authorized below, the Court will not permit the government to access the data collected until . . . the government is able to restore the Court's confidence that the government can and will comply with previously approved procedures for accessing such data.

Accordingly, it is HEREBY ORDERED:

1. The NSA may continue to acquire all call detail records of "telephony metadata" created by [REDACTED] in accordance with the orders entered in the above-captioned docket . . . ;

2. The government is hereby prohibited from accessing BR metadata acquired pursuant to FISC orders . . . except as described herein. The data may be accessed for the purpose of ensuring data integrity and compliance with the Court's orders. Except as provided in paragraph 3, access to the BR metadata shall be limited to the team of NSA data integrity analysts . . . and individuals directly involved in developing and testing any technological measures designed to enable the NSA to comply with previously approved procedures for accessing such data;

3. The government may request . . . that the Court authorize querying of the BR metadata for purposes of obtaining foreign intelligence on a case-by-case basis. However, if the government determines that immediate access is necessary to protect against an imminent threat to human life, the government may access the BR metadata for such purpose. . . .;

4. Upon completion of the government's end-to-end system engineering and process reviews, the government shall file a report with the Court, that shall, at a minimum, include:

a. an affidavit by the Director of the FBI . . . describing the value of the BR metadata to the national security of the United States and certifying that the tangible things sought are relevant to an authorized investigation (other than a threat assessment) to obtain foreign intelligence information not concerning a U.S. person or to protect against international terrorism or clandestine intelligence activities, and that such investigation of a U.S. person is not conducted solely on the basis of activities protected by the First Amendment;

b. a description of the results of the NSA's end-to-end system engineering and process reviews, including any additional instances of non-compliance identified therefrom;

c. a full discussion of the steps taken to remedy any additional non-compliance as well as the incidents described herein, and an affidavit attesting that any technological remedies have been tested and demonstrated to be successful; and

d. the minimization and oversight procedures the government proposes to employ should the Court decide to authorize the government's resumption of regular access to the BR metadata.

IT IS SO ORDERED, this 2nd day of March, 2009.

REGGIE B. WALTON

Judge, United States Foreign Intelligence Surveillance Court

Foreign Intelligence Surveillance Court, In Re Production of Tangible Things from [REDACTED], March 2, 2009 (citations in text and footnotes omitted) [declassified by the U.S. government on September 10, 2013, with updated declassified version released on March 28, 2014].

*Source:* Office of the Director of National Intelligence, IC on the Record, http://www.dni.gov/files /documents/0328/039.%20A4000915%20%20BR%2008-13%20%20Order%20%283-2-09%29%20 Redacted%2020140327.pdf.

*Made in the USA?*
*NSA Surveillance and U.S. Technology Companies*

# 8

# NSA MUSCULAR Program Briefing Slide

The *Washington Post* disclosed this NSA slide obtained from Snowden in October 2013. It formed part of a briefing on "Google Cloud Exploitation," through which the NSA accessed communications flowing between Google data centers located outside the United States. The *Post* story stated that the NSA did the same thing with Yahoo's foreign communication links. This activity formed part of the MUSCULAR program. In PRISM, Google and Yahoo received FISC-approved orders to provide information to the NSA. The exposure of MUSCULAR angered Google, Yahoo, and other U.S. technology companies, worsening their deteriorating relationship with the NSA and damaging their global reputation for providing secure services.

In the MUSCULAR program, neither company was aware that the NSA was accessing its foreign-based communications facilities, which raised questions about the NSA's authority to conduct this activity. The most likely source was the president's constitutional authority to conduct foreign intelligence, as regulated by Executive Order 12333, initially adopted in 1981, and considered a less restrictive set of rules than FISA. A former State Department official published an op-ed in July 2014 arguing that U.S. government collection and retention of communications by U.S. persons under Executive Order 12333 violated the Fourth Amendment. In August 2014, the Privacy and Civil Liberties Oversight Board decided to examine Executive Order 12333 for its implications for privacy and civil liberties, and the ACLU released documents in October 2014 on the executive order it obtained under the Freedom of Information Act as part of its effort to increase scrutiny of the order.

★ ★ ★

TOP SECRET//SI//NOFORN

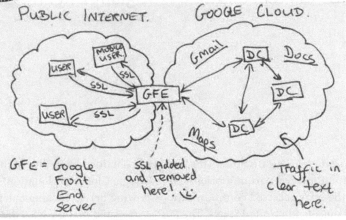

TOP SECRET//SI//NOFORN

★ ★ ★

NSA Briefing Slide on Collecting Information from Google's Foreign-Based Servers and Communications Links under the MUSCULAR Program (date unknown) [disclosed October 30, 2013].

*Source:* Barton Gellman and Ashkan Soltani, "NSA Infiltrates Links to Yahoo, Google Data Centers Worldwide, Snowden Documents Say," *Washington Post,* October 30, 2013, http://www .washingtonpost.com/world/national-security/nsa-infiltrates-links-to-yahoo-google-data-centers -worldwide-snowden-documents-say/2013/10/30/e51d661e-4166-11e3-8b74-d89d714ca4dd_story .html.

# 9

# Marissa Mayer, Yahoo CEO, Statement on Protecting Customer Information

The October 2013 revelations that the NSA had accessed traffic flowing in Google's and Yahoo's foreign networks without the companies' knowledge generated corporate backlash in Silicon Valley and beyond. U.S. technology companies already faced problems in global markets because of Snowden's disclosures of the targeting of foreign communications through NSA surveillance and U.S. spying on foreign governments, leaders, and companies. Leading U.S. technology companies responded to their growing credibility crisis by, among other things, implementing stronger encryption of data within, and of traffic flowing through, their networks. The encryption moves announced by Yahoo CEO Marissa Mayer in November 2013 had counterparts at other U.S. technology companies, including Google and Microsoft. In 2014, high-level law enforcement officials and intelligence authorities in the United States and the United Kingdom raised concerns that private-sector efforts to expand encryption of digital communications benefited criminals and terrorists and thus threatened national security.

# YAHOO!

## Our Commitment to Protecting Your Information

We've worked hard over the years to earn our users' trust and we fight hard to preserve it.

As you know, there have been a number of reports over the last six months about the U.S. government secretly accessing user data without the knowledge of tech companies, including Yahoo. I want to reiterate what we have said in the past: Yahoo has never given access to our data centers to the NSA or to any other government agency. Ever.

There is nothing more important to us than protecting our users' privacy. To that end, we recently announced that we will make Yahoo Mail even more secure by introducing https (SSL - Secure Sockets Layer) encryption with a 2048-bit key across our network by January 8, 2014.

Today we are announcing that we will extend that effort across *all* Yahoo products. More specifically this means we will:

- **Encrypt all information that moves between our data centers by the end of Q1 2014;**
- **Offer users an option to encrypt all data flow to/from Yahoo by the end of Q1 2014;**
- **Work closely with our international Mail partners to ensure that Yahoo co branded Mail accounts are https-enabled.**

As we have said before, we will continue to evaluate how we can protect our users' privacy and their data. We appreciate, and certainly do not take for granted, the trust our users place in us.

Marissa Mayer, Chief Executive Officer of Yahoo, Our Commitment to Protecting Your Information, November 18, 2013.

*Source:* Yahoo!, http://yahoo.tumblr.com/post/67373852814/our-commitment-to-protecting-your -information. Reproduced with permission of Yahoo. ©2014 Yahoo. Yahoo! and the Yahoo! logo are registered trademarks of Yahoo.

# 10

# Reform Government Surveillance, Surveillance Reform Principles and Open Letter from U.S. Technology Companies

By the end of 2013, the problems Snowden's disclosures about NSA surveillance were causing U.S. technology companies resulted in a group of prominent enterprises joining forces in an effort called Reform Government Surveillance. This document contains two products of this collaboration. First, the companies promulgated principles to guide the reform and operation of government surveillance activities worldwide. These principles included heading off data "localization" requirements that foreign government were considering in reaction to Snowden's disclosures about the scale and intensity of NSA surveillance. Second, the companies sent a joint communication to U.S. political leaders highlighting the urgent need for reforms to government surveillance laws and practices at home and abroad. Reform Government Surveillance subsequently engaged with proposals to reform U.S. surveillance laws, such as the USA FREEDOM Act passed by the House of Representatives in May 2014 (see Document 37 for a summary of this proposed legislation).

Reform Government Surveillance

Our CEOs sent a letter to the Senate, read it here.

# Global Government Surveillance Reform

The undersigned companies believe that it is time for the world's governments to address the practices and laws regulating government surveillance of individuals and access to their information.

While the undersigned companies understand that governments need to take action to protect their citizens' safety and security, we strongly believe that current laws and practices need to be reformed.

Consistent with established global norms of free expression and privacy and with the goals of ensuring that government law enforcement and intelligence efforts are rule-bound, narrowly tailored, transparent, and subject to oversight, we hereby call on governments to endorse the following principles and enact reforms that would put these principles into action.

★  ★  ★

## Global Government Surveillance Reform, The Principles

### *1 Limiting Governments' Authority to Collect Users' Information*

Governments should codify sensible limitations on their ability to compel service providers to disclose user data that balance their need for the data in limited circumstances, users' reasonable privacy interests, and the impact on trust in the Internet. In addition, governments should limit surveillance to specific, known users for lawful purposes, and should not undertake bulk data collection of Internet communications.

### *2 Oversight and Accountability*

Intelligence agencies seeking to collect or compel the production of information should do so under a clear legal framework in which executive powers are subject to strong checks and balances. Reviewing courts should be independent and include an adversarial process, and governments should allow important rulings of law to be made public in a timely manner so that the courts are accountable to an informed citizenry.

### 3 Transparency About Government Demands

Transparency is essential to a debate over governments' surveillance powers and the scope of programs that are administered under those powers. Governments should allow companies to publish the number and nature of government demands for user information. In addition, governments should also promptly disclose this data publicly.

### 4 Respecting the Free Flow of Information

The ability of data to flow or be accessed across borders is essential to a robust 21st century global economy. Governments should permit the transfer of data and should not inhibit access by companies or individuals to lawfully available information that is stored outside of the country. Governments should not require service providers to locate infrastructure within a country's borders or operate locally.

### 5 Avoiding Conflicts Among Governments

In order to avoid conflicting laws, there should be a robust, principled, and transparent framework to govern lawful requests for data across jurisdictions, such as improved mutual legal assistance treaty—or "MLAT"—processes [an international legal mechanism for law enforcement cooperation]. Where the laws of one jurisdiction conflict with the laws of another, it is incumbent upon governments to work together to resolve the conflict.

An Open Letter to Washington

Dear Mr. President and Members of Congress,

We understand that governments have a duty to protect their citizens. But this summer's revelations highlighted the urgent need to reform government surveillance practices worldwide. The balance in many countries has tipped too far in favor of the state and away from the rights of the individual—rights that are enshrined in our Constitution. This undermines the freedoms we all cherish. It's time for a change.

For our part, we are focused on keeping users' data secure—deploying the latest encryption technology to prevent unauthorized surveillance on our networks and by pushing back on government requests to ensure that they are legal and reasonable in scope.

We urge the US to take the lead and make reforms that ensure that government surveillance efforts are clearly restricted by law, proportionate to the risks, transparent and subject to independent oversight. To see the full set of principles we support, visit ReformGovernmentSurveillance.com

Sincerely,

AOL, Apple, Dropbox, Facebook, Google, LinkedIn, Microsoft, Twitter, Yahoo

AOL, Apple, Dropbox, Facebook, Google, LinkedIn, Microsoft, Twitter, and Yahoo, Reform Government Surveillance: Global Government Surveillance Reform—The Principles and an Open Letter to Washington, December 9, 2013.

*Source:* Reform Government Surveillance, https://www.reformgovernmentsurveillance.com/.

*Friend and Foe?*
*U.S. Espionage against Other Countries*

# 11

# NSA Briefing Slides on Brazilian President Dilma Rousseff and Petrobas Oil Company

The documents released by Snowden included many disclosures about U.S. intelligence activities directed against other countries. These NSA briefing slides, for example, provide evidence of U.S. government surveillance and espionage directed at Brazil's political leadership and national oil company, Petrobas. Snowden also leaked information about U.S. intelligence efforts targeting Afghanistan, Argentina, the Bahamas, Chile, China, Colombia, Costa Rica, El Salvador, France, Germany, Honduras, India, Iran, Italy, Japan, Kenya, Mexico, Nicaragua, North Korea, Pakistan, Panama, Paraguay, Peru, the Philippines, Russia, South Korea, Spain, Turkey, the Vatican, and Venezuela. Snowden-provided documents also indicated that the U.S. government spied on international institutions and their meetings, including the European Union, International Atomic Energy Agency, Organization of Petroleum Exporting Countries, Summit of the Americas, UN, UN Climate Change Conference, and the World Bank. These disclosures increased the displeasure of foreign governments, which were already upset about U.S. surveillance of foreign communications. Fellow democracies, such as Brazil, responded with particular pique to being targets of U.S. spying. These slides on Brazil also highlight (see bottom of each slide) the special relationship of the so-called "Five Eyes"—Australia, Canada, New Zealand, the United Kingdom, and the United States—among whom these slides (and other documents Snowden disclosed) circulated. These disclosures did not connect to Snowden's allegations that the NSA was violating the U.S. Constitution; instead they brought international law more directly into the debate about U.S. surveillance and espionage.

★ ★ ★

TOP SECRET//COMINT//REL TO USA, GBR, AUS, CAN, NZL

# (U//FOUO) S2C42 surge effort
# (U) Goal

(TS//SI//REL) An increased understanding of the communication methods and associated selectors of Brazilian President Dilma Rousseff and her key advisers.

TOP SECRET//COMINT//REL TO USA, GBR, AUS, CAN, NZL

NSA Briefing Slides on Brazil's President and Advisors, July 2012 [disclosed September 1, 2013] and Petrobas, Brazil's National Oil Company [disclosed September 8, 2013].

*Source:* Globo.com, http://g1.globo.com/fantastico/noticia/2013/09/veja-os-documentos -ultrassecretos-que-comprovam-espionagem-dilma.html and http://g1.globo.com/fantastico /noticia/2013/09/nsa-documents-show-united-states-spied-brazilian-oil-giant.html.

# 12

# James R. Clapper, Director of National Intelligence, Statement on Allegations of Economic Espionage

In response to the furor caused by the Brazilian media's dissemination of Snowden-provided information about U.S. spying against Petrobas, the Brazilian state-owned oil company, James Clapper, the director of national intelligence, issued this statement. The Petrobas disclosure prompted accusations that the U.S. government engaged in economic espionage, a practice it had long denied doing. Clapper responds to these accusations by acknowledging that the U.S. government collects economic and financial intelligence for national security purposes but restating the U.S. position that it does not steal the secrets of foreign companies for the benefit of American enterprises. As Cate and Fidler argue in this volume, Snowden's disclosures about U.S. economic and financial intelligence gathering undermined U.S. government efforts to distinguish its own actions from economic and commercial spying conducted by other countries, especially China. The U.S. government's position was not helped when Snowden later disclosed a secret report from 2009 in which the U.S. intelligence community identified a potential need to engage in "technology acquisition by all means," including cyber operations against foreign researchers and companies, in order to maintain the U.S. edge in innovation and technology.

It is not a secret that the Intelligence Community collects information about economic and financial matters, and terrorist financing.

We collect this information for many important reasons: for one, it could provide the United States and our allies early warning of international financial crises which could negatively impact the global economy. It also could provide insight into other countries' economic policy or behavior which could affect global markets.

Our collection of information regarding terrorist financing saves lives. Since 9/11, the Intelligence Community has found success in disrupting terror networks by following their money as it moves around the globe. International criminal organizations, proliferators of weapons of mass destruction, illicit arms dealers, or nations that attempt to avoid international sanctions can also be targeted in an effort to aid America's and our allies' interests.

What we do not do, as we have said many times, is use our foreign intelligence capabilities to steal the trade secrets of foreign companies on behalf of—or give intelligence we collect to—US companies to enhance their international competitiveness or increase their bottom line.

As we have said previously, the United States collects foreign intelligence— just as many other governments do—to enhance the security of our citizens and protect our interests and those of our allies around the world. The Intelligence Community's efforts to understand economic systems and policies and monitor anomalous economic activities is critical to providing policy makers with the information they need to make informed decisions that are in the best interest of our national security.

James R. Clapper, Director of National Intelligence, Statement on Allegations of Economic Espionage, September 8, 2013.

*Source:* Office of the Director of National Intelligence, http://www.dni.gov/index.php/newsroom /press-releases/191-press-releases-2013/926-statement-by-director-of-national-intelligence-james-r -clapper-on-allegations-of-economic-espionage.

# 13

# Dilma Rousseff, President of Brazil, Statement to United Nations General Assembly

The Snowden leaks that revealed U.S. surveillance against Brazilian government officials and companies provoked anger and diplomatic action from Brazil's president, Dilma Rousseff. She canceled an official visit to the United States in September 2013 and, in the same month, blasted the U.S. government in a speech at the UN. Brazil and Germany led efforts at the UN in November and December 2013 to adopt a resolution on the human right to privacy in the digital age (see Document 35 for the text of this resolution). The Snowden disclosures catalyzed the adoption of new legislation in Brazil in April 2014 strengthening privacy protections for Brazilians and ensuring equal access to the Internet. In April 2014, Brazil hosted NETmundial, a Global Multistakeholder Meeting on the Future of Internet Governance, which adopted a statement of Internet governance principles and a road map for the evolution of Internet governance.

. . .

I would like to bring to the consideration of delegations a matter of great importance and gravity.

Recent revelations concerning the activities of a global network of electronic espionage have caused indignation and repudiation in public opinion around the world.

In Brazil, the situation was even more serious, as it emerged that we were targeted by this intrusion. Personal data of citizens was intercepted indiscriminately. Corporate information—often of high economic and even strategic value—was at the center of espionage activity. Also, Brazilian diplomatic missions, among them the Permanent Mission to the United Nations and the Office of the President of the Republic itself, had their communications intercepted.

Tampering in such a manner in the affairs of other countries is a breach of International Law and is an affront to the principles that must guide the relations among them, especially among friendly nations. A sovereign nation can never establish itself to the detriment of another sovereign nation. The right to safety of citizens of one country can never be guaranteed by violating fundamental human rights of citizens of another country.

The arguments that the illegal interception of information and data aims at protecting nations against terrorism cannot be sustained.

Brazil, Mr. President, knows how to protect itself. We reject, fight and do not harbor terrorist groups.

We are a democratic country surrounded by nations that are democratic, pacific and respectful of International Law. We have lived in peace with our neighbors for more than 140 years.

As many other Latin Americans [have], I fought against authoritarianism and censorship, and I cannot but defend, in an uncompromising fashion, the right to privacy of individuals and the sovereignty of my country. In the absence of the right to privacy, there can be no true freedom of expression and opinion, and therefore no effective democracy. In the absence of the respect for sovereignty, there is no basis for the relationship among Nations.

We face, Mr. President, a situation of grave violation of human rights and of civil liberties; of invasion and capture of confidential information concerning corporate activities, and especially of disrespect to national sovereignty.

We expressed to the Government of the United States our disapproval, and demanded explanations, apologies and guarantees that such procedures will never be repeated.

Friendly governments and societies that seek to build a true strategic partnership, as in our case, cannot allow recurring illegal actions to take place as if they were normal. They are unacceptable.

Brazil, Mr. President, will redouble its efforts to adopt legislation, technologies and mechanisms to protect us from the illegal interception of communications and data.

My Government will do everything within its reach to defend the human rights of all Brazilians and to protect the fruits borne from the ingenuity of our workers and our companies.

The problem, however, goes beyond a bilateral relationship. It affects the international community itself and demands a response from it. Information and telecommunication technologies cannot be the new battlefield between States. Time is ripe to create the conditions to prevent cyberspace from being used as a weapon of war, through espionage, sabotage, and attacks against systems and infrastructure of other countries.

The United Nations must play a leading role in the effort to regulate the conduct of States with regard to these technologies.

For this reason, Brazil will present proposals for the establishment of a civilian multilateral framework for the governance and use of the Internet and to ensure the effective protection of data that travels through the web.

We need to create multilateral mechanisms for the worldwide network that are capable of ensuring principles such as:

1—Freedom of expression, privacy of the individual and respect for human rights.
2—Open, multilateral and democratic governance, carried out with transparency by stimulating collective creativity and the participation of society, Governments and the private sector.
3—Universality that ensures the social and human development and the construction of inclusive and non-discriminatory societies.
4—Cultural diversity, without the imposition of beliefs, customs and values.
5—Neutrality of the network, guided only by technical and ethical criteria, rendering it inadmissible to restrict it for political, commercial, religious or any other purposes.

Harnessing the full potential of the Internet requires, therefore, responsible regulation, which ensures at the same time freedom of expression, security and respect for human rights.

. . .

★ ★ ★

*Source:* Statement by H. E. Dilma Rousseff, President of the Federative Republic of Brazil, at the Opening of the General Debate of the 68th Session of the United Nations General Assembly, September 24, 2013, http://gadebate.un.org/sites/default/files/gastatements/68/BR_en.pdf.

# 14

# NSA Document on Cell Phone Surveillance of German Chancellor Angela Merkel

A document published by *Der Spiegel* in late October 2013 from information provided by Snowden was taken as evidence that the NSA had been monitoring German chancellor Angela Merkel's cell phone, probably since 2002. It appears to be a targeting record for Merkel, perhaps from an NSA database. An earlier, unrelated Snowden disclosure identified SYNAPSE as an NSA effort to analyze communications of foreign intelligence targets. German officials were already disturbed by previous Snowden disclosures that indicated that the NSA had engaged in mass surveillance of Germans' communications. These disclosures prompted Germany to support efforts to strengthen the right to privacy in international law, terminate a Cold War–era intelligence agreement with the United States, and engage in talks with the U.S. government to establish a new intelligence relationship. The revelation about Merkel's cell phone damaged U.S.-German relations significantly, and U.S.-German relations on intelligence continued to deteriorate. The German government did not renew a contract with Verizon, a U.S. company, because of concerns about security, and expelled the CIA station chief in Germany over allegations (not related to Snowden) that the CIA was attempting to get information through an employee of Germany's domestic intelligence service. The rancor over

Merkel's cell phone overshadowed other Snowden disclosures reported in the German press that indicated the NSA had close relations with German intelligence agencies, which raised questions in Germany about the activities of its own spies. Adding to the controversy, a German prosecutor investigating the alleged tapping of Merkel's cell phone stated in December 2014 that he had not found clear evidence the NSA engaged in such activity or even that the document in question came from the NSA.

★ ★ ★

SelectorType PUBLIC DIRECTORY NUM
SynapseSelectorTypeID    SYN_0044
SelectorValue
Realm 3
RealmName rawPhoneNumber
Subscriber GE CHANCELLOR MERKEL
Ropi S2C32
NSRL 2002-388*
Status    A
Topi F666E
Zip 166E
Country Name
CountryCode GE

★ ★ ★

NSA Document on Cell Phone Surveillance of German Chancellor Angela Merkel (date unknown) [disclosed October 27, 2013].

*Source:* Wikimedia Commons, http://commons.wikimedia.org/wiki/File:Chancellor_Merkel_rawPhoneNumber.jpg.

# 15

# Wanted by the FBI

In May 2014, the Department of Justice announced to great media attention that it had indicted five members of the Chinese military for violating U.S. criminal law on economic espionage, theft of trade secrets, and computer crimes by hacking computer networks of U.S. companies. The FBI issued wanted posters with the indictment. Commentators noted that the likelihood the U.S. government would prosecute these men was nil, raising questions about why the Obama administration would, in such a high-profile way and in the midst of ongoing Snowden-related turmoil, apply U.S. criminal law against Chinese military personnel. As Fred Cate observes in chapter 2, this indictment invited accusations of U.S. hypocrisy given the scale and intensity of U.S. surveillance and espionage against other countries. The U.S. government appeared to have two objectives in issuing the indictment. The indictment revived a major emphasis in U.S. foreign policy before Snowden came along, the contention that China was engaging in massive economic cyber espionage against companies in the United States and other Western countries. It also reminded other nations that despite the Snowden-generated controversies about U.S. behavior, China remained a clear and present cyber security threat. In this sense, the indictment represented an attempt by the U.S. government to go back on the offensive in international cyber politics while dealing with global fallout from its own spying.

★ ★ ★

**WANTED**
BY THE FBI

Conspiring to Commit Computer Fraud; Accessing a Computer Without Authorization for the Purpose of Commercial Advantage and Private Financial Gain; Damaging Computers Through the Transmission of Code and Commands; Aggravated Identity Theft; Economic Espionage; Theft of Trade Secrets

| Huang Zhenyu | Wen Xinyu | Sun Kailiang | Gu Chunhui | Wang Dong |

★ ★ ★

*Source:* Federal Bureau of Investigation, Wanted Poster, May 19, 2014, http://www.fbi.gov/news /news_blog/five-chinese-military-hackers-charged-with-cyber espionage-against-u.s.

# 16

# Chinese National Ministry of Defense, Statement on U.S. Indictment of Chinese Military Officers

China responded to the U.S. indictment of Chinese military officers in May 2014 with a statement condemning the action while also criticizing the United States in light of "the Snowden affair." While he was in Hong Kong in June 2013, Snowden had disclosed information about U.S. surveillance and espionage against Chinese government, corporate, university, and individual targets to the *South China Morning Post*. Later disclosures identified China as a target of U.S. intelligence efforts, which was reported in August 2013 stories identifying China as a primary target for U.S. intelligence activities and offensive cyber operations and in March 2014 stories in the U.S. and German press about NSA activities against Chinese government targets and the Chinese telecommunications company Huawei. The indictment gave the Chinese government the opportunity to use the Snowden disclosures to remind the world about the extent of U.S. surveillance and espionage against it. Such a reminder served deeper Chinese strategic interests in weakening U.S. ideas, interests, influence, and credibility in cyberspace and cyber security matters in international politics.

On May 19 Beijing time, the United States Department of Justice indicted five members of the Chinese military on charges of so-called commercial cybertheft. China expresses its strong indignation and staunch opposition to this, and already had made solemn representations to the United States.

China's stance on Internet security issues has been consistent and clear. China is a protector of Internet security, and the Chinese government and military have never engaged or participated in any theft of commercial secrets over the Internet. The United States' claims of so-called commercial cybertheft and so on have been spun out of thin air to bamboozle public opinion, and they have been made out of nefarious motives.

For a long time, the relevant agencies of the United States have relied on its advanced technology and infrastructure to carry out large-scale, organized cybertheft, bugging and monitoring against foreign politicians, businesses and individuals. These facts are known to all. The hypocrisy and double standards of the United States regarding Internet security issues have been abundantly obvious from WikiLeaks to the Snowden affair. The Chinese military is a serious victim of this kind of U.S. conduct. Statistics show that the Internet user terminals of the Chinese military have come under many attacks from abroad in recent years, and IP addresses show that a considerable number of these originated in the United States. China demands that the United States give it a clear explanation of its cybertheft, bugging and monitoring activities, and immediately stop such activity.

Chinese-U.S. military relations have been enjoying healthy development, and this step by the United States flics in the face of its vow to "strive to build healthy, stable and reliable military-to-military relations," and it has seriously damaged bilateral mutual confidence. The U.S. side should demonstrate true sincerity and take substantive actions to promote the healthy and stable development of Chinese-U.S. state-to-state and military-to-military relations.

Chinese National Ministry of Defense, Statement on U.S. Indictment of Chinese Military Officers, May 20, 2014.

*Source:* http://news.mod.gov.cn/headlines/2014-05/20/content_4510313.htm, English translation published in *New York Times,* May 20, 2014, http://sinosphere.blogs.nytimes.com/2014/05/20 /chinese-defense-statement-on-the-u-s-cyberspying-indictment/.

*A Secure and Reliable Cyberspace?*
*The NSA, Encryption, and Exploits*

# 17

# NSA's Project BULLRUN on
# Defeating Encryption

Another category of disclosures made by Snowden includes NSA activities concerning encryption of cyber communications and the use of software exploits against foreign intelligence targets. These activities raised concerns that the NSA was strengthening its signals intelligence mission at the expense of broader cyber security, a point made by Cate and Fidler elsewhere in this volume. This document is an excerpt from a classified description of Project BULLRUN, a secret effort through which the NSA worked to defeat encryption of cyber communications of foreign intelligence targets. Exposure of BULLRUN and related NSA decryption activities brought accusations that the NSA was engaged in a secret war against encryption, a key way to provide security for communications transiting the Internet.

## TOP SECRET//SI//REL TO USA, FVEY

**CLASSIFICATION GUIDE TITLE/NUMBER:** (U///FOUO) PROJECT BULLRUN/2-16

**PUBLICATION DATE:** 16 June 2010

**OFFICE OF ORIGIN:** (U) Cryptanalysis and Exploitation Services

**POC:** (U) Cryptanalysis and Exploitation Services (CES) Classification Advisory Officer

**PHONE:** ███████

**ORIGINAL CLASSIFICATION AUTHORITY:** ███████

1. (TS//SI//REL) Project BULLRUN deals with NSA's abilities to defeat the encryption used in specific network communication technologies. BULLRUN involves multiple sources, all of which are extremely sensitive. They include CNE, interdiction, industry relationships, collaboration with other IC entities, and advanced mathematical techniques. Several ECIs apply to the specific sources, methods, and techniques involved. Because of the multiple sources involved in BULLRUN activities, "capabilities against a technology" does not necessarily equate to decryption.

NSA, Classification Guide for Project BULLRUN on Defeating Encryption, June 16, 2010 [disclosed September 5, 2013].

*Source:* Electronic Frontier Foundation, https://www.eff.org/document/2013-09-05-guard-bullrun.

# 18

# NSA's SIGINT Strategy, 2012–2016

This document provides an excerpt from the leak of the NSA's top secret strategy for signals intelligence adopted in 2012 and intended to guide the agency through 2016. The *New York Times* described it as "essentially a National Security Agency mission statement with broad goals, including a desire to push for changes in the law to provide the agency with expanded surveillance powers." The strategy contains objectives underscoring the NSA's strategic interest in countering encryption challenges to its signals intelligence missions. It also contained language that NSA critics seized upon as evidence of the menace the agency presented to cyber security, such as the goals to "dramatically increase mastery of the global network" and to have the ability to collect signals intelligence "from anyone, anytime, anywhere." This latter phrase recalled Snowden's Moscow airport statement in July 2013 (see Document 5) in which he controversially asserted that, at the NSA, he had the power to read "[a]nyone's communications at any time."

TOP SECRET//SI//REL TO USA, AUS, CAN, GBR, NZL

. . .

SIGINT Goals for 2012–2016

1. (U//FOUO) Revolutionize analysis—fundamentally shift our analytic approach from a production to a discovery bias, enriched by innovative customer/partner engagement, radically increasing operational impact across all mission domains.

    1.1. (U//FOUO) Through advanced tradecraft and automation, dramatically increase mastery of the global network

    1.2. (U//FOUO) Conduct original analysis in a collaborative information space that mirrors how people interact in the information age

    1.3. (U//FOUO) Disseminate data at its first point of relevance, share bulk data, and enable customers to address niche requirements

    1.4. (U//FOUO) Drive an agile technology base mapped to the cognitive processes that underpin large scale analysis, discovery, compliance and collaboration

2. (U//FOUO) Fully leverage internal and external NSA partnerships to collaboratively discover targets, find their vulnerabilities, and overcome their network/communication defenses.

    2.1. (U//FOUO) Bolster our arsenal of capabilities against the most critical cryptanalytic challenges

        2.1.1. (S//SI//REL) Employ multidisciplinary approaches to cryptanalytic problems, leveraging and integrating mid-point and end-point capabilities to enable cryptanalysis

        2.1.2. (S//REL) Counter the challenge of ubiquitous, strong, commercial network encryption

        2.1.3. (TS//SI//REL) Counter indigenous cryptographic programs by targeting their industrial bases with all available SIGINT and HUMINT capabilities

        2.1.4. (TS//SI//REL) Influence the global commercial encryption market through commercial relationships, HUMINT, and second and third party partners

        2.1.5. (S//SI//REL) Continue to invest in the industrial base and drive the state of the art for High Performance Computing to maintain preeminent cryptanalytic capability for the nation

    2.2. (TS//SI//REL) Defeat adversary cybersecurity practices in order to acquire the SIGINT data we need from anyone, anytime, anywhere

    2.3. (S//SI) Enable discovery capabilities and advanced tradecraft in the collection architecture to enable the discovery of mission-critical persona, networks, accesses, signals and technologies

2.4. (S//SI) Integrate capabilities into the mission architecture, deepen workforce skill base in advanced network and signals analysis, and optimize processes and policies for the benefit of discovery

3. (S//SI//REL) Dynamically integrate endpoint, midpoint, industrial-enabled, and cryptanalytic capabilities to reach previously inaccessible targets in support of exploitation, cyber defense, and cyber operations

3.1. (C//REL) Drive the SIGINT mission architecture to underpin synchronized, integrated, multi-capability operations, extending it to mission partners

3.2. (TS//SI//REL) Integrate the SIGINT system into a national network of sensors which interactively sense, respond, and alert one another at machine speed

3.3. (U//FOUO) Continuously rebalance our portfolio of accesses and access capabilities based on current and projected contributions to key SIGINT missions

3.4. (S//SI//REL) Identify new access, collection, and exploitation methods by leveraging global business trends in data and communications services

. . .

NSA, SIGINT Strategy, 2012–2016 (February 23, 2012), 4 [disclosed November 22, 2013].

*Source:* "A Strategy for Surveillance Powers," *New York Times,* November 23, 2013, http://www.nytimes.com/interactive/2013/11/23/us/politics/23nsa-sigint-strategy-document.html.

# 19

## Office of the Director of National Intelligence and James R. Clapper, Director of National Intelligence, Statements on NSA Cryptological Capabilities

The disclosures about NSA efforts on encryption provoked the Office of the Director of National Intelligence and the director of national intelligence to issue statements in September and October 2013 about the NSA's interest in, and responsibilities to counteract, encryption used by U.S. adversaries. Shortly after exposure of the encryption projects, the *Guardian* ran stories based on Snowden-leaked documents exposing NSA efforts to compromise online anonymity provided by the TOR network. TOR, which stands for "The Onion Router," is a software program that helps web users anonymize cyber activities to strengthen the security and privacy of Internet searches and communications. The TOR stories prompted the director of national intelligence to explain why the NSA must address the problems that online anonymity, encryption, and other techniques pose for gathering needed foreign intelligence.

## Office of the Director of National Intelligence, Statement on the Unauthorized Disclosure of NSA Cryptological Capabilities, September 6, 2013

It should hardly be surprising that our intelligence agencies seek ways to counteract our adversaries' use of encryption. Throughout history, nations have used encryption to protect their secrets, and today, terrorists, cybercriminals, human traffickers and others also use code to hide their activities. Our intelligence community would not be doing its job if we did not try to counter that.

While the specifics of how our intelligence agencies carry out this cryptanalytic mission have been kept secret, the fact that NSA's mission includes deciphering enciphered communications is not a secret, and is not news. Indeed, NSA's public website states that its mission includes leading "the U.S. Government in cryptology . . . in order to gain a decision advantage for the Nation and our allies."

The stories published yesterday, however, reveal specific and classified details about how we conduct this critical intelligence activity. Anything that yesterday's disclosures add to the ongoing public debate is outweighed by the road map they give to our adversaries about the specific techniques we are using to try to intercept their communications in our attempts to keep America and our allies safe and to provide our leaders with the information they need to make difficult and critical national security decisions.

## James R. Clapper, Director of National Intelligence, Why the Intelligence Community Seeks to Understand Online Communication Tools & Technologies, October 4, 2013

Recently published news articles discuss the Intelligence Community's interest in tools used to facilitate anonymous online communication. The articles accurately point out that the Intelligence Community seeks to understand how these tools work and the kind of information being concealed.

However, the articles fail to make clear that the Intelligence Community's interest in online anonymity services and other online communication and networking tools is based on the undeniable fact that these are the tools our adversaries use to communicate and coordinate attacks against the United States and our allies.

The articles fail to mention that the Intelligence Community is only interested in communication related to valid foreign intelligence and counterintelligence purposes and that we operate within a strict legal framework that prohibits accessing information related to the innocent online activities of US citizens.

Within our lawful mission to collect foreign intelligence to protect the United States, we use every intelligence tool available to understand the intent of our foreign adversaries so that we can disrupt their plans and prevent them from bringing harm to innocent Americans.

In the modern telecommunications era, our adversaries have the ability to hide their messages and discussions among those of innocent people around the world. They use the very same social networking sites, encryption tools and other security features that protect our daily online activities.

Americans depend on the Intelligence Community to know who and what the threats are, and where they come from. They want us to provide policy makers with the information necessary to keep our nation safe, and they rightfully want us to do this without compromising respect for the civil liberties and privacy of our citizens.

Many of the recent articles based on leaked classified documents have painted an inaccurate and misleading picture of the Intelligence Community. The reality is that the men and women at the National Security Agency and across the Intelligence Community are abiding by the law, respecting the rights of citizens and doing everything they can to help keep our nation safe.

Office of the Director of National Intelligence, Statement on the Unauthorized Disclosure of NSA Cryptological Capabilities, September 6, 2013, and James R. Clapper, Director of National Intelligence, Why the Intelligence Community Seeks to Understand Online Communication Tools & Technologies, October 4, 2013.

*Source:* Office of the Director of National Intelligence, IC on the Record, http://icontherecord .tumblr.com/post/60428572417/odni-statement-on-the-unauthorized-disclosure-of and http:// icontherecord.tumblr.com/post/63103784923/dni-statement-why-the-intelligence-community.

# 20

# NSA Briefing Slides on the QUANTUM Project

Snowden provided journalists with information about various NSA technological and intelligence capabilities. This category of disclosures included documents on programs through which the NSA implanted software exploits onto target computers and networks, as shown by these briefing slides on implant capabilities in a project code named QUANTUM. The overarching effort is apparently called QUANTUMTHEORY, within which are techniques for using implants for computer network exploitation, defense, or attack. One of these techniques, QUANTUMINSERT, involves detecting a target's Internet activities, redirecting a target's Internet communications to NSA servers, injecting malware onto the target computer from the NSA servers, and monitoring or exploiting the target's computer through the implant. QUANTUMINSERT uses other NSA capabilities, including TURMOIL and TURBINE, as identified in the slides. TURMOIL is a surveillance system that detects web activity of a target, and TURBINE is the capability that permits redirection to NSA servers, which facilitates injection of implants. These capabilities give the NSA the ability to use tailored implants to achieve "industrial-scale exploitation," as another NSA document put it. The last slide notes QUANTUMINSERT's success and describes other techniques, including QUANTUMHAND, which allows NSA to "[e]xploit the computer of a target who uses Facebook." Exposure of these capabilities generated controversies about the impact of such activities on cyber security in the United States and around the world.

★  ★  ★

# QUANTUMTHEORY

= (TS//SI//REL) Extremely powerful CNE/CND/CNA network effects are enabled by integrating our passive and active systems:
  = *Resetting connections (QUANTUMSKY)*
  = *Redirecting targets for exploitation (QUANTUMINSERT)*
  = *Taking control of IRC bots (QUANTUMBOT)*
  = *Corrupting file uploads/downloads (QUANTUMCOPPER)*

= (TS//SI//REL) QUANTUMTHEORY dynamically injects packets into a target's network session to achieve CNE/CND/CNA network effects.
  = **Detect**: TURMOIL passive sensors detect target traffic & tip TURBINE command/control.
  = **Decide**: TURBINE mission logic constructs response & forwards to TAO node.
  = **Inject**: TAO node injects response onto Internet towards target.

= (TS//SI//REL) The propagation delay from tip-to-target determines the success rate of the network effect. ***Less Latency = More Success!***

TS//REL

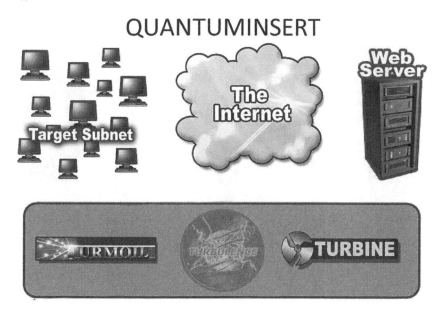

TS//REL

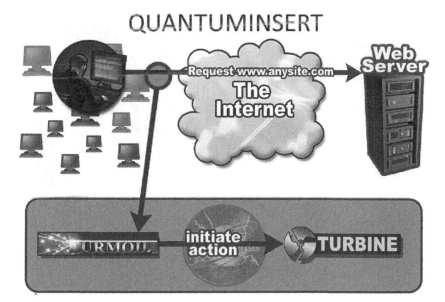

TS//REL

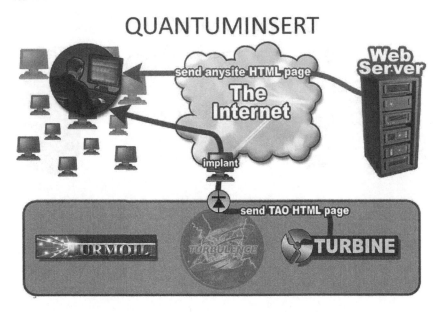

TS//REL

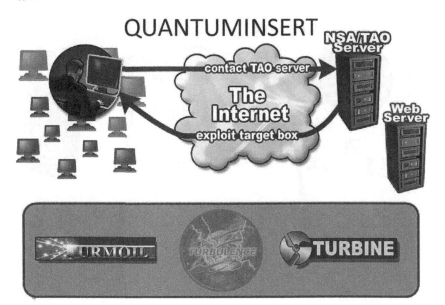

TS//REL

# QUANTUMINSERT

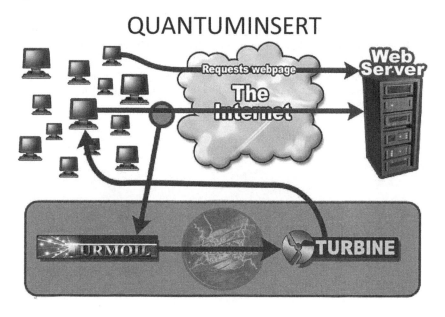

TOP SECRET//COMINT//REL USA, FVEY

## (U) There is More Than One Way to QUANTUM

TS//SI//REL

| Name | Description | Inception Date | Status | Operational Success |
|---|---|---|---|---|
| **CNE** | | | | |
| QUANTUMINSERT | • Man-on-the-Side technique<br>• Briefly hi-jacks connections to a terrorist website<br>• Re-directs the target to a TAO server (FOXACID) for implantation | 2005 | Operational | **Highly Successful**<br>(In 2010, 300 TAO implants were deployed via QUANTUMINSERT to targets that were un-exploitable by any other means) |
| QUANTUMBOT | • Takes control of idle IRC bots<br>• Finds computers belonging to botnets, and hijacks the command and control channel | Aug 2007 | Operational | **Highly Successful**<br>(over 140,000 bots co-opted) |
| QUANTUMBISCUIT | • Enhances QUANTUMINSERT's man-on-the-side technique of exploitation<br>• Motivated by the need to QI targets that are behind large proxies, lack predictable source addresses, and have insufficient unique web activity. | Dec 2007 | Operational | **Limited success at NSAW due to high latency on passive access**<br>(GCHQ uses technique for 80% of CNE accesses) |
| QUANTUMDNS | • DNS injection/redirection based off of A Record queries.<br>• Targets single hosts or caching name servers. | Dec 2008 | Operational | **Successful**<br>(High priority CCI target exploited) |
| QUANTUMHAND | Exploits the computer of a target who uses Facebook | Oct 2010 | Operational | **Successful** |
| QUANTUMPHANTOM | Hijacks any IP on QUANTUMable passive coverage to use as covert infrastructure. | Oct 2010 | Live Tested | **N/A** |
| **CNA** | | | | |
| QUANTUMSKY | Denies access to a webpage through RST packet spoofing. | 2004 | Operational | **Successful** |
| QUANTUMCOPPER | File download/upload disruption and corruption. | Dec 2008 | Live Tested | **N/A** |
| **CND** | | | | |
| QUANTUMSMACKDOWN | Prevents target from downloading implants to DoD computers while capturing malicious payload for analysis. | Oct 2010 | Live Tested | **N/A** |

TS//SI//REL

TOP SECRET//COMINT//REL USA, FVEY

1

NSA Briefing Slides on QUANTUMTHEORY, QUANTUMINSERT, and Other QUANTUM Techniques (dates unknown) [disclosed March 12, 2014].

*Source: Der Spiegel,* http://cdn1.spiegel.de/images/image-584098-galleryV9-jsgn.jpg; and *The Intercept,* https://firstlook.org/theintercept/document/2014/03/12/quantum-insert-diagrams/; https://firstlook.org/theintercept/document/2014/03/12/one-way-quantum/.

# 21

# NSA Public Affairs Office, Statement in Response to Press Allegations

Snowden's disclosures about the NSA's implant programs and capabilities brought a response from the NSA's Public Affairs Office. This terse statement reinforces themes in NSA reactions to the revelations by Snowden, namely that media reports include inaccurate information and allegations and that the NSA only exercises its capabilities for purposes, and within frameworks, anchored in policy-appropriate and lawfully authorized intelligence operations. On the same day this NSA statement appeared, Facebook founder and CEO Mark Zuckerberg, undoubtedly provoked by QUANTUMHAND's exploitation of Facebook, vented his displeasure with the NSA's activities, describing how he called President Obama "to express my frustration over the damage the government is creating for all of our future."

Recent media reports that allege NSA has infected millions of computers around the world with malware, and that NSA is impersonating U.S. social media or other websites, are inaccurate. NSA uses its technical capabilities only to support lawful and appropriate foreign intelligence operations, all of which must be carried out in strict accordance with its authorities. Technical capability must be understood within the legal, policy, and operational context within which the capability must be employed.

NSA's authorities require that its foreign intelligence operations support valid national security requirements, protect the legitimate privacy interests of all persons, and be as tailored as feasible. NSA does not use its technical capabilities to impersonate U.S. company websites. Nor does NSA target any user of global Internet services without appropriate legal authority. Reports of indiscriminate computer exploitation operations are simply false.

NSA Public Affairs Office, Statement in Response to Press Allegations, March 13, 2014.

*Source:* National Security Agency, Public Affairs Office, http://www.nsa.gov/public_info/_files /speeches_testimonies/2014_03_14_press_allegations_response.pdf.

*Norms of Responsible Behavior in Cyberspace?*
*U.S. Cyber Operations*

# 22

# Presidential Policy Directive 20 on U.S. Cyber Operations Policy

The third Snowden disclosure occurred on June 7, 2013, when the *Guardian* revealed Presidential Policy Directive/PPD-20, a top secret document under which President Obama established U.S. policy for cyber operations not involving foreign intelligence collection. The media focused on the provision instructing the government to identify potential targets for offensive cyber operations. But the directive also included guidance on defensive cyber operations, making it a comprehensive attempt to establish policy for cyber activities not involving intelligence. The Obama administration developed the directive in response to concerns that "rules of engagement" for U.S. cyber operations were not clear. The directive declared that all U.S. offensive and defensive cyber operations shall comply with U.S. and international law. The directive contains no information about specific U.S. cyber operations, but disclosures in August 2013 included information that the U.S. government conducted 231 offensive cyber operations in 2011 against government targets in China, Iran, North Korea, and Russia—the year before PPD-20 was adopted. This disputed information, along with PPD-20, connected these disclosures with alleged U.S. involvement in the Stuxnet cyber attack on Iranian nuclear centrifuges discovered in 2010. Fidler's chapter in this volume analyzes the foreign policy implications of PPD-20's disclosure, which include questions about how U.S. offensive cyber operations relate to the U.S. government's desire for "norms of responsible behavior in cyberspace."

★ ★ ★

TOP SECRET/NOFORN

PRESIDENTIAL POLICY DIRECTIVE/PPD-20

. . .

SUBJECT: U.S. Cyber Operations Policy (U)

. . .

I. Definitions (U)

The following terms are defined for the purposes of this directive and should be used when possible in interagency documents and communications on this topic to ensure common understanding. (U)

> Cyberspace: The interdependent network of information technology infrastructures that includes the Internet, telecommunications networks, computers, information or communications systems, networks, and embedded processors and controllers. (U)

> Network Defense: Programs, activities, and the use of tools necessary to facilitate them . . . conducted on a computer, network, or information or communications system by the owner or with the consent of the owner and, as appropriate, the users for the primary purpose of protecting (1) that computer, network, or system; (2) data stored on, processed on, or transiting that computer, network, or system; or (3) physical and virtual infrastructure controlled by that computer, network, or system. Network defense does not involve or require accessing or conducting activities on computers, networks, or information or communications systems without authorization from the owners or exceeding access authorized by the owners. (U)

> Malicious Cyber Activity: Activities, other than those authorized by or in accordance with U.S. law, that seek to compromise or impair the

confidentiality, integrity, or availability of computers, information or communications systems, networks, physical or virtual infrastructure controlled by computers or information systems, or information resident thereon. (U)

Cyber Effect: The manipulation, disruption, denial, degradation, or destruction of computers, information or communications systems, networks, physical or virtual infrastructure controlled by computers or information systems, or information resident thereon. (U)

Cyber Collection: Operations and related programs or activities conducted by or on behalf of the United States Government, in or through cyberspace, for the primary purpose of collecting intelligence—including information that can be used for future operations—from computers, information or communications systems, or networks with the intent to remain undetected. Cyber collection entails accessing a computer, information system, or network without authorization from the owner or operator of that computer, information system, or network or from a party to a communication or by exceeding authorized access. Cyber collection includes those activities essential and inherent to enabling cyber collection, such as inhibiting detection or attribution, even if they create cyber effects. (C/NF)

Defensive Cyber Effects Operations (DCEO): Operations and related programs or activities—other than network defense or cyber collection— conducted by or on behalf of the United States Government, in or through cyberspace, that are intended to enable or produce cyber effects outside United States Government networks for the purpose of defending or protecting against imminent threats or ongoing attacks or malicious cyber activity against U.S. national interests from inside or outside cyberspace. (C/NF)

Nonintrusive Defensive Countermeasures (NDCM): The subset of DCEO that does not require accessing computers, information or communications systems, or networks without authorization from the owners or operators of the targeted computers, information or communications systems, or networks or exceeding authorized access and only creates the minimum cyber effects needed to mitigate the threat activity. (C/NF)

Offensive Cyber Effects Operations (OCEO): Operations and related programs or activities—other than network defense, cyber collection, or DCEO—conducted by or on behalf of the United States Government, in or through cyberspace, that are intended to enable or produce cyber effects outside United States Government networks. (C/NF)

Cyber Operations: Cyber collection, DCEO (including NDCM), and OCEO collectively. (U)

Significant Consequences: Loss of life, significant responsive actions against the United States, significant damage to property, serious adverse U.S. foreign policy consequences, or serious economic impact on the United States. (U)

U.S. National Interests: Matters of vital interest to the United States to include national security, public safety, national economic security, the safe and reliable functioning of "critical infrastructure," and the availability of "key resources." . . . (U)

Emergency Cyber Action: A cyber operation undertaken at the direction of the head of a department or agency with appropriate authorities who has determined that such action is necessary, pursuant to the requirements of this directive, to mitigate an imminent threat or ongoing attack against U.S. national interests from inside or outside cyberspace and under circumstances that at the time do not permit obtaining prior Presidential approval to the extent that such approval would otherwise be required. (S/NF)

II. Purpose and Scope (U)

The United States has an abiding interest in developing and maintaining use of cyberspace as an integral part of U.S. national capabilities to collect intelligence and to deter, deny, or defeat any adversary that seeks to harm U.S. national interests in peace, crisis, or war. Given the evolution in U.S. experience, policy, capabilities, and understanding of the cyber threat, and in information and communications technology, this directive establishes updated principles and processes as part of an overarching national cyber policy framework. (C/NF)

The United States Government shall conduct all cyber operations consistent with the U.S. Constitution and other applicable laws and policies of the United States, including Presidential orders and directives. (C/NF)

The United States Government shall conduct DCEO and OCEO under this directive consistent with its obligations under international law, including with regard to matters of sovereignty and neutrality, and, as applicable, the law of armed conflict. (C/NF)

This directive pertains to cyber operations, including those that support or enable kinetic, information, or other types of operations. Most of this directive is directed exclusively to DCEO and OCEO. (S/NF)

> The United States Government has mature capabilities and effective processes for cyber collection. (S/NF)

> Therefore, this directive affirms and does not intend to alter existing procedures, guidelines, or authorities for cyber collection. (S/NF)

> This directive provides a procedure for cyber collection operations that are reasonably likely to result in "significant consequences." . . . (S/NF)

The principles and requirements in this directive apply except as otherwise lawfully directed by the President. With the exception of the grant of authority to the Secretary of Defense to conduct Emergency Cyber Actions as provided below, nothing in this directive is intended to alter the existing authorities of, or grant new authorities to, any United States Government department or agency (including authorities to carry out operational activities), or supersede any existing coordination and approval processes, other than those of NSPD-38. Nothing in this directive is intended to limit or impair military commanders from using DCEO or OCEO specified in a military action approved by the President and previously coordinated and deconflicted as required by existing processes and this directive. (S/NF)

In addition, this directive does not pertain to or alter existing authorities related to the following categories of activities by or on behalf of the United States Government, regardless of whether they produce cyber effects:

> Activities conducted under section 503 of the National Security Act of 1947 (as amended);

> Activities conducted pursuant to the Foreign Intelligence Surveillance Act, the approval authority delegated to the Attorney General (AG) by section 2.5 of Executive Order 12333 (as amended), or law enforcement authorities; however, cyber operations reasonably likely to result in significant consequences still require Presidential approval, and operations that reasonably can be expected to adversely affect other

United States Government operations still require coordination under established processes;

Activities conducted by the United States Secret Service for the purpose of protecting the President, the Vice President, and others as defined in 18 U.S.C. § 3056; however, cyber operations reasonably likely to result in significant consequences still require Presidential approval, and operations that reasonably can be expected to adversely affect other United States Government operations still require coordination under established processes;

The use of online personas and other virtual operations . . . undertaken exclusively for counterintelligence, intelligence collection, or law enforcement purposes—that do not involve the use of DCEO or OCEO;

Activities conducted in cyberspace pursuant to counterintelligence authorities for the purpose of protecting specific intelligence sources, methods, and activities;

Signals intelligence collection other than cyber collection as defined in this directive;

Open-source intelligence collection;

Network defense;

Traditional electronic warfare . . . activities;

The development of content to support influence campaigns, military deception, or military information support operations; or

Simple transit of data or commands through networks that do not create cyber effects on those networks. (S/NF)

III. Guiding Principles for DCEO and OCEO (U)

DCEO and OCEO may raise unique national security and foreign policy concerns that require additional coordination and policy considerations because cyberspace is globally connected. DCEO and OCEO, even for subtle or clandestine operations, may generate cyber effects in locations other than the intended target, with potential unintended or collateral consequences that may affect U.S. national interests in many locations. (S/NF)

The United States Government shall conduct DCEO and OCEO in a manner consistent with applicable values, principles, and norms for state behavior that the United States Government promotes domestically and internationally as described in the 2011 "International Strategy for Cyberspace." (C/NF)

> National-level strategic objectives and operational necessities shall dictate what the United States Government seeks to accomplish with DCEO and OCEO. (C/NF)

> The United States Government shall integrate DCEO and OCEO, as appropriate, with other diplomatic, informational, military, economic, financial, intelligence, counterintelligence, and law enforcement options, taking into account effectiveness, costs, risks, potential consequences, foreign policy, and other policy considerations. (C/NF)

> The United States Government shall reserve the right to act in accordance with the United States' inherent right of self defense as recognized in international law, including through the conduct of DCEO. (C/NF)

> The United States Government shall conduct neither DCEO nor OCEO that are intended or likely to produce cyber effects within the United States unless approved by the President. A department or agency, however, with appropriate authority may conduct a particular case of DCEO that is intended or likely to produce cyber effects within the United States if it qualifies as an Emergency Cyber Action as set forth in this directive and otherwise complies with applicable laws and policies, including Presidential orders and directives. (C/NF)

The United States Government shall obtain consent from countries in which cyber effects are expected to occur or those countries hosting U.S. computers and systems used to conduct DCEO or OCEO unless:

> Military actions approved by the President and ordered by the Secretary of Defense authorize nonconsensual DCEO or OCEO, with provisions made for using existing processes to conduct appropriate interagency coordination on targets, geographic areas, levels of effect, and degrees of risk for the operations;

DCEO is undertaken in accordance with the United States' inherent right of self defense as recognized in international law, and the United States Government provides notification afterwards in a manner consistent with the protection of U.S. military and intelligence capabilities and foreign policy considerations and in accordance with applicable law; or

The President—on the recommendation of the Deputies Committee and, as appropriate, the Principals Committee—determines that an exception to obtaining consent is necessary, takes into account overall U.S. national interests and equities, and meets a high threshold of need and effective outcomes relative to the risks created by such an exception. (S/NF)

The information revealed to other countries in the course of seeking consent shall be consistent with operational security requirements and the protection of intelligence sources, methods, and activities. (S/NF)

The United States Government, to ensure appropriate application of these principles, shall make all reasonable efforts, under circumstances prevailing at the time, to identify the adversary and the ownership and geographic location of the targets and related infrastructure where DCEO or OCEO will be conducted or cyber effects are expected to occur, and to identify the people and entities, including U.S. persons, that could be affected by proposed DCEO or OCEO. (S/NF)

Additional Considerations for DCEO (U)

The Nation requires flexible and agile capabilities that leverage the full resources of the United States Government to conduct necessary and proportionate DCEO. These operations shall conform to the following additional policy principles:

The United States Government shall reserve use of DCEO to protect U.S. national interests in circumstances when network defense or law enforcement measures are insufficient or cannot be put in place in time to mitigate a threat, and when other previously approved measures would not be more appropriate, or if a Deputies or Principals Committee review determines that proposed DCEO provides an advantageous degree of effectiveness, timeliness, or efficiency compared to other methods commensurate with the risks;

The United States Government shall conduct DCEO with the least intrusive methods feasible to mitigate a threat;

The United States Government shall seek partnerships with industry, other levels of government as appropriate, and other nations and organizations to promote cooperative defensive capabilities, including, as appropriate, through the use of DCEO as governed by the provisions in this directive; and

Partnerships with industry and other levels of government for the protection of critical infrastructure shall be coordinated with the Department of Homeland Security (DHS), working with relevant sector-specific agencies and, as appropriate, the Department of Commerce (DOC). (S/NF)

The United States recognizes that network defense, design, and management cannot mitigate all possible malicious cyber activity and reserves the right, consistent with applicable law, to protect itself from malicious cyber activity that threatens U.S. national interests. (S/NF)

The United States Government shall work with private industry— through DHS, DOC, and relevant sector-specific agencies—to protect critical infrastructure in a manner that minimizes the need for DCEO against malicious cyber activity; however, the United States Government shall retain DCEO, including anticipatory action taken against imminent threats, as governed by the provisions in this directive, as an option to protect such infrastructure. (S/NF)

The United States Government shall—in coordination, as appropriate, with DHS, law enforcement, and other relevant departments and agencies, to include sector-specific agencies—obtain the consent of network or computer owners for United States Government use of DCEO to protect against malicious cyber activity on their behalf, unless the activity implicates the United States' inherent right of self-defense as recognized in international law or the policy review processes established in this directive and appropriate legal reviews determine that such consent is not required. (S/NF)

Offensive Cyber Effects Operations (U)

OCEO can offer unique and unconventional capabilities to advance U.S. national objectives around the world with little or no warning to the adversary or target and with potential effects ranging from subtle to severely damaging. The development and sustainment of OCEO capabilities, however, may require considerable time and effort if access and tools for a specific target do not already exist. (TS/NF)

> The United States Government shall identify potential targets of national importance where OCEO can offer a favorable balance of effectiveness and risk as compared with other instruments of national power, establish and maintain OCEO capabilities integrated as appropriate with other U.S. offensive capabilities, and execute those capabilities in a manner consistent with the provisions of this directive. (TS/NF)

IV. Cyber Operations with Significant Consequences (U)

Specific Presidential approval is required for any cyber operations—including cyber collection, DCEO, and OCEO—determined by the head of a department or agency to conduct the operation to be reasonably likely to result in "significant consequences" as defined in this directive. This requirement applies to cyber operations generally, except for those already approved by the President, even if this directive otherwise does not pertain to such operations as provided in the "Purpose and Scope" section of this directive. (S/NF)

V. Threat Response Operations (U)

Responses to Persistent Malicious Cyber Activity (U)

Departments and agencies with appropriate authorities—consistent with the provisions set forth in this directive and in coordination with the Departments of State, Defense (DOD), Justice (DOJ), and Homeland Security; the Federal Bureau of Investigation (FBI); the Office of the Director of National Intelligence (DNI); the National Security Agency (NSA); the Central Intelligence Agency (CIA); the Departments of the Treasury and Energy (DOE); and other relevant members of the Intelligence Community (IC) and sector-specific agencies—shall establish criteria and procedures to be approved by the President for responding to persistent malicious cyber activity against U.S. national interests. Such criteria and procedures shall include the following requirements:

> The United States Government shall reserve use of such responses to circumstances when network defense or law enforcement measures are insufficient or cannot be put in place in time to mitigate the malicious cyber activity; and

Departments and agencies shall conduct these responses in a manner not reasonably likely to result in significant consequences and use the minimum action required to mitigate the activity. (S/NF)

Emergency Cyber Actions (C/NF)

The Secretary of Defense is hereby authorized to conduct, or a department or agency head with appropriate authorities may conduct, under procedures approved by the President, Emergency Cyber Actions necessary to mitigate an imminent threat or ongoing attack using DCEO if circumstances at the time do not permit obtaining prior Presidential approval (to the extent that such approval would otherwise be required) and the department or agency head determines that:

> An emergency action is necessary in accordance with the United States inherent right of self-defense as recognized in international law to prevent imminent loss of life or significant damage with enduring national impact on the Primary Mission Essential Functions of the United States Government, . . . U.S. critical infrastructure and key resources, or the mission of U.S. military forces;

> Network defense or law enforcement would be insufficient or unavailable in the necessary timeframe, and other previously approved activities would not be more appropriate;

> The Emergency Cyber Actions are reasonably likely not to result in significant consequences;

> The Emergency Cyber Actions will be conducted in a manner intended to be nonlethal in purpose, action, and consequence;

> The Emergency Cyber Actions will be limited in magnitude, scope, and duration to that level of activity necessary to mitigate the threat or attack;

> The Emergency Cyber Actions, when practicable, have been coordinated with appropriate departments and agencies, including State, DOD, DHS, DOJ, the Office of the DNI, FBI, CIA, NSA, the Treasury, DOE, and other relevant members of the IC and sector-specific agencies; and

The Emergency Cyber Actions are consistent with the U.S. Constitution and other applicable laws and policies of the United States, including Presidential orders and directives. (S/NF)

In addition, Emergency Cyber Actions that are intended or likely to produce cyber effects within the United States (or otherwise likely to adversely affect U.S. network defense activities or U.S. networks) must be conducted:

Under the procedures and, as appropriate, criteria for domestic operations previously approved by the President; and

Under circumstances that at the time of the Emergency Cyber Action preclude the use of network defense, law enforcement, or some form of DOD support to civil authorities that would prevent the threatened imminent loss of life or significant damage. (S/NF)

Department and agency heads shall report Emergency Cyber Actions to the President through the National Security Advisor as soon as feasible. If the coordination specified above is not practicable in the available time, then notification shall occur after the fact as soon as possible to inform subsequent whole-of-government response and recovery activities. (S/NF)

Until such time as any additional criteria for domestic operations are approved by the President, authorization by department and agency heads for Emergency Cyber Actions that are intended or likely to produce cyber effects within the United States (or otherwise likely to adversely affect U.S. network defense activities or U.S. networks) shall be granted only if the President has provided prior approval for such activity, or circumstances at the time do not permit obtaining prior approval from the President and such actions are conducted within the other constraints defined above. (S/NF)

VI. Process (U)

The National Security Staff (NSS) shall formalize the functions of the Cyber Operations Policy Working Group (COP-WG) as the primary United States Government forum below the level of an Interagency Policy Committee (IPC) for integrating DCEO or OCEO policy, including consideration of exceptions or refinements to the principles of this directive. The COP-WG shall work with other elements of the policy community as appropriate to the geographic or functional context of the DCEO- or OCEO-related policy discussion at the earliest opportunity. The COP-WG is not an operational group, but will address policy issues related to the conduct of operations raised by departments and agencies or the NSS. (S/NF)

Departments and agencies shall work through the COP-WG to raise unresolved or ambiguous policy questions in an integrated IPC meeting of all appropriate national and economic security stakeholders. The NSS shall use existing channels to elevate any unresolved policy conflicts to the Deputies and Principals Committees, as appropriate. (C/NF)

Departments and agencies shall continue to use existing operational processes for cyber operations, except as those processes are modified by or under this directive. Other types of operations that are supported or enabled by cyber operations shall use their existing operational processes. This continued use of existing operational processes applies, for example, to operations conducted under military orders that authorize DCEO or OCEO, including clandestine preparatory activities. (C/NF)

Departments and agencies, during planning for proposed cyber operations, shall use established processes . . . to coordinate and deconflict with other organizations—including, as appropriate, State, DOD, DOJ, DHS, members of the IC, and relevant sector specific agencies—and obtain any other approvals required under applicable policies, except as those processes are modified by or under this directive. Departments and agencies shall modify or enhance these processes as future circumstances dictate. (S/NF)

> Departments and agencies shall coordinate DCEO and OCEO with State and Chiefs of Station or their designees in countries where DCEO or OCEO are conducted or cyber effects are expected to occur. (S/NF)

Coordination of DCEO and OCEO with network defense efforts shall be sufficient to enable a whole-of-government approach to the protection of U.S. national interests and shall identify potential implications of proposed DCEO and OCEO for U.S. networks, including potential adversary responses or unintended consequences of U.S. operations for which the United States Government or the private sector would need to prepare. This coordination shall occur in a manner consistent with operational security requirements and the protection of intelligence sources, methods, and activities. (S/NF)

> Toward this end of ensuring a unified whole-of-government approach, departments and agencies shall coordinate and deconflict DCEO and

OCEO with network defense efforts of other departments and agencies as appropriate. (S/NF)

In addition, DCEO and OCEO with potential implications for U.S. networks shall be deconflicted as appropriate and coordinated with DHS, appropriate law enforcement agencies, and relevant sector-specific agencies. (S/NF)

The United States Government shall make all reasonable efforts to identify and notify, as appropriate, private sector entities that could be affected by DCEO and OCEO. (S/NF)

Policy Criteria (U)

Policy deliberations for DCEO and OCEO shall consider, but not be limited to, the following criteria:

Impact: The potential threat from adversary actions or the potential benefits, scope, and recommended prioritization of proposed U.S. operations as compared with other approaches—including, as appropriate, network defense by the United States Government or private sector network operators;

Risks: Assessments of intelligence gain or loss, the risk of retaliation or other impacts on U.S. networks or interests (including economic), impact on the security and stability of the Internet, and political gain or loss to include impact on foreign policies, bilateral and multilateral relationships (including Internet governance), and the establishment of unwelcome norms of international behavior;

Methods: The intrusiveness, timeliness, efficiency, capacity, and effectiveness of operational methods to be employed;

Geography and Identity: Geographic and identity aspects of the proposed activity, including the location of operations and the resulting effects, the identity of network owners and users that will be affected, and the identity or type—when known—of adversaries to be countered or affected by U.S. operations;

Transparency: The need for consent or notification of network or computer owners or host countries, the potential for impact on U.S.

persons and U.S. private sector networks, and the need for any public or private communications strategies before or after an operation; and

Authorities and Civil Liberties: The available authorities and procedures and the potential for cyber effects inside the United States or against U.S. persons. (S/NF)

Policy decisions shall be broad enough and include rationales in order to provide guidelines and direction for future proposals with the same operational and risk parameters. (C/NF)

. . .

★  ★  ★

Presidential Policy Directive/PPD-20 on U.S. Cyber Operations Policy, October 2012 [disclosed June 7, 2013] (footnotes omitted).

*Source:* "Obama Tells Intelligence Chiefs to Draw Up Cyber Target List—Full Document Text," *Guardian,* June 7, 2013, http://www.theguardian.com/world/interactive/2013/jun/07/obama -cyber-directive-full-text.

*"Worse than the U.S."?*
*Surveillance by the UK's Government*
*Communications Headquarters*

# 23

# GCHQ's TEMPORA Program

Snowden's disclosures revealed information not only about U.S. government intelligence, but also about the intelligence activities of other countries. These leaks included documents related to collaboration between the NSA and intelligence agencies in Australia, Canada, Germany, Israel, the Netherlands, Norway, Sweden, and the United Kingdom. Snowden also released information about the intelligence activities of some governments, including those of Australia, Canada, and the Netherlands. The majority of disclosures about foreign governments related to the UK's signals intelligence agency, GCHQ. In fact, Snowden said that GCHQ was "worse than the U.S." The documents below relate to what Snowden disclosed about GCHQ and reactions to what he made public. The first document is from GCHQ describing its TEMPORA capability. The *Guardian* disclosed TEMPORA in June 2013, early in the timing of Snowden's leaks. Under TEMPORA, GCHQ collects large volumes of metadata and communication content by accessing fiber-optic cables over which significant portions of the world's Internet and telephone traffic travels. GCHQ analysts then query the information by, for example, using XKEYSCORE, the powerful NSA tool shared with GCHQ for analyzing surveillance information collected by various means and held in different databases.

★　★　★

. . .

**BREAKING NEWS (May 2012)**—The second tranche of 'deep dive' processing capability at RPC [Remote Processing Centre] has gone live. . . .

This gives over 300 GCHQ and ~250 NSA analysts access to huge amounts of data to support the target discovery mission.

The MTI [Master the Internet] programme would like to say a big thanks to everyone who has made this possible . . . a true collaborative effort!

TEMPORA was delivered by the MTI Enhanced Discovery swimlane . . .

**TEMPORA**

**TEMPORA** is an Internet Buffer capability being delivered by MTI . . . for joint mission benefit. It builds upon the key success of the TINT experiment and will provide a vital unique capability. . . .

- TEMPORA is the codeword for GCHQ's internet buffer business capability as a whole—which is the ability to loosely promote a % of traffic across GCHQ's SSE [Special Source Exploitation] access into a repository which will keep the content (and its associated metadata) for periods of time (approximately 3 days for content and up to 30 days for metadata) to allow retrospective analysis and forwarding to follow on systems.
- TEMPORA as a capability is *agnostic* of the technologies used to promote that traffic and to store that traffic and so should not be used as a codeword for the individual components (e.g., XKS [XKEYSCORE], MVR [Massive Volume Reduction] etc).
- At the moment the components include, amongst others, GCHQ SSE Access, POKERFACE sanitisation, XKS (in various configurations) and it will include MVR in the very near future.
- TEMPORA also covers the management of the rules used to promote traffic into the internet buffer capability.
- TEMPORA is not processing centre specific. . . .

**A bit more detail**

**TEMPORA** are GCHQ's large-scale, Deep Dive deployments on Special Source access (SSE). Deep Dive XKeyscores work by promoting loose categories of traffic (e.g., all web, email, social, chat, EA, VPN [Virtual Private Network], VoIP

[Voice-over Internet Protocol] . . . ) from the bearers feeding the system and block all high-volume, low value traffic (e.g., P2P [Peer-to-Peer] downloads). This usually equates to ~30% of the traffic on the bearer. We keep the full sessions for 3 working days and the metadata for 30 days for you to query, using all the functionality that Keyscore offers to slice and dice the data. The aim is to put the best 7.5% of our access into TEMPORA's, comprising a mix of Deep Dive Keyscores and promotion of data based on IP [Internet Protocol] subnet or technology type from across the entire MVR. At the moment, users are able to access 46x10Gs of data via existing Internet Buffers. This is a lot of data! Not only that, but the long-running TINT program and our initial 3-month operation trial of the CPC [Cheltenham Processing Centre] Internet Buffer (the first operational Internet Buffer to be deployed) show that every area of ops can get real benefit from this capability, especially for target discovery and target development. Internet Buffers are different from TINT in that the latter is purely an experimental, research environment whereas Internet Buffers can be used operationally for EPR, Effects, enabling CNE [Computer Network Exploitation] etc.

. . .

★ ★ ★

GCHQ, Information about TEMPORA, May 2012 [disclosed June 18, 2014].

Source: Der Spiegel, http://www.spiegel.de/media/media-34103.pdf.

# 24

# NSA Memo on the TEMPORA Program

This document is an internal NSA communication about TEMPORA announcing that NSA analysts can get access to it through XKEYSCORE, an NSA system analysts use to search NSA databases for information on existing surveillance targets or to develop new foreign intelligence targets. It reveals not only the excitement of NSA analysts about getting access to a "massive site" containing "40 billion pieces of content a day," but also the deep intelligence cooperation taking place between NSA and the UK's GCHQ.

★ ★ ★

**(C//REL) TEMPORA -- "The World's Largest XKEYSCORE" -- Is Now Available to Qualified NSA Users**

FROM: (U//FOUO)
NSA Integree at GCHQ
Run Date: 09/19/2012

(U//FOUO) SIGINT analysts: We have all heard about Big Data; now you can get **Big Access** to Big Data.

(TS//SI//REL) What happens when one site contains more data than all other XKEYSCOREs combined? At more than 10 times larger than the next biggest XKEYSCORE,* **TEMPORA at GCHQ** is the world's largest XKEYSCORE and the NSA workforce is now getting greater access to it. This massive site uses over 1000 machines to process and make available to analysts more than 40 billion pieces of content a day. And starting today, skilled NSA XKEYSCORE users can get access to the TEMPORA database via the XKS-Central interface.

(TS//SI//REL) **What is TEMPORA?** TEMPORA is GCHQ's XKEYSCORE "Internet buffer" which exploits the most valuable Internet links available to GCHQ. TEMPORA provides a powerful discovery capability against Middle East, North African and European target sets (among others). Analysts who have benefited from GCHQ Special Source accesses like INCENSER or MUSCULAR will almost certainly benefit from TEMPORA.

(TS//SI//REL) **How valuable is TEMPORA?** The value and utility of TEMPORA were proven early into a 5-month evaluation that began this past March. With a limited user base of 300 analysts, TEMPORA became the second most valuable XKEYSCORE access for discovery. Additionally, this small group of analysts produced over 200 end-product reports and provided critical support to SIGINT, defensive, and cyber mission elements.

(TS//SI//REL) **Why TEMPORA?** TEMPORA provides the ability to do content-based discovery and development across a large array of high-priority signals. Similar to other XKEYSCORE deployments, TEMPORA effectively "slows down" a large chunk of Internet data, providing analysts with three working days to use the surgical toolkit of the GENESIS language to discover data that otherwise would have been missed. This tradecraft of **content-based discovery** using the GENESIS language is a critical tool in the analyst's discovery tool kit, and nicely complements the existing and well-known tradecrafts of strong selection targeting and bulk meta-data analysis.

(TS//SI//REL) **How do I get an account?** To comply with GCHQ policy and to ensure users are successful in such a large-scale environment, TEMPORA access requires users to be proficient with XKEYSCORE. At NSA this is achieved via the completion of various XKS Skilz achievements. Beginning today, users will see a new "TEMPORA" achievement, which requires users to have remained current with their UK Legalities training (OVSC1700), be a level 3 or higher XKS Skilz user, and have used GENESIS by either querying or authoring fingerprints. Users who meet those criteria will automatically be given TEMPORA access in their XKS Central account.

(S//SI//REL) **What do I need to know about using TEMPORA?** Although TEMPORA will appear as an additional database in XKS Central, there are some important items analysts need to be aware of when they search this database. Analysts are asked to pay close attention to details concerning the UK Legality requirements on the TEMPORA user-guidance wiki page. TEMPORA queries must comply with both UK and U.S. legal requirements, and the analytic community must ensure we are using this access wisely and compliantly.

(S//SI//REL) **How can I learn more about using XKEYSCORE?** If you'd like to get TEMPORA access but need some help fulfilling the proficiency requirements, the XKEYSCORE Outreach Team is ready to help. The team recently added an additional round of XKEYSCORE training sessions on ERS, which users can sign up for via this link. Also, analysts can find great tradecraft and training tips via the XKEYBLOG, or they can contact the team directly at DL XKS_Mentoring.

(U//FOUO) For more information **"go TEMPORA"** or contact █████████████████████ ████████████████████████

---

(U) Notes:

* (S//SI/REL) XKEYSCORE is a computer-network exploitation system that combines high-speed filtering with SIGDEV. XKEYSCORE performs filtering and selection to enable analysts to quickly find information they need based on what they already know, but it also performs SIGDEV functions such as target development to allow analysts to discover new sources of information.

NSA, TEMPORA—"The World's Largest XKEYSCORE"—Is Now Available to Qualified NSA Users, September 19, 2012 [disclosed June 18, 2014]. Page 4 of 4 is blank and not reproduced here.

*Source: Der Spiegel,* http://www.spiegel.de/media/media-34090.pdf.

# 25

# British Parliament's Intelligence and Security Committee, Statement on the U.S. PRISM Program

Snowden's disclosures of GCHQ activities spawned policy and legal controversies in the UK, including allegations that GCHQ had access to information the NSA collected under PRISM without authorization under British law. With access to PRISM information concerning foreigners located outside the United States, did GCHQ access and use PRISM data about British nationals that GCHQ could not, under British law, have or review? The Intelligence and Security Committee (ISC) of Parliament issued this statement in July 2013 summarizing its conclusions following a review of whether GCHQ acted illegally with respect to PRISM information shared by the U.S. government. The ISC is charged with providing parliamentary oversight of the British government's intelligence activities, including GCHQ. These functions make it the equivalent of the select committees on intelligence in the U.S. House of Representatives and Senate. Although the ISC found no wrongdoing in GCHQ's actions, its concluding thoughts revealed disquiet about the existing statutory framework and noted a need for further examination of whether this framework adequately protected private communications. In October 2013, the committee announced that it was broadening the scope of this examination to include the impact on privacy of the intelligence agencies' capabilities, and the committee's inquiry was continuing as of this writing.

★  ★  ★

# INTELLIGENCE AND SECURITY
# COMMITTEE OF PARLIAMENT

*Chairman: The Rt. Hon. Sir Malcolm Rifkind, MP*

## Statement on GCHQ's Alleged Interception of Communications under the US PRISM Programme

### Introduction

1.    Over the last month, details of highly classified intelligence-gathering programmes run by the US signals intelligence agency – the National Security Agency (NSA) – have been leaked in both the US and the UK. Stories in the media have focussed on the collection of communications data and of communications content by the NSA. These have included the collection of bulk 'meta-data' from a large communications provider (Verizon), and also access to communications content via a number of large US internet companies (under the PRISM programme).

2.    The legal arrangements governing these NSA accesses, and the oversight and scrutiny regimes to which they are subject, are matters for the US Congress and courts. However some of the stories have included allegations about the activities of the UK's own signals intelligence agency, GCHQ. While some of the stories are not surprising, given GCHQ's publicly acknowledged remit, there is one very serious allegation amongst them – namely that GCHQ acted illegally by accessing communications content via the PRISM programme.[1]

### What is the PRISM programme?

3.    PRISM is a programme through which the US Government obtains intelligence material (such as communications) from Internet Service Providers (ISPs). The US administration has stated that the programme is regulated under the US Foreign Intelligence Surveillance Act (FISA), and applications for access to material through PRISM have to be approved by the FISA Court, which is comprised of 11 senior judges. Access under PRISM is specific and targeted (not a broad 'data mining' capability, as has been alleged).

4.    Stories in the media have asserted that GCHQ had access to PRISM and thereby to the content of communications in the UK without proper authorisation. It is argued that, in so doing, GCHQ circumvented UK law. This is a matter of very serious concern: if true, it would constitute a serious violation of the rights of UK citizens.

### Our investigation

5.    The ISC has taken detailed evidence from GCHQ. Our investigation has included scrutiny of GCHQ's access to the content of communications, the legal framework which governs that access, and the arrangements GCHQ has with its overseas counterparts for sharing such information. We have received substantive reports from GCHQ, including:

---

[1] There are other matters arising from the leaks that we are considering, although we note that none alleges – as the PRISM story did – any illegality on the part of GCHQ.

- a list of counter-terrorist operations for which GCHQ was able to obtain intelligence from the US in any relevant area;
- a list of all the individuals who were subject to monitoring via such arrangements who were either believed to be in the UK or were identified as UK nationals;
- a list of every 'selector' (such as an email address) for these individuals on which the intelligence was requested;
- a list of the warrants and internal authorisations that were in place for each of these individual being targeted;
- a number (as selected by us) of the intelligence reports that were produced as a result of this activity; and
- the formal agreements that regulated access to this material.

We discussed the programme with the NSA and our Congressional counterparts during our recent visit to the United States. We have also taken oral evidence from the Director of GCHQ and questioned him in detail.

---

- **It has been alleged that GCHQ circumvented UK law by using the NSA's PRISM programme to access the content of private communications. From the evidence we have seen, we have concluded that this is unfounded.**

- **We have reviewed the reports that GCHQ produced on the basis of intelligence sought from the US, and we are satisfied that they conformed with GCHQ's statutory duties. The legal authority for this is contained in the Intelligence Services Act 1994.**

- **Further, in each case where GCHQ sought information from the US, a warrant for interception, signed by a Minister, was already in place, in accordance with the legal safeguards contained in the Regulation of Investigatory Powers Act 2000.**

---

## Next Steps

6.   Although we have concluded that GCHQ has not circumvented or attempted to circumvent UK law, it is proper to consider further whether the current statutory framework[2] governing access to private communications remains adequate.

7.   In some areas the legislation is expressed in general terms and more detailed policies and procedures have, rightly, been put in place around this work by GCHQ in order to ensure compliance with their statutory obligations under the Human Rights Act 1998. We are therefore examining the complex interaction between the Intelligence Services Act, the Human Rights Act and the Regulation of Investigatory Powers Act, and the policies and procedures that underpin them, further. We note that the Interception of Communications Commissioner is also considering this issue.

---

[2] The Intelligence Services Act 1994, the Human Rights Act 1998 and the Regulation of Investigatory Powers Act 2000.

## NOTES TO EDITORS

1.  The Intelligence and Security Committee of Parliament (ISC) is a statutory committee of Parliament that has responsibility for oversight of the UK intelligence community. The Committee was originally established by the Intelligence Services Act 1994, and has recently been reformed by the Justice and Security Act 2013.

2.  The Committee oversees the intelligence and security activities of the UK, including the policies, expenditure, administration and operations of the Security Service (MI5), the Secret Intelligence Service (MI6) and the Government Communications Headquarters (GCHQ). The Committee also scrutinises the work of other parts of the UK intelligence community, including the Joint Intelligence Organisation and the National Security Secretariat in the Cabinet Office; Defence Intelligence in the Ministry of Defence; and the Office for Security and Counter-Terrorism in the Home Office.

3.  The Committee consists of nine Members drawn from both Houses of Parliament. The Chair is elected by its Members. The Members of the Committee are subject to Section 1(1)(b) of the Official Secrets Act 1989 and are routinely given access to highly classified material in carrying out their duties. The current membership is:
    The Rt. Hon. Sir Malcolm Rifkind, MP (Chairman)
    The Rt. Hon. Hazel Blears, MP
    The Rt. Hon. Lord Butler KG GCB CVO
    The Rt. Hon. Sir Menzies Campbell CH CBE QC, MP
    Mr Mark Field, MP
    The Rt. Hon. Paul Goggins, MP
    The Rt. Hon. George Howarth, MP
    Dr. Julian Lewis, MP
    The Most Hon. The Marquis of Lothian PC QC DL

4.  The Committee sets its own agenda and work programme. It takes evidence from Government Ministers, the Heads of the intelligence Agencies, officials from the intelligence community, and other witnesses as required. The Committee is supported in its work by an independent Secretariat and an Investigator. It also has access to legal and financial expertise where necessary.

5.  The Committee produces an Annual Report on the discharge of its functions. The Committee may also produce Reports on specific investigations.

★ ★ ★

Intelligence and Security Committee of Parliament, Statement on GCHQ's Alleged Interception of Communications under the US PRISM Programme, July 17, 2013.

*Source:* Intelligence and Security Committee of Parliament, https://www.gov.uk/government/uploads/system/uploads/attachment_data/file/225459/ISC-Statement-on-GCHQ.pdf.

# 26

# European Court of Human Rights, Big Brother Watch and Others v. United Kingdom

Snowden's disclosures triggered resort to judicial tribunals by persons and organizations in the UK who argued that GCHQ violated British law. British law empowers an Investigatory Powers Tribunal (IPT) to investigate complaints that intelligence or law enforcement agencies breached human rights, including the right to privacy, in engaging in covert operations, such as secretly monitoring or intercepting communications. After Snowden's disclosures about GCHQ, the IPT received complaints from UK nongovernmental organizations alleging GCHQ's TEMPORA program and access to PRISM information violated the UK's obligations concerning the rights to privacy and freedom of expression under the European Convention on Human Rights (ECHR). The IPT began hearings in mid-July 2014, and, in December 2014, it ruled that GCHQ was not violating the ECHR. The nongovernmental organizations vowed to take their complaints to the European Court of Human Rights (ECtHR). The next document provides excerpts of the official summary of an earlier challenge by nongovernmental organizations to GCHQ's activities filed with the ECtHR in September 2013 alleging violations of the ECHR's right to privacy. The ECtHR has not issued a ruling in this case as of this writing.

* * *

## STATEMENT OF FACTS

### A. The circumstances of the case

The facts of the case, as submitted by the applicants, may be summarised as follows.

### 1. The applicants

Big Brother Watch (the first applicant) . . . operates as a campaign group to conduct research into, and challenge policies which threaten privacy, freedoms and civil liberties, and to expose the scale of surveillance by the State. Its staff members regularly liaise and work in partnership with similar organisations in other countries, communicating by email and Skype. As a vocal critic of excessive surveillance, and a commentator on sensitive topics relating to national security, the first applicant believes that its staff and directors may have been the subject of surveillance by or on behalf of the United Kingdom Government. Moreover, it has contact with internet freedom campaigners and those who wish to complain to regulators around the world, so it is conscious that some of those with whom it is in contact may also fall under surveillance.

English PEN (the second applicant) . . . promotes freedom to write and read, and campaigns around the world on freedom of expression, and equal access to the media and works closely with individual writers at risk and in prison. Most of its internal and external communications are by email and by Skype. Since many of those for and with whom English PEN campaigns express views on governments which may be controversial, English PEN believes that it, and those with whom it communicates, may be the subject of United Kingdom Government surveillance, or may be the subject of surveillance by other countries' security services which may pass such information to the United Kingdom security services (and vice-versa).

Open Rights Group (the third applicant) . . . operates as a campaign organisation, defending freedom of expression, innovation, creativity and consumer rights on the internet. It regularly liaises and works in partnership with other organisations in other countries. . . . Most of its internal and external communications are by email and Skype. For similar reasons to those expressed by the first and second applicants, it believes that its electronic communications and activities may be subject to foreign intercept conveyed to United Kingdom authorities, or intercept activity by United Kingdom authorities.

Dr Constanze Kurz (the fourth applicant) is an expert on surveillance techniques, based in Berlin, where she works at the University of Applied Sciences. . . . Dr Kurz has been outspoken in relation to the recent disclosures regarding United Kingdom internet surveillance activities, which continue to be a subject of significant concern in the German media. She fears that she may well have been the subject of surveillance either directly by the United Kingdom or by foreign security services who may have passed that data to the United Kingdom security services, not only because of her activities as a freedom of expression campaigner and hacking activist, but also because these security services may wish to learn from her and persons with whom she communicates, habitually in encrypted communications.

## 2. *The surveillance programmes complained about*

The applicants' concern was triggered by media coverage following the leak of information by Edward Snowden. . . . According to media reports, the NSA has in place a programme, known as PRISM, which allows it to access a wide range of internet communication content (such as emails, chat, video, images, documents, links and other files) and metadata (information permitting the identification and location of internet users), from United States corporations, . . . such as Microsoft, Google, Yahoo, Apple, Facebook, YouTube and Skype. Since global internet data takes the cheapest, rather than the most direct route, a substantial amount of global data passes through the servers of these American companies, including possibly emails sent by the applicants in London and Berlin to their international contacts. The applicants submit that the NSA also operates a second interception programme known as UPSTREAM, which provides access to nearly all the traffic passing through fibre optic cables owned by United States communication service providers such as AT&T and Verizon. Together, these programmes provide very broad access to the communications content and metadata of non-United States persons, to whom the provisions of the Fourth Amendment . . . [do not apply], and allow for this material to be collected, stored and searched using keywords. According to the documents leaked by Edward Snowden, the United Kingdom Government Communications Head Quarters (GCHQ) has had access to PRISM material since at least June 2010 and has used it to generate intelligence reports (197 reports in 2012).

In addition, the disclosures based on Edward Snowden's leaked documentation have included details about a United Kingdom surveillance programme called TEMPORA . . . by which GCHQ can access electronic traffic passing along fibre-optic cables running between the United Kingdom and North America. The data collected include both internet and telephone communications. GCHQ is able to access not only metadata but also the content of emails,

Facebook entries and website histories. The TEMPORA programme is authorised by certificates issued under section 8(4) of the Regulation of Investigatory Powers Act 2000 (RIPA: see below). The applicants allege that United States agencies have been given extensive access to TEMPORA information.

## B. Relevant domestic law

Section 1 of the Intelligence Services Act 1994 ("ISA") . . . provides a statutory basis for the operation of the United Kingdom's Secret Intelligence Service[.] . . . Section 2 of ISA provides for the control of the operations of the Intelligence Service by a Chief of Service, to be appointed by the Secretary of State. . . . Section 3 of ISA sets out the authority for the operation of GCHQ[.] . . .

The Regulation of Investigatory Powers Act 2000 (RIPA) came into force on 15 December 2000 . . . to ensure that the relevant investigatory powers were used in accordance with human rights.

Section 1(1) of RIPA makes it an offence for a person intentionally and without lawful authority to intercept, at any place in the United Kingdom, any communication in the course of its transmission by means of a public postal service or a public telecommunication system.

Section 8(4) and (5) allows the Secretary of State to issue a warrant for "the interception of external communications in the course of their transmission by means of a telecommunication system." At the time of issuing such a warrant, she must also issue a certificate setting out a description of the intercepted material which she considers it necessary to be examined, and stating that the warrant is necessary, *inter alia*, in the interests of national security, for the purpose of preventing or detecting serious crime or for the purpose of safeguarding the economic well-being of the United Kingdom and that the conduct authorised by the warrant is proportionate to what is sought to be achieved by that conduct.

RIPA sets out a number of general safeguards in section 15. . . . Section 16 sets out additional safeguards in relation to interception of "external" communications under certificated warrants[.] . . .

Part IV of RIPA provides for the appointment of an Interception of Communications Commissioner and an Intelligence Services Commissioner, charged with supervising the activities of the intelligence services.

Section 65 of RIPA provides for a Tribunal, the Investigatory Powers Tribunal, which has jurisdiction to determine claims related to the conduct of the intelligence services, including proceedings under the Human Rights Act 1998.

. . .

COMPLAINTS

The applicants allege that they are likely to have been the subject of generic surveillance by GCHQ and/or that the United Kingdom security services may have been in receipt of foreign intercept material relating to their electronic communications, such as to give rise to interferences with their rights under Article 8 of the [European] Convention [on Human Rights]. They contend that these interferences are not "in accordance with the law," for the following reasons.

In the applicants' submission, there is no basis in domestic law for the receipt of information from foreign intelligence agencies. In addition, there is an absence of legislative control and safeguards in relation to the circumstances in which the United Kingdom intelligence services can request foreign intelligence agencies to intercept communications and/or to give the United Kingdom access to stored data that has been obtained by interception, and the extent to which the United Kingdom intelligence services can use, analyse, disseminate and store data solicited and/or received from foreign intelligence agencies and the process by which such data must be destroyed.

In relation to the interception of communications directly by GCHQ, the applicants submit that the statutory regime applying to external communications warrants does not comply with the minimum standards outlined by the Court in its [Article 8] case-law. . . . They contend that section 8(4) of RIPA permits the blanket strategic monitoring of communications where at least one party is outside the British Isles, under broadly defined warrants, which are continuously renewed so as to form a "rolling programme." Although the Secretary of State is required to issue a certificate limiting the extent to which the intercepted material can be examined, the legislation also permits such certificates to be framed in very broad terms, for example, "in the interests of national security." The applicants claim, in particular, that the concept of "national security" in this context is vague and unforeseeable in scope. They consider that the safeguards set out in sections 15 and 16 of RIPA are of limited scope, particularly in the light of the broad definition of national security employed. They further contend that domestic law does not provide for effective independent authorisation and oversight.

The applicants further contend that the generic interception of external communications by GCHQ, merely on the basis that such communications have been transmitted by transatlantic fibre-optic cables, is an inherently disproportionate interference with the private lives of thousands, perhaps millions, of people.

## QUESTIONS TO THE PARTIES

1. Can the applicants claim to be victims of violations of their rights under Article 8 [of the European Convention on Human Rights]?

2. Have the applicants done all that is required of them to exhaust domestic remedies? In particular, . . . had the applicants raised their Convention complaints before the Investigatory Powers Tribunal, could the Tribunal have made a declaration of incompatibility under . . . the Human Rights Act 1998 . . . [which] should be regarded by the Court as an effective remedy which should be exhausted before bringing a complaint of this type before the Court . . . ?

3. In the event that the application is not inadmissible on grounds of non-exhaustion of domestic remedies, are the acts of the United Kingdom intelligence services in relation to:

(a) the soliciting, receipt, search, analysis, dissemination, storage and destruction of interception data obtained by the intelligence services of other States; and/or

(b) their own interception, search, analysis, dissemination, storage and destruction of data relating to "external" communications (where at least one party is outside the British Isles);

"in accordance with the law" and "necessary in a democratic society" within the meaning of Article 8 of the Convention . . . ?

European Court of Human Rights, Big Brother Watch and Others v. United Kingdom, Application No. 58170/13 (lodged September 4, 2013), Statement of Facts, Complaints, and Questions Presented, January 9, 2014.

*Source:* European Court of Human Rights, http://hudoc.echr.coe.int/sites/eng/pages/search .aspx?i=001-140713#{"itemid":["001-140713"]}

## B. Reviews and Recommendations

As awareness of the substance of Snowden's disclosures spread and debates over their implications grew, various governmental and international institutions undertook assessments of the issues raised by the revelations and reactions to them, and they developed recommendations to implement changes. This section provides documents containing analyses of legal and policy questions and/or recommendations for reform associated with engaging in foreign intelligence activities while respecting individual rights. These documents include U.S. federal court decisions on the telephone metadata program and Section 702 of FISA, reports from U.S. advisory and oversight bodies and the European Parliament, and a resolution from the United Nations General Assembly. These documents further illustrate the comprehensive and global impact Snowden's disclosures have had.

*U.S. Federal Court Decisions on NSA Programs*

# 27

## *Klayman v. Obama:*
## Issuing a Preliminary Injunction against the
## Telephone Metadata Program

Snowden's public disclosure of information about the NSA's telephone metadata program prompted litigation in U.S. federal courts about the program's legality under Section 215 of the USA PATRIOT Act and the Fourth Amendment. In *Klayman v. Obama,* subscribers of U.S. telecommunications and Internet companies brought suit, and Judge Richard J. Leon ruled on the plaintiffs' request for a preliminary injunction to stop the U.S. government from collecting their telephone metadata. His decision attracted significant attention. In asking for an injunction, the plaintiffs argued that Section 215 did not support the telephone metadata program and that the program violated the Fourth Amendment. Judge Leon held that the plaintiffs could not challenge the U.S. government's compliance with Section 215 under federal law. He ruled for the plaintiffs, however, on the constitutional issue. He determined that the plaintiffs met their burden of showing they would likely prevail at the merits stage of the case on their claim that the telephone metadata program violated the Fourth Amendment. Snowden, his supporters, and NSA critics celebrated the decision and Judge Leon's reasoning.

The U.S. government appealed the decision. The appellate court heard oral arguments in *Klayman* in early November 2014, but, as of this writing, it has not issued a ruling. Whether the appellate court overrules Judge Leon's decision, it will remain a memorable opinion in the judiciary's handling of litigation prompted by Snowden's disclosures.

★ ★ ★

. . .

## b. Plaintiffs Are Likely to Succeed on the Merits of Their Fourth Amendment Claim.

. . .

The threshold issue [under the Fourth Amendment] . . . is whether plaintiffs have a reasonable expectation of privacy that is violated when the Government indiscriminately collects their telephony metadata along with the metadata of hundreds of millions of other citizens without any particularized suspicion of wrongdoing, retains all of that metadata for five years, and then queries, analyzes, and investigates that data without prior judicial approval of the investigative targets. If they do—and a Fourth Amendment search has thus occurred—then the next step of the analysis will be to determine whether such a search is "reasonable." . . .

### i. The Collection and Analysis of Telephony Metadata Constitutes a Search.

The analysis of this threshold issue of the expectation of privacy must start with the Supreme Court's landmark opinion in *Smith v. Maryland* [1979] . . . , which the FISC has said "squarely control[s]" when it comes to "[t]he production of telephone service provider metadata." . . . In *Smith,* police were investigating a robbery victim's reports that she had received threatening and obscene phone calls from someone claiming to be the robber. . . . Without obtaining a warrant or court order, police installed a pen register [a device that records the numbers dialed from a specific telephone number], which revealed that a telephone in Smith's home had been used to call the victim on one occasion. . . . The Supreme Court held that Smith had no reasonable expectation of privacy in the numbers dialed from his phone because he voluntarily transmitted them to his phone company, and because it is generally known that phone companies keep such information in their business records. . . . The main thrust of the Government's argument here is that under *Smith,* no one has an expectation of privacy, let alone a reasonable one, in the telephony metadata that telecom companies hold as business records; therefore, the Bulk Telephony Metadata Program is not a search. . . . I disagree.

The question before me is *not* the same question that the Supreme Court confronted in *Smith*. To say the least, "whether the installation and use of a pen register constitutes a 'search' within the meaning of the Fourth Amendment," . . . under the circumstances addressed and contemplated in that case—is a far cry from the issue in this case.

Indeed, the question in this case can more properly be styled as follows: When do present-day circumstances—the evolutions in the Government's surveillance capabilities, citizens' phone habits, and the relationship between the NSA and telecom companies—become so thoroughly unlike those considered by the Supreme Court thirty-four years ago that a precedent like *Smith* simply does not apply? The answer, unfortunately for the Government, is now.

. . .

. . . [T]he Court in *Smith* was not confronted with the NSA's Bulk Telephony Metadata Program. Nor could the Court in 1979 have ever imagined how the citizens of 2013 would interact with their phones. For the many reasons discussed below, I am convinced that the surveillance program now before me is so different from a simple pen register that *Smith* is of little value in assessing whether the Bulk Telephony Metadata Program constitutes a Fourth Amendment search. To the contrary, . . . I believe that bulk telephony metadata collection and analysis almost certainly does violate a reasonable expectation of privacy.

First, the pen register in *Smith* was operational for only a matter of days . . . , and there is no indication from the Court's opinion that it expected the Government to retain those limited phone records once the case was over. . . . This short-term, forward-looking (as opposed to historical), and highly-limited data collection is what the Supreme Court was assessing in *Smith*. The NSA telephony metadata program, on the other hand, involves the creation and maintenance of a historical database containing *five years'* worth of data. And I might add, there is the very real prospect that the program will go on for as long as America is combatting terrorism, which realistically could be forever!

Second, the relationship between the police and the phone company in *Smith* is *nothing* compared to the relationship that has apparently evolved over the last seven years between the Government and telecom companies. . . . The Supreme Court itself has long-recognized a meaningful difference between cases in which a third party collects information and then turns it over to law enforcement, . . . and cases in which the government and the third party create a formalized policy under which the service provider collects information for law enforcement purposes, . . . with the latter raising Fourth Amendment concerns. In *Smith,* the Court considered a one-time, targeted request for data regarding an individual suspect in a criminal investigation, . . . which in no way resembles the daily, all-encompassing, indiscriminate dump of phone metadata that the NSA now receives as part of its Bulk Telephony Metadata Program. It's one thing to say that people expect phone companies to occasionally provide information to law enforcement; it is quite another to suggest that our citizens expect all phone companies to operate what is effectively a joint intelligence-gathering operation with the Government. . . .

Third, the almost-Orwellian technology that enables the Government to store and analyze the phone metadata of every telephone user in the United States is unlike anything that could have been conceived in 1979. In *Smith,* the Supreme Court was actually considering whether local police could collect one person's phone records for calls made after the pen register was installed and for the limited purpose of a small-scale investigation of harassing phone calls. . . . The notion that the Government could collect similar data on hundreds of millions of people and retain that data for a five-year period, updating it with new data every day in perpetuity, was at best, in 1979, the stuff of science fiction. By comparison, the Government has at its disposal today the most advanced twenty-first century tools, allowing it to "store such records and efficiently mine them for information years into the future." . . . And these technologies are "cheap in comparison to conventional surveillance techniques and, by design, proceed[ ] surreptitiously," thereby "evad[ing] the ordinary checks that constrain abusive law enforcement practices: limited police . . . resources and community hostility." . . .

Finally, *and most importantly,* not only is the Government's ability to collect, store, and analyze phone data greater now than it was in 1979, but the nature and quantity of the information contained in people's telephony metadata is much greater, as well. According to the 1979 U.S. Census, in that year, 71,958,000 homes had telephones available, while 6,614,000 did not. . . . In December 2012, there were a whopping 326,475,248 mobile subscriber connections in the United States, of which approximately 304 million were for phones and twenty-two million were for computers, tablets, and modems. . . . The number of mobile subscribers in 2013 is more than *3,000 times* greater than the 91,600 subscriber connections in 1984, . . . and more than *triple* the 97,035,925 subscribers in June 2000. . . . It is now safe to assume that the vast majority of people reading this opinion have *at least* one cell phone within arm's reach (in addition to other mobile devices). . . . In fact, some undoubtedly will be reading this opinion *on their cellphones.* . . . Cell phones have also morphed into multi-purpose devices. They are now maps and music players. . . . They are cameras. . . . They are even lighters that people hold up at rock concerts. . . . They are ubiquitous as well. Count the phones at the bus stop, in a restaurant, or around the table at a work meeting or any given occasion. Thirty-four years ago, *none* of those phones would have been there. Thirty-four years ago, city streets were lined with pay phones. Thirty-four years ago, when people wanted to send "text messages," they wrote letters and attached postage stamps.

Admittedly, what metadata *is* has not changed over time. As in *Smith*, the *types* of information at issue in this case are relatively limited: phone numbers dialed, date, time, and the like. But the ubiquity of phones has dramatically altered the *quantity* of information that is now available and, *more importantly*, what that information can tell the Government about people's lives. . . . Put simply, people in 2013 have an entirely different relationship with phones than they did thirty-four years ago. As a result, people make calls and send text messages now that they would not (really, *could not*) have made or sent back when *Smith* was decided. . . . This rapid and monumental shift towards a cell phone-centric culture means that the metadata from each person's phone "reflects a wealth of detail about her familial, political, professional, religious, and sexual associations," . . . that could not have been gleaned from a data collection in 1979. . . . Records that once would have revealed a few scattered tiles of information about a person now reveal an entire mosaic—a vibrant and constantly updating picture of the person's life. . . . Whereas some may assume that these cultural changes will force people to "reconcile themselves" to an "inevitable" "diminution of privacy that new technology entails," . . . I think it is more likely that these trends have resulted in a *greater* expectation of privacy and a recognition that society views that expectation as reasonable.

In sum, the *Smith* pen register and the ongoing NSA Bulk Telephony Metadata Program have so many significant distinctions between them that I cannot possibly navigate these uncharted Fourth Amendment waters using as my North Star a case that predates the rise of cell phones. . . . As I said at the outset, the question before me is not whether *Smith* answers the question of whether people can have a reasonable expectation of privacy in telephony metadata under all circumstances. Rather, the question that I will ultimately have to answer when I reach the merits of this case someday is whether people have a reasonable expectation of privacy that is violated when the Government, without any basis whatsoever to suspect them of any wrongdoing, collects and stores for five years their telephony metadata for purposes of subjecting it to high-tech querying and analysis without any case-by-case judicial approval. For the many reasons set forth above, it is significantly likely that on that day, I will answer that question in plaintiffs' favor.

### ii. There Is a Significant Likelihood Plaintiffs Will Succeed in Showing that the Searches Are Unreasonable.

Having found that a search occurred in this case, I next must "examin[e] the totality of the circumstances to determine whether [the] search is reasonable within the meaning of the Fourth Amendment." . . .

The Supreme Court has recognized . . . [that] "'special needs, beyond the normal need for law enforcement, make the warrant and probable-cause requirement impracticable[]'." . . . "Even where the government claims 'special needs,'" as it does in this case, "a warrantless search is generally unreasonable unless based on 'some quantum of individualized suspicion.'" . . . Still, a suspicionless search may be reasonable "'where the privacy interests implicated by the search are minimal, and where an important governmental interest furthered by the intrusion would be placed in jeopardy by a requirement of individualized suspicion.'" . . . As such, my task is to "'balance the [plaintiffs'] privacy expectations against the government's interests to determine whether it is impractical to require a warrant or some level of individualized suspicion in the particular context.'" . . . The factors I must consider include: (1) "the nature of the privacy interest allegedly compromised" by the search, (2) "the character of the intrusion imposed" by the government, and (3) "the nature and immediacy of the government's concerns and the efficacy of the [search] in meeting them." . . .

"Special needs" cases . . . form something of a patchwork quilt. For example, schools and government employers are permitted under certain circumstances to test students and employees for drugs and alcohol, . . . and officers may search probationers and parolees to ensure compliance with the rules of supervision. . . . The doctrine has also been applied in cases involving efforts to prevent acts of terrorism in crowded transportation centers. . . . To my knowledge, however, no court has ever recognized a special need sufficient to justify continuous, daily searches of virtually every American citizen without any particularized suspicion. In effect, the Government urges me to be the first non-FISC judge to sanction such a dragnet.

For reasons I have already discussed at length, I find that plaintiffs have a very significant expectation of privacy in an aggregated collection of their telephony metadata covering the last five years, and the NSA's Bulk Telephony Metadata Program significantly intrudes on that expectation. Whether the program violates the Fourth Amendment will therefore turn on "the nature and immediacy of the government's concerns and the efficacy of the [search] in meeting them . . .".

The Government asserts that the Bulk Telephony Metadata Program serves the "programmatic purpose" of "identifying unknown terrorist operatives and preventing terrorist attacks"—an interest that everyone, including this Court, agrees is "of the highest order of magnitude[.]. .". A closer examination of the record, however, reveals that the Government's interest is a bit more nuanced—it is not merely to investigate potential terrorists, but rather, to do so *faster* than other investigative methods might allow. Indeed, the affidavits in support of the Government's brief repeatedly emphasize this interest in speed. For example, according to SID [Signals Intelligence Directorate] Director Shea, the primary advantage of the bulk metadata collection is that "it enables the Government to *quickly* analyze past connections and chains of communication," and "increases the NSA's ability to *rapidly* detect persons affiliated with the identified foreign terrorist organizations." . . . (emphasis added)[.]

Yet, . . . the Government does *not* cite a single instance in which analysis of the NSA's bulk metadata collection actually stopped an imminent attack, or otherwise aided the Government in achieving any objective that was time-sensitive in nature. In fact, none of the three "recent episodes" cited by the Government . . . involved any apparent urgency. . . . In the first example, the FBI learned of a terrorist plot still "in its early stages" and investigated that plot before turning to the metadata "to ensure that all potential connections were identified." . . . Assistant [FBI] Director Holley does not say that the metadata revealed any new information—much less time-sensitive information—that had not already come to light in the investigation up to that point. . . . In the second example, it appears that the metadata analysis was used only after the terrorist was arrested "to establish [his] foreign ties and put them in context with his U.S. based planning efforts." . . . And in the third, the metadata analysis "revealed a previously unknown number for [a] co-conspirator . . . and corroborated his connection to [the target of the investigation] as well as to other U.S.-based extremists." . . . Again, there is no indication that these revelations were immediately useful or that they prevented an impending attack. Assistant [FBI] Director Holley even concedes that bulk metadata analysis only "*sometimes* provides information earlier than the FBI's other investigative methods and techniques." . . . Given the . . . utter lack of evidence that a terrorist attack has ever been prevented because searching the NSA database was faster than other investigative tactics—I have serious doubts about the efficacy of the metadata collection program as a means of conducting time-sensitive investigations in cases involving imminent threats of terrorism. . . . Thus, plaintiffs have a substantial likelihood of showing that their privacy interests outweigh the Government's interest in collecting and analyzing bulk telephony metadata and therefore the NSA's bulk collection program is indeed an unreasonable search under the Fourth Amendment.

I realize, of course, that such a holding might appear to conflict with other trial courts . . . and with longstanding doctrine that courts have applied in other contexts. . . . Nevertheless, in reaching this decision, I find comfort in the statement in the Supreme Court's recent majority opinion in [*United States v.*] *Jones* [(2012)] that "[a]t bottom, we must 'assur[e] preservation of that degree of privacy against government that existed when the Fourth Amendment was adopted.'" . . . Indeed, as the Supreme Court noted more than a decade before *Smith,* "[t]he basic purpose of th[e Fourth] Amendment, as recognized in countless decisions of this Court, is to safeguard the privacy and security of individuals against *arbitrary invasions by governmental officials.*" . . . The Fourth

Amendment . . . is offended by "general warrants" and laws that allow searches to be conducted "indiscriminately and without regard to their connection with [a] crime under investigation." . . . I cannot imagine a more "indiscriminate" and "arbitrary invasion" than this systematic and high-tech collection and retention of personal data on virtually every single citizen for purposes of querying and analyzing it without prior judicial approval. Surely, such a program infringes on "that degree of privacy" that the Founders enshrined in the Fourth Amendment. Indeed, I have little doubt that the author of our Constitution, James Madison, who cautioned us to beware "the abridgement of freedom of the people by gradual and silent encroachments by those in power," would be aghast.

. . .

## CONCLUSION

This case is yet the latest chapter in the Judiciary's continuing challenge to balance the national security interests of the United States with the individual liberties of our citizens. The Government, in its understandable zeal to protect our homeland, has crafted a counterterrorism program with respect to telephone metadata that strikes the balance based in large part on a thirty-four year old Supreme Court precedent, the relevance of which has been eclipsed by technological advances and a cell phone-centric lifestyle heretofore inconceivable. In the months ahead, other Article III courts, no doubt, will wrestle to find the proper balance consistent with our constitutional system. But in the meantime, for all the above reasons, I will grant Larry Klayman's and Charles Strange's requests for an injunction and enter an order that (1) bars the Government from collecting, as part of the NSA's Bulk Telephony Metadata Program, any telephony metadata associated with their personal Verizon accounts and (2) requires the Government to destroy any such metadata in its possession that was collected through the bulk collection program.

However, in light of the significant national security interests at stake in this case and the novelty of the constitutional issues, I will stay my order pending appeal. . . .

*Klayman v. Obama*, U.S. District Court, District of Columbia, December 16, 2013 (citations in the text and footnotes omitted).

Source: *Klayman v. Obama*, 957 F.Supp.2d 1 (D.D.C. 2013), 29–44.

# 28

# *ACLU v. Clapper:* Upholding the Legality of the Telephone Metadata Program

Eleven days after Judge Leon issued his ruling in *Klayman v. Obama,* Judge William H. Pauley III handed down his decision in *ACLU v. Clapper,* rejecting the request of the ACLU and other plaintiffs for a preliminary injunction and granting the government's motion to dismiss the case. Like Judge Leon, Judge Pauley held that federal law precluded the claim that Section 215 of the USA PATRIOT Act did not support the telephone metadata program. Judge Pauley stated, however, that even if the claim were not precluded, it would fail on the merits, and he analyzed how Section 215 authorized the telephone metadata program. On constitutional questions, Judge Pauley held that the program did not violate the First or Fourth Amendments, but he expressed unease with the Foreign Intelligence Surveillance Court only hearing the government's arguments given the nature of the legal issues. The plaintiffs appealed Judge Pauley's decision. A different federal court similarly rejected another claim the telephone metadata program was unconstitutional in *Smith v. Obama* in June 2014, and this decision was likewise appealed. The appellate courts considering *ACLU v. Clapper* and *Smith v. Obama* heard oral arguments in early September and early December 2014 respectively, but, as of this writing, neither has rendered a decision. As the excerpts in the next document help illustrate, the conflicting opinions from Judge Pauley in *ACLU v. Clapper* and Judge Leon in *Klayman v. Obama* mirrored divisions in the American body politic created by Snowden's revelations.

★ ★ ★

. . .

B. *Merits of the Statutory Claims*

Even if the statutory claim were not precluded, it would fail. . . . Here, the ACLU fails to demonstrate a likelihood of success on the merits of their statutory claim.

1. *Does the Stored Communications Act Prohibit the Collection of Telephony Metadata Under Section 215?*

Section 215 was enacted at the same time as an amendment to the Stored Communications Act. As amended, the Stored Communications Act prohibits communications providers from "knowingly divulg[ing]" a subscriber's records to a government entity unless one of several exceptions are met. . . . The Government may also obtain telephony metadata with a national security letter ("NSL"). . . . An NSL does not require judicial approval. . . .

By contrast, section 215 allows the government an order "requiring the production of any tangible thing." . . . The only limitation—relevant here—on the types of records that may be obtained with a section 215 order are that they be obtainable with a grand jury subpoena. . . . Section 215 contains nothing suggesting that it is limited by the Stored Communications Act. Nevertheless, Plaintiffs argue that section 215 should be interpreted narrowly to avoid any conflict with the Stored Communications Act.

But this court must attempt to interpret a statute "as a symmetrical and coherent regulatory scheme, and fit, if possible, all parts into an harmonious whole" and is "guided to a degree by common sense." . . . Read in harmony, the Stored Communications Act does not limit the Government's ability to obtain information from communications providers under section 215 because section 215 orders are functionally equivalent to grand jury subpoenas. Section 215 authorizes the Government to seek records that may be obtained with a grand jury subpoena, such as telephony metadata under the Stored Communications Act.

That conclusion is bolstered by common sense: to allow the Government to obtain telephony metadata with an NSL but not a section 215 order would lead to an absurd result. Unlike an NSL, a section 215 order requires a FISC judge to find the Government has provided a "statement of facts showing that there are reasonable grounds to believe that the tangible things sought are relevant" to a foreign intelligence investigation. . . .

. . .

### 2. Did Congress Ratify The Government's Interpretation of Section 215?

. . .

The Government argues Congress was aware of the bulk metadata collection program and ratified it by reenacting section 215. Before Congress reauthorized FISA, no judicial opinion interpreting relevance was public, which was in line with Congress's design. Congress passed FISA to engraft judicial and congressional oversight onto Executive Branch activities that are most effective when kept secret. To conduct surveillance under section 215, the Executive must first seek judicial approval from the FISC. . . . Then, on a semi-annual basis, it must provide reports to the Permanent Select Committee on Intelligence of the House of Representatives, the Select Committee on Intelligence of the Senate, and the Committees on the Judiciary of the House of Representatives and the Senate. . . . Those Congressional reports must include: (1) a summary of significant legal interpretations of section 215 involving matters before the FISC; and (2) copies of all decisions, orders, or opinions of the FISC that include significant construction or interpretation of section 215. . . .

. . . There is no doubt that the Congressional Committees responsible for oversight of this program knew about the FISC opinions and the Executive Branch's interpretation of section 215. But what about the rest of Congress?

In 2010 and 2011, Congress reauthorized section 215 without making any changes. Prior to the 2010 reauthorization, the Executive Branch made available *to all members of Congress* a classified, five-page document discussing the bulk telephony metadata program.

. . .

That classified document, which was made available prior to the vote for reauthorization and has now been declassified in part, informed the reader that "[section 215] orders generally require production of the business records . . . relating to *substantially all of the telephone calls* handled by the [telecommunications] companies, including both calls made between the United States and a foreign country and calls made entirely within the United States." . . .

The following year, when section 215 was again scheduled to sunset, senators were informed of an updated classified document available for their review. . . . Apparently some Senators did review it, while other Members of Congress did not. The House Intelligence Committee did not make the document available to members of the House. Dozens of House members elected in 2010 therefore never had an opportunity to review the classified document. While this is problematic, the Executive Branch did what it was required to do under the statutory scheme that Congress put in place to keep Congress informed about foreign intelligence surveillance.

And viewing all the circumstances presented here in the national security context, this Court finds that Congress ratified section 215 as interpreted by the Executive Branch and the FISC, when it reauthorized FISA. In cases finding ratification, it is fair to presume that Congress had knowledge of the statute's interpretation. . . .

### 3. *Is Bulk Telephony Metadata Collection Permitted By Section 215?*

To obtain a section 215 order, the Government must show (1) "reasonable grounds to believe that the tangible things sought are relevant to an authorized investigation" and (2) that the item sought must be able to be "obtained with a subpoena . . . in aid of a grand jury investigation or with any other [court] order . . . directing the production of records or tangible things." . . . The Government can obtain telephony metadata with grand jury subpoenas and other court orders. . . .

A grand jury subpoena permits the Government to obtain tangible things unless "there is no reasonable possibility that the category of materials the Government seeks will produce information relevant to the general subject of the grand jury's investigation." . . . The ACLU argues that the category at issue—all telephony metadata—is too broad and contains too much irrelevant information. That argument has no traction here. Because without all the data points, the Government cannot be certain it connected the pertinent ones. As FISC Judge Eagan noted, the collection of virtually all telephony metadata is "necessary" to permit the NSA, not the FBI, to do the algorithmic data analysis that allow the NSA to determine "connections between known and unknown international terrorist operatives." . . . And it was the FISC that limited the NSA's production of telephony metadata to the FBI. While section 215 contemplates that tangible items will be produced to the FBI, FISC orders require that bulk telephony metadata be produced directly—and only—to the NSA. And the FISC forbids the NSA from disseminating any of that data until after the NSA has identified particular telephony metadata of suspected terrorists. Without those minimization procedures, FISC would not issue any section 215 orders for bulk telephony metadata collection. . . .

"Relevance" has a broad legal meaning. The Federal Rules of Civil Procedure allow parties to obtain discovery "regarding any nonprivileged matter that *is relevant* to any party's claim or defense." . . . This Rule "has been construed broadly to encompass any matter that bears on, or that reasonably could lead to other matter that could bear on, any issue that is or may be in the case." . . .

Tangible items are "relevant" under section 215 if they bear on or could reasonably lead to other matter that could bear on the investigation.

Under section 215, the Government's burden is not substantial. The Government need only provide "a statement of facts showing that there are *reasonable grounds to believe* that the tangible things sought are relevant." . . . Because section 215 orders flow from the Government's grand jury and administrative subpoena powers, . . . the Government's applications are subject to deferential review. . . .

The concept of relevance in the context of an investigation does not require the Government to parse out irrelevant documents at the start of its investigation. Rather, it allows that Government to get a category of materials if the category is relevant. The question of the permissible scope is generally "variable in relation to the nature, purposes and scope of the inquiry." . . . Defining the reasonableness of a subpoena based on the volume of information to be produced would require the Government to determine wrongdoing before issuing a subpoena—but that determination is the primary purpose for a subpoena. . . . And in the context of a counterterrorism investigation, that after-the-attack determination would be too late.

Here, there is no way for the Government to know which particle of telephony metadata will lead to useful counterterrorism information. When that is the case, courts routinely authorize large-scale collections of information, even if most of it will not directly bear on the investigation. . . .

Any individual call record alone is unlikely to lead to matter that may pertain to a terrorism investigation. Approximately 300 seeds were queried in 2012 and only a "very small percentage of the total volume of metadata records" were responsive to those queries. . . . But aggregated telephony metadata is relevant because it allows the querying technique to be comprehensive. And NSA's warehousing of that data allows a query to be instantaneous. This new ability to query aggregated telephony metadata significantly increases the NSA's capability to detect the faintest patterns left behind by individuals affiliated with foreign terrorist organizations. . . . Armed with all the metadata, NSA can draw connections it might otherwise never be able to find.

The collection is broad, but the scope of counterterrorism investigations is unprecedented. National security investigations are fundamentally different from criminal investigations. They are prospective—focused on preventing attacks—as opposed to the retrospective investigation of crimes. National security investigations span "long periods of time and multiple geographic regions." . . . Congress was clearly aware of the need for breadth and provided the Government with the tools to interdict terrorist threats.

. . .

## III. *Constitutional Claims*

...

### A. *Fourth Amendment*

...

In *Smith v. Maryland* [1979], ... the Supreme Court held individuals have no "legitimate expectation of privacy" regarding the telephone numbers they dial because they knowingly give that information to telephone companies when they dial a number.... *Smith's* bedrock holding is that an individual has no legitimate expectation of privacy in information provided to third parties.

...

The privacy concerns at stake in *Smith* were far more individualized than those raised by the ACLU. *Smith* involved the investigation of a single crime and the collection of telephone call detail records collected by the telephone company at its central office, examined by the police, and related to the target of their investigation, a person identified previously by law enforcement.... Nevertheless, the Supreme Court found there was no legitimate privacy expectation because "[t]elephone users ... typically know that they must convey numerical information to the telephone company; that the telephone company has facilities for recording this information; and that the telephone company does in fact record this information for a variety of legitimate business purposes." ...

The ACLU argues that analysis of bulk telephony metadata allows the creation of a rich mosaic: it can "reveal a person's religion, political associations, use of a telephone-sex hotline, contemplation of suicide, addiction to gambling or drugs, experience with rape, grappling with sexuality, or support for particular political causes." ... But that is at least three inflections from the Government's bulk telephony metadata collection. First, without additional legal justification—subject to rigorous minimization procedures—the NSA cannot even query the telephony metadata database. Second, when it makes a query, it only learns the telephony metadata of the telephone numbers within three "hops" of the "seed." Third, without resort to additional techniques, the Government does not know who any of the telephone numbers belong to. In other words, all the Government sees is that telephone number A called telephone number B. It does not know who subscribes to telephone numbers A or B. Further, the Government repudiates any notion that it conducts the type of data mining the ACLU warns about in its parade of horribles.

The ACLU also argues that "[t]here are a number of ways in which the Government could perform three-hop analysis without first building its own database of every American's call records." ... That has no traction. At bottom, it is little more than an assertion that less intrusive means to collect and analyze telephony metadata could be employed. But, the Supreme Court has "repeatedly refused to declare that only the 'least intrusive' search practicable can be reasonable under the Fourth Amendment." . . .

The ACLU's pleading reveals a fundamental misapprehension about ownership of telephony metadata. In its motion for a preliminary injunction, the ACLU seeks to: (1) bar the Government from collecting "Plaintiffs' call records" under the bulk telephony metadata collection program; (2) quarantine "all of Plaintiffs' call records" already collected under the bulk telephony metadata collection program; and (3) prohibit the Government from querying metadata obtained through the bulk telephony metadata collection program using any phone number or other identifier associated with Plaintiffs. . . .

First, the business records created by Verizon are not "Plaintiffs' call records." Those records are created and maintained by the telecommunications provider, not the ACLU. Under the Constitution, that distinction is critical because when a person voluntarily conveys information to a third party, he forfeits his right to privacy in the information. . . . Second, the Government's subsequent querying of the telephony metadata does not implicate the Fourth Amendment—anymore than a law enforcement officer's query of the FBI's fingerprint or DNA databases to identify someone. . . . In the context of DNA querying, any match is of the DNA profile—and like telephony metadata additional investigative steps are required to link that DNA profile to an individual.

The collection of breathtaking amounts of information unprotected by the Fourth Amendment does not transform that sweep into a Fourth Amendment search. . . .

The ACLU's reliance on the concurring opinions in *Jones* is misplaced. In *Jones,* the police attached a GPS [Global Positioning System] tracking device to the undercarriage of a vehicle without a warrant and tracked the vehicle's location for the next four weeks. . . . The majority held that a "search" occurred because by placing the GPS device on the vehicle, "[t]he Government physically occupied private property for the purpose of obtaining information. . . . [S]uch a physical intrusion would have been considered a 'search' within the meaning of the Fourth Amendment when it was adopted." . . . In two separate concurring opinions, five justices appeared to be grappling with how the Fourth Amendment applies to technological advances. . . .

But the Supreme Court did not overrule *Smith*. And the Supreme Court has instructed lower courts not to predict whether it would overrule a precedent even if its reasoning has been supplanted by later cases. . . . Clear precedent applies because *Smith* held that a subscriber has no legitimate expectation of privacy in telephony metadata created by third parties. . . . Inferior courts are bound by that precedent.

Some ponder the ubiquity of cellular telephones and how subscribers' relationships with their telephones have evolved since *Smith*. While people may "have an entirely different relationship with telephones than they did thirty-four years ago," *Klayman* [2013], . . . this Court observes that their relationship with their telecommunications providers has not changed and is just as frustrating. Telephones have far more versatility now than when *Smith* was decided, but this case only concerns their use as telephones. The fact that there are more calls placed does not undermine the Supreme Court's finding that a person has no subjective expectation of privacy in telephony metadata. . . . Because *Smith* controls, the NSA's bulk telephony metadata collection program does not violate the Fourth Amendment.

## B. *First Amendment*

. . . Pervasive Government surveillance implicates not only the Fourth Amendment but also the First Amendment . . . [.]
. . .

The ACLU alleges that "[t]he fact that the government is collecting this information is likely to have a chilling effect on people who would otherwise contact Plaintiffs." . . . Significant impairments of first amendment rights "must withstand exacting scrutiny." . . . The Government contends, however, that "surveillance consistent with Fourth Amendment protections . . . does not violate First Amendment rights, even though it may be directed at communicative or associative activities." . . .

The Government's argument is well-supported. . . .

Here, it is unnecessary to decide whether there could be a First Amendment violation in the absence of a Fourth Amendment violation because . . . the bulk metadata collection does not burden First Amendment rights substantially. . . . There must be "a direct and substantial" or "significant" burden on associational rights in order for it to qualify as "substantial." . . . "Mere incidental burdens on the right to associate do not violate the First Amendment." . . .

Any alleged chilling effect here arises from the ACLU's speculative fear that the Government will review telephony metadata related to the ACLU's telephone calls. For telephony metadata to be "used to identify those who contact Plaintiffs for legal assistance or to report human-rights or civil-liberties violations," . . . it must actually be reviewed and the identities of the telephone subscribers determined. Fear that telephony metadata relating to the ACLU will be queried or reviewed or further investigated "relies on a highly attenuated chain of possibilities." . . . "[S]uch a fear is insufficient to create standing[.]" . . . Neither can it establish a violation of an individual's First Amendment rights.

## IV. *Remaining Preliminary Injunction Considerations*

For the reasons above, the ACLU has failed to state a claim and its case must be dismissed. But even if it could show a likelihood of success on the merits, a preliminary injunction would be inappropriate. . . .

Here, the balance of the equities and the public interest tilt firmly in favor of the Government's position. "Everyone agrees that the Government's interest in combating terrorism is an urgent objective of the highest order." . . .

The Constitution vests the President with Executive Power. . . . That power reaches its zenith when wielded to protect national security. . . . And courts must pay proper deference to the Executive in assessing the threats that face the nation. . . . Any injunction dismantling the section 215 telephony metadata collection program "would cause an increased risk to national security and the safety of the American public." . . . The "unique capabilities" of the telephony metadata collection program "could not be completely replicated by other means." . . .

The effectiveness of bulk telephony metadata collection cannot be seriously disputed. Offering examples is a dangerous stratagem for the Government because it discloses means and methods of intelligence gathering. Such disclosures can only educate America's enemies. Nevertheless, the Government has acknowledged several successes in Congressional testimony and in declarations that are part of the record in this case. In this Court's view, they offer ample justification:

- In September 2009, NSA discovered that an al-Qaeda-associated terrorist in Pakistan was in contact with an unknown person in the United States about efforts to perfect a recipe for explosives. NSA immediately notified the FBI, which investigated and identified the al-Qaeda contact as Colorado-based Najibullah Zazi. The NSA and FBI worked together to identify other terrorist links. The FBI executed search warrants and found bomb-making components in backpacks. Zazi confessed to conspiring to bomb the New York subway system. Through a section 215 order, NSA was able to provide a previously unknown number of one of the co-conspirators—Adis Medunjanin.
- In January 2009, while monitoring an extremist in Yemen with ties to al-Qaeda, the NSA discovered a connection with Khalid Oazzani in Kansas City. NSA immediately notified the FBI, which discovered a nascent plot to attack the New York Stock Exchange. Using a section 215 order, NSA queried telephony metadata to identify potential connections. Three defendants were convicted of terrorism offenses.
- In October 2009, while monitoring an al-Qaeda affiliated terrorist, the NSA discovered that David Headley was working on a plot to bomb a Danish newspaper office that had published cartoons depicting the

Prophet Mohammed. He later confessed to personally conducting surveillance of the Danish newspaper office. He was also charged with supporting terrorism based on his involvement in the planning and reconnaissance for the 2008 hotel attack in Mumbai. Information obtained through section 215 orders was utilized in tandem with the FBI to establish Headley's foreign ties and put them in context with U.S. based planning efforts.

. . .

Of course, the considerations weighing in favor of the ACLU's position are far from trivial. . . . Just as the Constitution gives the Executive the duty to protect the nation, citizens' right to privacy is enshrined in the Bill of Rights.

Fifteen different FISC judges have found the metadata collection program lawful a total of thirty-five times since May 2006. . . . The Government argues that "Plaintiffs are asking this Court to conclude that the FISC exceeded its authority when it authorized the NSA's bulk collection of telephony metadata, and that this Court (without the benefit of the classified applications and information available to the FISC) should substitute its judgment for the decisions that the FISC reached [35] times." . . .

This Court is bound only by the decisions of the Second Circuit and the Supreme Court. The decisions of other district courts are often persuasive authority. The two declassified FISC decisions authorizing bulk metadata collection do not discuss several of the ACLU's arguments. They were issued on the basis of *ex parte* applications by the Government without the benefit of the excellent briefing submitted to this Court by the Government, the ACLU, and *amici curiae.*

There is no question that judges operate best in an adversarial system. . . . At its inception, FISC judges were called on to review warrant applications, a familiar role and one well-suited for a judge to protect the rights of an individual in his absence. The FISC's role has expanded greatly since its creation in 1978.

As FISA has evolved and Congress has loosened its individual suspicion requirements, the FISC has been tasked with delineating the limits of the Government's surveillance power, issuing secret decisions without the benefit of the adversarial process. Its *ex parte* procedures are necessary to retain secrecy but are not ideal for interpreting statutes. This case shows how FISC decisions may affect every American—and perhaps, their interests should have a voice in the FISC.

## CONCLUSION

The right to be free from searches and seizures is fundamental, but not absolute. . . . Whether the Fourth Amendment protects bulk telephony metadata is ultimately a question of reasonableness. . . . Every day, people voluntarily surrender personal and seemingly-private information to transnational corporations, which exploit that data for profit. Few think twice about it, even though it is far more intrusive than bulk telephony metadata collection.

There is no evidence that the Government has used any of the bulk telephony metadata it collected for any purpose other than investigating and disrupting terrorist attacks. While there have been unintentional violations of guidelines, those appear to stem from human error and the incredibly complex computer programs that support this vital tool. And once detected, those violations were self-reported and stopped. The bulk telephony metadata collection program is subject to executive and congressional oversight, as well as continual monitoring by a dedicated group of judges who serve on the Foreign Intelligence Surveillance Court.

No doubt, the bulk telephony metadata collection program vacuums up information about virtually every telephone call to, from, or within the United States. That is by design, as it allows the NSA to detect relationships so attenuated and ephemeral they would otherwise escape notice. As the September 11th attacks demonstrate, the cost of missing such a thread can be horrific. Technology allowed al-Qaeda to operate decentralized and plot international terrorist attacks remotely. The bulk telephony metadata collection program represents the Government's counter-punch: connecting fragmented and fleeting communications to re-construct and eliminate al-Qaeda's terror network.

"Liberty and security can be reconciled; and in our system they are reconciled within the framework of the law." . . . The success of one helps protect the other. Like the 9/11 Commission observed: The choice between liberty and security is a false one, as nothing is more apt to imperil civil liberties than the success of a terrorist attack on American soil. . . . A court's solemn duty is "to reject as false, claims in the name of civil liberty which, if granted, would paralyze or impair authority to defend [the] existence of our society, and to reject as false, claims in the name of security which would undermine our freedoms and open the way to oppression." . . .

For all of these reasons, the NSA's bulk telephony metadata collection program is lawful. Accordingly, the Government's motion to dismiss the complaint is granted and the ACLU's motion for a preliminary injunction is denied. . . .

*ACLU v. Clapper,* U.S. District Court, Southern District of New York, December 27, 2013 (citations in the text and footnotes omitted).

Source: *ACLU v. Clapper,* 959 F.Supp.2d 724 (S.D.N.Y. 2013), 742–758.

# 29

# *United States v. Mohamud:* Upholding the Legality of Section 702 of FISA

This decision from a U.S. district court analyzed Section 702 of FISA—a key legal provision at the heart of controversies Snowden caused. Mohamed Mohamud, a U.S. citizen, was convicted in January 2013 for trying to set off a car bomb in Portland. Before sentencing, the U.S. government informed the court that it used information gathered under Section 702 as evidence in the trial. Surveillance under Section 702 against a foreign target had incidentally collected communications Mohamud made. Prosecutors had not disclosed this fact to Mohamud, who then challenged Section 702's constitutionality by arguing that it violated the separation of powers doctrine and the First and Fourth Amendments. These claims connected to controversies about Section 702's constitutionality in relation to the incidental collection of Americans' communications that arose before Snowden began his disclosures. In this case, Judge Garr King ruled that Section 702 is constitutional.

★  ★  ★

### III. *Alternative Motion for Suppression of Evidence and a New Trial Based on the Government's Introduction of Evidence at Trial and Other Uses of Information Derived from Unlawful Electronic Surveillance*

. . .

### B. *Separation of Powers*

As a threshold issue, defendant claims §702 violates the separation of powers doctrine. The Fourth Amendment inserts a neutral and detached magistrate between the subject of the search and the government. Defendant claims §702 procedures reduce the role of the judge to consulting with the Executive Branch with no case or controversy involving an adversary. He contends the FISC does not approve or disapprove proposals for §702 surveillance but instead has a role in designing them. Defendant characterizes the FISC's role as providing a non judicial advisory opinion, and he argues this violates the fundamental separation of powers function of the [Fourth Amendment's] Warrant Clause.

The government disagrees and analogizes the FISC role to numerous judicial functions not directly connected to adversarial proceedings.

. . .

The Supreme Court has approved numerous congressional delegations of power which did not upset the balance of power established in the Constitution:

> The nondelegation doctrine is rooted in the principle of separation of powers that underlies our tripartite system of Government. . . . We . . . have recognized . . . that the separation-of-powers principle, and the nondelegation doctrine in particular, do not prevent Congress from obtaining the assistance of its coordinate Branches. . . . So long as Congress "shall lay down by legislative act an intelligible principle to which the person or body authorized to [exercise the delegated authority] is directed to conform, such legislative action is not a forbidden delegation of legislative power." . . .

. . .

The statutory scheme Congress specified for §702 surveillance is sufficient to serve as the intelligible principle to which FISC judges must conform in reviewing applications. In particular, the FISC review must insure the surveillance will be conducted in a manner consistent with the Fourth Amendment. . . . The judiciary certainly is well-prepared to fulfill that function. Furthermore, determining if a statute is constitutional is not a prohibited executive or administrative duty which would violate the separation of powers doctrine. . . .

Indeed, as the government points out, the judiciary also issues search warrants and reviews wiretap applications, both of which are ex parte proceedings. . . . I am not persuaded the review of §702 surveillance applications interferes with the prerogatives of another branch of government beyond requiring the executive branch to conform to the statute. Review of §702 surveillance applications is as central to the mission of the judiciary as the review of search warrants and wiretap applications.

Moreover, I disagree with defendant's argument that the FISC judges only provide advisory opinions. The FISC judge reviews the certification, targeting procedures, and minimization procedures included in a §702 surveillance application and either approves the acquisition or orders the government to choose between correcting deficiencies within 30 days and ceasing or not beginning the acquisition. . . . Similarly, electronic communication service providers must follow directives to acquire communications or challenge the directive before the FISC; the opinions are not advisory. . . .

Although I am not a FISC judge, I disagree with defendant's argument that the FISC judges assist in designing §702 procedures. FISC opinions now declassified inform us that the court meets with senior officials at the Department of Justice to discuss information provided in the submissions. . . . The technology underlying the surveillance is so extremely complex there is likely little possibility of understanding it without question sessions like this. If the FISC disapproves a government submission, it explains why. The government can then make changes addressing the problems and resubmit the submission. This is the normal way courts operate—justice is not served if the court does not explain its decisions.

Finally, "[p]rior review by a neutral and detached magistrate is the time-tested means of effectuating Fourth Amendment rights." . . . Although the FISC is not reviewing a warrant application under §702, the FISC review of §702 surveillance submissions provides prior review by a neutral and detached magistrate. This strengthens, not undermines, Fourth Amendment rights.

Accordingly, I conclude §702 does not violate the separation of powers doctrine.

## C. Constitutionality of Section 702 under the First Amendment

Defendant contends the breadth and vagueness of §702 surveillance chill Americans' exercise of their First Amendment rights, causing many to change their habits in using the Internet and telephones. Defendant claims this chill is sufficient to create a First Amendment violation, invalidating §702.

The government responds that First Amendment interests in a criminal investigation are protected by the Fourth Amendment, and motions to suppress based on alleged First Amendment violations are analyzed under the Fourth Amendment and the exclusionary rule.

Defendant raises a significant point: "Where the materials sought to be seized may be protected by the First Amendment, the requirements of the Fourth Amendment must be applied with scrupulous exactitude." . . .

But the appropriate analysis is under the Fourth Amendment, not the First Amendment. . . .

. . .

### D. *Constitutionality of Section 702 under the Fourth Amendment*

. . .

The parties agree on one thing: The Fourth Amendment does not "apply to activities of the United States directed against aliens in foreign territory." . . . Section 702 is aimed at acquiring communications of non-U.S. persons outside the United States, and thus [who are] not entitled to Fourth Amendment protection. The dispute arises because communications of U.S. persons located in the United States can be incidentally acquired.

The government claims the §702 acquisition targeting non-U.S. persons outside the United States is constitutional because: (1) the incidental collection of communications of U.S. persons does not trigger the warrant requirement; (2) surveillance authorized under §702 falls within the foreign intelligence exception to the warrant requirement; and (3) surveillance authorized under §702 is a reasonable search under the Fourth Amendment.

Defendant strongly disagrees:

> [R]egardless of the nominal targeting of foreign persons abroad, the §702 programs routinely acquire huge numbers of American communications in America . . . [which] implicate[ ] the Fourth Amendment. This case is a test of fundamental American liberties: the Court should reject the claim that, simply because foreign persons are being targeted, Americans lose their rights as collateral damage.

. . .

### 1. *Warrant Requirement*

Defendant, a U.S. citizen, was not targeted under §702, but his communications were collected incidentally during intelligence collection targeted at one or more non-U.S. persons outside the United States.

The government contends the warrant requirement is not triggered by the incidental collection of non-targeted U.S. person communications during the lawful collection of communications of targeted non-U.S. persons located outside the United States. According to the government, the privacy interests of the U.S. persons are protected by the required minimization procedures. Application of a warrant requirement in this situation would be impracticable and inconsistent with decades of foreign-intelligence collection practice. The government notes that before starting surveillance of a foreign target, the government cannot know the identities of all people with whom the target will communicate, and there is always a possibility the target will communicate with a U.S. person. Thus, the government claims imposing a warrant requirement for any incidental interception of U.S. person communications would effectively require a warrant for all foreign intelligence collection, even though the foreign targets lack Fourth Amendment rights and their communications often involve only other foreigners. . . .

Defendant argues §702 violates the Fourth Amendment because it permits the "widespread capture, retention, and later querying, dissemination, and use of the communications of American citizens" without the protection afforded by a warrant. . . . Defendant notes the FISC's statement that the NSA acquires more than 250 million Internet communications each year under §702, including acquisitions from upstream and from Internet service providers. . . . Defendant speculates that a significant number of those acquisitions would be communications with U.S. persons located in the United States and thus implicate their Fourth Amendment rights sufficiently that the court should apply a warrant requirement.

. . .

. . . The §702 acquisition targeting a non-U.S. person overseas is constitutionally permissible, so, under the general rule, the incidental collection of defendant's communications with the extraterritorial target would be lawful. The one distinguishing factor is the possible vast number of incidental communications collected under §702. I stress the word "possible." It is equally likely that §702 surveillance of a non-U.S. person located outside the United States would acquire no incidental communications with a U.S. person. Consequently, I am unpersuaded incidental communications collected under §702 differ sufficiently from previous foreign intelligence gathering to distinguish prior case law, and I hold that §702 surveillance does not trigger the Warrant Clause.

Alternatively, as I explain in the next section, even if §702 surveillance triggers the Warrant Clause, no warrant is required because §702 surveillance falls within the foreign intelligence exception to the warrant requirement.

## 2. *Foreign Intelligence Exception*

Assuming the incidental collection of U.S.-person communications under §702 is subject to the same constitutional scrutiny as foreign intelligence collection targeting U.S. persons, the government contends the Fourth Amendment does not require a warrant for §702 surveillance because it falls within the foreign intelligence exception.

The Fourth Amendment's warrant requirement applies to domestic national security surveillance. . . . Defendant argues that even if there is a foreign national security exception to the Warrant Clause, the exception's scope is far narrower than the massive surveillance programs under §702. . . . Defendant is alarmed that the statutory definition of foreign intelligence information . . . includes information unrelated to any danger to the country. He also argues that even if the special needs doctrine covers the acquisition of the information, it should not also cover the retention and later querying of the information.

The government disagrees, arguing the special needs exceptions to the Warrant Clause include a foreign intelligence exception. The government cites numerous cases to support its argument and notes that . . . the cases involved the collection of foreign intelligence information from persons *inside* the United States. Because §702 targets non[-]U.S. persons reasonably believed to be *outside* the United States, the government contends the analysis in its cases applies even more strongly. . . .

. . .

Notably, the FISA Court of Review applied a foreign intelligence exception "when surveillance is conducted to obtain foreign intelligence for national security purposes and is directed against foreign powers or agents of foreign powers reasonably believed to be located outside the United States." . . . The court reasoned: (1) the purpose of the surveillance went well beyond any "garden-variety" law enforcement objective and involved the acquisition from overseas foreign agents of foreign intelligence to help protect national security; (2) the government's interest was "particularly intense"; and (3) there was a "high degree of probability that requiring a warrant would hinder the government's ability to collect time sensitive information and, thus, would impede the vital national security interests that are at stake." . . .

Precisely on point with the case before me, the FISC held that the foreign intelligence exception also applies to §702 surveillance, even though the court's understanding of the technical situation underlying the surveillance changed after the government released more information[.]

. . .

None of defendant's arguments persuade me to stray from the FISC's holding. . . . There is no reasonable argument the government's need for the acquisitions is merely routine law enforcement. The government's need for speed and stealth have not lessened since the FISC . . . found that application of the warrant requirement would be impracticable. When I balance the intrusion on the individual's interest in privacy, namely the incidental collection of U.S. persons' communications, against these special needs when the government targets a non-U.S. person believed to be outside the United States, I conclude the foreign intelligence exception applies and no warrant is required.

. . .

### 3. *Reasonableness*

Application of the foreign intelligence exception does not end the analysis: "even though the foreign intelligence exception applies in a given case, governmental action intruding on individual privacy interests must comport with the Fourth Amendment's reasonableness requirement." . . .

To analyze whether a government search is reasonable under the Fourth Amendment, the court examines the totality of the circumstances. . . . The court weighs "the promotion of legitimate governmental interests against the degree to which [the search] intrudes upon an individual's privacy." . . .

### a. *General Contentions*

Defendant claims §702 is presumptively unreasonable because it does not require a warrant, even though the acquired telephone calls and emails are within the core zone of privacy protected from government intrusion. . . .

Defendant claims the Warrant Clause is the key metric in determining reasonableness. He disputes that the programmatic authorizations and certifications from the FISC . . . offer the protections traditional warrants afford. . . .

Because §702 lacks these protections, defendant contends its use is either presumptively unreasonable or, alternatively, the extreme disconnect between §702 procedures and basic Fourth Amendment warrant protections shows the unreasonableness of searches and seizures under §702. Even though the FISC approves general programs and procedures under §702, defendant argues the FISC does not review the government's specific targeting decisions or its later access of seized communications. Defendant contends the government should not be allowed to read the contents of American citizens' electronic communications without a judicial finding of probable cause. Further, defendant argues the government interest in acquiring "foreign intelligence information" is unreasonable under the Fourth Amendment because the term is so broadly defined . . . , it goes well beyond threats to national security.

According to the government, surveillance under §702 satisfies the Fourth Amendment's general reasonableness test. It claims the significant interest in national security, in light of FISA's statutory safeguards, outweigh the privacy interests of U.S. persons whose communications are incidentally acquired. The government suggests U.S. persons have limited expectations of privacy in electronic communications with non-U.S. persons outside the United States.

. . .

## b. *Comparison of Section 702 to Protections Afforded by a Warrant*

I will first address defendant's arguments comparing the protections provided by a warrant to those provided under §702.
. . .

In specifically addressing arguments about prior judicial review, probable cause, and particularity, the FISA Court of Review refused to "reincorporate into the foreign intelligence exception the same warrant requirements that we already have held inapplicable." . . . The court explained, "the more a set of procedures resembles those associated with the traditional warrant requirements, the more easily it can be determined that those procedures are within constitutional bounds." . . . With this guidance in mind, I turn to the arguments.

Without the protections of the particularity requirement, defendant contends the communications of American citizens are swept up by §702 surveillance in a dragnet fashion prohibited by the Fourth Amendment. Defendant also contrasts the Warrant Clause's requirement of a supporting affidavit under oath with the §702 procedures for authorization. Defendant is concerned the §702 procedures fall far short of the oath or affirmation provision of the Warrant Clause, particularly because the certification does not deal with particular persons or events.

The government notes the Attorney General and DNI must certify that targeting and minimization procedures are in place which are consistent with the Fourth Amendment and that a significant purpose of the acquisition is to obtain foreign intelligence information. The government contends the certification requirement represents an important internal check on the actions of the Executive Branch . . . [and] argues the targeting procedures determine that "the user of the facility to be tasked for collection is a non-United States person reasonably believed to be located outside the United States." . . .

The lack of an oath requirement in §702, as well as any argument the government will not follow the law, is unpersuasive. Absent evidence of fraud or misconduct, a presumption of regularity attaches to obtaining a warrant. . . . I have seen no evidence of government fraud or misconduct in this case. . . .

Turning to the particularity requirement, §702 surveillance uses targeting and minimization procedures approved by the FISC. . . . Section 702 limits surveillance only to non-U.S. persons reasonably believed to be located outside the United States. . . . A significant purpose of the acquisition must be to obtain foreign intelligence information. . . .

The FISA Court of Review concluded . . . pre-surveillance procedures were sufficient to satisfy Fourth Amendment concerns. . . . Executive Order 12333 included a requirement that surveillance targeting U.S. persons reasonably

believed to be outside the United States had to be based on a finding by the
Attorney General of probable cause to believe the target was a foreign power
or agent of a foreign power. . . . Section 702, however, prohibits targeting a
U.S. person under any circumstances, even if the person is located outside the
United States and acting as a foreign power or agent of a foreign power. Consequently, I conclude this difference does not diminish the particularity to the
point of making the collections unreasonable under the Fourth Amendment.
. . .

In sum, I do not find the lack of procedures associated with warrants make
§702 searches unreasonable under the Fourth Amendment.

### c. *Balancing the Governmental Interests Against the Intrusion on Privacy*

I will now turn to balancing the legitimate governmental interests against
the intrusion on an individual's privacy.

It is undisputed the government's interest in protecting the national security is compelling. . . .

Defendant points to the statutory definition of foreign intelligence information to argue the government interest is too broadly defined, and thus intrudes
on individual privacy too much, to justify the mass acquisition of Americans'
electronic communications. The statute states:

(e) "Foreign intelligence information" means—
. . .
(?) information with respect to a foreign power or foreign territory that
relates to, and if concerning a United States person is necessary to—
    (A) the national defense or the security of the United States; or
    (B) the conduct of the foreign affairs of the United States.

. . .

. . . Defendant is concerned the government could interpret the "conduct of
the foreign affairs of the United States" broadly enough to cover such items as
international trade, rather than just threats to national security.

I note the discovery in this case all concerned protecting the country from
a terrorist threat and did not stray into the broader category of the conduct of
foreign affairs. . . .

Under §702, the intrusion of an individual's privacy is due to the incidental
collection of the individual's communications during the acquisition of the
communications from a targeted non-U.S. person reasonably believed to be
outside the United States. The government contends U.S. persons have limited

expectations of privacy when communicating electronically with non-U.S. persons outside the United States. The government reasons the U.S. person assumes the risk that the foreign recipient will give the information to others, leave it freely accessible to others, or that the U.S. or foreign government will obtain the information.

The Fourth Amendment does not prohibit the government from obtaining information a person revealed to a third party, even if revealed in confidence. . . . This concept also applies to electronic communications. . . .

Defendant offers the government cannot seize these communications without the consent of the recipient, which is an argument in favor of only the recipient's expectation of privacy in the communication. The sender's expectation of privacy has still been diminished.

Defendant also claims the minimization procedures for §702 surveillance . . . provide no meaningful protection because the exclusions from the minimization procedures swallow the rule. As a result, the illusory minimization procedures make §702 search and seizures unreasonable under the Fourth Amendment.

As I explain next, I conclude the minimization procedures contribute to the reasonableness of §702 under the Fourth Amendment.

The government refers to a recently declassified document to support the reasonableness of §702 minimization procedures. The government also notes the FISC has repeatedly found materially equivalent minimization procedures sufficient in the context of traditional FISA electronic surveillance and physical search. Because these searches target U.S. persons in the United States, they are more likely to capture communications of non-targeted U.S. persons than the foreign communications captured under §702. The government additionally relies on the . . . oversight provisions requiring regular reports to the FISC and congressional oversight committees on the implementation of minimization procedures and the FISC's Rule of Procedure . . . which requires the government to report all instances of non-compliance.

The FISC has concluded the §702 minimization procedures are consistent with the Fourth Amendment. . . .

Section 6 of the declassified minimization procedures discusses the retention and dissemination of foreign communications of or concerning United States persons, putting limits on both. For example, the identity of the United States person is deleted in any dissemination of the information unless certain requirements are met. I do not agree with defendant that the minimization procedures provide no meaningful protection. On the contrary, I agree with the FISC that the minimization procedures contribute to the reasonableness of §702 under the Fourth Amendment.

## d. *Querying After Acquisition*

I now turn to defendant's most persuasive argument. He argues that even if §702 warrantless surveillance is lawful, subsequent querying of the information after acquisition is a search requiring a warrant under the Fourth Amendment. . . .

The government strongly disagrees. It distinguishes defendant's cases as analyzing government action beyond the scope of the warrant (or warrant exception). I agree with this characterization. . . .

Unfortunately, I do not find much assistance in most of the government's analogies . . . . Law enforcement computer queries of license plates and driver's licenses take place in a highly regulated arena and, in the case of license plates, are based on information displayed for all to see. . . . DNA profiles retained in a database to allow later law enforcement searches are from people who have been arrested or convicted. . . . Neither of these limited invasions of privacy can be compared to the incidental acquisition of communications of U.S. persons.

The government also draws an analogy to minimization procedures under the Federal Wiretap Act which allow the government to use evidence from a wiretap to prove a crime unrelated to the original purpose for the wiretap. This analogy is more helpful because it addresses the use of communications obtained incidentally to those acquired by the wiretap. . . .

Because the government complied with all §702 procedures concerning targeting and minimization, the government contends its actions were within the scope of the relevant legal authority and are thus distinguishable from defendant's cases. In its view, subsequent queries of information lawfully obtained, which do not implicate any reasonable expectation of privacy beyond that implicated in the initial lawful collection, do not constitute separate searches under the Fourth Amendment. The government claims this is true even if U.S. person identifiers are used in the querying.

The government notes the minimization procedures compel it to review information lawfully collected under §702, which includes information about U.S. persons, to determine if the information should be retained or disseminated. . . .

In the government's view, it must conduct such queries to fulfill its compelling interest to detect and disrupt terrorist attacks by discovering potential links between foreign terrorist groups and people within the United States.

It is true, the FISC has approved minimization procedures which allow querying using U.S. person identifiers. . . . While the procedures previously imposed a "wholesale bar" on such queries, the new approved procedures allowed queries with U.S. person identifiers "subject to approval pursuant to internal NSA procedures and oversight by the Department of Justice." . . . The FISC reasoned it had approved FISA Title I applications targeting U.S. persons that used minimization procedures allowing queries with U.S. person identifiers.

. . .

This is a very close question. On the one hand, why not require a warrant when using a U.S. person identifier to search a database of information already gathered? That is not the test, however. Just because a practice might better protect Americans' privacy rights does not mean the Fourth Amendment requires the practice. Indeed, as the government argues, it must review information lawfully collected to decide whether to retain or disseminate it under the minimization procedures. . . . I do not find any significant additional intrusion past what must be done to apply minimization procedures. Thus, subsequent querying of a §702 collection, even if U.S. person identifiers are used, is not a separate search and does not make §702 surveillance unreasonable under the Fourth Amendment.

**e. *Summary***

. . .

Based on the statutory protections, I conclude the government's compelling interest in protecting national security outweighs the intrusion of §702 surveillance on an individual's privacy. Accordingly, §702, as applied to defendant, is reasonable under the Fourth Amendment.

. . .

*United States v. Mohamud,* U.S. District Court, District of Oregon, June 24, 2014 (citations in text and footnotes omitted).

Source: *United States v. Mohamud,* Criminal No. 3:10-CR-00475-KI-1, U.S. District Court, District of Oregon, June 24, 2014.

*Reports from U.S. Advisory and Oversight Bodies*

# 30

# Report of the President's Review Group on Intelligence and Communications Technologies, Executive Summary

In response to the controversies generated by Snowden's disclosures, President Obama established an expert group in August 2013 to review and develop recommendations on "how in light of advancements in communications technologies, the United States can employ its technical collection capabilities in a manner that optimally protects our national security and advances our foreign policy while respecting our commitment to privacy and civil liberties, recognizing our need to maintain the public trust, and reducing the risk of unauthorized disclosure." The group's report was released in mid-December 2013. It received worldwide attention, particularly because it advised ending the telephone metadata program, providing more protection for the privacy of foreign nationals, and changing the way the Foreign Intelligence Surveillance Court operates.

★ ★ ★

# Executive Summary

## Overview

The national security threats facing the United States and our allies are numerous and significant, and they will remain so well into the future. These threats include international terrorism, the proliferation of weapons of mass destruction, and cyber espionage and warfare. A robust foreign intelligence collection capability is essential if we are to protect ourselves against such threats. Because our adversaries operate through the use of complex communications technologies, the National Security Agency . . . is indispensable to keeping our country and our allies safe and secure.

At the same time, the United States is deeply committed to the protection of privacy and civil liberties—fundamental values that can be and at times have been eroded by excessive intelligence collection. After careful consideration, we recommend a number of changes to our intelligence collection activities that will protect these values without undermining what we need to do to keep our nation safe.

## Principles

We suggest careful consideration of the following principles:

### 1. The United States Government must protect, at once, two different forms of security: national security and personal privacy.

In the American tradition, the word "security" has had multiple meanings. In contemporary parlance, it often refers to *national security* or *homeland security*. . . . At the same time, the idea of security refers to a quite different and equally fundamental value, captured in the Fourth Amendment . . . : "The right of the people to be *secure* in their persons, houses, papers, and effects, against unreasonable searches and seizures, shall not be violated . . ." (emphasis added). Both forms of security must be protected.

### 2. The central task is one of risk management; multiple risks are involved, and all of them must be considered.

When public officials acquire foreign intelligence information, they seek to reduce risks, above all risks to national security. The challenge, of course, is that multiple risks are involved. Government must consider all of those risks . . . when it is creating sensible safeguards. In addition to reducing risks to national security, public officials must consider four other risks:

- Risks to privacy;
- Risks to freedom and civil liberties, on the Internet and elsewhere;
- Risks to our relationships with other nations; and
- Risks to trade and commerce, including international commerce.

### 3. The idea of "balancing" has an important element of truth, but it is also inadequate and misleading.

It is tempting to suggest that the underlying goal is to achieve the right "balance" between the two forms of security. The suggestion has an important element of truth. But some safeguards are not subject to balancing at all. In a free society, public officials should never engage in surveillance in order to punish their political enemies; to restrict freedom of speech or religion; to suppress legitimate criticism and dissent; to help their preferred companies or industries; to provide domestic companies with an unfair competitive advantage; or to benefit or burden members of groups defined in terms of religion, ethnicity, race, and gender.

### 4. The government should base its decisions on a careful analysis of consequences, including both benefits and costs (to the extent feasible).

In many areas of public policy, officials are increasingly insistent on the need for careful analysis of the consequences of their decisions, and on the importance of relying . . . on evidence and data. Before they are undertaken, surveillance decisions should depend (to the extent feasible) on a careful assessment of the anticipated consequences, including the full range of relevant risks. Such decisions should also be subject to continuing scrutiny, including retrospective analysis, to ensure that any errors are corrected.

### Surveillance of US Persons

With respect to surveillance of US Persons, we recommend a series of significant reforms. Under section 215 of the Foreign Intelligence Surveillance Act (FISA), the government now stores bulk telephony meta-data, understood as information that includes the telephone numbers that both originate and receive calls, time of call, and date of call. (Meta-data does not include the content of calls.) . . . Congress should end such storage and transition to a system in which such meta-data is held privately for the government to query when necessary for national security purposes.

In our view, the current storage by the government of bulk meta-data creates potential risks to public trust, personal privacy, and civil liberty. We recognize that the government might need access to such meta-data, which should be held instead either by private providers or by a private third party. This approach would allow the government access to the relevant information when such access is justified, and thus protect national security without unnecessarily threatening privacy and liberty. Consistent with this recommendation, . . . as a general rule and without senior policy review, the government should not be permitted to collect and store mass, undigested, non-public personal information about US persons for the purpose of enabling future queries and data-mining for foreign intelligence purposes.

We also recommend specific reforms that will provide Americans with greater safeguards against intrusions into their personal domain. We endorse new steps to protect American citizens engaged in communications with non-US persons. We recommend important restrictions on the ability of the Foreign Intelligence Surveillance Court (FISC) to compel third parties (such as telephone service providers) to disclose private information to the government. We endorse similar restrictions on the issuance of National Security Letters (by which the Federal Bureau of Investigation now compels individuals and organizations to turn over certain otherwise private records), recommending prior judicial review except in emergencies. . . .

We recommend concrete steps to promote transparency and accountability, and thus to promote public trust, which is essential in this domain. Legislation should be enacted requiring information about surveillance programs to be made available to the Congress and to the American people to the greatest extent possible (subject only to the need to protect classified information). . . . [L]egislation should be enacted authorizing telephone, Internet, and other providers to disclose publicly general information about orders they receive directing them to provide information to the government. Such information might disclose the number of orders that providers have received, the broad categories of information produced, and the number of users whose information has been produced. . . . [T]he government should publicly disclose, on a regular basis, general data about the orders it has issued in programs whose existence is unclassified.

## Surveillance of Non-US Persons

Significant steps should be taken to protect the privacy of non-US persons. In particular, any programs that allow surveillance of such persons even outside the United States should satisfy six separate constraints. They:

1) must be authorized by duly enacted laws or properly authorized executive orders;
2) must be directed *exclusively* at protecting national security interests of the United States or our allies;
3) must *not* be directed at illicit or illegitimate ends, such as the theft of trade secrets or obtaining commercial gain for domestic industries;

4) must not target any non-United States person based solely on that person's political views or religious convictions;

5) must not disseminate information about non-United States persons if the information is not relevant to protecting the national security of the United States or our allies; and

6) must be subject to careful oversight and to the highest degree of transparency consistent with protecting the national security of the United States and our allies.

. . .

## Setting Priorities and Avoiding Unjustified or Unnecessary Surveillance

To reduce the risk of unjustified, unnecessary, or excessive surveillance in foreign nations, including collection on foreign leaders, . . . the President should create a new process, requiring highest-level approval of all sensitive intelligence requirements and the methods that the Intelligence Community will use to meet them. This process should identify both the uses and the limits of surveillance on foreign leaders and in foreign nations.

. . . [T]hose involved in the process should consider whether (1) surveillance is motivated by especially important national security concerns or by concerns that are less pressing and (2) surveillance would involve leaders of nations with whom we share fundamental values and interests or leaders of other nations. With close reference to (2), . . . with a small number of closely allied governments, meeting specific criteria, the US Government should explore understandings or arrangements regarding intelligence collection guidelines and practices with respect to each others' citizens (including, if and where appropriate, intentions, strictures, or limitations with respect to collections).

## Organizational Reform

We recommend a series of organizational changes. With respect to the National Security Agency (NSA), we believe that the Director should be a Senate-confirmed position, with civilians eligible to hold that position; the President should give serious consideration to making the next Director of NSA a civilian. NSA should be clearly designated as a foreign intelligence organization. Other missions (including that of NSA's Information Assurance Directorate) should generally be assigned elsewhere. The head of the military unit, US Cyber Command, and the Director of NSA should not be a single official.

We favor a newly chartered, strengthened, independent Civil Liberties and Privacy Protection Board (CLPP Board) to replace the Privacy and Civil Liberties Oversight Board (PCLOB). The CLPP Board should have broad authority to review government activity relating to foreign intelligence and counterterrorism whenever that activity has implications for civil liberties and privacy. A Special Assistant to the President for Privacy should also be designated, serving in both the Office of Management and Budget and the National Security Staff. This Special Assistant should chair a Chief Privacy Officer Council to help coordinate privacy policy throughout the Executive branch.

With respect to the FISC, . . . Congress should create the position of Public Interest Advocate to represent the interests of privacy and civil liberties before the FISC. . . . [T]he government should take steps to increase the transparency of the FISC's decisions and . . . Congress should change the process by which judges are appointed to the FISC.

## Global Communications Technology

Substantial steps should be taken to protect prosperity, security, and openness in a networked world. A free and open Internet is critical to both self-government and economic growth. The United States Government should reaffirm the 2011 International Strategy for Cyberspace. It should stress that Internet governance must not be limited to governments, but should include all appropriate stakeholders, including businesses, civil society, and technology specialists.

The US Government should take additional steps to promote security, by (1) fully supporting and not undermining efforts to create encryption standards; (2) making clear that it will not in any way subvert, undermine, weaken, or make vulnerable generally available commercial encryption; and (3) supporting efforts to encourage the greater use of encryption technology for data in transit, at rest, in the cloud, and in storage. Among other measures relevant to the Internet, the US Government should also support international norms or agreements to increase confidence in the security of online communications.

For big data and data-mining programs directed at communications, the US Government should develop Privacy and Civil Liberties Impact Assessments to ensure that such efforts are statistically reliable, cost-effective, and protective of privacy and civil liberties.

## Protecting What We Do Collect

We recommend a series of steps to reduce the risks associated with "insider threats." . . . Classified information should be shared only with those who genuinely need to know. . . . The use of "for-profit" corporations to conduct personnel investigations should be reduced or terminated. Security clearance levels should be further differentiated. Departments and agencies should institute a Work-Related Access approach to the dissemination of sensitive, classified information. Employees with high-level security clearances should be subject to a Personnel

Continuous Monitoring Program. Ongoing security clearance vetting of individuals should use a risk-management approach and depend on the sensitivity and quantity of the programs and information to which individuals are given access.

The security of information technology networks carrying classified information should be a matter of ongoing concern by Principals, who should conduct an annual assessment with the assistance of a "second opinion" team. Classified networks should increase the use of physical and logical separation of data to restrict access, including through Information Rights Management software. Cyber-security software standards and practices on classified networks should be at least as good as those on the most secure private-sector enterprises.

## Recommendations

### Recommendation 1

We recommend that section 215 should be amended to authorize the Foreign Intelligence Surveillance Court to issue a section 215 order compelling a third party to disclose otherwise private information about particular individuals only if:
(1) it finds that the government has reasonable grounds to believe that the particular information sought is relevant to an authorized investigation intended to protect "against international terrorism or clandestine intelligence activities" and
(2) like a subpoena, the order is reasonable in focus, scope, and breadth.

### Recommendation 2

We recommend that statutes that authorize the issuance of National Security Letters should be amended to permit the[ir] issuance . . . only upon a judicial finding that:
(1) the government has reasonable grounds to believe that the particular information sought is relevant to an authorized investigation intended to protect "against international terrorism or clandestine intelligence activities" and
(2) like a subpoena, the order is reasonable in focus, scope, and breadth.

### Recommendation 3

We recommend that all statutes authorizing the use of National Security Letters should be amended to require the use of the same oversight, minimization, retention, and dissemination standards that currently govern the use of section 215 orders.

## Recommendation 4

We recommend that, as a general rule, and without senior policy review, the government should not be permitted to collect and store all mass, undigested, non-public personal information about individuals to enable future queries and data-mining for foreign intelligence purposes. Any program involving government collection or storage of such data must be narrowly tailored to serve an important government interest.

## Recommendation 5

We recommend that legislation should be enacted that terminates the storage of bulk telephony meta-data by the government under section 215, and transitions ... to a system in which such meta-data is held instead either by private providers or by a private third party. Access to such data should be permitted only with a section 215 order from the Foreign Intelligence Surveillance Court that meets the requirements set forth in Recommendation 1.

## Recommendation 6

We recommend that the government should commission a study of the legal and policy options for assessing the distinction between meta-data and other types of information. The study should include technological experts and persons with a diverse range of perspectives, including experts about the missions of intelligence and law enforcement agencies and about privacy and civil liberties.

## Recommendation 7

We recommend that legislation should be enacted requiring that detailed information about authorities such as those involving National Security Letters, section 215 business records, section 702, pen register and trap-and-trace, and the section 215 bulk telephony meta-data program should be made available on a regular basis to Congress and the American people to the greatest extent possible, consistent with the need to protect classified information. With respect to authorities and programs whose existence is unclassified, there should be a strong presumption of transparency to enable the American people and their elected representatives independently to assess the merits of the programs for themselves.

## Recommendation 8

We recommend that:

(1) legislation should be enacted providing that . . . non-disclosure orders may be issued only upon a judicial finding that there are reasonable grounds to believe that disclosure would significantly threaten the national security, interfere with an ongoing investigation, endanger the life or physical safety of any person, impair diplomatic relations, or put at risk some other similarly weighty government or foreign intelligence interest;

(2) nondisclosure orders should remain in effect for no longer than 180 days without judicial re-approval; and

(3) nondisclosure orders should never be issued in a manner that prevents the recipient of the order from seeking legal counsel in order to challenge the order's legality.

## Recommendation 9

We recommend that legislation should be enacted providing that, even when nondisclosure orders are appropriate, recipients of . . . orders issued in programs whose existence is unclassified may publicly disclose on a periodic basis general information about the number of such orders they have received, the number they have complied with, the general categories of information they have produced, and the number of users whose information they have produced in each category, unless the government makes a compelling demonstration that such disclosures would endanger the national security.

## Recommendation 10

We recommend that, building on current law, the government should publicly disclose on a regular basis general data about National Security Letters, section 215 orders, pen register and trap-and-trace orders, section 702 orders, and similar orders in programs whose existence is unclassified, unless the government makes a compelling demonstration that such disclosures would endanger the national security.

## Recommendation 11

We recommend that the decision to keep secret from the American people programs of the magnitude of the section 215 bulk telephony meta-data program should be made only after careful deliberation at high levels of government and only with due consideration of and respect for the strong presumption of transparency that is central to democratic governance. A program of this magnitude should be kept secret from the American people only if (a) the program serves a compelling governmental interest and (b) the efficacy of the program would be *substantially* impaired if our enemies were to know of its existence.

## Recommendation 12

We recommend that, if the government legally intercepts a communication under section 702, or under any other authority that justifies the interception of a communication on the ground that it is directed at a non-United States person who is located outside the United States, and if the communication either includes a United States person as a participant or reveals information about a United States person:

(1) any information about that United States person should be purged upon detection unless it either has foreign intelligence value or is necessary to prevent serious harm to others;

(2) any information about the United States person may not be used in evidence in any proceeding against that United States person;

(3) the government may not search the contents of communications acquired under section 702, or under any other authority covered by this recommendation, in an effort to identify communications of particular United States persons, except (a) when the information is necessary to prevent a threat of death or serious bodily harm, or (b) when the government obtains a warrant based on probable cause to believe that the United States person is planning or is engaged in acts of international terrorism.

## Recommendation 13

We recommend that, in implementing section 702, and any other authority that authorizes the surveillance of non-United States persons who are outside the United States, . . . the US Government should reaffirm that such surveillance:

(1) must be authorized by duly enacted laws or properly authorized executive orders;

(2) must be directed *exclusively* at the national security of the United States or our allies;

(3) must *not* be directed at illicit or illegitimate ends, such as the theft of trade secrets or obtaining commercial gain for domestic industries; and

(4) must not disseminate information about non-United States persons if the information is not relevant to protecting the national security of the United States or our allies.

In addition, the US Government should make clear that such surveillance:

(1) must not target any non-United States person located outside of the United States based solely on that person's political views or religious convictions; and

(2) must be subject to careful oversight and to the highest degree of transparency consistent with protecting the national security of the United States and our allies.

## Recommendation 14

We recommend that, in the absence of a specific and compelling showing, the US Government should follow the model of the Department of Homeland Security, and apply the Privacy Act of 1974 in the same way to both US persons and non-US persons.

## Recommendation 15

We recommend that the National Security Agency should have a limited statutory emergency authority to continue to track known targets of counterterrorism surveillance when they first enter the United States, until the Foreign Intelligence Surveillance Court has time to issue an order authorizing continuing surveillance inside the United States.

## Recommendation 16

We recommend that the President should create a new process requiring high-level approval of all sensitive intelligence requirements and the methods the Intelligence Community will use to meet them. This process should . . . identify both the uses and limits of surveillance on foreign leaders and in foreign nations. A small staff . . . should review intelligence collection for sensitive activities on an ongoing basis . . . and advise the National Security Council . . . when they believe that an unscheduled review by them may be warranted.

## Recommendation 17

We recommend that:

(1) senior policymakers should review not only the requirements in Tier One and Tier Two of the National Intelligence Priorities Framework, but also any other requirements that they define as sensitive;

(2) senior policymakers should review the methods and targets of collection on requirements in any Tier that they deem sensitive; and

(3) senior policymakers from the federal agencies with responsibility for US economic interests should participate in the review process because disclosures of classified information can have detrimental effects on US economic interests.

## Recommendation 18

We recommend that the Director of National Intelligence should establish a mechanism to monitor the collection and dissemination activities of the Intelligence Community to ensure they are consistent with the determinations of senior policymakers. To this end, the Director of National Intelligence should prepare an annual report on this issue to the National Security Advisor, to be shared with the Congressional intelligence committees.

## Recommendation 19

We recommend that decisions to engage in surveillance of foreign leaders should consider the following criteria:

(1) Is there a need to engage in such surveillance in order to assess significant threats to our national security?

(2) Is the other nation one with whom we share values and interests, with whom we have a cooperative relationship, and whose leaders we should accord a high degree of respect and deference?

(3) Is there a reason to believe that the foreign leader may be being duplicitous . . . or is attempting to hide information relevant to national security concerns from the US?

(4) Are there other collection means or collection targets that could reliably reveal the needed information?

(5) What would be the negative effects if the leader became aware of the US collection, or if citizens of the relevant nation became so aware?

## Recommendation 20

We recommend that the US Government should examine the feasibility of creating software that would allow the National Security Agency and other intelligence agencies more easily to conduct targeted information acquisition rather than bulk-data collection.

## Recommendation 21

We recommend that with a small number of closely allied governments, meeting specific criteria, the US Government should explore . . . intelligence collection guidelines and practices with respect to each others' citizens (including, if and where appropriate, intentions, strictures, or limitations with respect to collections). The criteria should include:

(1) shared national security objectives;
(2) a close, open, honest, and cooperative relationship between senior-level policy officials; and
(3) a relationship between intelligence services characterized both by the sharing of intelligence information and analytic thinking and by operational cooperation against critical targets of joint national security concern. Discussions of such understandings or arrangements should be done between relevant intelligence communities, with senior policy-level oversight.

## Recommendation 22

We recommend that:

(1) the Director of the National Security Agency should be a Senate-confirmed position;
(2) civilians should be eligible to hold that position; and
(3) the President should give serious consideration to making the next Director of the National Security Agency a civilian.

## Recommendation 23

We recommend that the National Security Agency should be clearly designated as a foreign intelligence organization; missions other than foreign intelligence collection should generally be reassigned elsewhere.

## Recommendation 24

We recommend that the head of the military unit, US Cyber Command, and the Director of the National Security Agency should not be a single official.

## Recommendation 25

We recommend that the Information Assurance Directorate—a large component of the National Security Agency that is not engaged in activities related to foreign intelligence—should become a separate agency within the Department of Defense. . . .

## Recommendation 26

We recommend the creation of a privacy and civil liberties policy official located both in the National Security Staff and the Office of Management and Budget.

*Recommendation 27*

We recommend that:

(1) The charter of the Privacy and Civil Liberties Oversight Board should be modified to create a new and strengthened agency, the Civil Liberties and Privacy Protection Board, that can oversee Intelligence Community activities for foreign intelligence purposes, rather than only for counter-terrorism purposes;

(2) The Civil Liberties and Privacy Protection Board should be an authorized recipient for whistle-blower complaints related to privacy and civil liberties concerns from employees in the Intelligence Community;

(3) An Office of Technology Assessment should be created within the Civil Liberties and Privacy Protection Board to assess Intelligence Community technology initiatives and support privacy-enhancing technologies; and

(4) Some compliance functions . . . should be shifted from the National Security Agency and perhaps other intelligence agencies to the Civil Liberties and Privacy Protection Board.

*Recommendation 28*

We recommend that:

(1) Congress should create the position of Public Interest Advocate to represent privacy and civil liberties interests before the Foreign Intelligence Surveillance Court;

(2) the . . . Court should have greater technological expertise available to the judges;

(3) the transparency of the . . . Court's decisions should be increased, including by instituting declassification reviews that comply with existing standards; and

(4) Congress should change the process by which judges are appointed to the . . . Court, with the appointment power divided among the Supreme Court Justices.

*Recommendation 29*

We recommend that, regarding encryption, the US Government should:

(1) fully support and not undermine efforts to create encryption standards;

(2) not in any way subvert, undermine, weaken, or make vulnerable generally available commercial software; and

(3) increase the use of encryption and urge US companies to do so, in order to better protect data in transit, at rest, in the cloud, and in other storage.

## Recommendation 30

We recommend that the National Security Council staff should manage an interagency process to review on a regular basis the activities of the US Government regarding attacks that exploit a previously unknown vulnerability in a computer application or system. These are often called "Zero Day" attacks because developers have had zero days to address and patch the vulnerability. US policy should generally move to ensure that Zero Days are quickly blocked, so that the underlying vulnerabilities are patched on US Government and other networks. In rare instances, US policy may briefly authorize using a Zero Day for high priority intelligence collection, following senior, interagency review involving all appropriate departments.

## Recommendation 31

We recommend that the United States should support international norms or international agreements for specific measures that will increase confidence in the security of online communications. Among those measures to be considered are:

(1) Governments should not use surveillance to steal industry secrets to advantage their domestic industry;
(2) Governments should not use their offensive cyber capabilities to change the amounts held in financial accounts or otherwise manipulate the financial systems;
(3) Governments should promote transparency about the number and type of law enforcement and other requests made to communications providers;
(4) Absent a specific and compelling reason, governments should avoid localization requirements that (a) mandate location of servers and other information technology facilities or (b) prevent trans-border data flows.

## Recommendation 32

We recommend that there be an Assistant Secretary of State to lead diplomacy of international information technology issues.

## Recommendation 33

We recommend that as part of its diplomatic agenda on international information technology issues, the United States should advocate for . . . a model of Internet governance that is inclusive of all appropriate stakeholders, not just governments.

## Recommendation 34

We recommend that the US Government should streamline the process for lawful international requests to obtain electronic communications through the Mutual Legal Assistance Treaty process.

## Recommendation 35

We recommend that for big data and data-mining programs directed at communications, the US Government should develop Privacy and Civil Liberties Impact Assessments to ensure that such efforts are statistically reliable, cost-effective, and protective of privacy and civil liberties.

## Recommendation 36

We recommend that for future developments in communications technology, the US should create program-by-program reviews informed by expert technologists, to assess and respond to emerging privacy and civil liberties issues, through the Civil Liberties and Privacy Protection Board or other agencies.

## Recommendation 37

We recommend that the US Government should move toward a system in which background investigations relating to the vetting of personnel for security clearance are performed solely by US Government employees or by a non-profit, private sector corporation.

## Recommendation 38

We recommend that the vetting of personnel for access to classified information should be ongoing, rather than periodic. A standard of Personnel Continuous Monitoring should be adopted, incorporating data from Insider Threat programs and from commercially available sources, to note such things as changes in credit ratings or any arrests or court proceedings.

## Recommendation 39

We recommend that security clearances should be more highly differentiated, including the creation of "administrative access" clearances that allow for support and information technology personnel to have the access they need without granting them unnecessary access to substantive policy or intelligence material.

## Recommendation 40

We recommend that the US Government should institute a demonstration project in which personnel with security clearances would be given an Access Score, based upon the sensitivity of the information to which they have access and the number and sensitivity of Special Access Programs and Compartmented Material clearances they have. Such an Access Score should be periodically updated.

## Recommendation 41

We recommend that the "need-to-share" or "need-to-know" models should be replaced with a Work-Related Access model, which would ensure that all personnel whose role requires access to specific information have such access, without making the data more generally available to cleared personnel who are merely interested.

## Recommendation 42

We recommend that the Government networks carrying Secret and higher classification information should use the best available cyber security hardware, software, and procedural protections against both external and internal threats. The National Security Advisor and the Director of the Office of Management and Budget should annually report to the President on the implementation of this standard. All networks carrying classified data, including those in contractor corporations, should be subject to a Network Continuous Monitoring Program, similar to the EINSTEIN 3 and TUTELAGE programs [that protect against intrusions into government civilian and military networks], to record network traffic for real time and subsequent review to detect anomalous activity, malicious actions, and data breaches.

## Recommendation 43

We recommend that the President's prior directions to improve the security of classified networks, Executive Order 13587, should be fully implemented as soon as possible.

## Recommendation 44

We recommend that the National Security Council Principals Committee should annually meet to review the state of security of US Government networks carrying classified information, programs to improve such security, and evolving threats to such networks. An interagency "Red Team" should report annually . . .

with an independent, "second opinion" on the state of security of the classified information networks.

## Recommendation 45

We recommend that all US agencies and departments with classified information should expand their use of software, hardware, and procedures that limit access to documents and data to those specifically authorized to have access to them. The US Government should fund the development of, procure, and widely use on classified networks improved Information Rights Management software to control the dissemination of classified data in a way that provides greater restrictions on access and use, as well as an audit trail of such use.

## Recommendation 46

We recommend the use of cost-benefit analysis and risk-management approaches, both prospective and retrospective, to orient judgments about personnel security and network security measures.

★ ★ ★

Liberty and Security in a Changing World: Report and Recommendations of the President's Review Group on Intelligence and Communications Technologies, December 12, 2013, Executive Summary, 14–42.

*Source:* White House, http://www.whitehouse.gov/sites/default/files/docs/2013 12-12_rg_final _report.pdf.

# 31

# Privacy and Civil Liberties Oversight Board, Report on the Telephone Metadata Program and FISC, Executive Summary

As Lee Hamilton described in chapter 3, the 9/11 Commission recommended in 2004 the establishment of an oversight board to ensure respect for civil liberties in counterterrorism policies, but years passed before the Privacy and Civil Liberties Oversight Board (PCLOB) was established and functioning. Within one week of the initial Snowden disclosures about the telephone metadata and Section 702 programs, members of Congress asked the PCLOB to investigate these programs to contribute to the debate Congress and the public were starting to have about the NSA's activities and civil liberties. The PCLOB issued its report on the telephone metadata program and the operations of the FISC on January 23, 2014. Although President Obama announced reforms to NSA activities in his January 17, 2014, speech (Document 36) and a presidential policy directive, the PCLOB's report still made waves by arguing that the telephone metadata program had no legal basis in Section 215 of the USA PATRIOT Act, violated other U.S. laws, raised serious constitutional concerns, and had not demonstrated any effectiveness as a counterterrorism tool.

★ ★ ★

# EXECUTIVE SUMMARY

The statute creating the Privacy and Civil Liberties Oversight Board ("PCLOB" or "Board") directs the Board to analyze and review actions taken by the executive branch to protect the nation from terrorism, "ensuring that the need for such actions is balanced with the need to protect privacy and civil liberties." In pursuit of this mission, the PCLOB has conducted an in-depth analysis of the bulk telephone records program operated by the National Security Agency ("NSA") under Section 215 of the USA PATRIOT Act ("Patriot Act"). The Board's examination has also included a review of the operation of the Foreign Intelligence Surveillance Court ("FISC" or "FISA court"). . . .

# I. Overview of the Report

## A. Background: Description and History of the Section 215 Program

The NSA's telephone records program . . . is intended to enable the government to identify communications among known and unknown terrorism suspects, particularly those located inside the United States. When the NSA identifies communications that may be associated with terrorism, it issues intelligence reports to other federal agencies, such as the FBI, that work to prevent terrorist attacks. The FISC order authorizes the NSA to collect nearly all call detail records generated by certain telephone companies in the United States, and specifies detailed rules for the use and retention of these records. Call detail records typically include much of the information that appears on a customer's telephone bill: the date and time of a call, its duration, and the participating telephone numbers. Such information is commonly referred to as a type of "metadata." The records collected by the NSA under this program do not, however, include the content of any telephone conversation.

After collecting these telephone records, the NSA stores them in a centralized database. Initially, NSA analysts are permitted to access the . . . records only through "queries" of the database. A query is a search for a specific number or other selection term within the database. Before any specific number is used as the search target or "seed" for a query, one of twenty-two designated NSA officials must first determine that there is a reasonable, articulable suspicion ("RAS") that the number is associated with terrorism. Once the seed has been RAS-approved, NSA analysts may run queries that will return the calling records for that seed, and permit "contact chaining" to develop a fuller picture of the seed's contacts. Contact chaining enables analysts to retrieve not only the numbers directly in contact with the seed number (the "first hop"), but also numbers in contact with all first hop numbers (the "second hop"), as well as all numbers in contact with all second hop numbers (the "third hop").

The Section 215 telephone records program has its roots in counterterrorism efforts that originated in the immediate aftermath of the September 11 attacks. The NSA began collecting telephone metadata in bulk as one part of . . . the President's Surveillance Program. From late 2001 through early 2006, the NSA collected bulk telephony metadata based upon presidential authorizations issued every thirty to forty-five days. In May 2006, the FISC first granted an application by the government to conduct the telephone records program under Section 215. . . .

On June 5, 2013, . . . the *Guardian* published an article based on unauthorized disclosures of classified documents by Edward Snowden, a contractor for the NSA, which revealed the telephone records program to the public. On August 29, 2013, FISC Judge Claire Eagan issued an opinion explaining the court's rationale for approving the Section 215 telephone records program. Although prior authorizations of the program had been accompanied by detailed orders outlining applicable rules and minimization procedures, this was the first judicial opinion explaining the FISA court's legal reasoning in authorizing the bulk records collection. . . .

Over the years, a series of compliance issues were brought to the attention of the FISA court by the government. However, none of these compliance issues involved significant intentional misuse of the system. Nor has the Board seen any evidence of bad faith or misconduct on the part of any government officials or agents involved with the program. Rather, the compliance issues were recognized by the FISC—and are recognized by the Board—as a product of the program's technological complexity and vast scope, illustrating the risks inherent in such a program.

## B. Legal Analysis: Statutory and Constitutional Issues

Section 215 is designed to enable the FBI to acquire records that a business has in its possession, as part of an FBI investigation, when those records are relevant to the investigation. Yet the operation of the NSA's bulk telephone records program bears almost no resemblance to that description. While the Board believes that this program has been conducted in good faith . . . , the Board concludes that Section 215 does not provide an adequate legal basis to support the program.

There are four grounds upon which we find that the telephone records program fails to comply with Section 215. First, the telephone records acquired . . . have no connection to any specific FBI investigation at the time of their collection. Second, because the records are collected in bulk—potentially encompassing all telephone calling records across the nation—they cannot be regarded as "relevant" to any FBI investigation as required by the statute without redefining the word relevant in a manner that is circular, unlimited in scope, and out of step with the case law . . . involving the production of records. Third, the program operates by putting telephone companies under an obligation to furnish new calling records on a daily basis . . . (instead of turning over records already in their possession)—an approach lacking foundation in the statute and one that is inconsistent with FISA as a whole. Fourth, the statute permits only the FBI to obtain items for use in its investigations; it does not authorize the NSA to collect anything.

In addition, . . . the program violates the Electronic Communications Privacy Act. That statute prohibits telephone companies from sharing customer records with the government except in response to specific enumerated circumstances, which do not include Section 215 orders.

Finally, we do not agree that the program can be considered statutorily authorized because Congress twice delayed the expiration of Section 215 during the operation of the program without amending the statute. The "reenactment doctrine," under which Congress is presumed to have adopted settled administrative or judicial interpretations of a statute, does not trump the plain meaning of a law, and cannot save an administrative or judicial interpretation that contradicts the statute itself. Moreover, the circumstances presented here differ in pivotal ways from any in which the reenactment doctrine has ever been applied, and applying the doctrine would undermine the public's ability to know what the law is and hold their elected representatives accountable for their legislative choices.

The NSA's telephone records program also raises concerns under both the First and Fourth Amendments. . . . We explore these concerns and explain that while government officials are entitled to rely on existing Supreme Court doctrine in formulating policy, the existing doctrine does not fully answer whether the Section 215 telephone records program is constitutionally sound. In particular, the scope and duration of the program are beyond anything ever before confronted by the courts, and as a result of technological developments, the government possesses capabilities to collect, store, and analyze data not available when existing Supreme Court doctrine was developed. Without seeking to predict the direction of changes in Supreme Court doctrine, the Board urges as a policy matter that the government consider how to preserve underlying constitutional guarantees in the face of modern communications technology and surveillance capabilities.

## C. Policy Implications of the Section 215 Program

The threat of terrorism . . . is real. The Section 215 telephone records program was intended as one tool to combat this threat. . . . However, . . . the Section 215 program has shown minimal value in safeguarding the nation from terrorism. Based on the information provided to the Board, including classified briefings and documentation, we have not identified a single instance involving a threat to the United States in which the program made a concrete difference in the outcome of a counterterrorism investigation. Moreover, we are aware of no instance in which the program directly contributed to the discovery of a previously unknown terrorist plot or the disruption of a terrorist attack. And we believe that in only one instance over the past seven years has the program arguably contributed to the identification of an unknown terrorism suspect. Even in that case, the suspect was not involved in planning a terrorist attack and there is reason to believe that the FBI may have discovered him without the contribution of the NSA's program.

The Board's review suggests that where the telephone records . . . have provided value, they have done so primarily in two ways: by offering additional leads regarding the contacts of terrorism suspects already known to investigators, and by demonstrating that foreign terrorist plots do *not* have a U.S. nexus. . . . But with respect to the former, our review suggests that the Section 215 program offers little unique value but largely duplicates the FBI's own information gathering efforts. And with respect to the latter, . . . we question whether the American public should accept the government's routine collection of all of its telephone records because it helps in cases where there is no threat to the United States.

The Board also has analyzed the Section 215 program's implications for privacy and civil liberties and has concluded that they are serious. Because telephone calling records can reveal intimate details about a person's life, particularly when aggregated with other information and subjected to sophisticated computer analysis, the government's collection of a person's entire telephone calling history has a significant and detrimental effect on individual privacy. The circumstances of a particular call can be highly suggestive of its content, such that the mere record of a call potentially offers a window into the caller's private affairs. Moreover, when the government collects *all* of a person's telephone records, storing them for five years in a government database that is subject to high-speed digital searching and analysis, the privacy implications go far beyond what can be revealed by the metadata of a single telephone call.

Beyond such individual privacy intrusions, permitting the government to routinely collect the calling records of the entire nation fundamentally shifts the balance of power between the state and its citizens. With its powers of compulsion and criminal prosecution, the government poses unique threats to privacy when it collects data on its own citizens. Government collection of personal information on such a massive scale also courts the ever-present danger of "mission creep." An even more compelling danger is that personal information collected by the government will be misused to harass, blackmail, or intimidate, or to single out for scrutiny particular individuals or groups. To be clear, the Board has seen no evidence suggesting that anything of the sort is occurring at the NSA and the agency's incidents of non-compliance with the rules approved by the FISC have generally involved unintentional misuse. Yet, while the danger of abuse may seem remote, given historical abuse of personal information by the government during the twentieth century, the risk is more than merely theoretical.

Moreover, the bulk collection of telephone records can be expected to have a chilling effect on the free exercise of speech and association, because individuals and groups engaged in sensitive or controversial work have less reason to trust in the confidentiality of their relationships as revealed by their calling patterns. Inability to expect privacy vis-à-vis the government in one's telephone communications means that people engaged in wholly lawful activities—but who for various reasons justifiably do not wish the government to know about their communications—must either forgo such activities, reduce their frequency, or take costly measures to hide them from government surveillance. The telephone records program thus hinders the ability of advocacy organizations to communicate confidentially with members, donors, legislators, whistleblowers, members of the public, and others. For similar reasons, awareness that a record of all telephone calls is stored in a government database may have debilitating consequences for communication between journalists and sources.

To be sure, detailed rules . . . limit the NSA's *use* of the telephone records it collects. . . . But in our view, they cannot fully ameliorate the implications for privacy, speech, and association that follow from the government's ongoing *collection* of virtually all telephone records of every American. Any governmental program that entails such costs requires a strong showing of efficacy. We do not believe the NSA's telephone records program conducted under Section 215 meets that standard.

## D. Operation of the Foreign Intelligence Surveillance Court

Congress created the FISA court in 1978 in response to concerns about the abuse of electronic surveillance. This represented a major restructuring of the domestic conduct of foreign intelligence surveillance, with constitutional implications. Prior to then, successive Presidents had authorized national security wiretaps and other searches solely on the basis of their executive powers under Article II of the Constitution. The Foreign Intelligence Surveillance Act ("FISA") of 1978 provided a procedure under which the Attorney General could obtain a judicial warrant authorizing the use of electronic surveillance in the United States for foreign intelligence purposes.

Over time, the scope of FISA and the jurisdiction of the FISA court have evolved. Initially, the FISC's sole role was to approve individualized FISA warrants for electronic surveillance relating to a specific person, a specific place, or a specific communications account or device. Beginning in 2004, the role of the FISC changed when the government approached the court with its first request to approve a program involving what is now referred to as "bulk collection." In conducting this study, the Board was told by former FISA court judges that they were quite comfortable hearing only from government attorneys when evaluating individual surveillance requests but that the judges' decision making would be greatly enhanced if they could hear opposing views when ruling on requests to establish new surveillance programs.

Upon the FISC's receipt of a proposed application, a member of the court's legal staff will review the application and evaluate whether it meets the legal requirements under FISA. The FISC's legal staff . . . serve as staff to the judges rather than as advocates. . . . The FISA court process for considering applications may include a hearing, and FISC judges have the authority to take testimony from government employees. . . . FISA does not provide a mechanism for the court to invite non-governmental parties to provide views on pending government applications or otherwise participate in FISC proceedings. . . .

FISA also established a Foreign Intelligence Surveillance Court of Review ("FISCR"). . . . Electronic communications service providers have some limited ability to appeal FISC orders, but FISA does not provide a way for the FISCR to receive the views of other non-governmental parties on appeals pending before it.

The FISC's *ex parte,* classified proceedings have raised concerns that the court does not take adequate account of positions other than those of the government. It is critical to the integrity of the process that the public has confidence in its impartiality and rigor. Therefore, the Board believes that some reforms are appropriate and would help bolster public confidence in the operation of the court. The most important reforms . . . are: (1) creation of a panel of private attorneys, Special Advocates, who can be brought into cases involving novel and significant issues by FISA court judges; (2) development of a process facilitating appellate review of such decisions; and (3) providing increased opportunity for the FISC to receive technical assistance and legal input from outside parties.

## E. Transparency Issues

In a representative democracy, the tension between openness and secrecy is inevitable and complex. The challenges are especially acute in the area of intelligence collection, where the powers exercised by the government implicate fundamental rights and our enemies are constantly trying to understand our capabilities in order to avoid detection. In this context, both openness and secrecy are vital to our survival, and we must strive to develop and implement intelligence programs in ways that serve both values.

Transparency is one of the foundations of democratic governance. Our constitutional system of government relies upon the participation of an informed electorate. This in turn requires public access to information about the activities of the government. Transparency supports accountability. It is especially important with regard to activities of the government that affect the rights of individuals, where it is closely interlinked with redress for violations of rights. In the intelligence context, although a certain amount of secrecy is necessary, transparency regarding collection authorities and their exercise can increase public confidence in the intelligence process and in the monumental decisions that our leaders make based on intelligence products.

In the aftermath of the Snowden disclosures, the government has released a substantial amount of information on the leaked government surveillance programs. Although there remains a deep well of distrust, these official disclosures have helped foster greater public understanding of government surveillance programs. However, to date the official disclosures relate almost exclusively to specific programs that had already been the subject of leaks, and we must be careful in citing these disclosures as object lessons for what additional transparency might be appropriate in the future.

The Board believes that the government must take the initiative and formulate long-term solutions that promote greater transparency for government surveillance policies . . . in order to inform public debate on technology, national security, and civil liberties going beyond the current controversy. In this effort, all three branches have a role. For the executive branch, disclosures about key national security programs that involve the collection, storage and dissemination of personal information . . . show that it is possible to describe practices and policies publicly, even those that have not been otherwise leaked, without damage to national security or operational effectiveness.

With regard to the legislative process, even where classified intelligence operations are involved, the purposes and framework of a program for domestic intelligence collection should be debated in public. During the process of developing legislation, some hearings and briefings may need to be conducted in secret to ensure that policymakers fully understand the intended use of a particular authority. But the government should not base an ongoing program affecting the rights of Americans on an interpretation of a statute that is not apparent from a natural reading of the text. In the case of Section 215, the government should have made it publicly clear in the reauthorization process that it intended for Section 215 to serve as legal authority to collect data in bulk on an ongoing basis.

There is also a need for greater transparency regarding operation of the FISA court. Prospectively, we encourage the FISC judges to continue the recent practice of writing opinions with an eye to declassification, separating specific sensitive facts peculiar to the case at hand from broader legal analyses. We also believe that there is significant value in producing declassified versions of earlier opinions, and recommend that the government undertake a classification review of all significant FISC opinions and orders involving novel interpretations of law.

... In addition, should the government adopt our recommendation for a Special Advocate in the FISC, the nature and extent of that advocate's role must be transparent to be effective.

It is also important to promote transparency through increased reporting to the public on the scope of surveillance programs. We urge the government to work with Internet service providers and other companies to reach agreement on standards allowing reasonable disclosures of aggregate statistics that would be meaningful without revealing sensitive government capabilities or tactics. We recommend that the government should also increase the level of detail in its unclassified reporting to Congress and the public regarding surveillance programs.

## II. Overview of the PCLOB's Recommendations

### A. Section 215 Program

*Recommendation 1: The government should end its Section 215 bulk telephone records program.*

The Section 215 bulk telephone records program lacks a viable legal foundation under Section 215, implicates constitutional concerns under the First and Fourth Amendments, raises serious threats to privacy and civil liberties as a policy matter, and has shown only limited value. As a result, the Board recommends that the government end the program.

Without the current Section 215 program, the government would still be able to seek telephone calling records directly from communications providers through other existing legal authorities. The Board does not recommend that the government impose data retention requirements on providers in order to facilitate any system of seeking records directly from private databases.

Once the Section 215 bulk collection program has ended, the government should purge the database of telephone records that have been collected and stored ..., subject to limits on purging data that may arise under federal law or as a result of any pending litigation.

The Board also recommends against the enactment of legislation that would merely codify the existing program or any other program that collects bulk data on such a massive scale regarding individuals with no suspected ties to terrorism or criminal activity. Moreover, the Board's constitutional analysis should provide a message of caution, and as a policy matter, given the significant privacy and civil liberties interests at stake, if Congress seeks to provide legal authority for any new program, it should seek the least intrusive alternative and should not legislate to the outer bounds of its authority.

The Board recognizes that [if] the government . . . need[s] a short period of time to . . . wind down the 215 program . . . it should follow . . . Recommendation 2 below.

*Recommendation 2: The government should immediately implement additional privacy safeguards in operating the Section 215 bulk collection program.*

The Board recommends that the government immediately implement several additional privacy safeguards to mitigate the privacy impact of the present Section 215 program. The recommended changes can be implemented without any need for congressional or FISC authorization. Specifically, the government should:

(a) reduce the retention period for the bulk telephone records program from five years to three years;
(b) reduce the number of "hops" used in contact chaining from three to two;
(c) submit the NSA's "reasonable articulable suspicion" determinations to the FISC for review after they have been approved by NSA and used to query the database; and
(d) require a "reasonable articulable suspicion" determination before analysts may submit queries to, or otherwise analyze, the "corporate store," which contains the results of contact chaining queries to the full "collection store."

## B. FISA Court Operations

*Recommendation 3: Congress should enact legislation enabling the FISC to hear independent views, in addition to the government's views, on novel and significant applications and in other matters in which a FISC judge determines that consideration of the issues would merit such additional views.*

Congress should authorize the establishment of a panel of outside lawyers to serve as Special Advocates before the FISC in appropriate cases. The Presiding Judge of the FISC should select attorneys drawn from the private sector to serve on the panel. The attorneys should be capable of obtaining appropriate security clearances and would then be available to be called upon to participate in certain FISC proceedings.

The decision as to whether the Special Advocate would participate in any particular matter should be left to the discretion of the FISC. The Board expects that the court would invite the Special Advocate to participate in matters involving interpretation of the scope of surveillance authorities, other matters presenting novel legal or technical questions, or matters involving broad programs of collection. The role of the Special Advocate, when invited by the court to participate, would be to make legal arguments addressing privacy, civil rights, and civil liberties interests. The Special Advocate would review the government's application and exercise his or her judgment about whether the proposed surveillance or collection is consistent with law or unduly affects privacy and civil liberties interests.

*Recommendation 4: Congress should enact legislation to expand the opportunities for appellate review of FISC decisions by the FISCR and for review of FISCR decisions by the Supreme Court of the United States.*

Providing for greater appellate review of FISC and FISCR rulings will strengthen the integrity of judicial review under FISA. Providing a role for the Special Advocate in seeking that appellate review will further increase public confidence in the integrity of the process.

*Recommendation 5: The FISC should take full advantage of existing authorities to obtain technical assistance and expand opportunities for legal input from outside parties.*

FISC judges should take advantage of their ability to appoint Special Masters or other technical experts to assist them in reviewing voluminous or technical materials, either in connection with initial applications or in compliance reviews. In addition, the FISC and the FISCR should develop procedures to facilitate amicus participation by third parties in cases involving questions that are of broad public interest, where it is feasible to do so consistent with national security.

## C. Promoting Transparency

*Recommendation 6: To the maximum extent consistent with national security, the government should create and release with minimal redactions declassified versions of new decisions, orders and opinions by the FISC and FISCR in cases involving novel interpretations of FISA or other significant questions of law, technology or compliance.*

FISC judges should continue their recent practice of drafting opinions in cases involving novel issues and other significant decisions in the expectation that declassified versions will be released to the public. The government should promptly create and release declassified versions of these FISC opinions.

*Recommendation 7: Regarding previously written opinions, the government should perform a declassification review of decisions, orders and opinions by the FISC and FISCR that have not yet been released to the public and that involve novel interpretations of FISA or other significant questions of law, technology or compliance.*

Although it may be more difficult to declassify older FISC opinions . . . , the release of such older opinions is still important to facilitate public understanding of the development of the law under FISA. The government should create and release declassified versions of older opinions in novel or significant cases to the greatest extent possible consistent with protection of national security. This should cover programs that have been discontinued, where the legal interpretations justifying such programs have ongoing relevance.

*Recommendation 8: The Attorney General should regularly and publicly report information regarding the operation of the Special Advocate program recommended by the Board. This should include statistics on the frequency and nature of Special Advocate participation in FISC and FISCR proceedings.*

These reports should include statistics showing the number of cases in which a Special Advocate participated, as well as the number of cases identified by the government as raising a novel or significant issue, but in which the judge declined to invite Special Advocate participation. The reports should also indicate the extent to which FISC decisions have been subject to review in the FISCR and the frequency with which Special Advocate requests for FISCR review have been granted.

*Recommendation 9: The government should work with Internet service providers and other companies that regularly receive FISA production orders to develop rules permitting the companies to voluntarily disclose certain statistical information. In addition, the government should publicly disclose more detailed statistics to provide a more complete picture of government surveillance operations.*

The Board urges the government to pursue discussions with communications service providers to determine the maximum amount of information that companies could voluntarily publish to show the extent of government surveillance requests they receive per year in a way that is consistent with protection of national security. In addition, the government should itself release annual reports showing in more detail the nature and scope of FISA surveillance for each year.

*Recommendation 10: The Attorney General should fully inform the PCLOB of the government's activities under FISA and provide the PCLOB with copies of the detailed reports submitted under FISA to the specified committees of Congress. This should include providing the PCLOB with copies of the FISC decisions required to be produced [to authorized congressional committees] under Section 601(a)(5) [of FISA].*

*Recommendation 11: The Board urges the government to begin developing principles and criteria for transparency.*

The Board urges the Administration to commence the process of articulating principles and criteria for deciding what must be kept secret and what can be released as to existing and future programs that affect the American public.

*Recommendation 12: The scope of surveillance authorities affecting Americans should be public.*

In particular, the Administration should develop principles and criteria for the public articulation of the legal authorities under which it conducts surveillance affecting Americans. If the text of the statute itself is not sufficient to inform the public of the scope of asserted government authority, then the key elements of the legal opinion or other documents describing the government's legal analysis should be made public so there can be a free and open debate regarding the law's scope. This includes both original enactments such as 215's revisions and subsequent reauthorizations. While sensitive operational details regarding the conduct of government surveillance programs should remain classified, and while legal interpretations of the application of a statute in a particular case may also be secret so long as the use of that technique in a particular case is secret, the government's interpretations of statutes that provide the basis for ongoing surveillance programs affecting Americans can and should be made public.

Privacy and Civil Liberties Oversight Board, Report on the Telephone Records Program Conducted under Section 215 of the USA PATRIOT Act and on the Operations of the Foreign Intelligence Surveillance Court, January 23, 2014, Executive Summary, 8–20 (footnotes omitted).

*Source:* Privacy and Civil Liberties Oversight Board, http://www.pclob.gov/library/215-Report_on _the_Telephone_Records_Program.pdf.

# 32

# Privacy and Civil Liberties Oversight Board, Report on Section 702 of FISA, Executive Summary

The PCLOB issued its report on Section 702 of FISA in July 2014. As the Snowden affair unfolded, NSA use of Section 702 was less controversial in the United States than the telephone metadata program. The use of Section 702 drew more criticism abroad, where it was perceived as the justification for mass surveillance programs that, as a matter of U.S. law and policy, did not address the privacy interests of non-U.S. persons. This PCLOB report gained both notoriety and praise in the United States and internationally for concluding that the NSA's use of Section 702 to gather foreign intelligence complied with FISA and the Fourth Amendment and contributed to U.S. government efforts to combat terrorism. The report avoided, however, making conclusions on the subject of international law and protection of the privacy of non-U.S. persons.

★ ★ ★

# EXECUTIVE SUMMARY

In 2008, Congress enacted the FISA Amendments Act, which made changes to the Foreign Intelligence Surveillance Act of 1978 ("FISA"). Among those changes was the addition of a new provision, Section 702 of FISA, permitting the Attorney General and the Director of National Intelligence to jointly authorize surveillance conducted within the United States but targeting only non-U.S. persons reasonably believed to be located outside the United States. The Privacy and Civil Liberties Oversight Board ("PCLOB") began reviewing implementation of the FISA Amendments Act early in 2013, shortly after the Board began operations as an independent agency. The PCLOB has conducted an in-depth review of the program now operated under Section 702, in pursuit of the Board's mission to review executive branch actions taken to protect the nation from terrorism in order to ensure "that the need for such actions is balanced with the need to protect privacy and civil liberties." . . .

# I. Overview of the Report

## A. Description and History of the Section 702 Program

Section 702 has its roots in the President's Surveillance Program developed in the immediate aftermath of the September 11th attacks. Under one aspect of that program, the Terrorist Surveillance Program ("TSP"), the President authorized interception of the contents of international communications from within the United States, outside of the FISA process. Following disclosures about the TSP by the press in December 2005, the government sought and obtained authorization from the Foreign Intelligence Surveillance Court ("FISA court") to conduct, under FISA, the collection that had been occurring under the TSP. Later, the government developed a statutory framework . . . to authorize this collection program. After the enactment and expiration of a temporary measure, the Protect America Act of 2007, Congress passed the FISA Amendments Act of 2008, which included the new Section 702 of FISA. The statute provides a procedural framework for the targeting of non-U.S. persons reasonably believed to be located outside the United States to acquire foreign intelligence information.

Section 702 permits the Attorney General and the Director of National Intelligence to jointly authorize surveillance targeting persons who are not U.S. persons, and who are reasonably believed to be located outside the United States, with the compelled assistance of electronic communication service providers, in order to acquire foreign intelligence information. . . . Executive branch authorizations to acquire designated types of foreign intelligence under Section 702 must be approved by the FISA court, along with procedures governing targeting decisions and the handling of information acquired.

Although U.S. persons may not be targeted under Section 702, communications of or concerning U.S. persons may be acquired in a variety of ways. An example is when a U.S. person communicates with a non-U.S. person who has been targeted, resulting in what is termed "incidental" collection. Another example is when two non-U.S. persons discuss a U.S. person. Communications of or concerning U.S. persons that are acquired in these ways may be retained and used by the government, subject to applicable rules and requirements. The communications of U.S. persons may also be collected by mistake, as when a U.S. person is erroneously targeted or in the event of a technological malfunction, resulting in "inadvertent" collection. In such cases, however, the applicable rules generally require the communications to be destroyed.

Under Section 702, the Attorney General and Director of National Intelligence make annual certifications authorizing this targeting to acquire foreign intelligence information, without specifying to the FISA court the particular non-U.S. persons who will be targeted. There is no requirement that the government demonstrate probable cause to believe that an individual targeted is an agent of a foreign power, as is generally required in the "traditional" FISA process under Title I of the statute. Instead, the Section 702 certifications identify categories of information to be collected, which must meet the statutory definition of foreign intelligence information. The certifications that have been authorized include information concerning international terrorism and other topics, such as the acquisition of weapons of mass destruction.

Section 702 requires the government to develop targeting and "minimization" procedures that must satisfy certain criteria. As part of the FISA court's review and approval of the government's annual certifications, the court must approve these procedures and determine that they meet the necessary standards. The targeting procedures govern how the executive branch determines that a particular person is reasonably believed to be a non-U.S. person located outside the United States, and that targeting this person will lead to the acquisition of foreign intelligence information. The minimization procedures cover the acquisition, retention, use, and dissemination of any non-publicly available U.S. person information acquired through the Section 702 program.

Once foreign intelligence acquisition has been authorized under Section 702, the government sends written directives to electronic communication service providers compelling their assistance in the acquisition of communications. The government identifies or "tasks" certain "selectors," such as telephone numbers or email addresses, that are associated with targeted persons, and it sends these selectors to electronic communications service providers to begin acquisition. There are two types of Section 702 acquisition: what has been referred to as "PRISM" collection and "upstream" collection.

In PRISM collection, the government sends a selector, such as an email address, to a United States-based electronic communications service provider, such as an Internet service provider ("ISP"), and the provider is compelled to give the communications sent to or from that selector to the government. PRISM collection does not include the acquisition of telephone calls. The National Security Agency ("NSA") receives all data collected through PRISM. In addition, the Central Intelligence Agency ("CIA") and the Federal Bureau of Investigation ("FBI") each receive a select portion of PRISM collection.

Upstream collection differs from PRISM collection in several respects. First, the acquisition occurs with the compelled assistance of providers that control the telecommunications "backbone" over which telephone and Internet communications transit, rather than with the compelled assistance of ISPs or similar companies. Upstream collection also includes telephone calls in addition to Internet communications. Data from upstream collection is received only by the NSA: neither the CIA nor the FBI has access to unminimized upstream data. Finally, the upstream collection of Internet communications includes two features that are not present in PRISM collection: the acquisition of so-called "about" communications and the acquisition of so-called "multiple communications transactions" ("MCTs"). An "about" communication is one in which the selector of a targeted person (such as that person's email address) is contained within the communication but the targeted person is not necessarily a participant in the communication. Rather than being "to" or "from" the selector that has been tasked, the communication may contain the selector in the body of the communication, and thus be "about" the selector. An MCT is an Internet "transaction" that contains more than one discrete communication within it. If one of the communications within an MCT is to, from, or "about" a tasked selector, and if one end of the transaction is foreign, the NSA will acquire the entire MCT through upstream collection, including other discrete communications within the MCT that do not contain the selector.

Each agency that receives communications under Section 702 has its own minimization procedures, approved by the FISA court, that govern the agency's use, retention, and dissemination of Section 702 data. Among other things, these procedures include rules on how the agencies may "query" the collected data. The NSA, CIA, and FBI minimization procedures all include provisions permitting these agencies to query data acquired through Section 702, using terms intended to discover or retrieve communications content or metadata that meets the criteria specified in the query. These queries may include terms that identify specific U.S. persons and can be used to retrieve the already acquired communications of specific U.S. persons. Minimization procedures set forth the standards for conducting queries. . . .

The minimization procedures also include data retention limits and rules outlining circumstances under which information must be purged. Apart from communications acquired by mistake, U.S. persons' communications are not typically purged or eliminated from agency databases, even when they do not contain foreign intelligence information, until the data is aged off in accordance with retention limits.

Each agency's adherence to its targeting and minimization procedures is subject to extensive oversight within the executive branch, including internal oversight within individual agencies as well as regular reviews conducted by the Department of Justice ("DOJ") and the Office of the Director of National Intelligence ("ODNI"). The Section 702 program is also subject to oversight by the FISA court, including during the annual certification process and when compliance incidents are reported to the court. Information about the operation of the program also is reported to congressional committees. Although there have been various compliance incidents over the years, many of these incidents have involved technical issues resulting from the complexity of the program, and the Board has not seen any evidence of bad faith or misconduct.

## B. Legal Analysis

The Board's legal analysis of the Section 702 program includes an evaluation of whether it comports with the terms of the statute, an evaluation of the Fourth Amendment issues raised by the program, and a discussion of the treatment of non-U.S. persons under the program.

. . . On the whole, the text of Section 702 provides the public with transparency into the legal framework for collection, and it publicly outlines the basic structure of the program. The Board concludes that PRISM collection is clearly authorized by the statute and that, with respect to the "about" collection, which occurs in the upstream component of the program, the statute can permissibly be interpreted as allowing such collection as it is currently implemented.

The Board also concludes that the core of the Section 702 program—acquiring the communications of specifically targeted foreign persons who are located outside the United States, upon a belief that those persons are likely to communicate foreign intelligence, using specific communications identifiers, subject to FISA court-approved targeting rules and multiple layers of oversight—fits within the "totality of the circumstances" standard for reasonableness under the Fourth Amendment. . . . Outside of this fundamental core, certain aspects of the Section 702 program push the program close to the line of constitutional reasonableness. Such aspects include the unknown and potentially large scope of the incidental collection of U.S. persons' communications, the use of "about" collection to acquire Internet communications that are neither to nor from the target of surveillance, and the use of queries to search for the communications of specific U.S. persons within the information that has been collected. With these concerns in mind, this Report offers a set of policy proposals designed to push the program more comfortably into the sphere of reasonableness, ensuring that the program remains tied to its constitutionally legitimate core.

Finally, the Board discusses the fact that privacy is a human right that has been recognized in the International Covenant on Civil and Political Rights ("IC-CPR"), an international treaty ratified by the U.S. Senate, and that the treatment of non-U.S. persons in U.S. surveillance programs raises important but difficult legal and policy questions.... The President's recent initiative under Presidential Policy Directive 28 on Signals Intelligence ("PPD-28") will ... address the extent to which non-U.S. persons should be afforded the same protections as U.S. persons under U.S. surveillance laws. Because PPD-28 invites the PCLOB to be involved in its implementation, the Board has concluded that it can make its most productive contribution in assessing these issues in the context of the PPD-28 review process.

## C. Policy Analysis

The Section 702 program has enabled the government to acquire a greater range of foreign intelligence than it otherwise would have been able to obtain—and to do so quickly and effectively. Compared with the "traditional" FISA process under Title I of the statute, Section 702 imposes significantly fewer limits on the government when it targets foreigners located abroad, permitting greater flexibility and a dramatic increase in the number of people who can realistically be targeted. The program has proven valuable in the government's efforts to combat terrorism as well as in other areas of foreign intelligence. Presently, over a quarter of the NSA's reports concerning international terrorism include information based in whole or in part on Section 702 collection, and this percentage has increased every year since the statute was enacted. Monitoring terrorist networks under Section 702 has enabled the government to learn how they operate, and to understand their priorities, strategies, and tactics. In addition, the program has led the government to identify previously unknown individuals who are involved in international terrorism, and it has played a key role in discovering and disrupting specific terrorist plots aimed at the United States and other countries.

The basic structure of the Section 702 program appropriately focuses on targeting non-U.S. persons reasonably believed to be located abroad. Yet communications of, or concerning, U.S. persons can be collected under Section 702, and certain features of the program implicate privacy concerns. These features include the potential scope of U.S. person communications that are collected, the acquisition of "about" communications, and the use of queries that employ U.S. person identifiers.

. . .

The government is presently unable to assess the scope of the incidental collection of U.S. person information under the program. For this reason, the Board recommends several measures that together may provide insight about the extent to which communications involving U.S. persons or people located in the United States are being acquired and utilized.

With regard to the NSA's acquisition of "about" communications, the Board concludes that the practice is largely an inevitable byproduct of the government's efforts to comprehensively acquire communications that are sent to or from its targets. Because of the manner in which the NSA conducts upstream collection, and the limits of its current technology, the NSA cannot completely eliminate "about" communications from its collection without also eliminating a significant portion of the "to/from" communications that it seeks. The Board includes a recommendation to better assess "about" collection and a recommendation to ensure that upstream collection as a whole does not unnecessarily collect domestic communications.

The Report also assesses the impact of queries using "United States person identifiers." At the NSA, for example, these queries can be performed if they are deemed "reasonably likely to return foreign intelligence information." No showing of suspicion that the U.S. person is engaged in any form of wrongdoing is required, but procedures are in place to prevent queries being conducted for improper purposes. The Board includes two recommendations to address the rules regarding U.S. person queries.

Overall, the Board finds that the protections contained in the Section 702 minimization procedures are reasonably designed and implemented to ward against the exploitation of information acquired under the program for illegitimate purposes. The Board has seen no trace of any such illegitimate activity associated with the program, or any attempt to intentionally circumvent legal limits. But the applicable rules potentially allow a great deal of private information about U.S. persons to be acquired by the government. The Board therefore offers a series of policy recommendations to ensure that the program appropriately balances national security with privacy and civil liberties.

## II. Recommendations

### A. Targeting and Tasking

*Recommendation 1: The NSA's targeting procedures should be revised to (a) specify criteria for determining the expected foreign intelligence value of a particular target, and (b) require a written explanation of the basis for that determination sufficient to demonstrate that the targeting of each selector is likely to return foreign intelligence information relevant to the subject of one of the certifications approved by the FISA court. . . . We expect that the FISA court's review of these targeting procedures in the course of the court's periodic review of Section 702 certifications will include an assessment of whether the revised procedures provide adequate guidance to ensure that targeting decisions are reasonably designed to acquire foreign intelligence information relevant to the subject of one of the certifications approved by the FISA court. Upon revision of the NSA's targeting procedures, internal agency reviews, as well as compliance audits performed by the ODNI and DOJ, should include an assessment of compliance with the foreign intelligence purpose requirement comparable to the review currently conducted of compliance with the requirement that targets are reasonably believed to be non-U.S. persons located outside the United States.*

### B. U.S. Person Queries

*Recommendation 2: The FBI's minimization procedures should be updated to more clearly reflect the actual practice for conducting U.S. person queries, including the frequency with which Section 702 data may be searched when making routine queries as part of FBI assessments and investigations. Further, some additional limits should be placed on the FBI's use and dissemination of Section 702 data in connection with non-foreign intelligence criminal matters.*

*Recommendation 3: The NSA and CIA minimization procedures should permit the agencies to query collected Section 702 data for foreign intelligence purposes using U.S. person identifiers only if the query is based upon a statement of facts showing that it is reasonably likely to return foreign intelligence information as defined in FISA. . . .*

### C. FISA Court Role

*Recommendation 4: To assist in the FISA court's consideration of the government's periodic Section 702 certification applications, the government should submit with those applications a random sample of tasking sheets and a random sample of the NSA's and CIA's U.S. person query terms, with supporting documentation. The sample size and methodology should be approved by the FISA court.*

*Recommendation 5: As part of the periodic certification process, the government should incorporate into its submission to the FISA court the rules for operation of the Section 702 program that have not already been included in certification orders by the FISA court, and that at present are contained in separate orders and opinions, affidavits, compliance and other letters, hearing transcripts, and mandatory reports filed by the government. To the extent that the FISA court agrees that these rules govern the operation of the Section 702 program, the FISA court should expressly incorporate them into its order approving Section 702 certifications.*

## D. Upstream and "About" Collection

*Recommendation 6: To build on current efforts to filter upstream communications to avoid collection of purely domestic communications, the NSA and DOJ, in consultation with affected telecommunications service providers, and as appropriate, with independent experts, should periodically assess whether filtering techniques applied in upstream collection utilize the best technology . . . to ensure government acquisition of only communications that are authorized for collection and prevent the inadvertent collection of domestic communications.*

*Recommendation 7: The NSA periodically should review the types of communications acquired through "about" collection under Section 702, and study the extent to which it would be technically feasible to limit, as appropriate, the types of "about" collection.*

## E. Accountability and Transparency

*Recommendation 8: To the maximum extent consistent with national security, the government should create and release, with minimal redactions, declassified versions of the FBI's and CIA's Section 702 minimization procedures, as well as the NSA's current minimization procedures.*

*Recommendation 9: The government should implement five measures to provide insight about the extent to which the NSA acquires and utilizes the communications involving U.S. persons and people located in the United States under the Section 702 program. Specifically, the NSA should implement processes to annually count the following: (1) the number of telephone communications acquired in which one caller is located in the United States; (2) the number of Internet communications acquired through upstream collection that originate or terminate in the United States; (3) the number of communications of or concerning U.S. persons that the NSA positively identifies as such in the routine course of its work; (4) the number of queries performed that employ U.S. person identifiers, specifically distinguishing the number of such queries that include names, titles, or other identifiers potentially associated with individuals; and (5) the number of instances in which the NSA disseminates non-public information about U.S. persons, specifically distinguishing disseminations that includes names, titles, or other identifiers potentially associated with individuals. These figures should be reported to Congress in the NSA Director's annual report and should be released publicly to the extent consistent with national security.*

## F. Efficacy

*Recommendation 10: The government should develop a comprehensive methodology for assessing the efficacy and relative value of counterterrorism programs.*

. . .

★　★　★

Privacy and Civil Liberties Oversight Board, Report on the Surveillance Program Operated Pursuant to Section 702 of the Foreign Intelligence Surveillance Act, July 2, 2014, Executive Summary, 8–15 (footnotes omitted).

*Source:* Privacy and Civil Liberties Oversight Board, http://www.pclob.gov/library/702-Report.pdf.

*International Institutions*

# 33

# Edward Snowden, Testimony to the European Parliament

In the wake of Snowden's disclosures, investigations of NSA activities began in a number of foreign legislative bodies, including Australia's Senate, Brazil's Senate, and Germany's Bundestag, and in international organizations, including the Council of Europe and European Parliament. In July 2013, the European Parliament tasked its Committee on Civil Liberties, Justice, and Home Affairs with conducting an inquiry into electronic mass surveillance of EU citizens. The committee submitted its report in February 2014. This report included a proposed European Parliament resolution on the NSA surveillance programs, surveillance activities in EU member states, and the impact on transatlantic cooperation and on the fundamental rights of EU citizens. As part of its consideration of the report, the European Parliament invited Snowden to provide testimony. From Russia, he submitted a written statement and answers to questions posed by EP members.

★ ★ ★

# Introductory Statement

I would like to thank the European Parliament for the invitation to provide testimony. . . . The suspicionless surveillance programs of the NSA, GCHQ, and so many others . . . endanger a number of basic rights which, in aggregate, constitute the foundation of liberal societies.

The first principle any inquiry must take into account is that despite extraordinary political pressure to do so, no western government has been able to present evidence showing that such programs are necessary. In the United States, the heads of our spying services once claimed that 54 terrorist attacks had been stopped by mass surveillance, but two independent White House reviews with access to the classified evidence . . . concluded it was untrue [President's Review Group and the PCLOB], as did a Federal Court [*Klayman v. Obama*].

. . . The most recent of these investigations, performed by the . . . Privacy and Civil Liberties Oversight Board, determined that the mass [telephone metadata] surveillance program investigated was not only ineffective—they found it had never stopped even a single imminent terrorist attack—but that it had no basis in law. In less diplomatic language, they discovered the United States was operating an unlawful mass surveillance program, and the greatest success the program had ever produced was discovering a taxi driver in the United States transferring $8,500 dollars to Somalia in 2007.

After noting . . . this unimpressive success . . . , the Board recommended that the unlawful mass surveillance program be ended. Unfortunately, we know from press reports that this program is still operating today.

I believe that suspicionless surveillance not only fails to make us safe, but it actually makes us less safe. By squandering precious, limited resources on "collecting it all," we end up with more analysts trying to make sense of harmless political dissent and fewer investigators running down real leads. I believe investing in mass surveillance at the expense of traditional, proven methods can cost lives, and history has shown my concerns are justified.

Despite the extraordinary intrusions of the NSA and EU national governments into private communications world-wide, Umar Farouk Abdulmutallab, the "Underwear Bomber," was allowed to board an airplane traveling from Europe to the United States in 2009. The 290 persons on board were not saved by mass surveillance, but by his own incompetence, when he failed to detonate the device. While even Mutallab's own father warned the US government he was dangerous in November 2009, our resources were tied up monitoring online games and tapping German ministers. That extraordinary tip-off didn't get Mutallab a dedicated US investigator. All we gave him was a US visa.

Nor did the US government's comprehensive monitoring of Americans at home stop the Boston Bombers [in April 2013]. Despite the Russians specifically warning us about Tamerlan Tsarnaev, the FBI couldn't do more than a cursory investigation—although they did plenty of worthless computer-based searching—and failed to discover the plot. 264 people were injured, and 3 died. The resources that could have paid for a real investigation had been spent on monitoring the call records of everyone in America.

This should not have happened. I worked for the United States' Central Intelligence Agency. The National Security Agency. The Defense Intelligence Agency. I love my country, and I believe that spying serves a vital purpose and must continue. And I have risked my life, my family, and my freedom to tell you the truth.

The NSA granted me the authority to monitor communications world-wide using its mass surveillance systems, including within the United States. I have personally targeted individuals using these systems under both the President of the United States' Executive Order 12333 [of December 4, 1981] and the US Congress' FAA 702 [FISA Amendments Act of 2008]. I know the good and the bad of these systems, and what they can and cannot do, and I am telling you that . . . I could have read the private communications of any member of this committee, as well as any ordinary citizen. I swear under penalty of perjury that this is true.

These are not the capabilities in which free societies invest. Mass surveillance violates our rights, risks our safety, and threatens our way of life.

If even the US government, after determining mass surveillance is unlawful and unnecessary, continues to operate to engage in mass surveillance, we have a problem. I consider the United States Government to be generally responsible, and I hope you will agree with me. Accordingly, this begs the question many legislative bodies implicated in mass surveillance have sought to avoid: if even the US is willing to knowingly violate the rights of billions of innocents—and I say billions without exaggeration—for nothing more substantial than a "potential" intelligence advantage that has never materialized, what are other governments going to do?

Whether we like it or not, the international norms of tomorrow are being constructed today, right now, by the work of bodies like this committee. If liberal states decide that the convenience of spies is more valuable than the rights of their citizens, the inevitable result will be states that are both less liberal and less safe.

Thank you.

I will now respond to the submitted questions. . . .

## Rapporteur Claude Moraes MEP, S&D Group

*Given the focus of this Inquiry is on the impact of mass surveillance on EU citizens, could you elaborate on the extent of cooperation that exists between the NSA and EU Member States in terms of the transfer and collection of bulk data of EU citizens?*

. . .

One of the foremost activities of the NSA's FAD, or Foreign Affairs [Director-ate], is to pressure or incentivize EU member states to change their laws to enable mass surveillance. Lawyers from the NSA, as well as the UK's GCHQ, work very hard to search for loopholes in laws and constitutional protections that they can use to justify indiscriminate, dragnet surveillance operations that were at best unwittingly authorized by lawmakers. These efforts to interpret new powers out of vague laws is an intentional strategy to avoid public opposition and lawmakers' insistence that legal limits be respected, effects the GCHQ internally described in its own documents as "damaging public debate."

In recent public memory, we have seen these FAD "legal guidance" opera-tions occur in both Sweden and the Netherlands, and also faraway New Zealand. Germany was pressured to modify its . . . law to appease the NSA, and it eroded the rights of German citizens under their constitution. Each of these countries received instruction from the NSA, sometimes under the guise of the US Depart-ment of Defense and other bodies, on how to degrade the legal protections of their countries' communications. The ultimate result of the NSA's guidance is that the right of ordinary citizens to be free from unwarranted interference is degraded, and systems of intrusive mass surveillance are being constructed in secret within otherwise liberal states, often without the full awareness of the public.

Once the NSA has successfully subverted or helped repeal legal restrictions against unconstitutional mass surveillance in partner states, it encourages part-ners to perform "access operations." Access operations are efforts to gain access to the bulk communications of all major telecommunications providers in their jurisdictions, normally beginning with those that handle the greatest volume of communications. Sometimes the NSA provides consultation, technology, or even the physical hardware itself for partners to "ingest" these massive amounts of data in a manner that allows processing, and it does not take long to access everything. Even in a country the size of the United States, gaining access to the circuits of as few as three companies can provide access to the majority of citizens' com-munications. In the UK, Verizon, British Telecommunications, Vodafone, Global Crossing, Level 3, Viatel, and Interoute all cooperate with the GCHQ, to include cooperation beyond what is legally required. . . .

By the time this general process has occurred, it is very difficult for the citi-zens of a country to protect the privacy of their communications, and it is very easy for the intelligence services of that country to make those communications available to the NSA—even without having explicitly shared them. The nature of the NSA's "NOFORN," or NO FOREIGN NATIONALS classification, when combined with the fact that the memorandum agreements between NSA and its foreign partners have a standard disclaimer stating they provide no enforceable rights, provides . . . the NSA with a means of monitoring its partner's citizens without informing the partner, and the partner with a means of plausible deniability.

The result is a European bazaar, where an EU member state like Denmark may give the NSA access to a tapping center on the (unenforceable) condition that NSA doesn't search it for Danes, and Germany may give the NSA access to another on the condition that it doesn't search for Germans. Yet the two tapping sites may be two points on the same cable, so the NSA simply captures the communications of the German citizens as they transit Denmark, and the Danish citizens as they transit Germany, all the while considering it entirely in accordance with their agreements. Ultimately, each EU national government's spy services are independently hawking domestic accesses to the NSA, GCHQ, FRA [Sweden's intelligence agency], and the like without having any awareness of how their individual contribution is enabling the greater patchwork of mass surveillance against ordinary citizens as a whole.

The Parliament should ask the NSA and GCHQ to deny that they monitor the communications of EU citizens, and in the absence of an informative response, I would suggest that the current state of affairs is the inevitable result of subordinating the rights of the voting public to the prerogatives of State Security Bureaus. The surest way for any nation to become subject to unnecessary surveillance is to allow its spies to dictate its policy.

The right to be free [from] unwarranted intrusion into our private effects—our lives and possessions, our thoughts and communications—is a human right. It is not granted by national governments and it cannot be revoked by them out of convenience. Just as we do not allow police officers to enter every home to fish around for evidence of undiscovered crimes, we must not allow spies to rummage through our every communication for indications of disfavored activities.

*Could you comment on the activities of EU Member States intelligence agencies in these operations and how advanced their capabilities have become in comparison with the NSA?*

The best testimony I can provide on this matter . . . is to point to the indications that the NSA not only enables and guides, but shares some mass surveillance systems and technologies with the agencies of EU member states. As it pertains to the issue of mass surveillance, the difference between, for example, the NSA and FRA is not one of technology, but rather funding and manpower. Technology is agnostic of nationality, and the flag on the pole outside of the building makes systems of mass surveillance no more or less effective.

*In terms of the mass surveillance programmes already revealed through the press, what proportion of the mass surveillance activities do these programmes account for? Are there many other programmes, undisclosed as of yet, that would impact on EU citizens rights?*

There are many other undisclosed programs that would impact EU citizens' rights, but I will leave the public interest determinations as to which of these may be safely disclosed to responsible journalists in coordination with government stakeholders.

## Shadow Rapporteur Sophie Int'Veld MEP, ALDE Group

*Are there adequate procedures in the NSA for staff to signal wrongdoing?*

Unfortunately not. The culture within the US Intelligence Community is such that reporting serious concerns about the legality or propriety of programs is much more likely to result in your being flagged as a troublemaker than to result in substantive reform. We should remember that many of these programs were well known to be problematic to the legal offices of agencies such as the GCHQ and other oversight officials. According to their own documents, the priority of the overseers is not to assure strict compliance with the law and accountability for violations of law, but rather to avoid, and I quote, "damaging public debate," to conceal the fact that for-profit companies have gone "well beyond" what is legally required of them, and to avoid legal review of questionable programs by open courts. . . .

In my personal experience, repeatedly raising concerns about legal and policy matters with my co-workers and superiors resulted in two kinds of responses.

The first were well-meaning but hushed warnings not to "rock the boat," for fear of the sort of retaliation that befell former NSA whistleblowers like [former NSA officials] [J. Kirk] Wiebe, [William] Binney, and [Thomas] Drake. All three men reported their concerns through the official, approved process, and all three men were subject to armed raids by the FBI and threats of criminal sanction. Everyone in the Intelligence Community is aware of what happens to people who report concerns about unlawful but authorized operations.

The second were similarly well-meaning but more pointed suggestions, typically from senior officials, that we should let the issue be someone else's problem. Even among the most senior individuals to whom I reported my concerns, no one at NSA could ever recall an instance where an official complaint had resulted in an unlawful program being ended, but there was a unanimous desire to avoid being associated with such a complaint in any form.

*Do you feel you had exhausted all avenues before taking the decision to go public?*

Yes. I had reported these clearly problematic programs to more than ten distinct officials, none of whom took any action to address them. As an employee of a private company rather than a direct employee of the US government, I was not protected by US whistleblower laws, and I would not have been protected from retaliation and legal sanction for revealing classified information about lawbreaking in accordance with the recommended process.

It is important to remember that this . . . legal dilemma did not occur by mistake. US whistleblower reform laws were passed as recently as 2012, with the US Whistleblower Protection Enhancement Act, but they specifically chose to exclude Intelligence Agencies from being covered by the statute [5 U.S.C. §2302(a)(2)(C)(ii)]. President Obama also reformed a key executive Whistleblower regulation with his [October] 2012 Presidential Policy Directive 19 [on Protecting Whistleblowers with Access to Classified Information], but it exempted Intelligence Community contractors such as myself. The result was that individuals like me were left with no proper channels.

*Do you think procedures for whistleblowing have been improved now?*

No. There has not yet been any substantive whistleblower reform in the US, and unfortunately my government has taken a number of disproportionate and persecutory actions against me. US government officials have declared me guilty of crimes in advance of any trial, they've called for me to be executed or assassinated in private and openly in the press, they revoked my passport and left me stranded in a foreign transit zone for six weeks, and even used NATO to ground the presidential plane of Evo Morales—the leader of Bolivia—on hearing that I might attempt to seek and enjoy asylum in Latin America.

*What is your relationship with the Russian and Chinese authorities, and what are the terms on which you were allowed to stay originally in Hong Kong and now in Russia?*

I have no relationship with either government.

## Shadow Rapporteur Jan Philipp Albrecht MEP, Greens Group

*Could we help you in any way, and do you seek asylum in the EU?*

If you want to help me, help me by helping everyone: declare that the indiscriminate, bulk collection of private data by governments is a violation of our rights and must end. What happens to me as a person is less important than what happens to our common rights.

As for asylum, I do seek EU asylum, but I have yet to receive a positive response to the requests I sent to various EU member states. Parliamentarians in the national governments have told me that the US, and I quote, "will not allow" EU partners to offer political asylum to me, which is why the previous resolution on asylum ran into such mysterious opposition. I would welcome any offer of safe passage or permanent asylum, but I recognize that would require an act of extraordinary political courage.

*Can you confirm cyber-attacks by the NSA or other intelligence agencies on EU institutions, telecommunications providers such as Belgacom and SWIFT, or any other EU-based companies?*

Yes. . . . I can confirm that all documents reported thus far are authentic and unmodified, meaning the alleged operations against Belgacom, SWIFT, the EU as an institution, the United Nations, UNICEF, and others based on documents I provided have actually occurred. And I expect similar operations will be revealed in the future that affect many more ordinary citizens.

## Shadow Rapporteur Cornelia Ernst MEP, GUE Group

*In your view, how far can the surveillance measures you revealed be justified by national security and from your experience is the information being used for economic espionage? What could be done to resolve this?*

Surveillance against specific targets, for unquestionable reasons of national security while respecting human rights, is above reproach. Unfortunately, we've seen a growth in untargeted, extremely questionable surveillance for reasons entirely unrelated to national security. Most recently, the Prime Minister of Australia, caught red-handed engaging in the most blatant kind of economic espionage, sought to argue that the price of Indonesian shrimp and clove cigarettes was a "security matter." These are indications of a growing disinterest among governments for ensuring intelligence activities are justified, proportionate, and above all accountable. We should be concerned about the precedent our actions set.

The UK's GCHQ is the prime example of this, due to what they refer to as a "light oversight regime," which is a bureaucratic way of saying their spying activities are less restricted than is proper. . . . Since that light oversight regime was revealed, we have learned that the GCHQ is intercepting and storing unprecedented quantities of ordinary citizens' communications on a constant basis, both within the EU and without. . . . There is no argument that could convince an open court that such activities were necessary and proportionate, and it is for this reason that such activities are shielded from the review of open courts.

In the United States, we use a secret, rubber-stamp Foreign Intelligence Surveillance Court that only hears arguments from the government. Out of approximately 34,000 government requests over 33 years, the secret court rejected only 11. It should raise serious concerns for this committee, and for society, that the GCHQ's lawyers consider themselves fortunate to avoid the kind of burdensome oversight regime that rejects 11 out of 34,000 requests. If that's what heavy oversight looks like, what, pray tell, does the GCHQ's "light oversight" look like?

Let's explore it. We learned only days ago that the GCHQ compromised a popular Yahoo service to collect images from web cameras inside citizens' homes, and around 10% of these images they take from within people's homes involve nudity or intimate activities. . . . In the same report, journalists revealed that this sort of webcam data was searchable via the NSA's XKEYSCORE system, which means the GCHQ's "light oversight regime" was used not only to capture bulk data that is clearly of limited intelligence value and most probably violates EU laws, but to then trade that data with foreign services without the knowledge or consent of any country's voting public.

We also learned last year that some of the partners with which the GCHQ was sharing this information, in this example the NSA, had made efforts to use evidence of religious conservatives' association with sexually explicit material of the sort GCHQ was collecting as a grounds for destroying their reputations and discrediting them. . . . The "Release to Five Eyes" classification of this particular report, dated 2012, reveals that the UK government was aware of the NSA's intent to use sexually explicit material in this manner, indicating a deepening and increasingly aggressive partnership. None of these religious conservatives were suspected of involvement in terrorist plots: they were targeted on the basis of their political beliefs and activism, as part of a class the NSA refers to as "radicalizers."

I wonder if any members of this committee have ever advocated a position that the NSA, GCHQ, or even the intelligence services of an EU member state might attempt to construe as "radical"? If you were targeted on the basis of your political beliefs, would you know? If they sought to discredit you on the basis of your private communications, could you discover the culprit and prove it was them? What would be your recourse?

And you are parliamentarians. Try to imagine the impact of such activities against ordinary citizens without power, privilege, or resources. Are these activities necessary, proportionate, and an unquestionable matter of national security?

A few weeks ago we learned the GCHQ has hired scientists to study how to create divisions amongst activists and disfavored political groups, how they attempt to discredit and destroy private businesses, and how they knowingly plant false information to misdirect civil discourse. . . .

To directly answer your question, yes, global surveillance capabilities are being used on a daily basis for the purpose of economic espionage. That a major goal of the US Intelligence Community is to produce economic intelligence is the worst kept secret in Washington.

In September, we learned the NSA had successfully targeted and compromised the world's major financial transaction facilitators, such as Visa and SWIFT, which released documents describe as providing "rich personal information," even data that "is not about our targets." . . . Again, these documents are authentic and unmodified—a fact the NSA itself has never once disputed.

In August, we learned the NSA had targeted Petrobras, an energy company. . . . It would be the first of a long list of US energy targets.

But we should be clear these activities are not unique to the NSA or GCHQ. Australia's DSD targeted Sri Mulyani Indrawati, a finance minister and Managing Director of the World Bank. . . . Report after report has revealed targeting of G-8 and G-20 summits. Mass surveillance capabilities have even been used against a climate change summit.

Recently, governments have shifted their talking points from claiming they only use mass surveillance for "national security" purposes to the more nebulous "valid foreign intelligence purposes." I suggest this committee consider that this rhetorical shift is a tacit acknowledgment by governments that they recognize they have crossed beyond the boundaries of justifiable activities. Every country believes its "foreign intelligence purposes" are "valid," but that does not make it so. If we are prepared to condemn the economic spying of our competitors, we must be prepared to do the same of our allies. Lasting peace is founded upon fundamental fairness.

The international community must agree to common standards of behavior, and jointly invest in the development of new technical standards to defend against mass surveillance. We rely on common systems, and the French will not be safe from mass surveillance until Americans, Argentines, and Chinese are as well.

The good news is that there are solutions. The weakness of mass surveillance is that it can very easily be made much more expensive through changes in technical standards: pervasive, end-to-end encryption can quickly make indiscriminate surveillance impossible on a cost-effective basis. The result is that governments are likely to fall back to traditional, targeted surveillance founded upon an individualized suspicion. Governments cannot risk the discovery of their exploits by simply throwing attacks at every "endpoint," or computer processor on the end of a network connection, in the world. Mass surveillance, passive surveillance, relies upon unencrypted or weakly encrypted communications at the global network level.

*If there had been better independent and public oversight over the intelligence agencies, do you think this could have prevented this kind of mass surveillance? What conditions would need to be fulfilled, both nationally and internationally?*

Yes, better oversight could have prevented the mistakes that brought us to this point, as could an understanding that defense is always more important than offense when it comes to matters of national intelligence. The intentional weakening of the common security standards upon which we all rely is an action taken against the public good.

The oversight of intelligence agencies should always be performed by opposition parties, as under the democratic model, they always have the most to lose under a surveillance state. Additionally, we need better whistleblower protections, and a new commitment to the importance of international asylum. These are important safeguards that protect our collective human rights when the laws of national governments have failed.

European governments, which have traditionally been champions of human rights, should not be intimidated out of standing for the right of asylum against political charges, of which espionage has always been the traditional example. Journalism is not a crime, it is the foundation of free and informed societies, and no nation should look to others to bear the burden of defending its rights.

## Shadow Rapporteur Axel Voss MEP, EPP Group

*Why did you choose to go public with your information?*

Secret laws and secret courts cannot authorize unconstitutional activities by fiat, nor can classification be used to shield an unjustified and embarrassing violation of human rights from democratic accountability. If the mass surveillance of an innocent public is to occur, it should be authorized as the result of an informed debate with the consent of the public, under a framework of laws that the government invites civil society to challenge in open courts.

That our governments are even today unwilling to allow independent review of the secret policies enabling mass surveillance of innocents underlines governments' lack of faith that these programs are lawful, and this provides stronger testimony in favor of the rightfulness of my actions than any words I might write.
. . .

*Are you aware that your revelations have the potential to put at risk lives of innocents and hamper efforts in the global fight against terrorism?*

Actually, no specific evidence has ever been offered, by any government, that even a single life has been put at risk by the award-winning journalism this question attempts to implicate.

The ongoing revelations about unlawful and improper surveillance are the product of a partnership between the world's leading journalistic outfits and national governments, and if you can show one of the governments consulted on these stories chose not to impede demonstrably fatal information from being published, I invite you to do so. The front page of every newspaper in the world stands open to you.

*Did the Russian secret service approach you?*

Of course. Even the secret service of Andorra would have approached me, if they had had the chance: that's their job.

But I didn't take any documents with me from Hong Kong, and . . . it doesn't take long for an intelligence service to realize when they're out of luck. I was also accompanied at all times by an utterly fearless journalist with one of the biggest megaphones in the world, which is the equivalent of Kryptonite for spies. As a consequence, we spent the next 40 days trapped in an airport instead of sleeping on piles of money while waiting for the next parade. But we walked out with heads held high.

I would also add, for the record, that the United States government has repeatedly acknowledged that there is no evidence at all of any relationship between myself and the Russian intelligence service.

. . .

## Shadow Rapporteur Timothy Kirkhope MEP, ECR Group

*You have stated previously that you want the intelligence agencies to be more accountable to citizens, however, why do you feel this accountability does not apply to you? Do you therefore, plan to return to the United States or Europe to face criminal charges and answer questions in an official capacity, and pursue the route as an official whistle-blower?*

Respectfully, I remind you that accountability cannot exist without the due process of law, and . . . the well-known gap in US law . . . deprived me of vital legal protections due to nothing more meaningful than my status as an employee of a private company rather than of the government directly. . . . Surely no one on the committee believes that the measure of one's political rights should be determined by their employer.

Fortunately, we live in a global, interconnected world where, when national laws fail like this, our international laws provide for another level of accountability, and the asylum process provides a means of due process for individuals who might otherwise be wrongly deprived of it. In the face of the extraordinary campaign of persecution brought against me by . . . the United States government on account of my political beliefs, . . . an increasing number of national governments have agreed that a grant of political asylum is lawful and appropriate.

Polling of public opinion in Europe indicates I am not alone in hoping to see EU governments agree that blowing the whistle on serious wrongdoing should be a protected act.

. . .

★ ★ ★

Edward Snowden, Testimony to the European Parliament, March 7, 2014 (citations in text omitted).

*Source:* European Parliament Committee on Civil Liberties, Justice, and Home Affairs, http://www.europarl.europa.eu/document/activities/cont/201403/20140307ATT80674/20140307ATT80674EN.pdf.

# 34

# European Parliament, Resolution on U.S. NSA Surveillance Program

Five days after Snowden's testimony, the European Parliament adopted a resolution based on the recommendations of its Committee on Civil Liberties, Justice, and Home Affairs. The resolution, summarized in the next document, represents an evaluation of the impact of NSA programs on the governments and peoples of its member states. The EU had been at odds with the United States over the protection of privacy long before Snowden's revelations. The resolution contains ambitious recommendations and an action agenda. Although the European Parliament does not have the same authority as a national legislature, it wields significant powers and can use these to advance its objectives. For example, it has the power to approve or reject international agreements on behalf of the EU. In the resolution, the European Parliament threatens to block approval of the proposed Transatlantic Trade and Investment Partnership (TTIP) Agreement between the EU and the United States if the United States does not abandon mass surveillance of EU citizens and spying on EU institutions. With TTIP negotiations still ongoing, it remains to be seen whether the European Parliament will carry through on this threat.

★ ★ ★

The European Parliament adopted by 544 votes to 78 with 60 abstentions, a resolution on the US NSA surveillance programme, surveillance bodies in various Member States and their impact on EU citizens' fundamental rights and on transatlantic cooperation in Justice and Home Affairs.

Parliament noted that in comparison to actions taken both by EU institutions and by certain EU Member States, the European Parliament had taken very seriously its obligation to shed light on the revelations on the indiscriminate practices of mass surveillance of EU citizens and instructed its Committee on Civil Liberties, Justice and Home Affairs to conduct an in-depth inquiry into the matter.

**Main findings:** Members considered that recent revelations in the press by whistleblowers and journalists, together with the expert evidence given during this inquiry, admissions by authorities, and the insufficient response to these allegations, have resulted in **compelling evidence of the existence of far-reaching, complex and highly technologically advanced systems** designed by US and some Member States' intelligence services to collect, store and analyse communication data, including content data, location data and metadata of all citizens around the world, on an unprecedented scale and in an indiscriminate and non-suspicion-based manner.

Parliament specifically pointed to:

- US NSA intelligence programmes allowing for the mass surveillance of EU citizens through direct access to the central servers of leading US internet companies (PRISM programme), the analysis of content and metadata (Xkeyscore programme), the circumvention of online encryption (BULLRUN);
- systems of the UK intelligence agency GCHQ such as the upstream surveillance activity (Tempora programme), etc.

Parliament emphasised that trust had been profoundly shaken between the two transatlantic partners. In order to rebuild trust, **an immediate and comprehensive response plan** comprising a series of actions which were subject to public scrutiny was needed.

Noting that several governments claim that these mass surveillance programmes were necessary to combat terrorism, Parliament stated that the fight against terrorism could never be a justification for untargeted, secret, or even illegal mass surveillance programmes. It strongly rejected the notion that all issues related to mass surveillance programmes were purely a matter of national security and therefore the sole competence of Member States. Discussion and action at EU level were not only legitimate, but also a matter of EU autonomy.

**Recommendations:** the US authorities and the EU Member States were called upon **to prohibit blanket mass surveillance activities.** Parliament intended to request strong political undertakings from the new Commission to implement the proposals and recommendations of this Inquiry.

Members States were called upon to:

- comprehensively evaluate, and revise where necessary, their national legislation and practices governing the activities of the intelligence services so as to ensure that they are subject to parliamentary and judicial oversight and public scrutiny;
- immediately fulfil their positive obligation under the European Convention on Human Rights to protect their citizens from surveillance contrary to its requirements, including when the aim thereof is to safeguard national security, undertaken by third states or by their own intelligence services, and
- ensure that the rule of law is not weakened as a result of extraterritorial application of a third country's law.

The United Kingdom, France, Germany, Sweden, the Netherlands and Poland were specifically asked to ensure that their current or future legislative frameworks and oversight mechanisms governing the activities of intelligence agencies were in line with the standards of the European Convention on Human Rights and European Union data protection legislation and to clarify the allegations of mass surveillance activities. Member States were also asked to shed light on US intelligence personnel and equipment on EU territory **without oversight on surveillance operations.**

The Commission was called upon to:

. . .

- present measures providing for the immediate suspension of . . . the Safe Harbour privacy principles [a 1998 agreement to facilitate the compliance of U.S. entities with the EU's Directive on Data Protection]. In this respect, the US authorities are urged to put forward a proposal for a new framework for transfers of personal data from the EU to the US which meets Union law data protection requirements and provides for the required adequate level of protection;
- present, by December 2014, a comprehensive assessment of the US privacy framework covering commercial, law enforcement and intelligence activities, and concrete recommendations based on the absence of a general data protection law in the US;
- engage with the US . . . to establish a legal framework providing for a high level of protection of individuals with regard to the protection of

their personal data when transferred to the US and ensure the equivalence of EU and US privacy frameworks;

- conduct, before the end of 2014, an in-depth assessment of the **existing
Mutual Legal Assistance Agreement;**
- immediately resume the negotiations with the US on the 'Umbrella
Agreement' [on protection of personal data transfers for law enforcement
and anti-terrorism], which should put rights for EU citizens on an equal
footing with rights for US citizens . . . ;
- react to concerns that three of the major computerised reservation
systems used by airlines worldwide are based in the US and that PNR
[Passenger Name Record] data are saved in cloud systems operating on
US soil under US law, which lacks data protection adequacy;
- present, by December 2014, a proposal for an EU security clearance procedure for all EU office holders;
- present draft legislation to ban the use of backdoors by law enforcement
agencies;
- present, by January 2015 at the latest, an **Action Plan to develop greater
EU independence in the IT sector,** including a more coherent approach
to boosting European IT technological capabilities (including IT systems,
equipment, services, cloud computing, etc);
- put forward by December 2014, legislative proposals to encourage
software and hardware manufacturers to introduce more security and
privacy by design and by default features in their products, including by
introducing disincentives for the undue and disproportionate collection
of mass personal data and legal liability on the part of manufacturers
for unpatched known vulnerabilities, faulty or insecure products or the
installation of secret backdoors enabling unauthorised access to and
processing of data;
- through funding in the **field of research and development**, support
the development of European innovative and technological capability
in IT tools, companies and providers (hardware, software, services and
network), including for purposes of cybersecurity and encryption and
cryptographic capabilities[.]

**Threat to block approval of the Transatlantic Trade and Investment Part-
nership Agreement (TTIP):** the resolution stressed that . . . the consent of the
European Parliament to the final TTIP agreement could be endangered as long
as the blanket mass surveillance activities and the interception of communications in EU institutions and diplomatic representations were not completely
abandoned and an adequate solution found for the data privacy rights of EU
citizens. Parliament might only consent to the final TTIP agreement provided the

agreement fully respected, inter alia, the fundamental rights recognised by the EU Charter, and provided the protection of the privacy of individuals in relation to the processing and dissemination of personal data remain governed by Article XIV of the GATS [the World Trade Organization's General Agreement on Trade in Services]. Parliament stresses that EU data protection legislation could not be deemed an 'arbitrary or unjustifiable discrimination' in the application of Article XIV of the GATS.

Parliament called for the setting up of a High-Level Group to propose, in a transparent manner and in collaboration with parliaments, recommendations and further steps to be taken for:

- enhanced democratic oversight, including parliamentary oversight, of intelligence services;
- increased oversight collaboration in the EU, in particular as regards its cross-border dimension;
- the possibility of **minimum European standards or guidelines** for the (ex ante and ex post) **oversight of intelligence services** on the basis of existing best practices and recommendations by international bodies;
- prepare a report for[,] and to assist in the preparation of[,] a conference to be held by Parliament with national oversight bodies . . . by the beginning of 2015.

Parliament decides to launch '**A European Digital Habeas Corpus**—protecting fundamental rights in a digital age' with the following 8 actions . . . :

- the adoption of the Data Protection Package in 2014;
- the conclusion of the EU-US Umbrella Agreement guaranteeing the fundamental right of citizens to privacy and data protection and ensuring proper redress mechanisms for EU citizens;
- the **suspension of Safe Harbour** . . . standards on data protection for non-EU businesses that send personal data of EU citizens to the US . . . until a full review has been conducted and current loopholes were remedied;
- the **suspension of the TFTP** agreement [EU-U.S. Terrorist Finance Tracking Programme Agreement] until: (i) the Umbrella Agreement negotiations have been concluded; (ii) a thorough investigation has been concluded on the basis of an EU analysis and all concerns raised by Parliament in its resolution of 23 October 2013 have been properly addressed;
- an examination from the Commission as to whether a future legislative proposal establishing an effective and comprehensive European

whistleblower protection programme. Member States should thoroughly examine the possibility of granting whistleblowers international protection from prosecution;

- the development of a European strategy for greater IT independence.

Lastly, the competent services of the Secretariat of the European Parliament were asked to carry out, by June 2015 at the latest, a thorough review and assessment of **Parliament's IT security dependability** . . . in order to achieve a high level of security for Parliament's IT systems.

. . .

★  ★  ★

European Parliament, Resolution on US NSA Surveillance Programme, Surveillance Bodies in Various Member States and Impact on EU Citizens' Fundamental Rights and on Transatlantic Cooperation in Justice and Home Affairs, March 12, 2014, Summary.

*Source:* European Parliament Legislative Observatory, http://www.europarl.europa.eu/oeil/popups /summary.do?id=1342393&t=e&l=en.

# 35

# United Nations Resolution on the Right to Privacy in the Digital Age

Revelations about the scale of U.S. surveillance of foreign communications provoked accusations that such activities violated the international human right to privacy. In one declassified opinion, the FISC stated that NSA surveillance targeting foreign nationals outside the United States had collected more than 250 million Internet communications annually. Brazil and Germany initiated UN actions to affirm the international human right to privacy and challenge mass surveillance of foreign communications. This effort resonated with Snowden's emphasis on the human right to privacy.

The resolution's negotiation proved controversial. The United States argued it had no international legal obligations concerning the privacy of foreign nationals outside its territory. Suggestive of the controversy, the General Assembly adopted the resolution without a vote. Even so, the resolution focused global attention on how the United States addressed privacy with respect to foreign communications the NSA collects, accesses, and retains under Section 702 of FISA and Executive Order 12333. The resolution initiated other UN activities on this issue, including the UN high commissioner for human rights' June 2014 report on *The Right to Privacy in the Digital Age* and a September 2014 report on mass digital surveillance from the UN special rapporteur on the promotion and protection of human rights and fundamental freedoms while countering terrorism.

### 68/167. The right to privacy in the digital age

*The General Assembly,*

*Reaffirming* the purposes and principles of the Charter of the United Nations,

*Reaffirming also* the human rights and fundamental freedoms enshrined in the Universal Declaration of Human Rights and relevant international human rights treaties, including the International Covenant on Civil and Political Rights and the International Covenant on Economic, Social and Cultural Rights,

*Reaffirming further* the Vienna Declaration and Programme of Action,

*Noting* that the rapid pace of technological development enables individuals all over the world to use new information and communication technologies and at the same time enhances the capacity of governments, companies and individuals to undertake surveillance, interception and data collection, which may violate or abuse human rights, in particular the right to privacy, as set out in article 12 of the Universal Declaration of Human Rights and article 17 of the International Covenant on Civil and Political Rights, and is therefore an issue of increasing concern,

*Reaffirming* the human right to privacy, according to which no one shall be subjected to arbitrary or unlawful interference with his or her privacy, family, home or correspondence, and the right to protection of the law against such interference, and recognizing that the exercise of the right to privacy is important for the realization of the right to freedom of expression and to hold opinions without interference, and is one of the foundations of a democratic society,

*Stressing* the importance of the full respect for the freedom to seek, receive and impart information, including the fundamental importance of access to information and democratic participation,

*Welcoming* the report of the Special Rapporteur on the promotion and protection of the right to freedom of opinion and expression, submitted to the Human Rights Council at its twenty-third session, on the implications of State surveillance of communications on the exercise of the human rights to privacy and to freedom of opinion and expression,

*Emphasizing* that unlawful or arbitrary surveillance and/or interception of communications, as well as unlawful or arbitrary collection of personal data, as highly intrusive acts, violate the rights to privacy and to freedom of expression and may contradict the tenets of a democratic society,

*Noting* that while concerns about public security may justify the gathering and protection of certain sensitive information, States must ensure full compliance with their obligations under international human rights law,

*Deeply concerned* at the negative impact that surveillance and/or interception of communications, including extraterritorial surveillance and/or interception of communications, as well as the collection of personal data, in particular when carried out on a mass scale, may have on the exercise and enjoyment of human rights,

*Reaffirming* that States must ensure that any measures taken to combat terrorism are in compliance with their obligations under international law, in particular international human rights, refugee and humanitarian law,

1. *Reaffirms* the right to privacy, according to which no one shall be subjected to arbitrary or unlawful interference with his or her privacy, family, home or correspondence, and the right to the protection of the law against such interference, as set out in article 12 of the Universal Declaration of Human Rights, and article 17 of the International Covenant on Civil and Political Rights;

2. *Recognizes* the global and open nature of the Internet and the rapid advancement in information and communications technologies as a driving force in accelerating progress towards development in its various forms;

3. *Affirms* that the same rights that people have offline must also be protected online, including the right to privacy;

4. *Calls upon* all States:

(a) To respect and protect the right to privacy, including in the context of digital communication;

(b) To take measures to put an end to violations of those rights and to create the conditions to prevent such violations, including by ensuring that relevant national legislation complies with their obligations under international human rights law;

(c) To review their procedures, practices and legislation regarding the surveillance of communications, their interception and the collection of personal data, including mass surveillance, interception and collection, with a view to upholding the right to privacy by ensuring the full and effective implementation of all their obligations under international human rights law;

(d) To establish or maintain existing independent, effective domestic oversight mechanisms capable of ensuring transparency, as appropriate, and accountability for State surveillance of communications, their interception and the collection of personal data;

5. *Requests* the United Nations High Commissioner for Human Rights to submit a report on the protect and promotion of the right to privacy in the context of domestic and extraterritorial surveillance and/or the interception of digital

communications and the collection of personal data, including on a mass scale, to the Human Rights Council at its twenty-seventh session and to the General Assembly at its sixty-ninth session, with views and recommendations, to be considered by Member States;

6. *Decides* to examine the question at its sixty-ninth session, under the subitem entitled "Human rights questions, including alternative approaches for improving the effective enjoyment of human rights and fundamental freedoms" of the item entitled "Promotion and protection of human rights."

UN General Assembly, The Right to Privacy in the Digital Age, Resolution 68/167, December 18, 2013 (footnotes omitted).

*Source:* UN General Assembly, Resolution 68/167, The Right to Privacy in the Digital Age, December 18, 2013, UN Doc. A/RES/68/167, distributed January 21, 2014.

## C. Reforms and a Reflection

Snowden intended his disclosures to stimulate public debate and reform of U.S. surveillance policies and laws, and many reactions to his revelations argued for or against reform. The reviews conducted and recommendations made in light of the disclosures contained reform ideas. The documents in this section focus on reforms made or proposed within the executive and legislative branches in the United States. President Obama implemented changes within the executive branch and proposed reforms that required congressional action. Surveillance reform is still a work in progress in the United States, and major legislation has not been adopted as of this writing. The final document gives Snowden the last word in a reflection he issued on the first anniversary of the first disclosures.

# 36

# President Barack Obama, Remarks on Review of Signals Intelligence

In explaining his motivations, Snowden emphasized his desire for the American people to have a public debate about NSA surveillance and, coming out of that debate, to demand reforms that would require the intelligence community to comply with his readings of the Fourth Amendment and international human rights law. President Obama gave a major speech on January 17, 2014, in which he announced reforms to the telephone metadata program and other changes contained in Presidential Policy Directive/PPD-28 on Signals Intelligence Activities, issued the same day. Some of the reform proposals would require legislative action by Congress. Snowden supporters and NSA critics viewed the president's acknowledgment of the need for reform as a victory, especially given that the White House and the intelligence community had been defending the status quo for months. While the president's decision to end the telephone metadata program represented a significant change, some observers concluded that the speech and the new policy directive contained less reform than at first it might have appeared because the president seemed committed to preserving the domestic and foreign surveillance capabilities at the root of the controversies. In both its clarity and craftiness, the speech constituted a landmark moment in the political saga Snowden created.

★  ★  ★

At the dawn of our Republic, a small, secret surveillance committee borne out of the "The Sons of Liberty" was established in Boston. And the group's members included Paul Revere. At night, they would patrol the streets, reporting back any signs that the British were preparing raids against America's early Patriots.

Throughout American history, intelligence has helped secure our country and our freedoms. In the Civil War, Union balloon reconnaissance tracked the size of Confederate armies by counting the number of campfires. In World War II, code-breakers gave us insights into Japanese war plans, and when Patton marched across Europe, intercepted communications helped save the lives of his troops. After the war, the rise of the Iron Curtain and nuclear weapons only increased the need for sustained intelligence gathering. And so, in the early days of the Cold War, President Truman created the National Security Agency, or NSA, to give us insights into the Soviet bloc, and provide our leaders with information they needed to confront aggression and avert catastrophe.

Throughout this evolution, we benefited from both our Constitution and our traditions of limited government. U.S. intelligence agencies were anchored in a system of checks and balances—with oversight from elected leaders, and protections for ordinary citizens. Meanwhile, totalitarian states like East Germany offered a cautionary tale of what could happen when vast, unchecked surveillance turned citizens into informers, and persecuted people for what they said in the privacy of their own homes.

In fact, even the United States proved not to be immune to the abuse of surveillance. And in the 1960s, government spied on civil rights leaders and critics of the Vietnam War. And partly in response to these revelations, additional laws were established in the 1970s to ensure that our intelligence capabilities could not be misused against our citizens. In the long, twilight struggle against Communism, we had been reminded that the very liberties that we sought to preserve could not be sacrificed at the altar of national security.

If the fall of the Soviet Union left America without a competing superpower, emerging threats from terrorist groups, and the proliferation of weapons of mass destruction placed new and in some ways more complicated demands on our intelligence agencies. Globalization and the Internet made these threats more acute, as technology erased borders and empowered individuals to project great violence, as well as great good. Moreover, these new threats raised new legal and new policy questions. For while few doubted the legitimacy of spying on hostile states, our framework of laws was not fully adapted to prevent terrorist attacks by individuals acting on their own, or acting in small, ideologically driven groups on behalf of a foreign power.

The horror of September 11th brought all these issues to the fore. Across the political spectrum, Americans recognized that we had to adapt to a world in which a bomb could be built in a basement, and our electric grid could be shut down by operators an ocean away. We were shaken by the signs we had missed leading up to the attacks—how the hijackers had made phone calls to known extremists and traveled to suspicious places. So we demanded that our intelligence community improve its capabilities, and that law enforcement change practices to focus more on preventing attacks before they happen than prosecuting terrorists after an attack.

It is hard to overstate the transformation America's intelligence community had to go through after 9/11. Our agencies suddenly needed to do far more than the traditional mission of monitoring hostile powers and gathering information for policymakers. Instead, they were now asked to identify and target plotters in some of the most remote parts of the world, and to anticipate the actions of networks that, by their very nature, cannot be easily penetrated with spies or informants.

And it is a testimony to the hard work and dedication of the men and women of our intelligence community that over the past decade we've made enormous strides in fulfilling this mission. Today, new capabilities allow intelligence agencies to track who a terrorist is in contact with, and follow the trail of his travel or his funding. New laws allow information to be collected and shared more quickly and effectively between federal agencies, and state and local law enforcement. Relationships with foreign intelligence services have expanded, and our capacity to repel cyber-attacks have been strengthened. And taken together, these efforts have prevented multiple attacks and saved innocent lives—not just here in the United States, but around the globe.

And yet, in our rush to respond to a very real and novel set of threats, the risk of government overreach—the possibility that we lose some of our core liberties in pursuit of security—also became more pronounced. We saw, in the immediate aftermath of 9/11, our government engaged in enhanced interrogation techniques that contradicted our values. As a Senator, I was critical of several practices, such as warrantless wiretaps. And all too often new authorities were instituted without adequate public debate.

Through a combination of action by the courts, increased congressional oversight, and adjustments by the previous administration, some of the worst excesses that emerged after 9/11 were curbed by the time I took office. But a variety of factors have continued to complicate America's efforts to both defend our nation and uphold our civil liberties.

First, the same technological advances that allow U.S. intelligence agencies to pinpoint an al Qaeda cell in Yemen or an email between two terrorists in the Sahel also mean that many routine communications around the world are within our reach. And at a time when more and more of our lives are digital, that prospect is disquieting for all of us.

Second, the combination of increased digital information and powerful supercomputers offers intelligence agencies the possibility of sifting through massive amounts of bulk data to identify patterns or pursue leads that may thwart impending threats. It's a powerful tool. But the government collection and storage of such bulk data also creates a potential for abuse.

Third, the legal safeguards that restrict surveillance against U.S. persons without a warrant do not apply to foreign persons overseas. This is not unique to America; few, if any, spy agencies around the world constrain their activities beyond their own borders. And the whole point of intelligence is to obtain information that is not publicly available. But America's capabilities are unique, and the power of new technologies means that there are fewer and fewer technical constraints on what we can do. That places a special obligation on us to ask tough questions about what we should do.

And finally, intelligence agencies cannot function without secrecy, which makes their work less subject to public debate. Yet there is an inevitable bias not only within the intelligence community, but among all of us who are responsible for national security, to collect more information about the world, not less. So in the absence of institutional requirements for regular debate—and oversight that is public, as well as private or classified—the danger of government overreach becomes more acute. And this is particularly true when surveillance technology and our reliance on digital information is evolving much faster than our laws.

For all these reasons, I maintained a healthy skepticism toward our surveillance programs after I became President. I ordered that our programs be reviewed by my national security team and our lawyers, and in some cases I ordered changes in how we did business. We increased oversight and auditing, including new structures aimed at compliance. Improved rules were proposed by the government and approved by the Foreign Intelligence Surveillance Court. And we sought to keep Congress continually updated on these activities.

What I did not do is stop these programs wholesale—not only because I felt that they made us more secure, but also because nothing in that initial review, and nothing that I have learned since, indicated that our intelligence community has sought to violate the law or is cavalier about the civil liberties of their fellow citizens.

To the contrary, in an extraordinarily difficult job—one in which actions are second-guessed, success is unreported, and failure can be catastrophic—the men and women of the intelligence community, including the NSA, consistently follow protocols designed to protect the privacy of ordinary people. They're not abusing authorities in order to listen to your private phone calls or read your emails. When mistakes are made—which is inevitable in any large and complicated human enterprise—they correct those mistakes. Laboring in obscurity, often unable to discuss their work even with family and friends, the men and women at the NSA know that if another 9/11 or massive cyber-attack occurs, they will be asked, by Congress and the media, why they failed to connect the dots. What sustains those who work at NSA and our other intelligence agencies through all these pressures is the knowledge that their professionalism and dedication play a central role in the defense of our nation.

Now, to say that our intelligence community follows the law, and is staffed by patriots, is not to suggest that I or others in my administration felt complacent about the potential impact of these programs. Those of us who hold office in America have a responsibility to our Constitution, and while I was confident in the integrity of those who lead our intelligence community, it was clear to me in observing our intelligence operations on a regular basis that changes in our technological capabilities were raising new questions about the privacy safeguards currently in place.

Moreover, after an extended review of our use of drones in the fight against terrorist networks, I believed a fresh examination of our surveillance programs was a necessary next step in our effort to get off the open-ended war footing that we've maintained since 9/11. And for these reasons, I indicated in a speech at the National Defense University last May that we needed a more robust public discussion about the balance between security and liberty. Of course, what I did not know at the time is that within weeks of my speech, an avalanche of unauthorized disclosures would spark controversies at home and abroad that have continued to this day.

And given the fact of an open investigation, I'm not going to dwell on Mr. Snowden's actions or his motivations; I will say that our nation's defense depends in part on the fidelity of those entrusted with our nation's secrets. If any individual who objects to government policy can take it into their own hands to publicly disclose classified information, then we will not be able to keep our people safe, or conduct foreign policy. Moreover, the sensational way in which these disclosures have come out has often shed more heat than light, while revealing methods to our adversaries that could impact our operations in ways that we may not fully understand for years to come.

Regardless of how we got here, though, the task before us now is greater than simply repairing the damage done to our operations or preventing more disclosures from taking place in the future. Instead, we have to make some important decisions about how to protect ourselves and sustain our leadership in the world, while upholding the civil liberties and privacy protections that our ideals and our Constitution require. We need to do so not only because it is right, but because the challenges posed by threats like terrorism and proliferation and cyber-attacks are not going away any time soon. They are going to continue to be a major problem.

And for our intelligence community to be effective over the long haul, we must maintain the trust of the American people, and people around the world.

This effort will not be completed overnight, and given the pace of technological change, we shouldn't expect this to be the last time America has this debate. But I want the American people to know that the work has begun. Over the last six months, I created an outside Review Group on Intelligence and Communications Technologies to make recommendations for reform. I consulted with the Privacy and Civil Liberties Oversight Board, created by Congress. I've listened to foreign partners, privacy advocates, and industry leaders. My administration has spent countless hours considering how to approach intelligence in this era of diffuse threats and technological revolution. So before outlining specific changes that I've ordered, let me make a few broad observations that have emerged from this process.

First, everyone who has looked at these problems, including skeptics of existing programs, recognizes that we have real enemies and threats, and that intelligence serves a vital role in confronting them. We cannot prevent terrorist attacks or cyber threats without some capability to penetrate digital communications—whether it's to unravel a terrorist plot; to intercept malware that targets a stock exchange; to make sure air traffic control systems are not compromised; or to ensure that hackers do not empty your bank accounts. We are expected to protect the American people; that requires us to have capabilities in this field.

Moreover, we cannot unilaterally disarm our intelligence agencies. There is a reason why BlackBerrys and iPhones are not allowed in the White House Situation Room. We know that the intelligence services of other countries—including some who feign surprise over the Snowden disclosures—are constantly probing our government and private sector networks, and accelerating programs to listen to our conversations, and intercept our emails, and compromise our systems. We know that.

Meanwhile, a number of countries, including some who have loudly criticized the NSA, privately acknowledge that America has special responsibilities as the world's only superpower; that our intelligence capabilities are critical to meeting these responsibilities, and that they themselves have relied on the information we obtain to protect their own people.

Second, just as ardent civil libertarians recognize the need for robust intelligence capabilities, those with responsibilities for our national security readily acknowledge the potential for abuse as intelligence capabilities advance and more and more private information is digitized. After all, the folks at NSA and other intelligence agencies are our neighbors. They're our friends and family. They've got electronic bank and medical records like everybody else. They have kids on Facebook and Instagram, and they know, more than most of us, the vulnerabilities to privacy that exist in a world where transactions are recorded, and emails and text and messages are stored, and even our movements can increasingly be tracked through the GPS on our phones.

Third, there was a recognition by all who participated in these reviews that the challenges to our privacy do not come from government alone. Corporations of all shapes and sizes track what you buy, store and analyze our data, and use it for commercial purposes; that's how those targeted ads pop up on your computer and your smartphone periodically. But all of us understand that the standards for government surveillance must be higher. Given the unique power of the state, it is not enough for leaders to say: Trust us, we won't abuse the data we collect. For history has too many examples when that trust has been breached. Our system of government is built on the premise that our liberty cannot depend on the good intentions of those in power; it depends on the law to constrain those in power.

I make these observations to underscore that the basic values of most Americans when it comes to questions of surveillance and privacy converge a lot more than the crude characterizations that have emerged over the last several months. Those who are troubled by our existing programs are not interested in repeating the tragedy of 9/11, and those who defend these programs are not dismissive of civil liberties.

The challenge is getting the details right, and that is not simple. In fact, during the course of our review, I have often reminded myself I would not be where I am today were it not for the courage of dissidents like Dr. King, who were spied upon by their own government. And as President, a President who looks at intelligence every morning, I also can't help but be reminded that America must be vigilant in the face of threats.

Fortunately, by focusing on facts and specifics rather than speculation and hypotheticals, this review process has given me—and hopefully the American people—some clear direction for change. And today, I can announce a series of concrete and substantial reforms that my administration intends to adopt administratively or will seek to codify with Congress.

First, I have approved a new presidential directive for our signals intelligence activities both at home and abroad. This guidance will strengthen executive branch oversight of our intelligence activities. It will ensure that we take into account our security requirements, but also our alliances; our trade and investment relationships, including the concerns of American companies; and our commitment to privacy and basic liberties. And we will review decisions about intelligence priorities and sensitive targets on an annual basis so that our actions are regularly scrutinized by my senior national security team.

Second, we will reform programs and procedures in place to provide greater transparency to our surveillance activities, and fortify the safeguards that protect the privacy of U.S. persons. Since we began this review, including information being released today, we have declassified over 40 opinions and orders of the Foreign

Intelligence Surveillance Court, which provides judicial review of some of our most sensitive intelligence activities—including the Section 702 program targeting foreign individuals overseas, and the Section 215 telephone metadata program.

And going forward, I'm directing the Director of National Intelligence, in consultation with the Attorney General, to annually review for the purposes of declassification any future opinions of the court with broad privacy implications, and to report to me and to Congress on these efforts. To ensure that the court hears a broader range of privacy perspectives, I am also calling on Congress to authorize the establishment of a panel of advocates from outside government to provide an independent voice in significant cases before the Foreign Intelligence Surveillance Court.

Third, we will provide additional protections for activities conducted under Section 702, which allows the government to intercept the communications of foreign targets overseas who have information that's important for our national security. Specifically, I am asking the Attorney General and DNI [Director of National Intelligence] to institute reforms that place additional restrictions on government's ability to retain, search, and use in criminal cases communications between Americans and foreign citizens incidentally collected under Section 702.

Fourth, in investigating threats, the FBI also relies on what's called national security letters, which can require companies to provide specific and limited information to the government without disclosing the orders to the subject of the investigation. These are cases in which it's important that the subject of the investigation, such as a possible terrorist or spy, isn't tipped off. But we can and should be more transparent in how government uses this authority.

I have therefore directed the Attorney General to amend how we use national security letters so that this secrecy will not be indefinite, so that it will terminate within a fixed time unless the government demonstrates a real need for further secrecy. We will also enable communications providers to make public more information than ever before about the orders that they have received to provide data to the government.

This brings me to the program that has generated the most controversy these past few months—the bulk collection of telephone records under Section 215. Let me repeat what I said when this story first broke: This program does not involve the content of phone calls, or the names of people making calls. Instead, it provides a record of phone numbers and the times and lengths of calls—metadata that can be queried if and when we have a reasonable suspicion that a particular number is linked to a terrorist organization.

Why is this necessary? The program grew out of a desire to address a gap identified after 9/11. One of the 9/11 hijackers—Khalid al-Mihdhar—made a phone call from San Diego to a known al Qaeda safe-house in Yemen. NSA saw that call, but it could not see that the call was coming from an individual already in the United

States. The telephone metadata program under Section 215 was designed to map the communications of terrorists so we can see who they may be in contact with as quickly as possible. And this capability could also prove valuable in a crisis. For example, if a bomb goes off in one of our cities and law enforcement is racing to determine whether a network is poised to conduct additional attacks, time is of the essence. Being able to quickly review phone connections to assess whether a network exists is critical to that effort.

In sum, the program does not involve the NSA examining the phone records of ordinary Americans. Rather, it consolidates these records into a database that the government can query if it has a specific lead—a consolidation of phone records that the companies already retained for business purposes. The review group turned up no indication that this database has been intentionally abused. And I believe it is important that the capability that this program is designed to meet is preserved.

Having said that, I believe critics are right to point out that without proper safeguards, this type of program could be used to yield more information about our private lives, and open the door to more intrusive bulk collection programs in the future. They're also right to point out that although the telephone bulk collection program was subject to oversight by the Foreign Intelligence Surveillance Court and has been reauthorized repeatedly by Congress, it has never been subject to vigorous public debate.

For all these reasons, I believe we need a new approach. I am therefore ordering a transition that will end the Section 215 bulk metadata program as it currently exists, and establish a mechanism that preserves the capabilities we need without the government holding this bulk metadata.

This will not be simple. The review group recommended that our current approach be replaced by one in which the providers or a third party retain the bulk records, with government accessing information as needed. Both of these options pose difficult problems. Relying solely on the records of multiple providers, for example, could require companies to alter their procedures in ways that raise new privacy concerns. On the other hand, any third party maintaining a single, consolidated database would be carrying out what is essentially a government function but with more expense, more legal ambiguity, potentially less accountability—all of which would have a doubtful impact on increasing public confidence that their privacy is being protected.

During the review process, some suggested that we may also be able to preserve the capabilities we need through a combination of existing authorities, better information sharing, and recent technological advances. But more work needs to be done to determine exactly how this system might work.

Because of the challenges involved, I've ordered that the transition away from the existing program will proceed in two steps. Effective immediately, we will only pursue phone calls that are two steps removed from a number associated with a terrorist organization instead of the current three. And I have directed the Attorney General to work with the Foreign Intelligence Surveillance Court so that during this transition period, the database can be queried only after a judicial finding or in the case of a true emergency.

Next, step two, I have instructed the intelligence community and the Attorney General to use this transition period to develop options for a new approach that can match the capabilities and fill the gaps that the Section 215 program was designed to address without the government holding this metadata itself. They will report back to me with options for alternative approaches before the program comes up for reauthorization on March 28th. And during this period, I will consult with the relevant committees in Congress to seek their views, and then seek congressional authorization for the new program as needed.

Now, the reforms I'm proposing today should give the American people greater confidence that their rights are being protected, even as our intelligence and law enforcement agencies maintain the tools they need to keep us safe. And I recognize that there are additional issues that require further debate. For example, some who participated in our review, as well as some members of Congress, would like to see more sweeping reforms to the use of national security letters so that we have to go to a judge each time before issuing these requests. Here, I have concerns that we should not set a standard for terrorism investigations that is higher than those involved in investigating an ordinary crime. But I agree that greater oversight on the use of these letters may be appropriate, and I'm prepared to work with Congress on this issue.

There are also those who would like to see different changes to the FISA Court than the ones I've proposed. On all these issues, I am open to working with Congress to ensure that we build a broad consensus for how to move forward, and I'm confident that we can shape an approach that meets our security needs while upholding the civil liberties of every American.

Let me now turn to the separate set of concerns that have been raised overseas, and focus on America's approach to intelligence collection abroad. As I've indicated, the United States has unique responsibilities when it comes to intelligence collection. Our capabilities help protect not only our nation, but our friends and our allies, as well. But our efforts will only be effective if ordinary citizens in other countries have confidence that the United States respects their privacy, too. And the leaders of our close friends and allies deserve to know that if I want to know what they think about an issue, I'll pick up the phone and call them, rather than turning to surveillance. In other words, just as we balance security and privacy at home, our global leadership demands that we balance our security requirements against our need to maintain the trust and cooperation among people and leaders around the world.

For that reason, the new presidential directive that I've issued today will clearly prescribe what we do, and do not do, when it comes to our overseas surveillance. To begin with, the directive makes clear that the United States only uses signals intelligence for legitimate national security purposes, and not for the purpose of indiscriminately reviewing the emails or phone calls of ordinary folks. I've also made it clear that the United States does not collect intelligence to suppress criticism or dissent, nor do we collect intelligence to disadvantage people on the basis of their ethnicity, or race, or gender, or sexual orientation, or religious beliefs. We do not collect intelligence to provide a competitive advantage to U.S. companies or U.S. commercial sectors.

And in terms of our bulk collection of signals intelligence, U.S. intelligence agencies will only use such data to meet specific security requirements: counterintelligence, counterterrorism, counter-proliferation, cybersecurity, force protection for our troops and our allies, and combating transnational crime, including sanctions evasion.

In this directive, I have taken the unprecedented step of extending certain protections that we have for the American people to people overseas. I've directed the DNI, in consultation with the Attorney General, to develop these safeguards, which will limit the duration that we can hold personal information, while also restricting the use of this information.

The bottom line is that people around the world, regardless of their nationality, should know that the United States is not spying on ordinary people who don't threaten our national security, and that we take their privacy concerns into account in our policies and procedures. This applies to foreign leaders as well. Given the understandable attention that this issue has received, I have made clear to the intelligence community that unless there is a compelling national security purpose, we will not monitor the communications of heads of state and government of our close friends and allies. And I've instructed my national security team, as well as the intelligence community, to work with foreign counterparts to deepen our coordination and cooperation in ways that rebuild trust going forward.

Now let me be clear: Our intelligence agencies will continue to gather information about the intentions of governments—as opposed to ordinary citizens—around the world, in the same way that the intelligence services of every other nation does. We will not apologize simply because our services may be more effective. But heads of state and government with whom we work closely, and on whose cooperation we depend, should feel confident that we are treating them as real partners. And the changes I've ordered do just that.

Finally, to make sure that we follow through on all these reforms, I am making some important changes to how our government is organized. The State Department will designate a senior officer to coordinate our diplomacy on issues related to technology and signals intelligence. We will appoint a senior official at the White House to implement the new privacy safeguards that I have announced today. I will devote the resources to centralize and improve the process we use to handle foreign requests for legal assistance, keeping our high standards for privacy while helping foreign partners fight crime and terrorism.

I have also asked my counselor, John Podesta, to lead a comprehensive review of big data and privacy [Executive Office of the President, *Big Data: Seizing Opportunities, Preserving Values* (May 2014)]. And this group will consist of government officials who, along with the President's Council of Advisors on Science and Technology, will reach out to privacy experts, technologists and business leaders, and look how the challenges inherent in big data are being confronted by both the public and private sectors; whether we can forge international norms on how to manage this data; and how we can continue to promote the free flow of information in ways that are consistent with both privacy and security.

For ultimately, what's at stake in this debate goes far beyond a few months of headlines, or passing tensions in our foreign policy. When you cut through the noise, what's really at stake is how we remain true to who we are in a world that is remaking itself at dizzying speed. Whether it's the ability of individuals to communicate ideas; to access information that would have once filled every great library in every country in the world; or to forge bonds with people on other sides of the globe, technology is remaking what is possible for individuals, and for institutions, and for the international order. So while the reforms that I have announced will point us in a new direction, I am mindful that more work will be needed in the future.

One thing I'm certain of: This debate will make us stronger. And I also know that in this time of change, the United States of America will have to lead. It may seem sometimes that America is being held to a different standard. And I'll admit the readiness of some to assume the worst motives by our government can be frustrating. No one expects China to have an open debate about their surveillance programs, or Russia to take privacy concerns of citizens in other places into account. But let's remember: We are held to a different standard precisely because we have been at the forefront of defending personal privacy and human dignity.

As the nation that developed the Internet, the world expects us to ensure that the digital revolution works as a tool for individual empowerment, not government control. Having faced down the dangers of totalitarianism and fascism and communism, the world expects us to stand up for the principle that every person has the right to think and write and form relationships freely—because individual freedom is the wellspring of human progress.

Those values make us who we are. And because of the strength of our own democracy, we should not shy away from high expectations. For more than two centuries, our Constitution has weathered every type of change because we have been willing to defend it, and because we have been willing to question the actions that have been taken in its defense. Today is no different. I believe we can meet high expectations. Together, let us chart a way forward that secures the life of our nation while preserving the liberties that make our nation worth fighting for.

Thank you. God bless you. May God bless the United States of America.

*Source:* White House, http://www.whitehouse.gov/the-press-office/2014/01/17/remarks-president -review-signals-intelligence.

# 37

# U.S. House of Representatives, USA FREEDOM Act

President Obama announced in March 2014 that the U.S. government would no longer collect or hold telephone metadata in bulk but would, instead, obtain such metadata from telecommunications companies pursuant to FISC orders approving queries about specific telephone numbers. This new approach would require legislation by Congress. In May 2014, the House of Representatives adopted the Uniting and Strengthening America by Fulfilling Rights and Ending Eavesdropping, Drag-Net Collection, and Online Monitoring Act, or USA FREEDOM Act. The bill ends bulk collection of telephone metadata, strengthens privacy protection for communications of U.S. persons, implements changes to the functioning of the FISC, and increases FISA transparency and reporting requirements. The next document contains a section-by-section description of the USA FREEDOM Act as passed by the House.

The bill was criticized by many in Congress and by civil liberties groups for not going far enough. In the Senate, Senator Patrick Leahy sponsored a version of the bill that contained stronger privacy protections, but, in November 2014, the Senate failed to bring this bill to a vote. In June 2014, the House approved an amendment to the defense appropriations bill for fiscal year 2015 prohibiting use of appropriated funds for two much-criticized NSA activities—so-called "backdoor" searches of information on a U.S. person gathered incidentally under Section 702 of FISA and U.S. government mandates that telecommunications companies alter their products and services to permit electronic surveillance. These House amendments were not included in the national defense appropriations act for fiscal 2015 passed by the House and Senate in December 2014. Failure of the USA FREEDOM Act in the Senate and removal of the House amendments from the final defense appropriations bill meant that, as of this writing, legislative reform of NSA surveillance activities has not occurred.

★ ★ ★

### TITLE I—FISA BUSINESS RECORD REFORMS

*Sec. 101—Additional requirements for call detail records.* On March 27, 2014, President Obama announced the need for legislation to reform the NSA's telephone metadata program. To that end, the Act preserves traditional operational capabilities exercised by the government to collect foreign intelligence information under Section 501 of FISA [i.e., Section 215 of the USA PATRIOT Act]. In addition, the Act prohibits the bulk collection of any business records under Section 501. The Act also creates a new, narrowly-tailored mechanism that prevents bulk collection of telephone metadata by the government but also preserves the government's ability to search telephone metadata for possible connections between foreign powers or agents of foreign powers and others, as part of an authorized investigation to protect against international terrorism and with the additional safeguards proposed by the President.

Under the Act, if the government can demonstrate a reasonable, articulable suspicion that a specific selection term is associated with a foreign power or an agent of a foreign power, the FISA court may issue an order for the production of call detail records created on or after the request for production and held by telephone companies in the normal course of business. The government may require the production of up to two "hops"—i.e., the call detail records associated with the initial seed and the call detail records associated with the records returned in the initial "hop." The prospective collection of call detail records (i.e., those created "after" the request for production) is limited to 180 days.

The Act defines "call detail record" to include "session identifying information (including originating or terminating telephone number, International Mobile Subscriber Identity number, or International Mobile Station Equipment Identity number), a telephone calling card number, or the time or duration of a call." The Act explicitly excludes from that term the contents of any communication; the name, address, or financial information of a subscriber or customer; and cell site location information.

The Act requires the entities involved in the production of call detail records to provide the government with technical assistance. The Act also requires the destruction of call detail records within 5 years of production, except for records that remain relevant to an ongoing counterterrorism investigation.

The Act does not require any private entity to retain any record or information other than in the ordinary course of business. However, nothing in current law or this Act prohibits the government and telecommunications providers from agreeing voluntarily to retain records for periods longer than required for their business purposes.

This new authority—designed to allow the government to search telephone metadata for possible connections to international terrorism—does not preclude the government's use of "traditional" business record orders under Section 501 to compel the production of business records, including call detail records.

*Sec. 102—Emergency authority.* This section creates a new emergency authority in Section 215. The Attorney General may authorize the emergency production of tangible things, provided that such an application is presented to the court within 7 days. If the court subsequently denies an emergency application, the government may not use any of the information obtained under the emergency authority except in instances of a threat of death or serious bodily harm.

*Sec. 103. Prohibition on Bulk Collection of Tangible Things.* The Act requires that each application for the production of tangible things include "a specific selection term to be used as the basis for the production." In so doing, the Act makes clear that the government may not engage in bulk collection under Section 501 of FISA.

The Act defines "specific selection term" to mean "a term used to uniquely describe a person, entity, or account."

This goes further than the President's plan in that it prohibits the bulk collection of all tangible things and not just telephone records. Section 501(b)(2)(A) of FISA will continue to require the government to make "a statement of facts showing that there are reasonable grounds to believe that the tangible things sought are relevant to an authorized investigation. . . ." The USA Freedom Act requires the government to provide a specific selection term as the basis for the production of the tangible things sought, thus ensuring that the government cannot collect tangible things based on the assertion that the requested collection "is thus relevant, because the success of [an] investigative tool depends on bulk collection." These changes restore meaningful limits to the "relevance" requirement of Section 501.

Although this Act eliminates bulk collection, the Act does not limit the government's use of Section 501 as it was designed, as a mechanism for intelligence agencies to obtain information, based on a statement of facts showing that there are reasonable grounds to believe that the tangible things sought are relevant to a national security investigation.

*Sec. 104—Judicial review of minimization procedures for the production of tangible things.* This section provides that the court may evaluate the adequacy of minimization procedures under Section 215. Under current law, the court is only empowered to determine whether or not the government has minimization procedures in place.

*Sec. 105—Liability protection.* This section provides liability protections to third parties who provide information, facilities, or technical assistance to the government in compliance with an order issued under Section 215. This provision mirrors the liability provisions in Titles I and VII of FISA.

*Sec. 106—Compensation for assistance.* This section explicitly permits the government to compensate third parties for producing tangible things or providing information, facilities, or assistance in accordance with an order issue[d] under Section 215. It is customary for the Government to enter into contractual agreements with third parties in order to compensate them for products and services provided to the Government.

*Sec. 107—Definitions.* This section provides definitions for "call detail records" and "specific selection term."

*Sec. 108—Inspector general reports on business records orders.* This section requires the Inspector General of the Department of Justice to conduct a comprehensive review of the use of Section 215 with respect to calendar years 2012 to 2014. It also requires the Inspector General of the Intelligence Community to assess the value and use of intelligence obtained under Section 215 over the same period.

*Sec. 109—Effective date.* This section provides that the new telephone metadata program, the new Section 215 emergency authority, and the prohibition on bulk collection of tangible things under Section 215 take effect 180 days after enactment.

## TITLE II—FISA PEN REGISTER AND TRAP AND TRACE DEVICE REFORM

*Sec. 201—Prohibition on bulk collection.* This section provides that the pen register and trap and trace device authority may not be used without a specific selection term as the basis for selecting the telephone line or other facility to which the pen register or trap and trace device is to be attached or applied.

*Sec. 202—Minimization procedures.* This section requires that the government adopt procedures that are reasonably designed to minimize the retention and prohibit the dissemination of nonpublic information about United States persons. It also explicitly authorizes the court to assess compliance with these procedures while a pen register or trap and trace device is in use.

## TITLE III—FISA ACQUISITIONS TARGETING PERSONS OUTSIDE THE UNITED STATES REFORMS

*Sec. 301—Restatement of Prohibition on Reverse Targeting.* Section 702(b)(2) of FISA provides that the government "may not intentionally target a person reasonably believed to be located outside the United States if *the* purpose of such acquisition is to target a particular, known person reasonably believed to be within the United States." The Act clarifies this prohibition to state that the government "may not intentionally target a person reasonably believed to be located outside the United States if *a* purpose of such acquisition is to target a particular, known person reasonably believed to be within the United States."

This change is meant to simply clarify and restate Congress' original intent in enacting Section 702 of the FISA Amendments Act that this authority cannot be used as a pretext to target U.S. persons inside the United States.

*Sec. 302—Minimization Procedures.* The Act codifies procedures already adopted by the government for the minimization of domestic communications. Specifically, the Act requires that the government minimize the acquisition, and prohibit the retention and dissemination, of any wholly domestic communication acquired by the government under Section 702. The Act also prohibits the government from using communications to or from a United States person or a person who appears to be located in the United States, except where the communication relates to a target under Section 702 or to protect against an immediate threat to human life.

*Sec. 303—Limits on use of unlawfully obtained information.* This section provides that the government may not use information acquired outside the scope of court-approved targeting and minimization procedures.

## TITLE IV—FOREIGN INTELLIGENCE SURVEILLANCE COURT REFORMS

*Sec. 401—Appointment of amicus curiae.* This section provides that both the FISA court and the FISA Court of Review shall, if deemed appropriate, appoint an individual to serve as amicus curiae in a case involving a novel or significant interpretation of law. In addition, this section permits the court to appoint amicus curiae in any case.

The presiding judges of the courts will designate five individuals who are eligible to serve as amicus curiae. These individuals shall possess expertise in privacy and civil liberties, intelligence collection, telecommunications, or any other area of law that may lend legal or technical expertise to the courts, and shall possess appropriate security clearances.

*Sec. 402—Declassification of decisions, orders, and opinions.* This section requires the Attorney General to conduct a declassification review of each decision, order, or opinion of the FISA court that includes a significant construction or interpretation of law. In the interest of national security, the Attorney General may provide a summary of the decision rather than a declassified copy.

## TITLE V—NATIONAL SECURITY LETTER REFORM

*Sec. 501—Prohibition on bulk collection.* This section prohibits the use of various national security letter authorities without the use of a specific selection term as the basis for the national security letter request.

## TITLE VI—FISA TRANSPARENCY AND REPORTING REQUIREMENTS

*Sec. 601—Additional reporting on orders requiring production of business records.* In addition to existing annual reporting requirements, this section requires the government to report on the number of requests made for call detail records under the new telephone metadata program.

*Sec. 602—Business records compliance reports to Congress.* This section requires the government to provide to Congress any compliance reports related to the use of Section 215.

*Sec. 603—Annual report by the Director of the Administrative Office of the United States Courts on orders Entered.* This section requires the Director of the Administrative Office of the United States Court to make an annual report on the number of orders issued under sections 105, 304, 402, 501, 702, 703, and 704 of FISA, as well as the number of appointments of individuals to serve as amicus curiae to the FISA court.

*Sec. 604—Reporting requirements for decisions of the Foreign Intelligence Surveillance Court.* This section requires the Attorney General to provide to the relevant committees, within 45 days of each decision, order, or opinion that includes a significant construction or interpretation, a copy of each such decision and a brief statement of the relevant background.

*Sec. 605—Submission of reports under FISA.* This section includes the House Judiciary Committee in several existing reporting requirements.

## TITLE VII—SUNSETS

*Sec. 701—USA PATRIOT Improvement and Reauthorization Act of 2005.*
This section aligns the sunset of the three sun-setting provisions of the USA
PATRIOT Act with the sunset of the FISA Amendment Act on December 31,
2017.

U.S. House of Representatives, Committee on the Judiciary's Section-by-Section
Analysis of the USA FREEDOM Act, passed by the House, May 22, 2014 (footnotes omitted).

*Source:* House of Representatives, Committee on the Judiciary Report on the USA FREEDOM Act,
Report 113–452, 24–29, May 15, 2014, https://beta.congress.gov/113/crpt/hrpt452/CRPT
-113hrpt452-pt1.pdf.

# 38

# Edward Snowden, One Year Later

On June 4, 2014, one year after the *Guardian* published the first of his disclosures, Edward Snowden released this statement in an e-mail to supporters of the American Civil Liberties Union. This book has attempted to convey important events and issues generated by Snowden's revelations about the surveillance activities of the United States and other governments. It is appropriate to end with Snowden's own reflections on a year of unprecedented events.

It's been one year.

Technology has been a liberating force in our lives. It allows us to create and share the experiences that make us human, effortlessly. But in secret, our very own government—one bound by the Constitution and its Bill of Rights—has reverse-engineered something beautiful into a tool of mass surveillance and oppression. The government right now can easily monitor whom you call, whom you associate with, what you read, what you buy, and where you go online and offline, and they do it to all of us, all the time.

Today, our most intimate private records are being indiscriminately seized in secret, without regard for whether we are actually suspected of wrongdoing. When these capabilities fall into the wrong hands, they can destroy the very freedoms that technology should be nurturing, not extinguishing. Surveillance, without regard to the rule of law or our basic human dignity, creates societies that fear free expression and dissent, the very values that make America strong.

In the long, dark shadow cast by the security state, a free society cannot thrive.

That's why one year ago I brought evidence of these irresponsible activities to the public—to spark the very discussion the U.S. government didn't want the American people to have. With every revelation, more and more light coursed through a National Security Agency that had grown too comfortable operating in the dark and without public consent. Soon incredible things began occurring that would have been unimaginable years ago. A federal judge in open court called an NSA mass surveillance program likely unconstitutional and "almost Orwellian." Congress and President Obama have called for an end to the dragnet collection of the intimate details of our lives. Today legislation to begin rolling back the surveillance state is moving in Congress after more than a decade of impasse.

I am humbled by our collective successes so far. When the *Guardian* and the *Washington Post* began reporting on the NSA's project to make privacy a thing of the past, I worried the risks I took to get the public the information it deserved would be met with collective indifference.

One year later, I realize that my fears were unwarranted.

Americans, like you, still believe the Constitution is the highest law of the land, which cannot be violated in secret in the name of a false security. Some say I'm a man without a country, but that's not true. America has always been an ideal, and though I'm far away, I've never felt as connected to it as I do now, watching the necessary debate unfold as I hoped it would. America, after all, is always at our fingertips; that is the power of the Internet.

But now it's time to keep the momentum for serious reform going so the conversation does not die prematurely.

Only then will we get the legislative reform that truly reins in the NSA and puts the government back in its constitutional place. Only then will we get the secure technologies we need to communicate without fear that silently in the background, our very own government is collecting, collating, and crunching the data that allows unelected bureaucrats to intrude into our most private spaces, analyzing our hopes and fears. Until then, every American who jealously guards their rights must do their best to engage in digital self-defense and proactively protect their electronic devices and communications. Every step we can take to secure ourselves from a government that no longer respects our privacy is a patriotic act.

We've come a long way, but there's more to be done.

—Edward J. Snowden, American

★  ★  ★

*Source:* American Civil Liberties Union, A Message from Edward Snowden, One Year Later, June 4, 2014, https://www.aclu.org/blog/national-security/message-edward-snowden-one-year-later.

# Contributors

FRED H. CATE is Distinguished Professor and the Ben C. Dutton Professor of Law at Indiana University's Maurer School of Law. He specializes in information privacy and security law issues. Professor Cate served as director of the Indiana University Center for Applied Cybersecurity Research from 2003 until 2014, and he is the director of the Institute for Information Policy Research and codirector of the Center for Law, Ethics & Applied Research in Health Information.

NICK CULLATHER is Professor of History and of International Studies at Indiana University. He is a historian of U.S. foreign relations, specializing in the history of intelligence, development, and nation building. His books include *The Hungry World: America's Cold War Battle Against Poverty in Asia*. His current research project, *First Line of Defense*, is investigating the early history of the Central Intelligence Agency.

DAVID P. FIDLER is the James Louis Calamaras Professor of Law at the Indiana University Maurer School of Law and is a Senior Fellow with the Center for Applied Cybersecurity Research. He specializes in international law, cyber security, cyberspace, counterinsurgency, biosecurity, weapons of mass destruction, and global health. He currently chairs the International Law Association's Study Group on Cyber Terrorism and International Law. During 2015, Professor Fidler was a Visiting Fellow for Cybersecurity at the Council on Foreign Relations.

LEE H. HAMILTON is director of the Center on Congress, Professor of Practice in the School of Public and Environmental Affairs, and Distinguished Scholar in the School of Global and International Studies at Indiana University. From 1965 to 1999, he served the State of Indiana in the U.S. House of Representatives, where his chairmanships included the Committee on Foreign Affairs and the Permanent Select Committee on Intelligence. Representative Hamilton was the Vice Chairman of the National Commission on Terrorists Attacks Upon the United States (the 9/11 Commission), and he is a member of the President's Homeland Security Advisory Council, the CIA External Advisory Board, and the U.S. Department of Homeland Security Task Force on Preventing the Entry of Weapons of Mass Effect on American Soil.

WILLIAM E. SCHEUERMAN is Professor and Director of Graduate Studies in the Department of Political Science at Indiana University. His research and teaching focus on modern political thought, German political thought, democratic theory, legal theory, and international political theory. His books include *The Realist Case for Global Reform, Hans J. Morgenthau: Realism and Beyond,* and *Liberal Democracy and the Social Acceleration of Time.*

# Index